For My Darling
Shantimama

Wishing you a
very happy birthday

All our love,
Mini xx
Rishi & Raju & Rooh

28 . X . 18

The
Bengalis

Also by Sudeep Chakravarti

Non-fiction

*Clear.Hold.Build: Hard Lessons of Business and
Human Rights in India* (2014)

Highway 39: Journeys Through a Fractured Land (2012)

Red Sun: Travels in Naxalite Country (2008)

Fiction

The Avenue of Kings (2010)

Tin Fish (2005)

The Bengalis

A PORTRAIT OF A COMMUNITY

SUDEEP CHAKRAVARTI

ALEPH

ALEPH

ALEPH BOOK COMPANY
An independent publishing firm
promoted by *Rupa Publications India*

First published in India in 2017
by Aleph Book Company
7/16 Ansari Road, Daryaganj
New Delhi 110 002

ISBN: 978-93-86021-04-5

3 5 7 9 10 8 6 4 2

Printed at Parksons Graphics Pvt. Ltd, Mumbai

To
Peter, Indrani, Swapan, Sreemati, Azam, Rahul, Nasreen,
Soma, Nazly, Sumangali, Hirak, Erika, Navid
My brothers, sisters—and fellow survivors
And variously jéthu, pishi, kāku, aunt, uncle to Maya,
an inheritor of a rainbow family

'...a hell full of good things'

—Fourteenth century CE Moroccan traveller Abu Abdullah Muhammad Ibn Abdullah al-Lawati al-Tanji Ibn Battuta, recounting a description of Bengal

Dāngāy bāgh, jolé kumir.
(Tiger on the shore, crocodile in the water)

—Bengali proverb

'Ever known a Bengali to move ahead?'

—Badal Sircar, in the play *Michhil (Procession)*

Néi māmār chéyé kānā māmā bhālō
(Better to have a blind uncle than no uncle)

—Bengali proverb

'Āmār shōnār Bānglā, āmi tōmāy bhālōbāshi'
(My golden Bengal, I love you)

—Rabindranath Tagore

Contents

A Note on Bānglā

There is deliberate use of Bānglā phonetics in this book. To familiarize readers who are unfamiliar with the language and yet wish to taste it and pronounce it in a way that does not require them to use the expertise of the linguist and scholar (Bānglā in Roman script is a complicated matter), I have simplified some established norms after consulting linguists and scholars.

This has meant avoiding transliteration and what is called the International Phonetic Alphabet, and staying closer to transcription. The arrangement is not perfect, but is intended to reach an audience beyond that of the linguist, scholar and reader of Bānglā.

To reduce confusion it is applied mostly to a few vowels.

An example: if Bānglā were to be written as Bangla, then those familiar with pronunciation in English but unfamiliar with the language of the Bengalis may pronounce it as Bang (as in 'hang') la. The emphasis on ā removes both that possibility and the need to write it as the more cumbersome Baangla. Besides, to the Bengali 'bang' is frog, quite removed from the stately, Sanskrit-laden Vanga or Banga, which we pronounce as Bongō.

For 'aw' as in 'thaw' the capital or lower-case 'o' is employed, distinct from the 'o' as in 'go'—which is shown in this book as 'ō'. So it is Bongōbōndhu, friend of Bengal, the honorific associated with Bangladesh's liberation hero, Mujibur Rahman; and roshōgōllā, the dessert some of us would go to war over to defend its provenance and honour.

For the 'ay' sound I have used 'é', for instance in 'ké?'—who?

'U' and 'i' are left alone. So 'u' is used both for the softer and extended 'oo' that Bānglā has, for, say, our staple fish, rui, or unish, nineteen, in which 'u' is not pronounced as you would in 'punish'; but as you might 'put' and 'moot'. Both these Bānglā words also take in the 'i' for the soft and extended 'ee' (as you would the 'i' in 'indicate' and the extended 'ee' sound in 'unleash.') I was advised that use of diacritic in 'u' and 'i' would complicate matters—best to keep things as simple as possible. But for a few extended 'ee' sounds for which 'i' is entirely inadequate, as in sheem, the broad bean that is for us a delicacy, a double 'ee' as in 'seem' appeared to be the judicious way.

The 'ch' sound as in 'chamber' is left alone. The explosive 'chh', common in Indic languages, is left to itself, as in chhānā, our word for hung curd or paneer. The sound for 't' remains as in 'tea', 'th' being used as with the softer aspect in 'theme' and also for a harder aspect as in 'though'. Similarly, 'k' remains as in 'kind, while 'kh' is like a soft cough, as in 'khomā', to forgive.

Bānglā does not possess a sharp 's' as in set (the equivalent would be shét, though we do have a soft, harder and hard 'sh' sounds depicted by distinct consonants). For simplicity the book employs 'sh' for all such.

We don't have a 'v' either, the closest consonant resembling it is 'bho', as in 'Bhutan', the country, or bhālōbāshā, one of our words for affection and love. Revolver in Bānglā would be a less impressive-sounding, but equally deadly, rebholbhār.

Or a 'w': we don't have that either. English (Ingréji) accented with Bānglā would have 'would' close to 'ood' and 'work' as something like 'uork'.

For names of people the book employs Anglicized versions, quite the established fashion among Bengalis, occasionally offering the Bānglā alongside for flavour—Rabindranath and Rōbindrōnāth, for example. Wherever I have used archival sources in Bānglā, the names of books, authors and references from the book employ Bānglā phonetics.

For names of places too the book uses Anglicized versions with the occasional Bānglā phonetic for flavour, except Kolkata, which has officially jettisoned 'Calcutta'—used here in that form only when quoting archival sources. Similarly, while quoting from archival sources I have remained faithful to the spellings of the original, as in Dacca for Dhaka; or Cutwa for Katwa, near the colonial-flavoured Burdwan—now generally spelled Bardhaman, but in Bānglā pronounced Bordhōmān.

Bānglā, entirely phonetic and logical in its own universe, was never meant to be English—a language comprising a seemingly random, bewildering nightmare of rules, a language that many urbanized Bengalis habitually use for emphasis both in perfect English or heavily accented by Bengali. But if you did not taste the language we love and cherish, a language we fought for and even died for, how would you know us?

And, so, Bānglā it is.

Prologue

Āmrā Ké?
Who, What, Why?

If you are Bengali, you may know much of what you read here.

Equally, if you are Bengali, you may be ignorant of some of these matters, or banish such thoughts and realities of being Bengali to the furthest recesses of your consciousness on the assumption that, if such things do not matter to you, a Bengali by birth and assiduous practice, they may not matter at all.

If you are not Bengali, to the Bengali you may not matter at all, even though this book is written as much for you as any Bengali, to know us and engage with us, although that engagement is a fraught exercise. To begin, you are what Bengalis call 'non-Bengali'. It is closer to non-person than persona non grata, but that would be splitting hairs, which the Bengali can perform even when asleep. By illogical extension, ethnically, intellectually, culturally and historically your every not-Bengali fibre, provenance, present and future may be construed by the Bengali chauvinist as being one of colossal insignificance.

All this naturally derives from a grand sense of the Bengali self.

The Chinese have for long deluded themselves into thinking they form the centre of this benighted world. The Japanese attempted, in vain, to conquer China to purloin that claim. The British did what they do best, exploit the ego of others to build up their own, and construct an empire to go with it. That is now gloriously absent. Others conquer their language, and their tiny island is mainly notable for some fine meadows, teas from Bengal, a much-photographed clock tower, royalty dressed in stolen jewels and an economy largely built on purloined assets—grand theft that began with depredations of the British East India Company in Bengal. Rome is a city of ruins and manicured people in mannequin clothes; their age of empire has come and gone, leaving in its wake judicial language and gluten intolerance tempered by superior salads. The Egyptians were fine: their monuments and mannerisms look fetching in photographs and when transported by Hollywood accents enunciated through excellent dental work. We are all fascinated by mummies.

Were there any others? With those of extremist predilection rampaging across West Asia, North Africa and within sighting distance of the ancient Silk Route, wiping out thousands of years of history at the touch of sword, bullet and explosive, who can tell?

In South Asia, in India—the land east of the Indus or Sindhu, Industan–Sindhustan–Hindustan–India, or Bharat after a pious brother in the mythological tour de force, the Ramayana—the dynasties of the Mauryas, Guptas, Kushanas, Cholas, Mughals, and the decorative plumage of the Hanovers (Victoria, Empress of India), and Saxe–Coburg and Gotha-turned-Windsors (a series of Georges, Emperors of India) have come and gone. Now a subcontinent of mostly poor and yet desperately ambitious countries make up a fractious South Asia.

In it there is us, Bengalis, the jewels of our own crown.

A quarter of a billion of us, and growing, the largest ethno-linguistic group after the Han Chinese and Arab, occupying some of the most fertile, bountiful and yet, some of the poorest, most densely populated, and socio-politically fragile spaces on the planet. Our homeland, geographical and linguistic—Bengali counts globally among the largest language groups—is spread across two countries, India and Bangladesh—literally, the country of Bengalis, and their language, Bāṅglā. It's a teeming, heaving, raucous space where empires have been won and lost, civilization celebrated and ground to dust, a place of lucid intellects and terrible illiteracy and intellectual poverty, of great reformation and great wretchedness, where emotion seems to be as much a cachet as education.

In this confounding acre are Nobel laureates. Three, as I write this, Rabindranath Tagore of literature, Amartya Sen of economics and Muhammad Yunus of microfinance and the Grameen Bank in Bangladesh, a model of women- and rural-empowerment that is today lauded the world over. More will surely follow, in literature, the sciences, economics and development initiatives: ours is a continual wellspring of thought, hope and initiative. (A Bengali who works? Indeed.) We have geniuses of science, among them one who collaborated with Einstein and another who kept pace with Marconi—was even a bit ahead, by some tellings. We have free thinkers and philosophers and literary minds (although Tagore is obsessively institutionalized as our cultural beacon) and cinematic icons and innovators.

We have revolutionaries: indeed, ours was a cradle of revolution against British colonialism, and of the Tebhaga and Naxalite rebellions, the domino effects of which continue to this day. We helped to create for South Asia the schizophrenic romanticism of the terrorist-revolutionary decades before Che Guevara embarked on his motorcycle journeys of erudition and indoctrination across South America, several decades before he became a cap and then a T-shirt. We are told about revolutionaries in our childhood lessons; they form the bedrock of our self-aggrandizing glory and are brickworks in our racial and national mythology. A Bengali child would almost always know the honorific 'Netaji', by which Subhas Chandra Bose is commonly known: Respected Leader, the Bengalis' dear and sadly departed leader and a man whom many Bengalis still think ought to have been free India's first prime minister, a man, as some folk legends have it, who really didn't die of burns after his transport, a Mitsubishi aircraft provided by the Japanese government, crashed in Formosa—later Taiwan—but lived on for decades in India in several guises, eyeing askance India's troubled birth and growth.

That child would rarely question this Congress leader who

wished peace in Greater Bengal, this great unfavourite of Mohandas Gandhi taking up with the Axis powers in World War II, against Allied forces, in a desperate bid to win for India freedom from British colonialism. That act alone is evidently all-encompassing, all-forgiving.

And what began in Bengal at the turn of the previous century to peak with the myth of Netaji continues as tradition in Bangladesh, where hagiography sometimes makes it appear as if nothing of import existed before 1971, the year Bangladesh was born. The year Bongōbōndhu, Friend of Bengal, won independence from Pakistan on the back of his charisma, an unstoppable momentum of identity politics that created history over the blood sacrifice of an estimated 3 million proto-Bangladeshis and the generous help of India. Sheikh Mujibur Rahman is Bangladesh's folkloric George Washington by vision and verve, Gandhi and Abraham Lincoln by assassination, and Stalin by his advocating of a one-party state, among several factors that brought about his death, and the rebirth of radical Islam that Bangladesh thought it had buried in 1971. Or was it 1964? Or 1950? Or 1947?

◆

Ours is a playground of the perpetual beauty and brutality of nature, and the goodness of humanity married to genocidal inhumanity during the Partition of India and after, mostly by men and some women who self-importantly interpreted scripture, norm and necessity on behalf of our various gods and their prophets; who thrive on bigotry and fear.

We are worthy of every cliché, every twist of confounding history and confusing present and uncertain future, every joy and tragic pursuit, every exultation and horror made at the hands of nature and the nature of man. We are at once lovers of poetry and despoilers and killers of children, women and men. At once renaissance people and ravagers of humanity.

Here, an animated discussion on the future of mankind can

be as commonplace as an animated discussion on the best way to cook fish—the best ways are all ours, naturally, but even in this cuisine-art apex there are superior and inferior ways of preparation, recipes of taste and ego. What is the best way to cook fish? A not-Bengali person might ask. There are a hundred and more different ways, a Bengali will reply, but what fish do you mean, exactly? There are so many excellent ways, all Bengali, to cook every kind of fish, several dozen varieties of freshwater fish that regularly form our diet, and a couple of dozen species of the sea, and a variety of dried fish—shuntki māchh—from both sea and freshwater that remains in limbo between culinary niche-heaven and olfactory hell. It can border on the obsessive.

A passionately presented point of view—does the Bengali know any other?—over politics, or sport, even in that welcoming arena of the āddā, the clubby Bengali equivalent of Circus Maximus for the opinionated and argumentative that lives alike in small town community centres and sprawling urban salons, can lead to injury. At the least, passionate preferences and arguments over them can end friendships. I lost a Bengali friend not long ago after confessing that I also liked Sri Lankan teas, and the finest from Nuwara Eliya possess fragrance not unlike—she cut me off mid-delusion. To her there was no civilized option to the very Bengali oeuvre of Darjeeling tea, and that narrowed down to the offerings of two particular estates, Makaibari and Lopchu. (I hadn't had the heart to point out to her that, while politically- and ethnically-charged Darjeeling was for the moment indeed in territorial West Bengal, and while Makaibari indeed retained Bengali ownership, Lopchu had for three generations been owned and curated by a Marwari family. It was too easy and ungentlemanly a way to score a point, to even suggest West Bengal could conceivably lose Darjeeling; and that the prized 'Darjeeling' of the Bengalis, one appreciated even by upper-class Bengali communists—again, among our peculiarities—is owned by among the more reviled not-Bengali species, the Marwari businessman.)

In a penetrating yet humorous article triggered by a book on the French by Oxford historian Sudhir Hazareesingh, Ramachandra Guha offered some quirks of the French as being those of the Bengali. He quoted the French historian Jules Michelet's description of the French: 'We gossip, we quarrel, we expend our energy in words; we use strong language, and we fly into great rages over the smallest of subjects.'

Guha then offered a palliative, using the French love of words, of letters, knowledge, thought and argument. 'When I lived and worked in Calcutta, one went to the National Library not knowing whether the adjoining desk would be occupied by a fellow academic or by a railway clerk seeking to his improve his mind,' Guha wrote in a column in *The Telegraph* of Kolkata. 'The film and bridge clubs I belonged to, which in Delhi or Bangalore would have been the preserve of the Westernized elite, here had as their members babus from Burdwan'—Bardhaman—'sub-inspectors from Howrah, and the like.'

(It is appropriate here to declare, perhaps to the disappointment of some of his fans in what I like to call Banglasphere that Guha, a cricket maven, writer of history and civil rights activist is not Bengali. Evidently, during his student years in northern India, unfamiliarity with southern norms which would have had it as Guha Ramachandra turned this Tamil gentleman's name into a fine Bengali one.)

The writer Nirad Chaudhuri was not as kind as Guha. He extended the characteristic of being argumentative, even querulous, to being divisive. 'The Bengalis, and more specifically the Bengalis of Calcutta, were and still remain some of the finest virtuosi of factiousness,' he wrote in *The Autobiography of an Unknown Indian*, first published in 1951, even suggesting that, 'The stasis of Plato and the asabiya of Ibn Khaldun were as milk and water compared with this distilled spirit of factiousness.'

It permeated every activity, Nirad-babu wrote with forthrightness for which species of Speak-no-ill-of-us and Who-is-he-to-write-this? Bengalis took offence at the time, and since: 'Municipalities, universities, learned societies, political parties, public offices, business concerns, clubs, and even schools are rent by cliques, and are always splitting up like protozoa.' The 'latest' consequence of such factiousness, he wrote with some prescience, 'now that political power has come into the hands of these clique-ridden creatures, is going to be chronic political instability.'

◆

To posit to the average Kolkata or Dhaka Bengali that the planets revolve around a sun beyond the metropolitan suns of Kolkata and Dhaka (indeed, to suggest to such a Kolkata person that Dhaka is the true sun, and the other way round, because each is generally blind to Banglasphere beyond the limits of these cities) is to invite invective. Our identity lies as often in our divisiveness as it does in uneasy unity over grand and trivial matters alike; even if it is to fight over the two most crowded, chaotic, filthy and decrepit metropolises in the world. There are socio-cultural charms, fetching quaintness, pockets of great liberalism and warmth to be found in both cities. In abundance, if not appreciation of cultural activities (ranging from concerts of various musical genres to theatre to cinema to book fairs), Kolkata has a distinct edge over Dhaka thanks to the roots planted in colonial times from the so-called Bengal Renaissance onwards and, since Independence, propelled by a determined veneer of secular activity and celebration. All this is worth argument and commentary, but to attempt to win over the other? There can be no victor here, only a confederacy of the blind.

It is vital to consider Bangladesh—if possible, visit Bangladesh—to get a complete sense of Bengal, of the Bengali, I have maintained with friends, acquaintances and complete strangers, 'West' Bengali and not, over the years.

Why bother? is usually the answer I receive from several of them, mostly Bengali Hindus from West Bengal with no roots in Bangladesh, or those with a family history of upheaval in Bangladesh.

Even the apparently educated and aware among them insist that most Bengalis have come away from there. I have to remind them that Bangladesh fought to be Bengali—the language and the people—and were butchered by the millions, Mussulman and Hindu alike, for that right. 'Bengalis in India have a province,' I have taken to telling them, paraphrasing the teasing remark of the sassy writer and editor Kazi Anis Ahmed, who now lives in Dhaka after several years in the United States. 'The Bengalis in Bangladesh have a country.' Since 1971, the language and the people have been firmly entrenched in the very etymology of the country. Nearly two-thirds of the world's Bengalis live here.

Ah, the critics remark. But aren't they mainly Mushōlmān? Haven't they driven out most Hindus? Don't these Mussulmans destroy temples? Don't they kill Hindus?

The answer is a qualified 'yes', and it drives this very real divide—as generally seen from West Bengal and, in a very real way, in Bangladesh.

Is the Bengali a bigot?

No?

Éktu? Just a little?

◆

Bengalis may vociferously disagree but the sobering truth is that, besides the liberal minority in both West Bengal, Bangladesh and elsewhere in Banglasphere, counting among them both practising and non-practising Hindu and Mussulman—a gloriously vocal and fearless collective that carries the torch of the stereotypical Bengali liberal—the answer to whether Bengalis are tolerant can be a qualified 'yes'. There is a generally silent multitude which has for several hundred years practised the sort of live-and-let-live religion that even encourages token—but staggeringly important, from the perspective of amity—participation in religious festivities of another faith. Musician-mendicants like the Bauls bring together a mutli-religious approach that might have put a California hippie out to grass. Across greater Bengal, and the vast deltas in particular, worship of a nature-driven deity transcends a particular religion to that of a religion of survival against all odds, and surviving it together. But our histories are leavened by the insecurities and ambitions of politics and religion and their cynical practitioners: an incestuous marriage of church and state that drives territorial and electoral politics of identity. Then anger is generated, and blood made to flow. It begins easily but ends uneasily.

In West Bengal, among Bengali Hindus, it goes something like this. Here we have Bengalis, Hindu and Mussulman alike, though fewer of the latter. In today's supercharged atmosphere (and, for some, since the supercharged atmosphere of the 1940s), the Bengali Mussulman is seen as Mussulman first and Bengali later. India's secular constitution, applied in West Bengal as elsewhere in India, is seemingly irrelevant: Constitutions don't rule over sore history, and sore hearts and minds. In Bangladesh the Bengali Mussulman is overwhelmingly present, nearly 90 per cent of a country that is now constitutionally Islamic. History, an international border in between, and a divisive present have nudged many Bengali Hindus and Bengali Mussulmans of both West Bengal and Bangladesh, to move from being Bengali into another space of existence altogether: the hyphenated space of religion-ethnicity.

Narrow conventional wisdom in West Bengal views Bangladesh as a country where people speak, read and write Bangla; sing a national anthem in Bengali, the first line of which is 'Āmār shōnār Bānglā, āmi tōmāy bhālōbāshi', composed by Tagore, one of Bengal's—and South Asia's—greatest poet-song writers; the national language is Bānglā, but that's inadequate culture-cred. The Bengali in Bangladesh—in Ōpār Bānglā, Bengal on the other bank as opposed to Ēpār Bānglā, the Bengal of 'this bank', our bank, in the Bengal within India—who institutionally sings 'My golden Bengal, I love you' is a Bangladeshi. The Bengali in India who rarely sings this song publicly except at the odd cultural fête, is a Bengali. Here the point is not that the government of Bangladesh encourages its people to call themselves Bangladeshi, but a sort of rejection by one lot of Bengalis of another lot of Bengalis.

I would go so far as to suggest the greatest differentiator among Bengalis today is not that of the economically robust and the poor, or literate and illiterate, but that of Hindu and Mussulman, the unity of language and shared purpose rent by religion, a process that began several hundred years ago, became more pronounced during the Raj and has not stopped growing since Partition. The creation of Bangladesh forged further disunity among those who shared a language but not socio-cultural-political or religious purpose. Bangladesh's recent war with its own identity that has seen pitched battles between a devout and yet liberal Islam, and a literal, Wahhabist, unforgiving, assimilate-or-be-annihilated syndrome exhibited in both petty and grand terrors, has driven that wedge further between perception and reality.

And another thing that the viciously communal among us, the Bengali Hindu and the Bengali Mussulman, do to each other, besides the established menu of death and destruction. The vicious Bengali Hindu, like some co-religionists across India, might disparagingly refer to the Bengali Mussulman and Mussulmans in general to signify a religion that mandates circumcision. The vicious Bengali Mussulman might return the favour, call the Bengali Hindu malaun. Rooted in Arabic, it means deprived or bereft of God's mercy, or simply cursed—accursed, and so on. In times of hatred it has remained common parlance among Mussulmans in Bangladesh and a few parts of West Bengal.

It's Partition vocabulary.

◆

And yet, beyond this great divide, there are so many more points of unity, of being Bengali than I have shared at the outset.

We are garrulous; argumentative—and liberal, conservative and moderate, often in the course of the same argument—opinionated; often contemptuous of those not-Bengali; eager to be appreciated by those not-Bengali; blithely unmindful of such hypocrisy; intensely curious—not merely curiosities; feminists; chauvinists; misogynists; ultra-leftist; leftist; rightist; ultra rightist; haters of colonialists; lovers of colonialism bashers; lovers of colonialists (in a range from Britain to Pakistan); lovers of bashers of colonialism-bashers; revolution-minded in theory and sometimes in practice; entirely evolution-minded in practice; among the gentlest people on earth; among the most vicious people on earth; creators and perpetuators of the most vicious gangs and political gangsterism; lovers of love; lovers of hatred; lovers of life; lovers of death; lovers of our land; lovers of the lands of those not-Bengali; lovers of rivers and rain; vastly literate; vastly illiterate; lovers of words, literature, poetry, theatre, cinema, art, any art form worth a form; lovers of witty comebacks and innuendo; populous—not to be confused with popular, although we can sometimes be that, too; pompous; quick to anger; quick to laughter; loud; noisy; eager transporters of such noise to some of the quietest places on earth; inveterate travellers; perhaps the greatest users of that odd phrase: sinikbewty; exhibitionists; drama queens; often colour-blind when attempting Western clothing and interior decor; exquisite wielders of colour in art; sufferers of some of the greatest famines—the phrase bhookha Bāngāli, the hungry, starving Bengali, still endures in northern India and Pakistan; fanatical about food; creators and worshippers of some of the most delicately flavoured foods on earth; fanatical about football; strangely fanatical about Argentine and Brazilian football players, nobody else matters except occasionally the French or Portuguese; terrible losers; weavers of the most exquisite fabrics of form and colour; wearers and exporters of such exquisite fabrics of exquisite design; lately, wearers of the most exquisite fabrics rendered hideous with overwrought design; unarguably the greatest users of balaclavas in the world other than terrorists and special operations personnel, they sometimes call their Hollywood-stamped versions ski masks, we call our simpler version mānkicap...

We are confounding.

And, as you already know, we are legion.

◆

Who or what is the Bengali, really, beyond a roiled history, schizophrenic emotion and heightened sense of self? What are the Bengali and the Bengali homelands all about, stereotypically and beyond stereotypes? What defines us? What are our defining moments? What makes us who we are?

To answer these questions we may need to seek the path of recorded history, clinical and unswerving in our pursuit. And yet, we may need to ask in a stream of consciousness way as Jean-Paul Sartre that tortured philosopher and iconic Parisien whom several generations of modernist Bengalis have studied, sometimes worshipped, and even wondered if this not-Bengali man did not possess a cordon bleu Bengali heart—might have:

Āmi ké?

A Bengali of impeccable credentials of universalism will immediately follow that up with a mirrored query in English, a language Bengalis use to amplify gravitas and self-esteem:

Who am I?

Because, where some of us yearned for a state, all of us yearn for a state of mind.

This is as complicated as it seems. It should, however, come as little surprise. The Bengali is at once an existentialist delight and nightmare, cast in perpetual drama.

◆

As an emotive people with great self-belief in individuality, our diverse reaction to anything is legion, as are we. A book about Bengalis will likely not be viewed clinically by a Bengali. When it comes to the Bengalis, a passionate and argumentative people, a telling with warts and all is perhaps a fraught project from inception, let alone its execution (our emotive nature is a cliché that bears repetition). There can be no book on a people, except something hagiographical, a kowtowing to all that is good and celebrated by every imaginable school of thought that can please them. Were a Bengali to write a book about Bengalis, it would perhaps never be clinically written—entirely, at any rate. On this rides the risk of anyone, Bengali—in any case even being Bengali is not enough expertise to write about Bengalis!—let alone a not-Bengali presuming to write omnisciently about our collective.

That is not my intention. There can be no absolute, definitive story about a people, Bengali or otherwise. My goal is more modest—to tell the story of my people as seen through my eyes, Bengali by birth, cosmopolitan by practice though steeped in default Bengaliness for practically my entire life, and especially so in the years it took me to research and write this book.

◆

Growing up Bengali was for me like a series of expectations, a continuous examination of beliefs in the middle of grand histories, grand tragedies and grand expectations.

Since the age of seven or so, in a relatively privileged home in Kolkata, that eternal citadel of Bengali lore, about a year before a movement for being Bengali birthed an entire country, Bangladesh, I became fully aware of the cardinal truth that a lesser people might call unfettered delusion—there are Bengalis, and there is the world. (A corollary quickly followed—there is Kolkata, and there is the world.)

At this time, what lesser people might call a tender age, I already attempted to abide by a list of expectations. These included impeccable table manners—expected of me, it seemed, immediately after birth, and especially after graduating onnōprāshōn, an elaborate ceremony in which an infant is fed solid food for the first time, usually a morsel of our quite unparalled preparation of pāyésh of rice with thickened milk, and sweetened with jaggery. (The colloquialism is mukhé-bhāt, literally, rice in the mouth, usually offered by a maternal uncle—māmā.) That is also when, in many households, the infant is ceremonially shown a future diet, including impeccably displayed rice, vegetables and fish, evidently in the hope of an unimpeded journey along our Eightfold Path that venerates desire and usually begins with food.

That was followed by expectations of impeccable handwriting in Bānglā and English, reading which included Western classics and little of the Eastern except, naturally, Bengali; speech with erudition; musicianship with at least one classical instrument (for me, toblā and later, shétār). Then there was trivia, for a Bengali akin to *The Fifth Element*. A random sample: knowledge of the names of countries and their capitals—What is the capital of Upper Volta? Ougadougou, thank you, Titu-kāku; what is the Rōbindrōshōngeet exponent Debabrata Biswas's nickname? George, thank you, Papa (Papa? We were an Ingō-Bongō household, employing English and Bānglā with equal fervour, a home where roast chicken with gravy and potatoes was as much a treat as the chātni of tomato, dates and raisins made by Dādu-mā, as we called my paternal grandmother Nirupama—the incomparable, unique). There had to be knowledge of epic fantasies like the Mahabharata—Mohābhārōt—that we, naturally, narrated best (Who were the tragic warrior Abhimanyu's parents? The incomparable archer Arjuna and Krishna's sister Subhadra, thank you, Dādu-mā).

Alongside arrived knowledge of the names of our classical artists if not appreciation of their art—at seven it would have been too much even for a Bengali child—Abanindranath Tagore, or Obōn Thākur, nephew of Rabindranath; Jamini Roy and Nandalal Bose. Seamlessly from the same fount of knowledge arrived executive summaries and demonstration of another, no less appreciated art form, the major varieties of fish that we ate, and hand-to-mouth expertise with which to devour these; the seasons in which certain varieties of spinach became available and the precise proportion of rice and precise dash of kāshundi—the incomparable mustard that can brighten even a luminous Bengali meal—to eat these with, and the protocol of always beginning with vegetables, bitters first, then moving along in that order to dāl, fish, then meat, and chātni before dessert, and to never, on pain of death or, at least, denial of family inheritance, to *never* vary from such progression or, the horror, mix one course with another; the protocol, meaning and importance of behavioural nuance at family gatherings, whose feet to touch in what order, when to smile, when to remain dignified, or deadpan (Thank you, Mā-mōni, you jewel among mothers).

The state of politics was always abysmal; so were national priorities—in which the Bengali would always rule best, had he or even she ever been permitted to rule in the first place (Thank you all, family and friends of the family, the barber, the family doctor, the dentist, the orthopaedic surgeon, the homeopathy consultant, the neighbourhood chemist, the neighbourhood newspaper and magazine vendor and bookseller, the neighbourhood dry-cleaner, the neighbourhood grocer, Monōhor-babu, our chauffeur...).

My sister, who was three at the time, had less expected of her. She had merely to smile beguilingly at everyone; sing the national anthem of India and another paean to the pride of identity and hope that would shortly become the national anthem of Bangladesh—both written by Rabindranath Tagore, the first Bengali to win a Nobel prize; begin a charming rendering of these songs and recitation of the Bānglā alphabet in front of guests, who would dutifully smile; some ladies would, in turn, lightly hold her chin and then bring that flowerbud of fingers of their right hand to their lips in a loud smack, appreciation of such regimented but undeniable sweetness, and say, 'Ki mishti'. Besides, she would need to behave impeccably at the table.

More knowledge would quickly follow. More awareness. More theories. More truths. More absolute truths. More contradictions. Meanwhile, the world revolved around us, the Bengalis—that much was axiomatic. I cannot speak for my sister (but, of course, I shall—imprinted in our cultural double helix is the right to speak on behalf of entire civilizations, what is a mere individual, even a sibling?) but it all seemed like we were part of a grand experiment. At the very least, we were a part of something interesting, of which we understood little but saw much. The world around us was in churn. Kolkata was a violent place, a geography of urban warfare between left-wing rebels and police and the government's henchmen. Our parents and family would speak in low tones about trouble brewing in East Pakistan, maybe a war. Why didn't anything seem to work in Kolkata? Why were there so many poor in our city, and wherever we went outside the city? Why were cinema halls closed down so often? Why were red flags everywhere? How could we be such a great people and yet, as Father kept repeating, in clipped Ingréji, be 'going to the dogs'?

◆

More often than not, books showed us the way to a universe of adventure and longing, and a way out of doubt and trouble—as books so often do. As I have said, we began to read the vast range of Bengali classics early. It was hardly exceptional—we were among a multitude. But we read works from other cultures, too, mostly Western as these were at the time the more popular translations: as a culture that generally looked to the West if at all we looked anywhere beyond the homeland, and so we often saw the world as the West saw the world.

In 1974, our cousin Hirak, gifted my sister Sumangali a book of stories, *Golpér Bisshōmelā*. (I still have the book with notes scribbled in a child's scrawl.) Such gifts were commonplace, and such books printed by the thousands, even tens of thousands, ahead of Durga Pujō. For children it was the literary and cultural gateway to the country and the world, perhaps even the seed that infects so many Bengalis with travel-madness. This global festival of stories carried chatty translations in Bānglā of excerpts or short stories by, among others, Luigi Pirandello, Somerset Maugham, Arthur Conan Doyle,

Leo Tolstoy, Nikolai Gogol, Alexander Pushkin, Ernest Hemingway, Daphne du Maurier, William Faulkner, Vicente Blasco Ibáñez, and a particularly disturbing auto-da-fé gem by Count de Villiers de l'Isle-Adam. Both Hirak and my sister were seven at the time. I was eleven, and arrogant, having moved on to reading such works and more modern writing in English, the cadet-bhodrōlōk's linguistic holy grail. But, of course, I surreptitiously devoured the book on the very next vacation from boarding school in faraway Rajasthan—my first real mingling with people and cultures other than Bengali.

It wasn't always such serious reading. We knew also to laugh at ourselves—some of the time, anyway; even as children.

Some of it was just pure fun, nonsense and satire in a delightful mix as in that children's staple, *Ābōl-Tābōl* and *Ho-Jo-Bo-Ro-Lo*, nonsense rhymes of the first collection written as early as 1914, the second, a tale, in 1922. These were created by Sukumar Ray, father to our Satyajit, the film-maker. Where else except in a universe touched by the likes of Edward Lear or Lewis Carroll, will you find what Satyajit termed 'whimsical compounds'—the Storkoise, Whalephant, Parakizard, Liontelope. Where but in *A Topsy-Turvy Tale* would we find humour in arithmetic as when a crow earnestly asks 'What's seven times two?' right after a handkerchief turns into a cat and, to avoid the heat, directs children to Tibet ('Here's Kolkata, and here's Diamond Harbour a little to the south, and here's Ranaghat a little to the north, and then—you're in Tibet!'):

> I wondered what it could be this time. As I looked about me, the voice came again: 'Why aren't you answering? What's seven times two?' I looked up and saw a jungle-crow scribbling something on a slate and bobbing his head towards me. 'Seven times two is fourteen,' I answered.
> He shook his head very hard and said, 'Wrong answer! No marks!'
> 'Of course I'm right!' I protested. 'Seven ones are seven, seven twos are fourteen, seven threes are twenty-one.'

The Crow didn't answer for a while, but just sat there sucking his pencil.

Then he began muttering, 'Seven twos are fourteen, put down four and carry the pencil.'

'Well then!' said I...

'It wasn't quite fourteen when you spoke,' answered the Crow. 'At that point it was only 13 rupees 14 annas and 3 pice. If I hadn't put down 14 just at the right moment, it would have got to 14 rupees 1 anna and 9 pice by now.'

'I've never heard such rubbish,' I told him. 'If seven twos make fourteen, it's always fourteen, an hour ago or ten days from now.'

The Crow looked shocked and said, 'Don't you count the cost of time in your country?'

Following close on exhilarating satire was exhilarating exaggeration. There's a charming slang for it—gul. The endemic gul mārār jāygā pāōni? is a phrase most in Bengal grow up with or have frequently heard relatives, teachers, elders, or friends tell someone—even themselves. 'Couldn't find another place to fib?' can in East Bengali dialect be gul mārtāsé or gul ditāsé—literally, hitting with a fib, and giving a fib. I've even heard chāp ditāsé, 'giving' pressure, chāp, a colloquialism that is typically applied to giving someone a hard time. There's nothing to beat a sometime staple at Jadavpur University in Kolkata, where the other favourite fib-slang, dhop— say it like gawp—is used masterfully. Along with your chā and ghughni you get to eat dhop-ér chop. It's a fine counterpoint to a saying in Bānglā: Golpō bōli tōh olpō kyanō? If I have to tell a story, why stop short?

As children there was enough joyous gul, particularly in short stories in Durga Pujō annuals. That's how I met Boglā-mama one day in the early 1970s, just shy of ten, in a story called 'Boglā-mama versus Dracula'. It was peppered with gul twinned with adventure, a staple irresistible to a child—and funny enough to chuckle to as

Sudeep Chakravarti

I read it again as a middle-aged man. I found the book in a trunk of my childhood things my parents had preserved.

The story by Rajkumar Maitra featured a bunch of youngsters hanging around in a colliery township near Kolkata, studies jettisoned with schools and colleges closed on account of the bombing of Kolkata by the Japanese. In the course of the story Boglā-mama and his young cohort of hangers-on—shāngō-pāngō, in colloquial Bānglā—conquer the reawakened dead, the ghoulish remnant of a noble scion who had murdered his uncle. Naturally, Boglā-mama led the fearless troupe. The setting for it was Rajmahal, a small town by the widening Ganga in the borderlands of Bengal and Jharkhand, not far from the Farakka barrage that now dams the river before it flows into Bangladesh. Boglā-mama's heroism ended with an exchange during a post-adventure āddā. It went something like this:

> Nāru said, 'Boglā-mama really saved us this time. Didn't he, Hābu?'
> Hābu stayed quiet.
> Boglā-mama then turned to us, his face stern. 'Let me tell you a true story,' he said after a while. 'This Second World War would never have started if Chamberlain-shāhéb had responded to my letter. I had written to shāhéb five years earlier: find some way to entice Hitler-shāhéb out of Germany, get him to India, make him a guard in the railways. Bas! Hitler would never ever think of Germany. He'd spend the rest of his life blowing whistles and waving flags.'
> Calmly, Boglā-mama lit a cigarette.
> 'Chamberlain-shāhéb didn't even bother replying to my letter. And so Hitler started the war.'

◆

The Bengalis is a freewheeling, unabashedly empathetic and yet, I hope, unswervingly critical (and if this makes me Bengali non grata, so be it!) account of a people that have, for better and worse, helped shape a subcontinent. They are continuing to help shape a subcontinent and an appreciable slice of the world outside it. In their homelands, Bangladesh and the state of West Bengal in India, in a slice of Assam, the usurped province of Tripura and in other places on the Indian subcontinent and elsewhere in the world where reside minimal or substantial numbers of Bengalis— Banglasphere in mind, body and spirit—they are attempting to trump the downsides of history, often a history of their own making, by trying emphatically to reach for a future with more fortitude and foresight than is perhaps granted them.

To the not-Bengali (I cannot bear to call you 'non-Bengali'), part-Bengali, and Bengali alike: This is my story of Bengal, the land of my birth if not immaculate belonging (not always, at any rate), even though Bengal is in me deeply, beyond carry-forward history; beyond the ability to speak, read and write Bānglā; beyond frequent visits to Bengal and other geographies of Banglasphere; the love of various forms of art and literature; and the perennial hot-button of our cuisine in memory and welcome reality that triggers a condition a Bengali knows in all its inelegance and truth: jibhé jol éshé jāy. To unashamedly salivate, figuratively, at the thought of our fine food, any fine food, is our way.

This is a personalized, often anecdotal journey about being Bengali that attempts to embrace history, politics, conflict, culture, and aspects of our homeland in the western and eastern part of Bengal—once East Bengal, then violently East Pakistan and, since a horrific, genocidal war in 1971, Bangladesh—the country that was born because it wanted to be Bengali, as much as speak it. My personal history, like that of several million Bengalis, is deeply rooted in both West Bengal and Bangladesh.

My journey includes several 'non-resident' years across India, at study and work in Rajasthan and Delhi, a year's non-prōbāshi hiatus in Kolkata grappling with an intensely trying culture of work and yet culturally energized 'play', followed by nearly fifteen years of work in Delhi (with two years of inadvertent residency in the city's so-called Mini Bengal of Chittaranjan Park), then to my adoptive home of Goa for more than a decade to pursue independent research and writing, and now a life in the borderlands of Tamil Nadu and Kerala. When I was done, I discovered that *The Bengalis* had become a story of magical simplicities, of miasma, of loves, passions and dreams, of deep hatreds, of secured insecurities, of grand and terrible histories, of grand riches and terrible poverty of both wealth and wisdom, of entire civilizations lost, won and lost in the blink of history's eye. It is a story about the hearts and minds of my people, our aspirations and foibles, stunning achievements and massive destructive force.

S. C.
The Velliangiri Hills
August 2017

Book I
Utshō
Genesis and More

.... ⌐ ....

1

Jonmō shutrō
Immaculate conceptions

The emergence of the Bengali can sometimes appear to be an immaculate misconception. If we go by what is broadcast by Bengali chauvinists as a self-evident truth it would seem as though the Bengali race emerged from some superior, grandly endowed chrysalis in the form of a blindingly beautiful butterfly, charming and dominating the world of intellect and culture with a flurry of delicate, artfully wrought wings. The truth is somewhat different. The Bengali race and culture was more the result of an immense mixing, an aggregation of numerous races and religions which arrived in the subcontinent for survival and conquest; a gradual accumulation of ways, wisdom and waywardness like the sure flow and conjoining of three great river systems in eastern India and present-day Bangladesh—the Brahmaputra, the Ganga and the Meghna, and their bewildering network of tributaries and distributaries.

This is what defines our land. *The History of Bengal*, the landmark series co-edited by Ramesh Chandra Majumdar, the first comprehensive history of our land and our people seen from the perspective of the modern Bengali, is remarkably humble in its acceptance of our place. Published in 1943 by the University of Dhaka (or Dacca, as English phonetics and spelling decreed it then), a scant three years before religious barbarity would tear apart Bengal, *The History* declared:

The province of Bengal lacks some of the extraordinary varieties of physical aspect for which the great sub-continent, of which it is an integral part, is justly famous. It has no deserts or hills or ridges except on the fringe in the extreme north, east and west. It cannot boast of anything comparable to the purple waters of the Kashmirian lakes which reflect the splendours of Haramukh, the gushing streams of Central India which leap into falls amidst the marble rocks near Jubbulpore, or the backwaters and cascades of Malabar that lend charm to the scenery...

It can, however, justly take pride in the snow-capped peaks with golden crests in the northern district of Darjeeling, a vast riverine plain which forms the focus of three great river-systems where the country 'widens out into a panorama of irrigated fertility', of swamps and flats in the south cut up by hundreds of coves and creeks, once the 'royal throne of kings', now the residence of the lord of the jungles.

Bengalis have for long claimed the Darjeeling hills and the superlative embroidery of the Himalaya beyond as their own even though they have no ethnic or linguistic claim whatsoever to those lands settled by the Lepcha or Rongpa, later inundated by those of Nepali extraction, among others. Darjeeling and its superb teas are administrative and commercial legacies of the British to Bengal—to West Bengal. But, yes, the river systems are indisputably us.

These rivers brought the bounty of silt and connectivity as a gift of ages. The Yarlung Tsangpo, 'water flowing from the crest', all the way from Tibet, arcing its way east into India's eastern extremity and then making a sharp turn west through Arunachal Pradesh as the Siang, and Assam as Brahmaputra—son of the creator, Brahma—for a run of over 900 kilometres, before turning south into Bangladesh. Here it changes name and gender to the Yamuna—Jōmunā to us, sister of the god of death: Jom in Bānglā, Yama to the not-Bengali—for the journey south to the Bay of Bengal, a journey of nearly 3,000 kilometres from Tibet to tail. But it does so with a riverine sibling, the Ganga, mythically brought down from the heavens to purify spirits on earth and nourish the land as Mother Ganga. Mā Gongā to the devout Bengali Hindu, she arrives from the western Himalaya, feeding and watering a great swathe of the Indian subcontinent for nearly 2,000 kilometres before weaving into Bangladesh. Then she becomes the Padma (we call her Poddā, lotus, but with the bounty she brings she is perhaps more Mā Lōkkhi—the goddess of wealth, Lakshmi—who is usually depicted as seated or standing on a lotus) her boon sustaining tens of millions of farmers and fisherfolk.

The Padma joins the Yamuna in central Bangladesh, northwest of Dhaka, and subsumes her. Yamuna-née-Brahmaputra-née-Tsangpo takes on the name of Padma.

Meanwhile, the Ganga leaves a significant branch in West Bengal, the Bhagirathi (daughter of Bhagirath) named for the penitent prince Bhagirath who invited Ganga from the heavens with a transit through Shiva's topknot to reduce her force, to weave its way past Kolkata—indeed, spawning Kolkata—before reaching the Bay of Bengal.

The Bhagirathi is today better known as the Hooghly, an inelegant name also ascribed to a town that became home to medieval Portuguese traders and pillagers who, like so many, flocked to Bengal, smelling riches in textiles, farm products and slaves—this last a lucrative side-business. The Bengalis came to call the often piratical Portuguese firingee (or phiringi), a name that many Bengalis still call them by, instead of Pōrtugij, denying these brilliantly canny and exploring louts any formal nationality in an inadvertent revenge of nomenclature damning them with the generic Persian word for the European foreigner. In contrast, the trading and visiting colonial and post-colonial French have remained Phorāshi, the Dutch, Ōlōndāj, the overlordly English, Ingréj. The American, to whom some latter-day Marx–Mao- and Ho Chi Minh-worshipping Bengalis have added the hyphenation 'neo-colonial', remain Mārkin. And those of the emergent superpower with its geopolitical dragon claws in Bangladesh, but perceptibly reduced in Kolkata to a race selling shoes, offering services such as dry cleaning, and some of the tastiest food in South Asia, are Chiné.

There is a third great river, perhaps less grand than her siblings but supremely generous with her waters and silt, the Meghna. Meaning 'of the clouds', she has her headwaters in the hills of the state of Meghalaya, the gloriously named 'abode of clouds' that embroiders the northern boundaries of the Bengali homeland, and the plains of Bengal. (It is for me always Bengal, never the split personalities of West Bengal and Bangladesh in geographical features. It seems natural to leave the trying aspect of borders and divisions to the discussion of political features and recent history.) This river system, taking names along the way from principal streams and tributaries—the Surma, as it winds past Sylhet in Bangladesh; the Barak, as it emerges from Assam after a journey through the Indian provinces of Manipur and Mizoram—grows in stature, births both the Surma and the Barak's southern stream, Kushiara, and grows into the Meghna. When the Meghna merges with the Padma (already merged with the Yamuna) south of Dhaka, this enormous hydra of a river system adopts Meghna's name as it barrels south into the Bay of Bengal.

There are more than 700 large, medium and small rivers that feed into the Padma-Yamuna-Meghna (and the Bhagirathi as Hooghly). The Teesta emerges from the eastern Himalaya and traverses the northern plains of West Bengal as a major river, but it merges into the several-kilometres-wide Yamuna in Bangladesh. The Ganga-Padma is already fed by scores of rivers as it travels eastwards through the Indo-Gangetic plains. But even the relatively humbler Bhagirathi-Hooghly is watered by great rivers in the province of West Bengal, the Damodar, Ajay, Roopnarayan—to us Dāmōdor, Ojoy, Roopnārāyon—that descend from the Chota Nagpur Plateau and hills further west, before being absorbed in the flow of what for many Bengalis remains the true branch of the Ganga as it flows to the sea. (Whatever the history of shifting river courses and science of mapping of rivers and riverbeds may show, this Ganga helps Bengali Hindus with their religiosity. For them, the Ganga couldn't possibly be anywhere but in West Bengal with its majority Hindu population, the waters of the Bhagirathi-Hooghly as sacred as the waters of the Ganga as descended from Gangotri in the Himalaya, as pure and good for ceremonial purpose even though it flushes the filth of India during its passage through West Bengal. The Hooghly needs to be Hindu enough, not just a giver of life—and, occasionally, death—in order to sustain the stream of myth that flows from it. In Bangladesh, despite its growing oeuvre of fundamentalist Islam, rivers with most un-Islamic of names have thus far remained secular!)

This riverine collective made the vast plains of Bengal and an immense delta, and is fringed to the south by the mangroves and island-laden Sundarbans—Shundōrbōn, a 'beautiful forest', if you prefer the literal translation; or a forest of sundari trees, a species of mangrove. This is the remarkable forest and the 'tide country' described so eloquently and brought to the world by the novelist Amitav Ghosh as both a geographical feature as well as a historically charged microcosm decanted into the creation myths and realities and politics of Bengal. 'For this I have seen and confirmed many times,' Nirmal, the tortured, heartbroken conscience-keeper of Ghosh's searching work, *The Hungry Tide*, writes in his journal, 'that the mudbanks of the tide country are shaped not only by rivers of silt, but by rivers of language: Bengali, English, Arabic, Hindi, Arakanese and who knows what else? Flowing into each other they create a proliferation of small worlds that hang suspended in the flow. And so it dawned on me: the tide country's faith is like something of one of its great mohonas, a meeting not just of many rivers, but a circular roundabout people can use to pass in many directions—from country to country and even between faiths and religions.'

The force of the sea is so powerful in the Sundarbans that

before the rains takes over in June, bringing with them swollen rivers and cyclones, a time of spectacular death, destruction and destitution, tides bring seawater a hundred or more kilometres inland, flavouring the water and low-lying land with brackish water. Ghosh's rich telling spans an evocative slice of the forest and its spiderweb of rivers in a tiny part of West Bengal. But there is a whole lot more, literally, to the Sundarbans which spans nearly 10,000 square kilometres, mostly in Bangladesh. It is the largest delta in the world, stretching just shy of 400 kilometres from west to east, and is home, among numerous species of land and marine creatures, to the Royal Bengal Tiger, as regal as any Bengali ruler, and perhaps a lot cleverer in the way it maps its territory and conducts its hunt and survival. To visit the tide country, let alone live there, is to become a changed person. The scale of the rivers, the often-immeasurable horizon, the otherworldly life of water and jungle touched by natural elements of sun and dark and mist and rain and storm cloud and raging storm, take a day and transform it into an event.

These rivers and plains attracted, fed and groomed immigrants of numerous races and religions who gradually claimed indigeneity.

Early travellers to Bengal were impressed by what they found. The fourteenth-century chronicler, whose travels were as extensive as his name, Abu Abdullah Muhammad Ibn Abdullah al-Lawati al-Tanji Ibn Battuta, wrote in his *Rihla*, after a visit in 1345, during the reign of Sultan Muhammad bin Tughluq, his host and for some years his patron: 'I have seen no country in the world where provisions are cheaper than in this country.' This Moroccan traveller described 'Bengala' as 'vast' and 'abounding in rice'.

We attracted traders, our boon and then our bane. The writer Madhusree Mukerjee reminds us how foreign merchants 'worked the wholesale markets, offering to buy produce in exchange of silver'. They could trade in goods, because Bengal was in need of 'virtually nothing':

Bengal's rice was exported to Sri Lanka and the Maldives, its sugar to Arabia and Mesopotamia, and its silks to Europe; ships at its ports were loaded with such exports as wheat biscuits and salted meats, opium, varnish, wax, musk, spices, preserved fruits and clarified butter. Bengal's cottons, supplied to much of the world, were astonishing in variety and quality: twenty yards of a delicate muslin could be stuffed into a snuffbox. One can only imagine for what sublime piece of fabric...a seventeenth-century visitor, Mirza Nathan [a familiar of the Mughal prince Khurram, later the emperor Shahjahan, and credited with writing *Baharistan-i-Ghaibi*, a chronicle of Mughal adventures in eastern India] paid 4,000 rupees, given that a single rupee bought a score of chickens.

As you will read in several fine retellings of aspects of our history by Bengalis, from a Ramesh Majumdar to Ashok Mitra and Nitish Sengupta to Madhusree Mukerjee and numerous near-faultless and faulty scholarly works in between, people who represent diverse generations, ideologies and persuasions, we are fond of quoting the travels of the French physican François Bernier who, like Mirza Nathan, visited us in the seventeenth century, a year before Shah Jahan died, in 1666. Aurangzeb was then the grand Mughal. Bernier described 'Bengale' as the 'finest and most fruitful country in the world'. The merchants of Bengal lived lavishly with their brocades and jewellery, eating off gold and silver plates. From his account, those closer to the earth ate well too, a mix of vegetables and rice, some ghee, 'purchased for the merest trifle'. Fish and meat, then as now integral to the Bengali diet, were abundant. 'Bengale abounds with every necessity of life' and this 'rich exuberance', as Bernier put it wonderingly—and a bit joyously—as it provided also the welcome corollary of the 'beauty and amiable disposition of the native women'. All taken together, wrote the charmed Frenchman, it has 'given rise to a proverb in common use among the Portuguese, English and Dutch, that the kingdom of Bengale has a hundred gates open for entrance, but not one for departure'.

The British, of course, knew this well. They took a while to leave, arriving emphatically in the seventeenth century and leaving a few hundred years later. Bengal their major bank and resource for financing the industrial revolution and irrepressible empire.

Thomas Babington Macaulay, the intellectual architect of among the most influential moves in British India, who said that the 'English language might be well and thoroughly taught' to the 'native', was as effusive in his praise of Bengal as he was withering in his criticism of the Bengali. In an essay on Bengal's corporate conqueror Robert Clive for the *Edinburgh Review* in 1840, Macaulay wrote an excellent raison d'être for the East India Company's initial focus on Bengal, and for General Clive's persistence:

> Of the provinces which had been subject to the house of Tamerlane, the wealthiest was Bengal. No part of India possessed such natural advantages, both for agriculture and for commerce. The Ganges, rushing through a hundred channels to the sea, has formed a vast plain of rich mould which, even under the tropical sky, rivals the verdure of an English April. The rice fields yield an increase such as is elsewhere unknown. Spices, sugar, vegetable oils, are produced with marvellous exuberance. The rivers afford an inexhaustible supply of fish. The desolate islands along the seacoast, overgrown by noxious vegetation, and swarming with deer and tigers, supply the cultivated districts with abundance of salt. The great stream which fertilises the soil is, at the same time, the chief highway of Eastern commerce. On its banks, and on those of its tributary waters, are the wealthiest marts, the most splendid capitals, and the most sacred shrines of India. The tyranny of man had for ages struggled in vain against the overflowing bounty of nature. In spite of the Mussulman despot, and of the Mahratta freebooter, Bengal was known through the East as the garden of Eden, as the rich kingdom. Its population

multiplied exceedingly. Distant provinces were nourished from the overflowing of its granaries; and the noble ladies of London and Paris were clothed in the delicate produce of its looms.

◆

It's easy to get carried away in Bengal—about Bengal. A counterpoint is sobering, and necessary.

Ibn Battuta was a master at delivering praise as subtle coup de grâce: 'But it is muggy…' he wrote of Bengal, and recounted the natter of those who came from the drier parts of Central Asia, for instance, who 'call it a hell full of good things'. Truer words to describe the Bengali homeland are difficult to find.

The horrors of humidity and much more, tropical insects and infestations, as described by Ibn Battuta and his contemporaries, conquistadors and settlers alike, are of course merely partial horrors. There have been hells beyond imagining, with Bengalis visiting horrors on each other as much as they had horrors visited upon them by non-Bengalis—the British, for instance. These plains, these deltas, are what made Bengal, made the Bengali. Some day in a not-too-distant and quite paranoid future I subscribe to in moments of concern, these deltas and plains could see the unmaking of Bengal, and the morphing of the Bengali into a creature not of cultural superiority but of pure survival, transcending ethnicity, and making religion at best a means to that survival.

That is a thought for later. Now is for nature, beauty before the beast.

◆

Have you seen—felt—our seasons? Life on earth must begin with Boshōntō, our crisp spring that lends its name to both man and woman, and rituals of renewal of land and nature, a time of bounty. Our Grishshō will drain you as it does us, baking us, boiling us, and then bringing tantalizing, terrifying storms, the Kālbōishākhi, presaging a season that makes us and sometimes breaks us, our life-giving, life-taking force of Borshā, monsoon rain. So much of it—curing, caring, cleansing, cruel rain in a land where lightning is known to strike at the same place more than once.

Shorōt arrives next, a still-damp autumn like a sigh of relief, gifting us back our skies, lands and waterways. (Like Boshōntō, Shorōt too is one that we have named our children after: my great-grandmother was named Shorōtkāmini, as beautiful, as desirable as Shorōt). The damp reduces during Hémontō, another etymological root and the time of festivals for so many of us, the time of ritual worship of the Mother—the Woman—as Goddess. Sheet or winter visits us after, with our vast wetlands and waterways adding surprising chill and damp to Himalayan breezes that often travel our way, for a month or more, cooling even our immense metropolises, our teeming cities.

Bengal makes us elemental.

Have you been on our rivers? In the early morning, when mist washes over them, white over fading dark before the sun, paler in winter and fiery in summer, arrives in streams of gold as you sit on the prow of a simple wooden nōukō with a curved roof of latticed bamboo, or greet the day from the deck of a launch as you search for the impossibly far banks in the Sundarbans? Have you walked by our fields of green or golden rice with its heavy fragrance, and found meaning in abstractions of māti, mrittikā—Mother Earth? Have you seen our greens, the Bengal greens, greener than all the greens of our mind's eye and superior to every shade born of industry? Paddy-green, mango-green, jackfruit-green, bamboo-green, guava-green, chilli-green, bayleaf-green, moss-green, banyan-green?

Have you seen our hibiscus-red, shāri-red and Durga-red, draping our women—a species our men at once cherish and chastise—from the simplest beauty to awe-inspiring, even frightening vehicle for the deliverance of justice?

Or our riot-red, or our rebellion-red? Our pomegranate-pink? Our grapefruit-orange? Our lemon-yellow?

Have you seen the absolute majesty of our cloud-grey and cloud-black that bring with them the promise of the densest rain, giver of our way of life, and sometimes the fiercest storms that erase life by the hundreds, thousands, hundreds of thousands? The rainbow of our chhāu, the mesmeric, near-martial dance from far-western Purulia with its primal folk rhythms that bring alive the epics, and life itself, with colour, devotion and energy beyond imagining? The pink-purple-white shāplā in a nearby pukur or beel that open to the sun, prettily, eerily sentient in the way they follow our lifegiver with their petals? Or the kaleidoscopic kingfisher that waits to feed, the blackest cormorant which, after feeding, spreads its wings to dry with the majesty of an eagle? The silver sparkle of fish in muddy waters, free, or caught and served—our stereotypical protein? Our darkest nights lit with the yellow-green fluorescence of fireflies, the folkloric vehicle of restless spirits which lead the unwary to a mesmerized death? Our darkest hearts that we have fought against for a hundred years and more, in our ongoing claim on culture and humanity?

Beauty *and* the beast.

These are the ingredients of our songs, our poetry, our writing, our revolutions. This is what we carry with us to our homes and hearts in some of the densest forests of concrete and cacophony to be found anywhere in the world where so many of us now live and love, our cramped rooms the sky, tiny potted plants all the bounty of our fields, and a hint of rain all the rivers of Bengal. If so many tens of millions of us didn't have this dream-reality we would be mere husks of Bengalis. Make-believe-Bengal, Bengal-in-our-minds is a crucial life force for a Bengali, our precious store of who we are.

Journey with me.

◆

I have had my breath taken away by a peerless sight, standing on the plateau of Meghalaya, a land that in parts is so lush as to make a Bengali who knows green, blue and brown as well as any inhabitant of the tropic, soak up its beauty in awed silence. From where I stood it seemed as though all the shops of the world had been emptied of colour and poured into this landscape. At other times it was like watching the floor of an ocean. I have also flown over this plateau—observing the cascades of blue from a great height on a clear summer or winter day, it was more like watching the floor of an ocean—a descent from continental shelf to abyssal plains.

From here the rivers of Bengal are ribbons. They work their way to the Bay of Bengal, no mere bay named by colonial imagination but a vast sea, too far to perceive even from a great height, but not difficult to imagine as it merges into the blue in the far horizon of the mind's eye, at the end of this land shaped roughly like an inverted, busy candelabra. Here there is no hint of the cacophony of life, of the quarter of a billion of humanity and inhumanity caught in the ebb and flow of history past—and history as-we-make-it—that mark the Bengali as palimpsest as much as people.

This is the cradle of our birth, our imagination, our very own tale of genesis.

◆

The proto-Bengali appears to have had a bit of an unsavoury reputation in those ancient times. We learn in Majumdar's *The History* that 'Jaina [Jain] writers of the *Āchārānga-sūtra* describe the land of the Lādhas (Rādha) in West Bengal as a pathless country inhabited by rude folk who attacked peaceful monks.' Our seemingly loutish ancestors are believed to have even set dogs upon such self-confessedly gentle folk, even the Jain spiritual great Vardhamana Mahavira during his sixth century BCE South Asian ramble. '[M]any natives attacked him, and dogs ran at him. Few people kept off the attacking beasts. Striking the monk they cried "*chu chchhu*" and made the dogs bite him.' Other mendicants had to make do with 'rough food' when visiting. It appears that our ancestors contributed handsomely to the frugality of such monks.

Perhaps—who can tell?—they even helped to inject some fortitude into this enduring religious stream.

Our regions of Pundravardhana and Vanga were also evidently much outside the civilizational posh of Aryavarta that was watered by the Upper Ganga and Yamuna rivers and bound by the Himalaya to the north and Vindhyas to the south—according to troubadours of Aryan supremacy who have driven racial perception management in India for over two thousand years. Along with Kalinga (a region in ancient Odisha) and Sauvira (southern Punjab and Sind), ancient Bengal's regions were 'altogether regarded as outside the pale of Vedic culture. Persons who lived amidst these folks even for a temporary period were required to go through expiatory rites.'

Such ancient humiliation for the eventual Bengali, now so proud of the Aryan mote in his subcontinental eye, seems to have been alleviated in later times by inclusion in the Hindu epics, when our ancestors were 'no longer shunned as impure barbarians'. In the Ramayana, for instance, we learn that the Vangas 'entered into intimate political relations with the high-born aristocrats of Ayodhya'—in that game of thrones it doesn't take much to imagine what intimacy in political relations signified. And, that search parties for the abducted heroine Sita were also counselled to look east to Pundra, which approximates to northwestern Bengal. (Though if such easterly lands are equated with places where the wondrous Sita, consort of the semi-divine Ārjōputrō Rām could have been abducted to, like the Aryan-free and Aryan-demonized land of Lanka to which she was ultimately traced, it doesn't speak well of our intimate 'political' relations with these Aryan sons.)

In the Mahabharata, proto-Bengalis are mentioned but not as a salutary species. Our ancestors were mythically invaded and pillaged, not by the marauding Mussulman and Christian that are favourite villains of latter-day proponents of cultural domination of the Bengali Hindu by sword and religion, but by the creamy layer of the Hindus' very own battering ram. In an early mythical play of what Marathas would visit upon the western fringes of Bengal in the eighteenth and nineteenth centuries CE, the righteous Pandava brother Bhima (or Bheem, as Bengalis know him) visited us. 'Having killed the king of Modāgiri [equated with presented-day Monghyr in Bihar] he fell upon the mighty lord of the Pundras as well as the potentate who ruled on the banks of the river Kosi [a tributary of Ganga that descends from Nepal and runs through north-eastern Bihar].' *The History* interprets for us this self-righteous mayhem, as well as subsequent mayhem visited upon all manner of proto-Bengalis. The Pandavas' holier-than-thou aura didn't prevent general conquest and slaughter even before the epic battle of the Mahabharata.

'Having defeated them he attacked the king of the Vangas.' Next he reduced to subjection the lords of Tāmralipta (modern Tamluk in East Medinipur district of West Bengal) and Karvata, apparently a neighbouring place, as well as the ruler of the Suhmas (in Hooghly district), those who lived in maritime regions, and all the hordes of outlandish barbarians (Mlechchhas). 'Having conquered these territories and despoiling them of their riches'—an unadulterated shade for nearly all invaders and traders to Bengal; I imagine this to be an early reference to raiding the nature derived and artisan-driven wealth of Bengal—'the mighty victor advanced to the Lauhitya (Brahmaputra)'.

Besides being driven to loss by this muscle-bound Pandava, and also, presumably, to subsequent gain (Aryan-glory tellings are rarely without white-man's-burden references), such texts tell us that Karna, the dispossessed Pandava, who on account of a quirk of fate signed on with his cousins, the Kauravas, had a go at us as well. And Krishna, too, who counselled his wards, the Pandavas, as to the necessity of just warfare, whatever its cost in death and destruction. Unfortunately, we were on the losing side—the king of Vanga was a Kaurava ally, evidently driven by the proto-Bengali king's hatred of the Pandavas on account of their hammering away at the kingdoms of his neighbours, several of whom also signed up with Kauravas. Nevertheless, it appeared to have been a heck of a ride while it lasted. Some history texts record the *Bhishma*

Parva's lively description of a battle in which the 'mighty ruler of the Vangas' faced off against the Pandavas to stand resolutely by his Kaurava patron, the prince Duryodhana:

> Beholding that lance levelled at Duryodhana, the lord of the Vangas quickly arrived on the scene with his elephant that towered like a mountain. He covered the Kuru king's chariot with the body of the animal. Ghatotokacha, [the shape-shifting son of our tormentor, the terminator Bheem, and the she-demon Hidimba], his eyes reddened with rage, flung his upraised missile at the beast. Struck with the dart the elephant bled profusely and fell down dead. The rider quickly jumped down from the falling animal...

And then Duryodhana quickly came to the rescue.

The epic tells us that some kings of Bengal fought on elephant-back; others preferred 'ocean-bred steeds of the hue of the moon'. All, however, had 'fierce energy'.

Not too shabby, courage-wise, for a people ridiculed as bhitu, kāpurush or cowardly, in particular by the British. An epic outing is an epic outing even if it comes from balladeers and historians eager to establish Bengalis were present with the best, or worst of them, with unflinching honour. That matters to us. We love the idea of courage and honour even though the modern world has historically—the stereotype driven by the British and in turn perpetated by others in South Asia—seen us as a lot of clerks and troublemakers.

Basically, people who *talk* a lot more than they *do*.

◆

There isn't much recorded history to go by for this time of the ancients, for regions and kingdoms, or for the root of the word Banga (pronounced Bongō, as in Pōshchim Bongō for West Bengal and Purbō Bongō for East Bengal, now Bangladesh). It's also the root of who we are, Bāngāli as we call ourselves, and the language we speak, Bānglā.

This brings us to Ibn Battuta's Bengala which is also the Bangala of Duarte Barbosa, a scrivener with the Portuguese in India in the early part of the sixteenth century, who wrote of the 'great city of the Moors, which they call Bangala'—a likely reference to Chittagong; though some historians have interpreted it as possibly being Sonargaon, near Dhaka, or Gaur, the ancient-medieval kingdom and capital in northern Bengal. Barbosa's naming followed a quite common tradition, and confusion, in those times of conflating the port with a kingdom or geographical region. There is even a suggestion that the name itself, Banga or Vanga, had added to it the suffix 'āl', Bānglā for dikes and earthen dividers that still marks this low-lying country. This is attributed to the Mughal emperor Akbar's wazir, minister at court, Abul Fazl in his chronicles of the emperor's rule, *Akbarnama*—specifically the third part of the chronicles that deals with law, *Ain-i-Akbari*.

Then, of course, there is the very English 'Bengal'. In early seventeenth century, the Elizabethan ambassador Thomas Roe tried to secure a firman from the Mughal emperor Jahangir to include Bengal in the East India Company's ambit of trade, to establish a post, but the Company would need to wait several decades for the royal decree. Anyhow the name in English has stuck—for the region, the subsequent British province, and the anglicized versions of Bāngāli—the Bengali people—and also near-universally to denote our language, Bānglā, as Bengali.

◆

The Bengali genesis is not easy to pin down as it is difficult to date the earliest settlers of the Bengal region. Clay, bamboo and thatch, shifting and flooding rivers and great tidal action from the oceans don't make for lasting remains. Tools, even dolmens, have been found largely in the hill and plateau areas that border West Bengal and Bangladesh. Archaeologists and historians date such things, and evidence of farming to well before 1500 BCE, during the so-called

Bronze Age culture of the Indus Valley era; there were also several cases of flourishing cultures in the Stone Age, and the Chalcolithic Age—the age between the Stone and Bronze ages. In the Bengal plains matters are fuzzy beyond that on account of the absence of evidence and also the limited archaeological and historical focus on ancient Bengal until well into the twentieth century. But between the mythological validation that people existed in the region of Bengal—even though dismissed by racist texts as being non-Aryan and therefore of lesser value—and Islamic-era validations from Ibn Battuta, there are several indicators of what Bengal used to be.

This land was in ancient times split broadly into four regions—'Grand divisions', *The History* describes it. The northwestern part of Greater Bengal (in West Bengal, a line north of the Farakka barrage on the Ganga up to the Cooch Behar area, and the Rajshahi division of Bangladesh, with the Brahmaputra-Yamuna marking the eastern border) was known as Pundravardhana. The Bardhaman region (Vardhamana to classicists, Burdwan to the politically and commercially agile but linguistically tone-deaf British) west of the Bhagirathi-Hooghly was the ancient Radha—or Rarh. The region to the east of this area, and bound by Pundravardhana, as it were, was a vast area that included most of southcentral West Bengal including present-day Kolkata, and the region from Dhaka southwards, including the Meghna estuary—essentially, the Bengal delta.

This area, *The History* tells us, 'was known to Pliny and Ptolemy'—the former chronicler being a first century CE Roman, the latter his second century CE geographer-genius colleague, Klaudios Ptolemaios, a Greco-Egyptian. They called it Gangaridai—there are linguistic variations—for instance, Gangaridum, Gangaridae. Some historians consider the Sanskrit for the heart, or hridai, of the Ganga being the genesis. According to the fourth-fifth century CE poet-playwright Kalidasa (here I am avoiding arguments as to whether there was one Kalidasa or several writers composed as one—a Shakespearean twist to ancient Indian literary history!)

those of 'the land of the Vanga' were noteworthy for their skill in handling boats. The fourth 'grand' division, east of the Meghna in present-day Chittagong (Chottōgrām in Bānglā) was the kingdom of Samatata. It appears the fourth century BCE creator of formal Sanskrit grammar, Panini, who was from Gandhara in present northwest Pakistan, knew of a Gaudapura—which is a pleasing leap of faith for us, Gauda approximating to Gaur, an eventual Bengali kingdom, and capital. His brilliant intellectual inheritor, Patanjali, mentioned Vanga.

Archaeological efforts have in the past hundred years greatly added to our picture of the life and times of ancient and early medieval Bengal—significant sites in both Bangladesh and West Bengal, in Mainamati, Mahasthangarh, Paharpur, Pandu Rajar Dhibi, Chandraketugarh and Mangalkot record thriving societies. Mahasthangarh near Bogura in northwest Bangladesh is today acknowledged as the capital or citadel of Pundravardhana based on the Chinese monk-traveller-chronicler Xuanzang's writings—and an Ashoka-era stone tablet in Brahmi script found in the ruins of the large fortified city that referred to it as Pudanagala or Pundranagara. The language of the script is Prakrit, a root language, along with Sanskrit, from which Bānglā evolved into its own from about the tenth century CE onwards.

Mainamati near Comilla has yielded an archaeological treasure trove of brick structures and copper and terracotta plates from the time of the Pal dynasty of Bengal as the seat of three local royal houses, Buddhists like the Pals—the Khadga, Deva and Chandra. Indeed, Mainamati is named after the queen of Manik Chandra. And visiting Paharpur—northwest from Bogura—is to me somewhat like visiting the ancient Buddhist redoubt of Nalanda in Bihar, with its massive eighth century CE monastery complex, a mahavihara; it is counted among the most significant Buddhist archaeological sites in South Asia. (Significantly, these sites, as many others in Bangladesh, have benefited from diligent application by the pre-Independence Archaeological Survey of India and subsequently by the archaeological surveys of both Pakistan and Bangladesh—a country that continues to be an underrated destination for the archaeological-tourist and museum-tourist.)

The partly-excavated gem of Chandraketugarh, an extensive ruin a short drive northeast of Kolkata, has been steadily looted in the absence of proper security, though some priceless seals, plaques and statues are fortunately preserved at the West Bengal government-run archaeological gallery in Kolkata. It shows various strata of preservation and plunder that ranges across six major periods, from the pre-Mauryan times of seventh century BCE, to thirteenth century CE. As I write this, there is an effort to establish a locally-sited museum for the place some historians have attempted to portray as the capital city of Ptolemy's 'Gangaridai'. A rare place too is Mangalkot, about an hour's drive to the north of Bardhaman (and a similar distance from Santiniketan) with a chronological range of structures and artefacts from a period similar to early findings at Chandraketugarh and on till seventeenth century CE.

Another gem is Pandu Rajar Dhibi in the valley of the Ajay River, south of Santiniketan (or more precisely, Bolpur, its semi-urban cousin), considered to be the most significant among several Chalcolithic and Iron Age sites in the region. This collective of sites in a mesh of rivers is really our Indus Valley—I say this only for effect to stress the site's importance in Bengal's history, with records going back to before 1600 BCE. This site, believed to have an association with the mythical King Pandu of Hastinapur, has yielded the picture of a likely trading hub by a river source, a flourishing civilization—house plans, urban layout, pottery, ornaments, fish hooks, weapons, figurines, coins, even skeletal remains—that includes ancestors of some of the Ādibāshī tribes of Bengal.

◆

Around the sixth and seventh centuries CE, we began to have the first real evidence of an indisputably Bengali civilization. There is numismatic and inscriptive evidence of the evidently short-lived kingdom of Banga—and the arrival of Sasanka and the kingdom of Gaur, which likely steamrolled the Banga kings, and is credited with advancing a distinct identity of early medieval Bengal extending from northern to southern Bengal and parts of Odisha—and of the eventual Bengali. Until then, the regions of Bengal were under the sway of a series of powerful northern Indian empires for a thousand years from the Mauryan Empire from the fourth century BCE, followed by that of the Sunga nearly up to the beginning of the Common Era. There was a brief interlude with the Kushan empire that came as far east as Pataliputra—ancient Patna, the cradle of the Mauryan and Sunga empires—till about the middle of the fourth century CE, before becoming a part of the sprawling Gupta empire till the latter half of the sixth century CE.

Sasanka had a reputation as a Buddhist-basher, which some historians attribute to his extended feud with Emperor Harshavardhana of Kannauj and the emperor's ally in Kamrup, located in present-day Assam. Xuanzang, an admirer of Harshavardhana and a visitor to his court, wrote about Sasanka in stern terms, and the king was accused by his detractors—a matter pointed out as exaggeration and unreliable by Bengali historians who minimize Sasanka's anti-Budhhist bias—of destroying Buddhist stupas and issuing what amounted to a fatwa against Buddhist monks.

After Sasanka's death in 637 CE, Harshavardhana and Kamrup's monarch, Bhaskarvarman, shared Gaur's empire. We learn from Xuanzang's accounts of his visit to the area in the following year, and historians who have studied the period, that Harshavardhana, the emperor who ruled from Kannuaj in the far west, had sway over the 'Bengal' regions of Pundravardhana, Karnasuvarna—Sasanka's capital—Samatata and the thriving regional and quite globalized port city of Tamralipta—as we know, present-day Tamluk.

But it was largely a time of flux, with repeated invasions into Bengal after the death of Harshavardhana, including by a Tibetan king and another ruler of Kannauj, Yashovarman, who invaded both Gaur and nearby Banga (there's now a University of Gour Banga in the district headquarters of Malda in West Bengal, not far from the ruins of the capital of ancient Gaur that straddle the border of West Bengal and Bangladesh). Sengupta's lucid retelling of this aspect of history, drawn greatly from Majumdar's work, as is so much of the chronicling of Bengal's ancient history, sums up this period which in dynastic and political terms is a bit of a black hole:

> There are also some copper plates of this period alluding to a certain Kharga dynasty in (the) Dhaka-Tippera area of East Bengal. The Tibetan monk Taranath, vaguely refers to a Chandra dynasty ruling in East Bengal... What is most certain is that Bengal was in a state of political disintegration until...the rise of the Pala [or Pal] dynasty.

This happened in the middle of the eighth century CE.

The Pals are generally held up as among the greatest ever (certainly the most politically emphatic) rulers of Bengal, rivalling the Rashtrakuta empire of the time in central and western India, on account of their direct control over the entire territory of Bengal, parts of Odisha (Utkal) and Assam (Kamrup), vast areas of Bihar (Magadh) and a string of vassalage that ran across nearly the entire Gangetic plain. This stretch of more than 400 years—from the establishing of the dynasty by Gopal in 750 CE to its successive golden-era moments of Bengal's history with Dharmapal, Devpal and Mahipal I, and its disintegration after the death of Madanpal in 1161 CE—is also seen by many as a socio-cultural apex of early Bengali civilization. Even the rapidly evolving Bānglā language flowed from this era.

'By the middle of the 10th century, to which the earliest extant specimens of Bengali can be referred, the Bengali language may be said to have become distinctive, as the expression of the life and religious aspirations of the people of Bengal, with the nucleus of a literature uniting the various dialectical areas,' wrote Suniti Kumar Chatterji in his seminal *The Origin and Development of the Bengali Language*, considered by many as the most definitive such work in modern times. It encompassed an extensive introduction, phonology, morphology and index of Bāngla words, and was published by Calcutta University in 1926. 'A new speech entered into being, to give expression, later in its life, to some of the highest flights of human spirit in the regions of poetic imagination and perception.'

Much of the Pals' mojo is based on conquests by Dharmapal, Devapal and Mahipal I, who reclaimed for the dynasty, territory lost through the slippage of governance, control, and subsequent attacks by numerous kingdoms and a series of weak kings between Devapal and Mahipal I.

The dynasty patronized Buddhism and some of the most significant archaeological remains in Bengal date from the time of the Pals, who were great patrons of the universities at Nalanda and Vikramshila. In addition, Mahipal is known to have sponsored the repair and upkeep of shrines in Bodh Gaya and Sarnath, and undertaken major waterworks and established new towns. Perhaps Bengal's greatest export to Buddhism and the art of travel, the scholar-monk Ātish Diponkor—the world knows him as Atisa Dipankara Srigyan—was a product of these times.

After Mahipal I, the dynasty slid into chaos with on-again off-again control by a series of successors—and a decades-long hiatus when Mahipal II was killed during what is called the Kaibarta rebellion, led by those of the so-called fisherman caste—before the last significant Pal ruler, Rampal, wrested Varendra from Kaibarta control and offered the empire a brief fling with its former glory before it finally petered out in 1161 CE. Ghaznavid, Ghurid and Turkic raiders had already begun their forays of loot and and eventual stay deep into northern India, the southern Indian Chalukyas had been aggressively nibbling at Bengal's doors, and smaller rulers in Bengal, such as the Barmans of Bikrampur in eastern Bengal, had made their break from Pal dominance.

Into this stepped the Sens, chieftains of southern Indian provenance—Karnataka, according to historians—who had ridden on the coat-tails of the Pals before emerging to claim control of

Bengal. Vijayasen, who is credited with beginning the dynasty, had already, during the reign of the last Pals, cleaned up in southern Bengal and stepped up his consolidation of territory in central and east Bengal during the decades-long implosion of the Pals who by that time were restricted to northern Bengal.

Vijaysen's son, Ballalsen, shored up his father's acquisitions and added a few of his own across all Bengal. At the same time, he is believed to have kept alive links with southern India by taking as consort a Chalukyan princess. This is also the time Bengal appears to have begun its shift away from its centuries-old espousal of Buddhism to orthodox Hinduism—the region had for long displayed opposition to what some historians term 'north Indian Aryan Brahmanism'. Liberal historians mention this time as when Brahmins really came into their own in Bengal, beginning a cycle of domineering religion that encouraged insularity. 'It was from the Sen period that greater Bengal became a narrower Bengal,' insists the bureaucrat-historian Sengupta, who doesn't pull his punches when it comes to discussing religion, culture or politics of Bengal and Bengalis—East Bengal and Bangladesh included—and is part of a refreshingly forthright school of approach not engaged in chauvinistically talking up or needlessly talking down the traits and histories of East or West Bengal, or histories derived from Bengal's dominant religions. Exchanges with the outside world were discouraged, and Bengal 'was turned into a frog in the well'. But military adventure continued for another generation, with Lakshmansen providing the last hurrah for the dynasty, a spread of command and control that hagiographical records of the time say included Gaur, from which the last remnants of the Pals were wiped out, and Kamrup, and Kashi—Varanasi—and Kalinga.

But the dominance of the Sens was jolted by a seismic development during Laskhmansen's lifetime, one that would visibly drive the course of Bengal for the next 500 years and more; and, after giving over to British domination for 150 years or so from 1757, would again seismically shape the region. That was the arrival in Bengal of Islam as a power, when Muhammad Bakhtiyar Khilji, an advenuturer—some would say, misdaventurer, after a disastrous Tibetan campaign towards the end of life—cut a swathe through Lakshmansen's faltering empire in 1201, when he took over the Nabadwip area and, over the following couple of years, moved to take control of Lakhnauti (Lakshamanvati) or Gaur, and with that northern Bengal.

Those were momentous times. The Rajput king Prithviraj Chauhan had been defeated in Delhi a decade earlier by Mohammad of Ghor. This Ghurid invader's general and appointed administrator, Qutb-ud-Din Aibak, governed the north and moved steadily through the plains of the Ganga and Yamuna—different from our Jōmunā. In turn, as Aibak's general, Bakhtiyar led the Turkic-Afghan juggernaut eastwards, before arriving in Bengal as much as the spearhead of empire as—for all practical purposes—the spearhead of Islam. He had built up a formidable reputation as destroyer of other cultures, having been credited with overrunning and destroying the Buddhist university and library at Nalanda; some dissenting historians maintain that Nalanda was already in decline, though that hardly merits a sacking, and others, that Bakhtiyar bypassed Nalanda as it wasn't on a practical route into Bengal.

Whatever the interpretations driven by chauvinistic, religious or nationalistic lenses of the subcontinent, the undisputed fact remains that Bakhtiyar's raids poured yet another series of dominant political and literal DNA into Bengal's steadily accumulating and morphing cultural gene pool, adding the Turkic, Afghan and Pathan strains. The conquest of western and northern Bengal would in a few short decades spread across all Bengal. Even though the Mussulman rulers of Bengal, as both governors of sultans and emperors of Delhi, would every so often fight for their territory's autonomy for reasons of both power and ethnicity (the Turk, Afghan and Pathan did not always sit comfortably with each other or, later, with Mughal domination), till the battle of Polāshi, or Plassey in 1757, Islamic rule would be the dominant force.

Islam would spread, driven by zeal of its preachers and travelling mendicants—in the early days of conquest, warrior-saints, too, were sometimes a feature. There was a blowback against orthodox Hinduism that made socio-economic and socio-cultural slaves of those of lower castes, and expansion driven by the relatively relaxed, encompassing, folksy attitude of itinerant preachers and some sedentary clergy who permitted their Hindu converts to adapt everyday social, cultural and even some religious practices of their previous faith and customs.

Eventually, there was a revivalism of their original faith among the Hindus of Bengal, symbolized in large part by the medieval saint Chaitanya (Chōitonnō Mohāprōbhu, or great spiritual leader, to the Bengali devout) who birthed a stream of Vaishnavism that today finds large groups of adherents across eastern India, northern and western India, some pockets of Bangladesh and the Northeast, especially in Assam, and among the Meitei community in Manipur. The so-called Hare Krishna movement too can be traced back to Sri Chaitanya. The relatively liberal attitude of Chaitanya's Vaishnavism was remarkable for its time, hardly presaging the massive hardening of attitudes and religious orthodoxy in a few short centuries—the worship of Krishna and his consort, Radha, for example, welcomed women as equal-opportunity devotees, and the path of devotion and salvation was open to all castes and even those beyond the pale of caste.

Bengal, as we know it, had begun to form. Bengali, as we know it, had begun to gather momentum, helped along by the patronage of several Islamic rulers who saw it as a language beyond the court, a language of the people—Mussulmans and Hindus alike.

Bengal's resentments, as we know them, began to form, too, the ways of the conqueror and conquered chafing and colliding alongside welcome stretches of coexistence.

◆

Navigating the roots of the Bengali people is made easier by the work of historians like Ramesh Chandra Majumdar who, alongside the Mughal-era specialist Jadunath Sarkar, surely counts as among the greatest historians of Bengali origin, and among the greatest historians in twentieth-century India.

Majumdar, a specialist in ancient Indian history is generally known for helming the eleven-volume *The History and Culture of the Indian People*, writing and editing several volumes on ancient India, and the contrarian *History of the Freedom Movement in India*— maintaining, among other things, that the conflagration of 1857 was a mutiny or 'great outbreak' against the British, not quite the first war of Indian independence.

Sarkar's Mughal journey (the result was a formidable four-volume history, *The Fall of the Mughal Empire*, besides histories of the Maratha chieftain Shivaji, and of the kingdom of Jaipur) took him first to the study of Arabic, Persian, Marathi, Rajasthani, French and Portuguese before a twenty-five-year pursuit of researching and writing this work. It was an effort born of the 'liberal high culture of Hindu Bengal', observes the historian Premen Addy, 'and the liberal high culture of Britain and its empiricist thinkers, from Locke to Burke to Bertrand Russell...' and undoubtedly groomed by his birth into a zamindari family in Natore. Sarkar wrote forcefully of '...the imbecility and vices of our rulers, the cowardice of their generals, and the selfish treachery of their ministers', of it being 'a tale that which makes every true son of India hang his head in shame'. (And perhaps every daughter and son of Bengal, West Bengal and Bangladesh, were Sarkar's prescient observation extended to the present day.)

This man who Addy described as having admired Britain but was nonetheless 'critical of the constricted vision and selfish workings of British imperialism in India', a Hindu and yet scornful of 'ossified Hinduism dreaming only of the past', has not seen the worth of his work diminished even by the rise of the so-called 'Marxist approach' of historiography in India with a dedication to social history (the state of peasants, for instance, as opposed to the traditional and overwhelming focus on dynasty and myth). Several generations of historians and those who read history at school or university benefited from the foundations established by the likes of Majumdar and Sarkar, and latter-day schools of approach and enquiry. I certainly did.

Majumdar and Sarkar's companion volumes of *The History of Bengal*—Majumdar edited the first volume on the 'Hindu Period', Sarkar the second, which addressed the 'Muslim Period'—brought Bengal alive for me, gave me a sense and understanding of the past and explained so much of the proximity of confusion and violence that was present when I was growing up. These volumes also gave me an understanding of the era of my parents, born in the 1930s—their roots and foundations of their firm politico-religious attitudes, for example. For Bengalis of the twentieth century, it was the first such history made available to them, tainted if at all by Bengali aspiration, not colonial sleight of words.

The History of Bengal is a remarkable effort for reasons that extend beyond content. It was a history of Bengal—still politically and ethnically united though that would be torn apart three years after the series was published in 1943. It was published by the University of Dhaka that was at the time still considered an upstart by many at the premier, well-established Calcutta University who were leery of it attracting government funds, and for offering itself since 1921 as a second hub for the highest level of education in Greater Bengal. As I read in some books of history written in India, Bengali Hindu worthies associated with Calcutta University went to the extent of successfully pressuring the colonial government of India to deny an annual grant of five lakh rupees, a huge sum at the time, to Dhaka University.

Abul Kasem Fazlul Huq, who had emerged as a leader of farmers and would by the 1940s be a towering figure in the politics of Bengal, was scathing in his criticism of the pettiness of Calcutta University's grandees and what Sengupta termed 'educated Hindu opinion'. 'To my mind the Dhaka University has become an eyesore to the men at the helm of the Calcutta University ever since Lord Hardinge proclaimed its establishment', Huq complained during a debate of the Bengal Legislative Council, as I read in Sengupta's *Bengal Divided: The Unmaking of a Nation*. Huq warned: 'I do not want to say much but I would caution my friends of West Bengal who put up objections whenever any money is proposed to be spent for Dhaka—Beware; if you persist in this attitude, it will only create differences between the two communities which will cause serious harm to the administration.' Subsequent events would prove this to be an understatement.

The History of Bengal project was also remarkable for its meshing of Hindu and Mussulman contributors, accomplished historians and academicians, a singular achievement in those fraught times. An early advocate of such a history was Sarkar, who proposed it during a lecture in mid-1933. It was pushed along by a new vice-chancellor, Sir A. F. Rahman, when he took office in 1934. Majumdar, who was born at the opposite end of the socio-economic spectrum of Sarkar, to a poor family in Faridpur in present-day Bangladesh, took up the project in 1935, after completing his work on ancient Indian colonies in the Far East. Already an established and respected historian, along with Rahman and Sarkar, he joined the History of Bengal Publication Committee at a meeting in Rahman's house the same year. Rahman was chair. (The others committee members were N. K. Bhattasali, S. N. Bhattacharyya, K. R. Quanungo and Hakim Habibur Rahman. At the time of its publication in 1943, Majumdar had only recently moved on as vice-chancellor of the Dhaka University; he would after Partition take up tenure at Banaras Hindu University.)

Such collaboration would soon be a dream. Matters of state intervened.

◆

By most accounts, the Muslim Period of Bengal that lasted about five centuries before the British began their period of conquest and dominance, was frenetic and yet a time of gradual consolidation. It effectively had two major outcomes and a third quite interesting one. One was the firmer establishing of the Bengali identity and language that carried on directly the legacy of the Sen and Pal kingdoms. The second was a centuries-long, sometimes overt, sometimes stealthy—for the Hindu establishment which felt ambushed, at any rate—spread of Islam and Islamization of vast areas of Bengal. And for me the interesting outcome was a near-continuous straining at the bit by Bengal rulers against domination by northern power centres of the subcontinent, traces of which extended well into the twentieth century.

Lakhnaoti, or Gaur, continued to be the centre of the action for more than three centuries from the early thirteenth century to well into the sixteenth century, as a mix of governors and de facto rulers—through the reigns of Aibak, the Khiljis, the Balban and Tughlaq dynasties, then the Sayyids and the Lodis—strenuously attempted to and succeeded in maintaining their autonomy from Delhi. They also attempted to extend their sway steadily southwards and westwards through conquest and a series of alliances that took in most of Bengal.

Of these Sultan Jalal-ud-din, the son of the chieftain-king Raja Ganesh, is among a few to find mention as a ruler of significance. It's a curious story of some hazy history. Raja Ganesh took wing for seven years or so in the early fifteenth century, a Hindu blip in the near continuous stream of Mussulman rule. Interpretations project this zamindar—jōmidār—of some note in north Bengal, and courtier to several Mussulman rulers as having taken over the reins of Gaur after the death of Shihab-ud-din Bayazid Shah. He is believed to have unleashed a reign of some brutality in an attempt to end Mussulman domination of Bengal, but it backfired when his professed enemies regrouped and led a countermove in the name of Islam. According to history-lore détente arrived only when the raja agreed to have his pre-teen son Jadu convert to Islam. He would later become Sultan Jalal-ud-din, and rule from

1415 to 1431. From most accounts Jalal-ud-din offered an even-handed administration, with positions of honour in the civil and military administration open to Hindus as well. The Sultan is also believed to have referred to himself as Gaureshwar (Gōuréshhor), Sanskrit for the 'ruler of Gaur', which historians offer as another of his stellar qualities besides bringing an era of peace and prosperity over much of Bengal, and maintaining robust trade and diplomatic relations with the Far East.

This reign segued after some decades into what is sometimes referred as the coming of age of Bengal. This is on account of a series of significant rulers as well as the emergence of a definite Bengali identity. Indeed, it is also the time of, unarguably, the greatest religious influence in Bengal after Shah Jalal, the birth and flourishing of Sri Chaitanya, Chōitonnō Mohāprōbhu to many, whom I have touched upon earlier in this chapter. He was born in 1486, in Nabadwip, and died in Puri, Odisha, in 1534. He and his school of what is called Gaudiya Vaishnavism, thrived during the rule of two enlightened Mussulman rulers of Gaur, Ala-ud-din Hussain Shah (r.1493–1519) and his son Nusrat Shah (r.1519–1532).

Nusrat Shah, whose death would plunge Bengal back into a cycle of massive intrigue and power-grabbing, concluded a peace treaty with the first Mughal emperor Babur, who took over Delhi from the Lodi dynasty in 1526, a treaty which historians maintain was done as one between equals. This Mughal attitude would change after consolidation and the empire's inexorable spread, but for some years it brought the Gaur kingdom and its people several crucial decades to go about their business. Meanwhile, the son built on with his father's legacy of extending their influence across most of what became latter-day Bengal, and bringing in local-born talent, both Hindu and Mussulman, in the administration and the army; and consolidated the trading hubs of Sonargaon and Chittagong. Indeed, the two—which some folkloric and historical references credit with being part-Bengali, including being dark-complexioned!—are also credited with allowing Bānglā and Bānglā literature to flourish, in a way taking ahead the legacy of the Pals. A contemporary hagiographic reference to Hussain Shah by the Vaishnav poet Parameshwar (quoted by Sengupta, in turn quoting Dinesh Chandra Sen's *History of Bengali Language and Literature*) marks him as an avatar of Krishna in Kali Yug. According to this telling the 'Great Khan ruled the kingdom with sons and grandsons listening gladly to the Puranas'.

Bengal's history remained a whirl for the next two centuries—not that what followed after 1757 right up to the birth of India and Pakistan is any less of a fractured whirl, but that was a time when Bengal came under the sway of the singular compulsion of the British East India Company which expanded rapidly from its grant of the 'zemindari' of 24 Parganas, or revenue districts, after the battle at Polāshi.

Historical high-water marks from the time of the Hussain Shahi sultans until the time of the British were few. Sher Shah Suri was one, the Afghan—Pashtun—military and administrative genius who was for Bengal a relevant factor besides displacing the Mughal emperor Humayun for several years during his direct rule as emperor from 1540 to 1545; his largely ineffectual successors would rule for another ten years before Humayun's return as emperor.

Before becoming emperor of India, Sher Shah née Sher Khan née Farid Khan won Gaur after moving eastwards from his den in present-day Bihar. Indeed, he was crowned Sultan of Gaur in 1538 after defeating Sultan Mahmud Shah, and in effect bolstered himself financially and militarily with this victory, ultimately defeating Humayun when the beleagured Mughal came chasing after Sher Khan. (Mahmud Shah had been in alliance with Humayun—who inevitably looked eastwards at Bengal, then as well upon his return as emperor, as did his successors. The province would financially fuel the Mughal empire and would literally feed vast parts of it by the time of Aurangzeb's rule.) The so-called Grand Trunk Road that traversed the subcontinent from the east to the northwest was established by Sher Shah, who greatly improved upon the Mauryan-era passageway and extended the eastern end of this outstanding link to the region of present-day Chittagong.

The Mughal emperor Akbar's rule was in the Bengal region characterized more by resistance to the central authority than acquiescing in Delhi's wishes. Primary resistance would be provided by both powerful Mussulman (of Turkic, Afghan, Pathan provenance) and Hindu landlords—warlords, really—an adamant dozen, the Bārō Bhuiyān who ran the core of Bengal, and formed a loose confederacy of shifting loyalties to keep out those they saw as outsiders, usurpers. Most did not hesitate to take on Akbar's famed generals, including Raja Man Singh of Jaipur, and would give little respite to any subahdar (to us shubédār, imperial governor of a subah or province) that Akbar sent along, or even his son who would become the emperor Jahangir.

Another singularity of sorts was provided during the reign of Jahangir's successor Shah Jahan and then the emperor Aurangzeb, which saw a string of governors who essentially ruled over most of Bengal as it came to be known in the modern era. This provided close to a hundred years of administrative stability which also had an effect (quite unlike that during the Company's run and during British rule), of Bengal largely benefiting from its own bounty—in particular during the governorship of Shah Shuja, a son of Shah Jahan who was governor for two decades until 1659 when he tried to take on his brother, the newly-minted emperor Aurangzeb, in battle at Khajuha, in present-day Uttar Pradesh. He lost and had to retreat all the way back to Dhaka (an increasingly important hub in Bengal that saw a dip in importance after the ascendancy of Kolkata in British colonial times) and then to Arakan, where he would be executed on a charge of conspiring against the local ruler.

The Portuguese were ejected from their stronghold in Hooghly, and the Arakanese from Chittagong—this during the early years of Aurangzeb's rule, under the governorship of Shayesta Khan. This playboy subahdar was Clive-like in his taste for wealth and ostentation—the man also leveraged trade monopolies for his own gain. At one point he even chased Company traders from their base in Hooghly after the Company actually declared hostilities against the Mughal governor—and, by extension, the Mughal empire—after a dispute over customs duties. The Company would return soon after the end of Shayesta's governorship in 1688, and establish its famous base in Kolkata.

Credit for establishing Kolkata in 1690 is given to Job Charnock, a Company employee who went somewhat 'native', as it were, evidently besotted with his common-law Indian wife; but in 2003, a bench of Calcutta High Court blew that hoary assertion right out of the water, of the Hooghly or any other source for that matter, on the basis of a litigation in the 'public interest' by a group of descendants of one of the 'original' families which petitioned the court as Sabarna Roychowdhury Paribar Parishad. I read in the Court's sesquicentennial souvenir of 2013:

> In May 2003, the High Court accepting the report of an Expert Committee of Historians headed by Prof. Nemai Sadhan Bose, held that Calcutta does not have a 'birth day' nor one simple 'founder'. It was a process in the 17th century in which Charnock, who settled in Sutanuti, Eyre and Goldsborough, on Englishside, and Lakshmikanta Majumdar who developed the tract; the Sett and Bysack families who lived in Gobindapur, and Sabarna Choudhuri who sold the villages to the English were all involved in the process of establishing Calcutta.

For some years everyone of consequence in Bengal would have to contend with Shayesta, who even spawned a common phrase in Bānglā for defeating someone, dominating a situation: shāyéstā korā.

After Shayesta's departure from Bengal to Delhi during the latter half of Aurangzeb's reign, the churning resumed in Bengal, the political equations now also irrevocably tied to trade equations and ambitions of transnational corporate empires. Weakening of control in Delhi after Aurangzeb's death in 1707 led directly to the effective independence of the Mughal subahdar of Bengal, much like several other subahs of this remarkable empire now for all practical purpose in free-fall. Murshid Quli Khan, a person held to be of personal integrity on account of his outing a previous subahdar's massive corruption—a nest egg for post-Aurangzeb chaos—led the de facto independence from the Mughals. The trend would hold from 1717, when Murshid Quli was appointed subahdar by the Mughal emperor Bahadur Shah, until the impetuous and ultimately tragic run of Siraj-ud-Daulah in 1757, whose army's defeat in Polāshi at the hands of Clive proved to be of seismic import for Bengal and the subcontinent.

Meanwhile, the Honourable East India Company, with its crafty indemnity from god—Deo ducente nil nocet, proclaimed John Company's elaborate logo: When (or Where) god leads, nothing can harm—was hardly the only transnational interest fishing in Bengal. With permission of Mughal emperors and rulers of Bengal, the Portuguese had marked their presence within twenty-five years of Afonso de Albuquerque conquering Goa in 1510, for decades indulging in trade and pillage from the mouth of the Hooghly all the way east to Chittagong. The Dutch came ashore at Chinsurah, the location of one of its key factories, established in 1656. The French established operations and a colony in Chandannagar (Chandernagore), north of Kolkata, in 1673. After a failed attempt, the Danes were finally established at Serampore—Srirampur—in 1755.

With business came politics. The battles that would ultimately, irrevocably divide Bengal had began in earnest. It seems the only ones who didn't realize it until it was far too late were Bengalis.

◆

There is much history between the arrival of the European as overlord and the division of the lands of the Bengalis and several significant aspects of it are examined throughout the book. Here, as we are looking at the origins of the Bengalis and their homelands, let me focus on two significant players who contributed to the utshō, genesis, of West Bengal and East Pakistan-to-be-Bangladesh.

Those who revel in—as much as those who revile—the rise of Hindu nationalists in present-day India may want to hold a candle up to the contributions of Syama Prasad Mookerjee in Banglasphere and out of it. Mookerjee founded the Jan Sangh in 1951—and within a year had won seats in elections to India's parliament. The Jan Sangh is a precursor to the Bharatiya Janata Party, or BJP, which has since the late 1980s emerged as an increasingly confident, and often-belligerent vehicle of Hindu politics.

As the Indian right-wing political commentator and politician Swapan Dasgupta observes, the Jan Sangh and BJP are the real inheritors of the ideology of 'political Hindutva' espoused by Vinayak Damodar Savarkar, leader of the Hindu Mahasabha and, indeed, nurturer of 'the creature that has come to be known as the political Hindu—an uncompromising modernist who, at the same time, shuns the melting pot of cosmopolitanism'. As his politics became increasingly more radicalized, Mookerjee left the Indian National Congress to join the Hindu Mahasabha in Bengal and became its 'working president' in 1940. (This followed remarkable interludes: being called to the bar at Lincoln's Inn, London, and in 1934 becoming the youngest ever vice-chancellor of Calcutta University, aged thirty-three.)

Flush in the middle of Partition politics that had already begun to be aired by the Muslim League, Mookerjee, a blue-chip bhodrōlōk began to make his voice heard. In 1941, he is believed to have told a rally that, if Mussulmans wanted to live in Pakistan they should 'pack' and 'leave India...' Two years later, he became the all-India president of the Hindu Mahasabha. Meanwhile, he also was part of the charge against Mohandas Gandhi and the Indian National Congress's Quit India Movement of 1942, believing that it would create internal disorder at a time the colonial government was engaged with World War II. It didn't exactly endear him to his former colleagues of the Congress, and it is still employed as an example of unpatriotic behaviour by those who question the roots of BJP's ultra-nationalism. (For the record, the Muslim League and India's communist parties were also ranged against the Quit India Movement: both Congress and BJP talking-heads use this as a polemical battering ram!)

If today there is a West Bengal, it is because Mookerjee was a key participant of the charge that demanded that Hindu majority areas of Bengal should remain with India after Partition. This ran strongly against the narrative of the Muslim League that all Bengal be part of Pakistan. There was even a proposal by some members of the League and Subhas Chandra's brother Sarat Bose for a united Bengal that would be independent of both India and Pakistan. It ran aground in the face of conservative Hindu and Mussulman opposition, especially from the Muslim League, certainly, even though it was said Muhammad Ali Jinnah gave tacit approval for this plan as it would effectively hand the League control of the province—Mookerjee and even some key leaders of the Indian Congress saw through that ruse.

After India's independence, he, to the surprise of many, joined the cabinet of Prime Minister Jawaharlal Nehru, as minister for industry and supply, for nearly three years. But he resigned in April 1950 after bitterly disagreeing with the government's approach to Kashmir—according it special status, with its own flag, power to its premier and a separate constitution. Mookerjee tried to break the cordon and enter Kashmir to protest, despite a ban on his entry. He was arrested and jailed. His iconic status for Hindu nationalists was sealed when he died in June 1953, in custody.

◆

If West Bengal exists because of the energy of those like Mookerjee, then Bangladesh—I would stress here that 'Bānglā'—exists because of the energy of those like Abul Kasem Fazlul Huq, who morphed from being a socialist-minded leader of peasants with his popular

Krishak Praja Party to being a leading light of the Muslim League (and this, after being repeatedly criticized and undercut by League supremo Muhammad Ali Jinnah, to whom he would not kowtow) which changed after Partition into being a leading light of the language movement in East Pakistan. The triple degree holder in mathematics, chemistry and physics from Kolkata's Presidency College is iconized in Bangladesh as Shér-é-Bānglā, the tiger of Bengal, though another nuance, if one were to continue in the style of hyperbole that has for long been the flavour of political Bangladesh, could be—the tiger for Bānglā.

And to think Mookerjee and Huq were once colleagues in government! This was over 1941 and 1942, when Huq was prime minister of the province of Bengal and political confusion, connivance, conspiracy and the outright bizarre had begun to peak, and the fight for the future of Bengal—and the idea of a separate homeland for the Mussulmans of the subcontinent—had gained great momentum.

Those were politically bizarre and expedient times. The Krishak Praja Party—well Huq, really—had initially resisted giving up control to the League and Jinnah for Mussulman minds and votes. It had fought elections to the Bengal Assembly in 1937 against the League, and won it with the tacit support of the local Congress. When results were declared in this election of diarchy—in which the electorate was divided by religion into two separate vote-banks—the Congress declined to be part of the government as it was not in the majority. Its Bengal unit was thus barred by Congress policy of a Mohandas Gandhi-influenced Congress from being part of government wherever it wasn't in majority. (It was a miscalculation on its part, as it led eventually to the League's domination of politics in Bengal and contributed to Bengal's eventual split when Mookerjee and his colleagues fought to retain a slice of Hindu-majority Bengal in India. Wheels within wheels.)

For the sake of expediency, the Muslim League allied with Huq to form the government in Bengal, seeing it also as an opportunity to both extend the hold of the League over the governance of Bengal as well as erode Huq's hold from inside out. Eventually, League ministers resigned from Bengal's provincial government. That's when Mookerjee, who was elected as an independent member of Bengal's assembly, joined Huq's government as finance minister, as part of a coalition that included other Hindu members. But Mookerjee soon left. And Huq was by then increasingly isolated.

◆

Indeed, Huq's hold over the Krishak Praja Party and Bengal politics was already slipping. Even though he transparently rooted for the interests of the Bengali Mussulmans he said he was really fighting for the upliftment of disadvantaged Mussulmans who, according to him, were being brutalized and marginalized by both Hindu and Mussulman zamindars, and were objects of derision of the gentrified ashraf of Kolkata and Dhaka who spoke Urdu and drew their lineage from West Asia by way of what is now Pakistan and Afghanistan. The peasant had been treated as a lesser mortal. Huq, through his party, offered what was a basic platform of 'dāl-bhāt'; it called for the abolition of the zamindari system and even asked for self rule in decidedly un-Muslim League language: swaraj. There are several fascinating accounts of this period. A particularly lucid one is by the Cambridge historian Joya Chatterji, who writes of how Huq's party 'was making the running in the countryside'. Krishak Praja rallies sometimes rang to the dual cry of 'Āllāhō Akbor' and various Bānglā versions of 'down with zamindari'.

Huq certainly took on the domination of Hindu landlords of Bengal, but he was also critical of Muslim gentry like Khwaja Nazimuddin (a future governor general of Pakistan), related to the nawab of Dhaka; the Nawab Kazi Golam Mohiuddin Faroqui, zamindar of Ratanpur; and the Nawab of Dhaka, Khwaja Habibullah—whose family was among the largest zamindars of Bengal. Another formidable opponent he tilted at was Huseyn Shaheed Suhrawardy, a future prime minister of Pakistan who descended from, as the Pakistani columnist Khaled Ahmed observed, 'the famous Suhrawardy saints of Baghdad and Multan and grew up as a scion of a family of great lawyers in Dhaka'.

The political commentator Nikhil Chakravarty, who worked as secretary to a Muslim League official in Kolkata, had a more colourful take on Suhrawardy in Joya Chatterji's book, *Bengal Divided: Hindu Communalism and Partition, 1932–1947.* Chakravarty, who claimed to know the inner workings of the League, described Suhrawardy as 'totally unscrupulous, but not communal or religious. He ate ham and drank Scotch and married a Russian actress', Well, he did marry the actress Vera Alexandrovna Tiscenko of the Moscow Art Theatre in 1940, the year the Lahore Declaration of the League for a separate homeland for Mussulmans was 'moved' at a conference, of all people, by Huq!

It was indicative of the cat and mouse game the League and Huq played for control of the Mussulman vote in Bengal. Huq played to his gallery of peasantry and the poor. The League played to all Mussulmans. Slowly but surely, Huq was squeezed out. Jinnah wanted a single party for Mussulmans. That animosity of the Mussulman gentry Huq upset, and the gradual but sure erosion of Huq's base that shifted to the League could have only one outcome, even as he fought for control and independence every inch of the way. The Krishak Praja Party was trounced by the League in the elections of 1945. And so it all came to nothing for Huq, though the League was vastly energized by the expansion of its base created by Huq's party.

In the end, Huq too was for the Partition of India when every alternative had been exhausted—and even for the partition of Bengal when all options of one Bengal foundered. He served subsequently as the chief minister of East Bengal—as it was still termed for some years after Partition, and as governor of East Pakistan. He died in 1962. His grave and memorial in Dhaka has some curious companions—Suhrawardy, who would forever be associated with the Great Calcutta Killings of 1946, in which over 4,000 people were estimated to have been killed and over 100,000 rendered homeless, and Khwaja Nazimuddin, one of the founding fathers of Pakistan.

Maybe Huq did achieve what he set out to do. He finally broke away from the League, and worked in the interest of East Pakistan and Bengali Mussulmans after the done deal of Partition and the birth of Pakistan. In 1954, the United Front he was part of defeated the League in East Bengal—it is how Huq came to be chief minister. He helped to firmly plant the seed of a Bengali nation in East Pakistan, and demanded the inclusion of Bānglā as a national language of Pakistan alongside Urdu—that happened in 1956, riding on major protests that began with pro-Bānglā demonstrators being killed by police on 21 February 1952—now known simply as Ékushé, Twenty-first, a national holiday in Bangladesh.

Huq infected several people with his thoughts, among them a relatively young and ambitious Muslim League member who later became a more ambitious colleague, an aide to Suhrawardy and, in time, president of the breakaway Awami League—Sheikh Mujibur Rahman.

◆

And what of ordinary people in our extraordinary chain of genesis and evolution, the people on whose behalf Bengal's historical luminaries have claimed to rule, to fight, to free, to purify? They are our ancestors too.

Into Bengal flowed all manner of people. First in were the early indigenous of Austric stock whose descendants are today's Dom, Chandala, Hadi, Pulinda, Kol and Sabara communities, among others. A word for our earliest ancestors is Nishada—a sort of mixed caste or hybrid. The impure Mlechhas were lumped with this lot. The superiority complex, begun by early racist interpreters, which placed such people at the bottom of the social heap, continues to this day. There was also for a while measuring of skulls and noses to establish a variety of racial provenance: medium and round heads, flattened and recessed foreheads, longer heads and sharper

Sudeep Chakravarti

Upper India features (creamy layer Aryan features), flat, medium and sharp noses, and such.

There are a wide variety of views that obtain among ethnographers and historians regarding the origin and composition of the Bengali race. Some of colonial British provenance held that Bengalis arrived from an 'admixture' of Dravidian and Mongoloid (Mon-Khmer) stock. Some Bengali contemporaries preferred to focus on racial purity and insisted that a heavy infusion of Aryan genes characterized the Bengali. One person in particular, Rama Prasad Chanda, who carried the title Rai Bahadur, maintained that Bengalis were descended from the *Homo alpinus* stock of Indo-Europeans in extraction and speech, with round heads, broad foreheads and stocky build, who had arrived from the 'Pamirs and the Taklamakan desert'.

Ergo, no matter who you listen to, we're pretty much mongrel. We're made more so by the steady infusion of Turkic, Afghan, Pathan and other Islam-driven streams into the Bengali double helix over the past 800 and more years.

The net result is a people who have a range of features and skin colour that can envelop much of the world. In my own family, while my father's lot largely appear to display very fair skin and a mix of so-called Aryan and near Eastern features, my mother's people contribute a heavy dose of Dravidian. Both sides claim high Brahmin lineage, as race is further layered with caste! My child, her mother and I have, over the years, been variously taken for (besides Bengali), Odia, Assamese, Malayali, Burmese, southern and eastern Thai, Malay, Sinhala, Tamil, and, on some occasions, as Israelis of North African origin. While in the United Kingdom we're sometimes described in a straightforward racist way as 'Paki'—reflecting that country's patchy familiarity with South Asia, in the United States many of us earn another hesitant layer—Latino. A Bengali cousin of mine did quite well socially in Western Europe by pretending for some years to be Brazilian. In the whiter parts—whiter minds—of South America I'm taken for Indio—their Nishada, as much on account of my facial features as my brown skin.

◆

'Gāér rong moylā kintu mukh-tā bésh mishti' is a standard operating statement among Bengal's racists—colourists would be too elegant a tag for people with ugly habits. I've heard women of my father's family, stolidly upper-caste and generally affluent, in eternal search of phorshā or fair skin, speak similarly, indulgently, of a girl come of age, sometimes a child of an unfortunate relative, perhaps a prospect for match-making, as being dark-skinned. That is a generous translation: moylā is also used for 'dirt' and 'dirty'. Kintu mukh-tā bésh mishti—'but she is sweet-faced'—is a saving grace. A médhābi or studious, academically talented girl such as this may be disparaged for her rong, colour of skin, but the statement will often be 'graciously' suffixed with 'kintu porāshōnā-é bhālō—but she's good at studies. The attitude is hardly restricted to the affluent or the illiterate.

Even the great Satyajit Ray fell prey to perpetuating that stereotype in one of his movies known to several generations of Bengali children since the 1960s, *Goopy Gyne Bagha Byne*, which is, even with this slip, an utterly absorbing movie. The movie ran for a stunning 102 weeks in Kolkata after its release in May 1969. My sister and I saw it twice at the Bijōli cinema in Bhobānipur—Bhowanipore to engaged Macaulay-putrā and Macaulay-putri—and would have seen it thrice if Mother hadn't intervened with Father, damning our petition with one of her short but effective you-will-go-straight-to-hell speeches. A true East Bengali, she seldom used the word norōk, with its Sanskrit root. We would always be a step closer to jāhannom, the far more impressive-sounding hell derived from Arabic. Anyway, there is a scene after the two lead characters, Goopy the singer and Bagha the dhōl player, have been promised by a king a princess each in marriage if they are able to avert the loss of the kingdom to an invading army. As they walk close to the palace they see a lady in one of the high balconies.

Sudeep Chakravarti

'Mōnimālā?' Bagha wonders.

'Jhee-tee noy tōh?' Goopy cautions, in his heart hoping she isn't a servant girl.

Bagha knows best. 'Can a jhee be so fair?'

♦

For all their claim to progressive thought and action, Bengalis, especially Bengali Hindus, are obsessed with race and racial superiority. Factor in caste and things get downright messy. Racial obsession wasn't and isn't merely a Hindu affliction. I've come across Bengali Mussulmans in Kolkata whose claim to higher being-ness is not that he is Bengali, or Mussulman, or Indian, but that he is Turki or Afghāni or Mōgōl—the Mussulman Aryan, as it were, descended from invaders of Bengal of Turkish or Afghan ancestry, and sometimes the Mughal. Even the love and practice of Islam will generally not bring such a specimen or upper-caste Mussulman into active social contact, let alone marriage, with a lower-caste Mussulman with an ancestry or surname signifying a jōla, or weaver, for instance, or a koshai, butcher, or the straightforward down-the-ladder chāshā, peasant.

These racially elitist worthies exist in West Bengal as freely as they do in Bangladesh. The architects of East Pakistan were nearly all of this ilk, ashraf, a sort of Mussulman kulin—mirrors of that upper-caste Hindu being, whose depredations against minor girls and attitudes of patriarchy were among the things the Bengal Renaissance tried to combat.

It is, therefore, a relief to come across findings such as the one by scientist and statistician Prasanta Chandra Mahalanobis, who, among other things, in a brilliant career co-founded the Indian Statistical Institute, analysed anthropometric data to arrive at a blessedly even-handed—some chauvinists would even venture to say, socialist—conclusion about the vaunted Bengali Brahmin, as well as several other castes prevalent in Bengal, Kayastha, Sadgopa, Kaivarta, and such. To sum up his thinking: 'The Bengal Brahmans resemble the other Bengal castes far more closely than they (the Brahmans) resemble castes outside Bengal, including the Brahmans.' While the Brahmans are shown as the apex predator of the social food chain, and other high castes sort of anthropometrically creep up to this Brahamanical mean—'the higher the social status the greater is the resemblance with the Bengal Brahmans'—such a conclusion also shows the peculiar nature of the Bengali animal. And that despite the genetic and socio-economic ebb and flow through these lands at some point the mongrel nation had begun to assume the characteristics of an ethno-linguistically distinct Bengali nation.

Of course the racially and ethnically elitist exist across the world. For all their progressiveness, an unhealthy percentage of Bengalis are up there with the worst of them.

2

Bāṅglā

Inceptions, impositions

What was Jinnah thinking?
On 21 March 1948, the man who helped to conjure up Pakistan, now the country's governor general carrying the formal sobriquet of Great Leader—Quaid-i-Azam—visited Dhaka. There Muhammad Ali Jinnah addressed a public meeting at the city's Racecourse Maidan, which set the tone for his speech at the convocation of the University of Dhaka some days later. Jinnah's erudition would ignite a second firestorm of identity in the subcontinent in less than two years. And, ultimately, contribute quite handsomely to the birth of Bangladesh, when Jinnah's two nations, Pakistan and India, became three.

Already aware of severe tensions in his brand new country, in particular a growing resentment against the Muslim League and provincial acrimony between West Pakistan and its more populous and nature-blessed cousin in the East, Jinnah spoke about the primacy of Pakistan and the Muslim League, a party which he put above all else—'a sacred trust in your hands', as he termed it. He then addressed matters of provincialism.

'Now I ask you to get rid of this provincialism because as long as you allow this poison to remain in the body politic of Pakistan, believe me, you will never be a strong nation, and you will never be able to achieve what I wish you could achieve. Please do not think that I do not appreciate the position. Very often it becomes a vicious circle. When you speak to a Bengali he says "Yes, you are right, but the Punjabi is so arrogant"; when you speak to the Punjabi or a non-Bengali he says "Yes, but these people do not want us here, they want to get us out." Now this is a vicious circle, and I do not think anybody can solve this Chinese puzzle.'

But it is worth trying, Jinnah pleaded, as much a man who didn't exactly suffer from a common touch could. He spoke of the province relying on good sense and sensibilities, practical considerations of nation-building, 'statesmanlike' behaviour that would set apart the more conscientious as 'rendering the greatest service to Pakistan'.

Then he added fuel to an already lit fire, claiming that a demand to grant Bānglā the status of a national language was an attempt by 'political saboteurs or their agents' to 'create disruption among the Mussulmans'. Just the previous month an opposition legislator from East Bengal, Dhirendranath Datta, had moved an amendment in Pakistan's Constituent Assembly to make Bānglā the second official language, after Urdu. It would, after all, only be fair as it was spoken by 56 per cent of Pakistan. It was rejected; and it greatly angered the League leaders including Prime Minister Liaquat Ali Khan. I read in chronicles of the time that three days after this incident, on 26 February 1948, students of Dhaka University went on strike in protest.

Several years later, Dhaka University would, on the night of 25 March 1971, feel the brunt of an attack by several battalions of Pakistan's army. Aided by tanks and automatic weapons, soldiers would converge on staff quarters and students' hostels and, as part of the opening moves of Operation Searchlight, kill several hundred students and staff, both Mussulman and Hindu. Datta, eighty-five at the time and retired from active politics, would be picked up from his residence in Comilla four days later, and 'disappeared'. Some accounts say he was taken to the cantonment at Mainamati (or Moynamōti) in eastern Bangladesh, where lie the stunning ruins of a great Buddhist culture, and tortured to death. That would be just a few days adrift of the day in March that Jinnah had spoken to East Bengal more than twenty years earlier:

Sudeep Chakravarti

Whether Bengali should be the official language of this province is a matter for the elected representatives of the people of this province to decide. I have no doubt that this question should be decided solely in accordance with the wishes of the inhabitants of this province at the appropriate time. Let me tell you in [the] clearest language that there is no truth [in rumours] that your normal life is to be touched or disturbed, so far as your Bengali language is concerned. But ultimately it is for you, the people of this province, to decide what should be the language of your province.

But let me make it clear to you that the state language of Pakistan is going to be Urdu and no other language. Anyone who tries to mislead [you] is merely the enemy of Pakistan. Without one state language, no nation can remain tied up solidly together and function. Look at the history of other countries. There[fore] so far as the state language is concerned, Pakistan's language should be Urdu; but, as I have said, it will come in time.

Wrong move.

The insanity of political cartography in creating countries was one thing. To demand that a massive part of the country, that for several hundred years hadn't experienced as a language of the people anything other than Bāṅglā, acknowledge without recourse what was practically a foreign language presaged an attitude that some had feared, colonialism of a sort. It didn't play well in a region that had only just rid itself of British colonialism, and—ironically, arranged in great part by Muslim League—also shaken off the bogey of neo-colonialism by a Hindu-majority India. Intellectuals—writers, journalists, academicians—were at the forefront of this revolt. The noted Bangladeshi academic Anisuzzaman highlights a tongue-in-cheek and quite angry response to the suggestion by a vice-chancellor of Aligarh Muslim University, Ziauddin Ahmed, that, just as Hindi was going to be made the state language of India, Urdu be made the state language of Pakistan: 'Dr Muhammad Shahidullah, doyen of the academics in East Pakistan, countered his arguments and suggested that Bānglā, the language of the majority, should be the state language of Pakistan, but if there was a scope for a second State language, then Urdu should be awarded that position.'

Shahidullah's words counted. He was more than just a 'doyen of academics in East Pakistan', he was a phenomenon. A scholar of Bānglā and Sanskrit, he earned a bachelor's degree in Sanskrit from Calcutta City College, and a master's in comparative philology from the University of Calcutta. He followed this up with a doctorate at the Sorbonne in Paris on dialects of the Charyapad, a mystical Buddhist text with tantric overtones—some call it 'songs of realization'—that various historians place between the eighth and twelfth centuries CE and with language affinities with early Bānglā and Odia, even Assamese. (This somewhat mysterious text was discovered in Nepal by another Bengali scholar, Harprasad Shastri, in the first decade of the twentieth century.) Shahidullah later taught at the University of Dhaka.

He was also associated with an influential Islamic cultural organization called Tāmāddun Mōjlis, which had begun to campaign for Bānglā in 1947, publishing important pamphlets and holding meetings with leading intellectuals and political personalities. The moving force of the Mōjlis was Mohammad Abul Kashem, a professor of physics at the university who was generally known as Principal Abul Kashem. The Mōjlis was emphatic in its stand—again, a key signal Jinnah and his colleagues deliberately or inadvertently misread—that its approach was vastly different from the leftists and others who were politically motivated. To its mind the almost entirely Bengali East Bengal (soon to be formally known as East Pakistan) simply could not have any language other than Bānglā for instruction, and official and judicial purposes. In its opinion Urdu could be the second language of the East—say, kept for the purpose of those wishing to live and work in West Pakistan—with English accorded third priority; again, a language of specific purpose.

The Mōjlis emerged as a prime mover in formation of the Rāshtrōbhāshā Shongrām Pōrishod, a council for the movement for the national language. Shongrām usually sits better as 'struggle' or 'battle'.

Jinnah died in September 1948, leaving behind a divided country. His colleagues would run headlong into the Great Bāngla Wall, as they remained adamant over the premier status of Urdu for all Pakistan. There was an attempt to introduce the Arabic script for written Bāngla which even Khwaja Nazimuddin, born into the Nawab of Dhaka's family, who became governor general of Pakistan after Jinnah's passing, supported alongside the absolute primacy of Urdu. All it did was raise the temperature in the east, and in time fracture the hold of the Muslim League, beginning the transformation of a vast part of Pakistan from the cause of religion, identity and livelihood to the cause of language, identity and livelihood. The Maulana Abdul Hamid Khan Bhashani, a staunch and powerful League supporter, moved away from the party in 1949, formed the Awami Muslim League—it would later morph into Awami League—and placed his heft behind Bāngla.

Nearly four years after Jinnah's speech in Dhaka, matters snowballed into a crisis. An umbrella all-party committee for Bāngla chaired by Bhashani called for a hortāl, a general strike on 21 February 1952. The plan was to lead a procession to the East Bengal Legislative Assembly to coincide with a session that day, as well as stage protests across the east. The government banned demonstrations and prohibited the assembly of more than four persons—backed by a legal code which Pakistan and India seamlessly inherited from their colonial overlords.

Though the committee voted to accept the prohibitory order, based on political calculations that also factored in a promise of general elections the following year, students had other ideas. They gathered in large numbers at Dhaka University. A group attempted to force its way into the nearby Assembly building.

The police opened fire. Several people were injured. Five would die, including students, a worker, and a nine-year-old boy—some accounts describe him as a teenager. The idea of Bangladesh had its first martyrs.

Dhaka erupted. East Bengal—East Pakistan—erupted. The creation of East Bengal—later East Pakistan—and West Bengal in 1947, somewhat reprising the partition of 1905, was not about language, but largely about carving out territory in which the Bengali Hindu or Bengali Mussulman was in the majority—much like Partition that ultimately tore apart the province of Punjab into dominions of Pakistan and India. But it had now become a matter of language-identity and pride.

A poem by the young student-poet Abdul Gaffar Choudhury— later a writer and commentator—became an instant classic, carrying as it did the emotion of the time basted by the very Bengali respect for blood sacrifice and revolution. 'Ékushér gān', the song of the Twenty-first, was soon set to music by Altaf Mahmud and Abdul Latif and is sung today in Bangladesh and wherever Bangladeshis live on nearly every occasion commemorating the language movement. Indeed, it now identifies an entire genre called Ékushér gān. I prefer the original as a stirring recitation to the deceptively soft melody that so much of classical and modern Bānglā singing is, but that's a quibble with a work replete with protest. Its opening lines are captivating in any form:

> *Āmār bhāiyér rokté rāngānō Ékushé Phébruāri*
> *Āmi ki bhūlité pāri?*
> How can I ever forget
> The twenty-first of February painted with the blood
> of my brother?

Ōrā édéshér noy, the poem urged, they are not of this land—those who barter its future, those who snatch away our food, clothing, our peace. Dārūn krōdhér āguné ābār jālbō Phébruāri. We shall again set February afire with our fierce anger.

♦

Ékushé quickly changed the political landscape of Pakistan, certainly its eastern aspect. In the provincial elections in 1954, the Muslim League was routed. It won 7 seats in the 309-member Assembly. The United Front coalition of five parties won 228, the Awami Muslim League accounting for more than half that number. (The following year it would recast itself as the Awami League—its present name—in a move designed to attract non-Mussulmans to the party.) The Front's plank was the so-called 21-Point Programme, which covered vast ground, from demanding Bānglā as a state language of Pakistan to a complete overhaul and rejuvenation of the political, administrative and economic system of East Pakistan—indeed, except for defence matters, foreign affairs and the currency, for all practical purposes the East wished to be autonomous.

Ékushé, Twenty-first, as we have seen is the day Bangladesh celebrates as the day of its spiritual birth, when the country which as you know wanted to speak Bengali as much as be Bengali, was born in the minds and hearts of its people. Aptly there is now even a series of Ékushé free Unicode 'open type' Bānglā fonts. Bangladesh has dedicated Shōhid Mīnār, the country's iconic martyrs' monument, to this day. The Ékushé Podōk is the country's second highest civilian award. Ékushé is celebrated with as much gravitas and nearly as much pomp as 26 March, the day Bangladesh celebrates its formal independence day—on that day in 1971 a declaration of independence by Sheikh 'Mujib' was proclaimed over the radio in Chittagong by one of his key supporters. (A day later a modified proclamation would be repeated at what was called the Independent Bangla Revolutionary Radio Centre at Kalurghat, north of Chittagong by a young major, Ziaur Rahman, who had thrown in his lot with freedom fighters. After a beleaguered and by then discredited and somewhat megalomaniacal Mujib and most of his family were assassinated by some army officers and their loyalists in 1975 after a series of counter coups, Rahman would assume office as martial law administrator. And shortly thereafter, as president. He would be assassinated, too, in 1981, by a faction of the army, in Chittagong.)

◆

That is only part of the story of Bangladesh's blood-soaked birth (and rebirth, if one were to take Partition as causing the initial incarnation). As we know, language was crucial tinder for the future Bangladesh. But there is a backstory beyond Bānglā that drove 3 million people to die for this future to materialize.

As it turned out Pakistan had got it terribly wrong about Bengalis right from the moment of its birth, when it assumed a compact of religion would suffice for command and control of East Pakistan. Nearly 1,400 kilometres and the bulk of India separated West and East Pakistan. It hampered governance and movement of people and goods on account of distance as well as intermittent tension and wars with India, but there were other thorny issues as well.

While western Pakistan retained all the important offices of government, the armed forces, and the central bank, the East had the numbers, literally, of population—the majority of Pakistanis, 56 per cent, were in its eastern part. This heft wasn't reflected in the country's government—at its peak 75 per cent of bureaucrats were from the West—or armed forces, where the ratio was even more skewed, or in the way resources were allocated. To many in East Pakistan, it seemed like the reprising of a colonial story, a sentiment Choudhury's inflammatory poem had perceptively, even presciently, captured.

Aid, a lynchpin of the early years of the country's socio-economic development, flowed more to the West than East—some economists estimate at 70 per cent to the East's 30 per cent. The United States and the World Bank had committed $1 billion in aid in the early 1960s for development works in the West. Investment mandated by the country's early decades of a planned economy was similarly skewed. Rehman Sobhan, among Bangladesh's best-known economists and a person who extensively tracked and commented on the economic affairs of West and East Pakistan for several decades, maintained in an essay published in 1970 that East Pakistan paid for West Pakistan's deficit by appropriating the East's share of aid and by passing on inflationary pressure to the East. Between 1950 and 1960, between 22 and 40 per cent of West Pakistan's fixed investments were financed by the East. Economic growth was quicker in the West than the East. Per capita income was higher in the West than the East by a wide margin. Indeed, an already poorer East's per capita income decreased while it rose in the West.

◆

Married to economic deprivation was political deprivation. It became clear very quickly that East Pakistan—the Bengalis—would find scant proportional representation in Pakistan. West Pakistan's political elite simply wouldn't permit it. Neither would its military elite. Various formulae for the province's fair representation in the country's national assembly came to nothing—and it would in any case take until 1970 for national general elections to be held, with seismic implications!

Meanwhile there was controlled chaos. The provincial elections of 1954 in East Pakistan would soon be pointless (beyond its singular achievement of demolishing old political links and creating new tribes), as within months the United Front government would be dismissed by the governor general ostensibly on account of secessionism, and Governor's Rule imposed—direct rule by the central government. By 1954, the military-bureaucratic elite had begun the process of diminishing the elected civilian government of Pakistan. In April the prime minister of Pakistan was dismissed by the governor general. In October, the Constituent Assembly was dismissed, and a new one constituted the following May.

When the first constitution was promulgated in 1956, the Awami League, disagreeing with its contents and implications for East Pakistan, had already walked out. By 1958, such action would again prove meaningless (beyond registering its complaint and underscoring its position of being firmly pro-East) as in October 1958 Pakistan's army formally took over in a coup d'état. Field Marshal Ayub Khan began his absolutist reign. Pakistan's constitution was abrogated and political parties were banned. In 1960, a farcical, controlled election under a servile system called Basic Democracies elected Ayub Khan president of Pakistan. (Those who near-unanimously elected him were called Basic Democrats.) His advisers described the dictator's version of democracy quite colourfully as a 'democracy suited to the genius of the people'. One such adviser was Zulfikar Ali Bhutto, who would later become president of Pakistan and, by numerous accounts, Bangladeshi and not, a key player behind the 1971 genocide.

Meanwhile, the stature of Sheikh Mujib had begun to grow. By the time of the language movement Mujib had evolved from a charismatic student leader to a key member of the Awami Muslim League, marching by the side of Maulana Abdul Hamid Khan Bhashani, barefoot like others in respect to those killed on Ékushé. In a short while he became general secretary of the party, a post he held until early 1966 under the presidentship of the Maulana, and his two successors, Huseyn Shaheed Suhrawardy and Abdur Rashid Tarkabagish—'Torkōbāgish' literally means expert debater, or floridly 'the supremely argumentative one', an honorific common in Bengal from medieval times. In January of that year, Mujib formally took over the reigns of the Awami League as its president. Though he had been the driving force of the party for some years—he was instrumental in building the opposition to Ayub Khan, for instance, with the figurehead of Fatima Jinnah, Muhammad Ali's sister, in the presidential elections of 1964—it was now that Mujib's moment had arrived.

Ayub Khan won the elections in 1964, but it proved to be a pyrrhic victory in several ways. Social reforms were undercut by the continuing economic slide in the East. An educational reforms commission appointed by him had meanwhile rekindled the fires of the Bānglā language movement by recommending Urdu be made compulsory and Bānglā be written in Arabic script. A war with India that began in the Rann of Kutch in April 1965 had spiralled by September that year into a misadventure in Kashmir that he had been urged to undertake by his generals and Bhutto, foreign minister of Pakistan at the time. It backfired. Pakistan was militarily humiliated. On 10 January 1966, Pakistan was compelled into the conciliatory Tashkent Agreement with India.

In February, Mujib pounced. The Awami League announced in Lahore the Six Point Programme which basically sought to create an autonomous East Pakistan. It demanded a federal system and parliamentary democracy built on universal adult franchise; that provinces would be completely autonomous from governance to raising taxes, except with regard to matters of defence and foreign relations; either separate, convertible currencies for West and East Pakistan or a common currency with the assurance to stop the draining of wealth from the East to the West, and foreign exchange earned by each wing—and each wing would be free to trade with any country—would be for its own use. By May, Mujib and thousands of Awami League workers were in jail.

In January 1968, the government accused Sheikh Mujib, some government officials and a motley crew of former and serving armed forces personnel, several of them in quite lowly positions, of conspiring with India to break East Pakistan away from Pakistan. *The State vs Sheikh Mujibur Rahman and Others* came to be called the Agartala Conspiracy Case, after the eastern Indian city where conspirators were alleged to have met Indian Army officials. Mujib and others were hauled away to jail in Dhaka in May and a trial, presided over by a special tribunal, began that June, in Dhaka's cantonment.

Instead of demolishing Mujib and his growing appeal, the widely publicized arrest and trial had the opposite effect of igniting popular imagination and protest. It was seen as a blatant attempt to further dominate the aspirations of Bengali East Pakistanis by the not-Bengali West. Unrest, with a distinctly socialist flavour, began to grow in East Pakistan, a workers' and students' movement that focused on more benefits for farmers and industrial workers, driven in part by the goings-on in West Bengal and elsewhere in eastern India—this was the time of growing labour unrest (the spark of the radical Naxalite movement had been lit)—but mostly on angst driven by diminished circumstance and the feeling of repeatedly being taken for granted or insulted by West Pakistan. It also fed off a growing resentment across much of Pakistan of Ayub's regime.

Matters came to a head in the East on 15 February 1969, eight months into the trial, when a guest house in which a top official of the tribunal was staying in Dhaka, was burnt down. Two days later, the presiding judge left Dhaka—the trial was effectively shut down. On 22 February, a day after Ayub Khan announced his retirement, Mujib and the others were released. A day later Mujib would be given the enduring honorific of Bongōbōndhū—Friend of Bengal—at a massive gathering of students in Dhaka.

Events began to gallop.

In March, Ayub was gone, discredited even by his own support base; his place was taken by the chief of Pakistan's army, Yahya Khan. The move from one dictator to another only strengthened the call for more democracy. Yahya finally relented, and called for the country's first general elections to the national assembly for 1970, an event pushed to December of that year by devastating monsoon floods in East Pakistan, which killed an estimated half a million people. The government came in for intense criticism for its failure to cope with the disaster. In East Pakistan it only added fuel to the fire.

The economist Rehman Sobhan had this to say in a brilliant essay in the journal *Forum*, in early November 1970, writing under the nom de plume Rashed Akhter:

Within its fold the Awami League embraces various views and

diverse pressures for it has come to mean all things to all men. While the bourgeois look for permits, its student wing and younger elements see it as the vanguard of emancipation—an engine of social revolution. *Matbars* join it to save their skins, peasants to destroy the hold of the matbar with the help of the students. Much of what will happen to Bānglā Desh will depend on what happens within the Awami League...

'Whether one supports the Sheikh or mistrusts him only a fool would underestimate him,' Sobhan wrote, concluding with a prescient chill: 'He today symbolises the tide of the moment. Like all symbols his appeal rests on his ability to articulate the basic emotions which put him on his pinnacle. This should temper any illusions he may have of his personal charisma. History has singled him out to lead Bengal's struggle to fulfilment. If he fails his trust history may simply pass him by.'

◆

The Awami League and Mujib went flat out in their effort to win the elections to the 300-seat national assembly, targeting the 162 seats allocated to the East based on proportional representation. Very quickly, the Awami League remained the only credible choice in that province after several smaller left-leaning parties decided to boycott the elections when their demand to immediately secede from Pakistan and all its institutions, including elections, was rejected. The Awami League won a staggering 160 seats, all in the East. Bhutto's Pakistan Peoples Party won 81, the Abdul Qayyum faction of Pakistan Muslim League came in third with 9 seats.

Even more staggering was the fact that the Awami League, a party of Bengalis from East Pakistan, now held a majority in the national assembly, contrary to the calculations of Pakistan's establishment and intelligence agencies which, as several commentators have written, had hoped for lesser numbers (which would then force the Awami League to climb down from its Six-Point stand in order to share power).

As its leader, Sheikh Mujibur Rahman would, in any democracy, have been invited to lead the national government as prime minister. Of course nothing of the sort happened. Pakistan's—West Pakistan's—entrenched power structure wouldn't permit the unthinkable that had now become electorally possible. Bhutto demanded a share in the spoils, to which Mujib wasn't agreeable. Bhutto then petitioned the president to postpone the session of the assembly, to be held in Dhaka, which he had already threatened to boycott. On 28 February, Bhutto had in a public speech threatened 'not only large-scale civil disobedience throughout West Pakistan… but also "liquidation" of those who might participate in the forthcoming Assembly session.'

When Yahya Khan announced the postponement on 1 March, it created pandemonium in East Pakistan. Clashes broke out between security forces and protestors, several died. The army was out in large numbers; these would soon get larger in what was transparently martial law in everything but name. Curfew was progressively imposed in several places across the East. Still hoping to form the government Mujib and his party adopted the path of non-cooperation, bringing East Pakistan to a near-standstill for several weeks. They demanded that the army be withdrawn to its barracks, an enquiry into the deaths of those who had been killed, and a transfer of power. Mujib wouldn't budge from Dhaka, forcing senior Pakistani officials to make the trip to the city, even Yahya and Bhutto, who hurriedly arrived on 21 March after news circulated that Yahya and Mujib had arrived at an understanding that would, in exchange for Yahya remaining president, give in to most of Mujib's demands.

Bhutto and Mujib met at the Intercontinental Hotel—now the Sheraton—in Dhaka. Nothing came of the meeting. Yahya was still present, and, evidently, swinging back to the hardline approach of limiting the influence of Awami League and the East.

On 23 March, Pakistan Day, to mark the Muslim League's adoption of the Lahore Resolution in 1940 to demand Pakistan, and the day that country adopted its constitution in 1956, the flag of Bangladesh was hoisted in Dhaka by a group of students. On the evening of 25 March, Yahya left the city; Bhutto had already departed earlier that day, after announcing at a press conference that the Awami League's demands went way beyond autonomy. By then the fate of both Pakistan and Bangladesh were cast in stone. Over the night of 25 March and early morning of 26 March, Operation Searchlight, planned and executed with precision by Pakistan's army, went into play. With Mujib and his colleagues in jail, the massacres began. They wouldn't end for several months.

On 26 March, the United States' Defence Intelligence Agency would write a memo to the White House Situation Room (The *Dhaka Courier* printed a facsimile of the declassified document in March 2010):

> Pakistan was thrust into civil war today when Sheikh Mujibur Rahman proclaimed the east wing of the two-part country to be 'the sovereign independent People's Republic of Bangla Desh'. Fighting is reported heavy in Dacca and other eastern cities where the 10,000 man paramilitary East Pakistan Rifles has joined police and private citizens in conflict with an estimated 23,000 West Pakistani regular army troops. Continuing reinforcement by sea and air combined with the government's stringent martial law regulation illustrates Islamabad's commitment to preserve the union by force... Because of logistical difficulties, the attempt will probably fail, but not before heavy loss of life results.

◆

'Thank God,' Bhutto exclaimed, upon hearing of the operation (reportedly he felt 20,000 deaths in the East ought to sort things out). 'Pakistan is saved.'

◆

My cousin Nasreen—Bibi to the family—remembers 25 March 1971 with the crystal clarity that horror etches into a young mind. Bibi is the daughter of my mother's younger sister, Fatima, Tolly-māshi to us, and Quamrul Anam Khan, who once co-owned and ran the newspaper *Azad*. He was ejected from its control in 1969 by disgruntled members of his family, in conjunction with Pakistan's administration. His cousin was an officer in Pakistan's Army and had leveraged government contacts, so goes the family legend, to grab the newspaper and attendant property by foisting a case of attempted murder on Quamrul—he was accused of attempting to murder his own workers. The cloak-and-dagger stuff was typical of East Pakistan in the 1960s. Quamrul was finally acquitted several years later, after Liberation.

Azad was for long seen as a conservative newspaper. The founder, and Quamrul-méshō's father, Maulana Akram Khan, had been a well-known figure in the Muslim League in Kolkata, and had moved to Dhaka on account of Partition. The maulana had retained his basic conservatism which he had injected into his newspaper, but *Azad* had during Quamrul's tenure as managing director published pro-Bengali (and by default, anti-Pakistan) articles and editorials. My cousin Bibi recalls pro-Bengali activists taking shelter in the family home in the late 1960s, a dangerous practice for Quamrul in very dangerous times.

Anyway, on 25 March, Bibi was at our granny Lila's house with her older brother Azam—Bāpi. The house was in Shantinagar, in the Purana Paltan Lines area of central Dhaka. Granny Lila lived there at the time with her eldest son, Sunil Roy Paladhy, second eldest daughter, Nellie, her youngest son, Sujit, and youngest daughter, Padma. Bibi's mother Fatima, my aunt, whom Quamrul worshipped as Pōrineeta, the complete one—in English this Sanskrit-flavoured word receives less than its lyrical due—were there too. They lived in the faraway northern suburb of Savar, but Granny Lila's was home to the extended family for several months of the war.

Bibi recalls loud sounds late that night, later identified by the family as coming from busy rifles and machine guns, followed by a massive fire that, she says, 'lit up the whole sky' to the right of the house in the direction of Rajarbagh police headquarters. The Pakistan Army had set fire to it. The main road could be seen across a large field, and it was crawling with army trucks. The family was worried as Sunil, who had as usual gone to his guru's ashram, hadn't yet returned. An executive with the Dutch airline KLM, Sunil would visit his guru Sri Brōjānondō at his ashram near Dhaka University, and would typically return home after the guru retired for the night. Bibi recalls Sunil—called Patel by the family as he was thought to resemble the Congress leader Vallabhbhai Patel—furtively returning home much later that night.

The family rushed to greet him. Bibi says the first thing everyone noticed was how his shoes had blood on them. He told them he'd had to walk through lanes strewn with the dead, awash in their blood. (Sunil, whom we called Borō-māmu, the traditional address in eastern Bengal for the eldest maternal uncle—in the West it's usually Borō-māmā—changed the subject when I asked him about this many years later. But he did graphically recount several incidents of Bengali Hindu families being attacked, and shot dead. He isn't the only one from these times to bury trauma, and move on to sanity by seeking spirituality and a monkish life.)

A few days later, Shantinagar's market was set on fire. Over the next several weeks such destruction, looting and killing—and its heightened avatar, genocide—became commonplace. Curfew was strictly enforced, though deaths on account of the violation were a mockery. The army and the militias would come for you anyway, whenever they wished.

One day in late May 1971, the army came for the family.

It was evening, Bibi recalls. The family was home. Upon hearing trucks moving up the lane, the family moved in a well-coordinated but ultimately futile manner. Bāpi moved with Sujit, our youngest maternal uncle—Chhōtō-māmu—to one toilet and attempted to hide under a pile of dirty linen and clothes—younger males were usually among the first to be killed or taken away, to be eventually tortured and then killed, or just killed outright if the soldiers were merciful. Bibi moved to a room furthest from the entrance, beyond the living room and main bedrooms with our aunt Padma, as younger women were easy targets for molestation and subsequent 'disposal'. ('You should have seen her then, she was a real beauty', Bibi would speak of our aunt to me several years later.) The rest were present when troopers barged in, followed by an officer.

Her father decided to be the interlocutor, Bibi recalls. Fluent in Urdu, Quamrul engaged the officer, and fended off his queries about having heard this was a 'Hindu house'. There was no differentiator between Hindu and Mussulman at this point, only those who were Bengali and those who were pro-Pakistan, but hunting the Hindu was as much sport as diktat in 1971.

Quamrul's work was made somewhat easier as Granny Lila, Didu to us children, had removed every trace of her pujō accessories—idols, flowers, vermilion, holy books—from the house in March. She had stopped wearing teep, or 'dot' in the typical identifier for a Hindu lady—though in East Paskistan at the time many Mussulman ladies wore teep (now in Bangladesh an Islamic conservative resurgence frowns at the practice). A photograph of granny in the living room showing her undeniably as a Hindu in the way she wore her sari and other accoutrements including teep, one in a row of four portraits, had been removed.

What remained confused the soldiers. Bejoy, Granny Lila's long deceased father-in-law, had been photographed with his flowing beard, looking more like a fōkir. Giving him company was my eldest aunt Dolly's husband, an Englishman who worked as a senior officer in East Pakistan's fire service, and who had passed on. Dolly—borō-māshi—was at home with us in Kolkata. Their son Peter Holden, who used to be in a band with our uncle Sujit, moving around Dhaka in a Volkswagen van in the era's statement of ultimate 'cool', had only months earlier moved to Dublin. (He married an Irish girl, Susan. They still live in Dublin. Peter is father and grandfather to a vast family with a great love of dāl, bhāt and chātni which he cooks.) Then there was the photograph of Grandfather Sukumar, Lila's husband, in suit and tie, back-brushed hair and horn-rimmed glasses, looking every inch a Muslim League intellectual.

This distracted the soldiers for a while, but eventually things appeared to be heading towards some bloodletting. The males, including my youngest uncle and Bibi's brother who were hiding in the toilet, were discovered and herded with other males into the courtyard. The women were gathered in the main bedroom. Quamrul was still desperately playing diplomat.

When the tension had become unbearable, and almost everyone in the family had resigned themselves to being killed, with some torture and molestation thrown in, Bibi says the officer's eye fell upon some cupboards. That's when the looting began, of money and jewellery in the house, of bric-à-brac that caught their fancy. That's when Quamrul turned to Granny Lila, Bibi recalls, and softly told her all would be well. Looting had won the day over massacre.

Bibi and her family soon left for Savar. Quamrul refused to stay in Shantinagar any longer, saying it was too dangerous. They survived.

Granny Lila and her family in Shantinagar also survived 1971. They don't exactly know how they came through the roulette of politics and genocide though they credit the aura of their guru Brōjānondō. The guru's residence and ashram where he greeted disciples and visitors—also dhām, in Bāngla—was attacked on 26 March, and several acolytes protecting the ashram were killed by the army and their not-Bengali associates. But Brōjānondō managed to escape to his disciples among a nearby colony of sweepers and scavengers. They were left alone. There was a lot of cleaning up to do in Dhaka. Blood and bodies were everywhere.

◆

The life and death struggle over language and identity was not limited to Bangladesh. Let me tell you another story. The numbers aren't much going by the numbing mayhem that led to the creation of Bangladesh. But eleven dead is still eleven too many for the right to speak, write and work in a particular language.

This is the nearly forgotten story of Cachar, a district of present-day Assam. Some say: a forgotten Bengal, so forgotten that its Bengali residents are often confused by Bengalis elsewhere as being prōbāshi. Some even call it Bāhirbongō, outside the territory of Bengal, east or west.

Like the Ékushé of Bangladesh they have their Unishé—the Nineteenth.

Every 19 May since 1961, when protesters demanding Bānglā as the first language of instruction and government were set upon by Assam's police, and were killed and injured, the Bengalis of Cachar, and specifically the district headquarters of Silchar, remind themselves of it, and to hell with what other Bengalis think of them—or not.

◆

They grow some fine tea in these parts. It isn't 'Darjeeling', but historically it's not even 'Assam'. And, in any case, the snobs of Assam's tea business maintain that the Upper Assam areas, in the upper plains of Brahmaputra, produce teas superior to teas in the Bengali-heavy areas of Cachar in the Barak Valley to the south of that state. Let me then continue to play provocateur and call it Bengali tea; it has some fine cousins in similar latitudes just across the international border in Bangladesh, in Sylhet, and a little to the south in Sreemangal. (Less gratuitously, and correctly, it ought to be called Cachari Tea, to honour the homelands of indigenous Cachari tribes, whose lives were irrevocably changed even before the insanity of political cartography around Partition when plantation-economy and resettlement came calling. Few among the High Assamese, as it were, and even the local Bengali, tell their stories.)

I've learned about the twists and turns of the history of Bengal, Bangladesh and Bengalis from numerous sources—family, academic, historical, cultural, folk, literary, and those often described as people-on-the-street—but the matter of Cachar was highlighted most succinctly for me by an essay by New Delhi-based sociologist and academic Nabanipa Bhattacharjee. 'Negotiating Marginality', as she aptly titled it, tells the story of the Bengali speakers of Assam, nearly 30 per cent of the population, the largest linguistic minority in that state.

The East India Company wrapped up its conquest of Assam in 1826 with that of Cachar six years later, and merged them with its mint, as it were—the Bengal Presidency. After administrative reorganization following the usurpation of John Company's powers by the British Crown after the 1857 mutiny, the largely Bengali speaking districts of Sylhet, Cachar, and Goalpara—in what is known as Lower Assam, and another present-day tea-growing area of the province—were with some hill districts merged into the new 'Chief Commissioner's Province' of Assam.

The reason Sylhet and Cachar were merged with the new province, claims Bhattacharjee in an article in the weekly *Mainstream*, was to meet the 'inadequate revenue potential of Assam'. It cut off Bengali speakers from Bengal, besides isolating the fiercely proud Sylheti who tend to identify themselves as Sylheti first before associating with any other nationalistic (Indian, Bangladeshi, British…), linguistic (Bānglā) or religious (generally Muslim or Hindu) entity. The merger also had an unintended, and awkward, effect—of clubbing Bengali-speaking areas to Assam when hiving off Assam was also done to assuage Assamese needs of identity. 'The situation for the Assamese was nothing less than paradoxical,' Bhattacharjee writes. 'The move was a moment of liberation from Bengal, but hardly from the Bengalis; the much needed and desired freedom and right to articulate and nurture the Assamese identity seemed sabotaged from the start.'

Matters became messier with the partition of India. In 1947, much of Muslim-majority Sylhet went over to newly-born Pakistan after a referendum that year, except for the areas that fell within the jurisdiction of approximately three-and-a-half police thanas that were of a majority Bānglā-speaking area and with a substantial population of Hindus, which remained with Assam—and India. Trouble began to brew with this legacy, this outcrop of Bengalis, cut-off from West Bengal—and from the very Bengali East Pakistan.

From the early twentieth century, there was a steady trickle of Bengali agricultural migrants into Assam, encouraged by the colonial government to settle along the Brahmaputra, but Partition unlocked a flood of Bengali Hindu refugees into eastern Indian territories from East Pakistan, a movement further spurred by anti-Hindu riots there in 1950. There was a massive influx into West Bengal and Tripura (with its own set of consequences, which I refer to elsewhere), but the influx was also severe in Assam, which had never hidden its dislike of Bānglā-speaking people—brought about in no small measure by the historical arrogance of Bengalis towards the Assamese from the time of the existence of Greater Bengal under the East India Company. While Assam's Congress government under the charismatic Gopinath Bordoloi accepted the inevitable after some months, a circular it issued on 4 May 1948, as I read in Bhattacharjee's essay (here she refers to the work of the scholar S. Choudhury) basically sent out a personae non grata message as to immigration and land settlement in Assam, citing the purpose of 'peace, tranquillity and social equilibrium in towns and villages', and that, 'in no circumstances' should any settlement of land be made to those not indigenous. The definition of non-indigenous people extended to 'non-Assamese settlers in Assam though they already have lands and houses of their own and have made Assam their home to all intents and purposes'.

Things were so chaotic—to be fair, no administration in eastern India had planned for an influx of several million—that a refugee board for Cachar in June 1950 made a representation to Syama Prasad Mookerjee. The Bengali politician, who had in the 1930s and 1940s established his conservative credentials as a leading light of the Hindu Mahasabha, and a reputation as a protector of Hindu Bengalis when he supported the Partition of Bengal in 1946 to ensure Hindu-majority areas of Bengal remained with India, was at the time a political loose cannon. As we have seen, he had fallen out with Jawaharlal Nehru over the Indian prime minister's overture to Pakistan, and what he perceived as pandering to Kashmiri nationalists, among other things, and had resigned his post as India's first minister of industry and supply in April 1950. Mookerjee could do little for the Bengalis in Assam.

Things were about to get worse for Bengalis in Cachar. The Assam (Official) Language Act, 1960, promulgated in December of that year, made Assamese the official language of Assam. This touched a raw nerve, especially as it followed what came to be called the Bongal Kheda campaign: get rid of Bengalis. Beginning mid-1960, Bengalis—including the district magistrate of Guwahati and a senior police officer—were attacked in the Brahmaputra Valley. They were stabbed by mobs. Depending on Assamese or Bengali sources, it is estimated that between 50,000 and ten times that number fled the Brahmaputra Valley to seek shelter, primarily in Bengali-majority Cachar, elsewhere in far-eastern India, and West Bengal. The word Bongal came to mean outsiders in general, but at the core of it lay the prime meridian of the agitation, Bengalis.

This fleeing was a move of the twice-displaced, Bengalis who had escaped the horrors of Partition and now the excesses of Assamese nationalism. Besides the historical reasons I've mentioned, the hatred of Bengalis was also brought about by the entrepreneurial, managerial and survival spirit of the middle-class Bengali—in this case largely the 'East Bengali'. There were large, successful islands of mini-Bengal in the heart of Assam. These were highly visible and, to hear some of my Assamese friends tell it, boastful, leery of indigenous Assamese—an attitude long resented locally. 'In the towns of Gauhati, Tezpur, Nowgong, Jorhat, Dibrugarh, Tinsukia etc., almost half the population consists of Bengalis,' wrote K. C. Chakravarti in a July 1960 issue of *Economic Weekly* (precursor of the *Economic and Political Weekly*). 'They have their own clubs where Bengali plays are staged. Many of them own cinema houses where Bengali pictures are shown. Bengali dailies from Calcutta enjoy a large circulation in these towns. In some of them Bengali schools are flourishing well. Many Bengalis are thriving as doctors, lawyers, teachers, clerks and occasionally as traders.'

The idyll didn't last long. 'These Bengalis in general and the Bengali employees of the oil refinery at Gauhati in particular have of late become objects of hostility and humiliation. In the past they used to be jeered at and sometimes even assaulted and stabbed. The culprits, very often, would be students. They were being incited by Assamese job-seekers and protected by college and university authorities. The local police often felt helpless…'

Some Bengali observers, with Partition fresh in their minds, were driven to dramatically describe the manner in which Bongal Kheda came to be executed as similar to Direct Action adopted by the Muslim League in Kolkata in 1946—when the League effectively encouraged violence against Hindus to drive an irretrievable wedge into the idea of unified India, knowing fully well there would be retaliation, and matters would roll a step closer to the creation of a separate homeland for Mussulmans of the subcontinent—Pakistan. It was a conspiracy of complicity. 'On the language issue, which practically aims at driving the Bengalis from the Assam Valley, all Assamese are unanimous,' wrote Chakravarti. 'Congress and non-Congress leaders, politicians of all shades of opinion, Rightists, Leftists, Hindus, Muslims, poets, priests, men of letters, sober educationists, unruly students—all have wonderfully cooperated. The town of Gauhati was divided into a number of zones. Zonal leaders were stationed with their student followers in each zone. If the police entered one zone, the other zone would become active. In fact, some Government officials too—Assamese and non-Assamese—have made their own contribution, each according to his capacity, either through active participation or through inaction.'

There was some talk—and such talk continues in academic and argumentative circles—that the law of the land permitted a unilingual approach only if an ethnic group counted for 70 per cent of the total population. In Assam's case, going by the 1951 census, it was 55 per cent, and much of Assam's area at the time constituted non-Assamese ethnicities. Meghalaya, for instance, the state for Khasi, Garo and Jaintia people, was yet to be. But it was clearly a case of reclaiming an ethnic identity as much as anything else. Moreover, several Assamese writers and thinkers of the time fully justified the move to make Assamese the only language of the state. 'Bengali has been declared as the State Language for the Darjeeling District of West Bengal where it is spoken only by about 16 per cent of the population,' maintained P. C. Goswami in the same issue of the *Economic Weekly* in which Chakravarti made his case for Bengalis in Assam. 'So there should be no hesitation in declaring Assamese as the State Language of Assam for fear of offending the people of Cachar and Hill Districts, particularly when adequate safeguards are provided for the minorities.'

The Bongal Kheda violence was not focused on Cachar, the Bengali redoubt fatefully clubbed with Assam—being majority Bengali had that ethnic advantage. But language remained an issue, a domination, a perceived violence. The government of Assam considered adequate safeguards within its official language such as permitting the use of Bāṅglā for 'administrative and other official purposes' in Cachar district at the sub-divisional and municipal board level; but it needed a two-thirds majority of the members 'present and voting' to 'decide in favour of adoption of the official language for use in the district for the aforesaid purposes'. For the Bengalis of Cachar, this was an insult—the government of Assam was clearly trying to contain the language genie by tying it up in legal knots. In any case it was seen as an imposition of Assamese in a place that had never been Assamese.

By February 1961, a resistance began to coalesce under the direction of the Cachar Gana Sangram Parishad—the Cachar Peoples' Struggle Committee. Within a month the movement to oppose the language law had spread from Silchar to the other significant towns of Barak Valley, Karimganj (which is today a district headquarters of an eponymous district) and Hailakandi (also the district headquarters of an eponymous district). Processions were taken out. An ultimatum of a hortāl was given for 19 May, if the language law wasn't modified to include the full-fledged use of Bānglā in Cachar. The government struck back, first arresting the leaders of the movement, and ordering troopers of the Assam Rifles, an adjunct of the Indian Army (which had acquired a controversial reputation for its strong-arm handling of civilians) and paramilitaries of the Central Reserve Police Force to conduct flag marches from mid-May.

On 19 May, Cachar was shut down. Numerous protesters were arrested. When a truck carrying some of them passed by Silchar's railway station in the area of Tarapur, protesters gathered nearby were drawn to it. They freed the detainees, and set the truck on fire. Security forces promptly arrived and engaged with the mob, wading into it with batons and freely using rifle butts. Shots were fired. Nine protesters died immediately; two died later. Bānglā had more martyrs.

No amount of curfew could hold back subsequent protests. The government of Assam realized it had misplayed its hand. Negotiations followed. In October 1961 the Language Act was amended to include, only for Cachar, Bānglā as an official language on par with Assamese. The business of government could here be conducted in Bānglā, so could education—even higher education. When Karimganj, where Sylheti is the prevalent dialect, and tiny Hailakandi—it has an area of less than 1,400 square kilometres— were hived off from Cachar as districts, the pro-Bengali privileges of Cachar also passed to them.

(Other districts of Assam, 'Lower Assam', as it is known, like Dhubri and Goalpara which today have large Bengali-speaking populations, do not have similar linguistic benefits; there, growth in Bengali-speaking populations has occurred since Cachar's language movement. In terms of percentage, fully a third of the people in

Assam use Bengali as a first language, a factor of Partition and ceaseless migration—and a matter in Assam of the greatest political, ethnic and religious volatility.)

◆

But this hasn't prevented a marginalization in Banglasphere, even the pining of a people that is close to 2 million in an island of someone else's making. Bhattacharjee mentions this near-desperate search to validate a definite identity within Banglasphere. Tritiyō Bhubon, or the Third World, is one—presumably a world beyond West Bengal and Bangladesh. Ishan Bānglā, or Northeast Bengal, is another; Barak Bongō—loosely, Bengal in Barak—yet another. '[T]he Bangla speakers of Barak Valley relentlessly try to "examine" and "explain" their relationship with the larger Bangla speaking community,' maintains Bhattacharjee. 'The urgency is reflected in the everyday articulations as well as the literature published from the region.'

She shares one such by Bijit Bhattacharya in the Hailakandi-based Bānglā journal *Shahittō* from 2010 which Bhattacharjee interprets as a plea to recognize that, 'what is generally conceptualized as "Bengal and Bengali culture" ought to be re-thought so that cultures are not necessarily viewed as tied to "fixed territorial regions".' As she quotes Bhattacharya in translation:

> The British in order to weaken the Bengali community broke up Bengal into numerous parts. The two main ones, Bangladesh and West Bengal, are the most important pilgrimages of Bengalis. But outside these, the small fragments of Bengal are also the *swasthan* [own territory], *pithasthan* [pilgrimage] of Bengalis—not *Bahirbanga* [Bengal outside territorial Bengal, in effect the Bengali Diaspora]… We only refer to the numerous small Bengals [like Barak Valley] as *Bahirbanga* when we assume that West Bengal is the only Bengal. We forget that prefixed by the word 'west' it too

becomes part of the original Bengal. To designate the Bangla speaking regions outside West Bengal as *Bahirbanga* is unjust and is the handiwork of the state and a section of the West Bengal-based intelligentsia.

As eloquently argued as this is, for me the more eloquently practical remains the argument of Amitabha Deb Choudhury in the *Bāhirbongō Pōtrikā* around mid-2000. He threw down the argumentative gauntlet by suggesting that instead of Bāhirbongō, Barak Valley should perhaps be termed Bhongōbongō, or Fragmented Bengal. Deb Choudhury is forceful in denying that Bengalis in Barak Valley are in any way prōbāshi—a presumption by those in West Bengal and, frankly, Bangladesh, where I have encountered similar ideas among my generation and those younger who are less mindful of the ancient history of the 1960s in a place already delinked geographically and politically, in body if not soul. 'All inhabitants of Barak Valley know that this is misleading… Barak Valley's Bengalis are not like ones who live in Madhya Pradesh, Hyderabad or New Delhi for these were never part of Bengal. But Sylhet and Cachar were…'

'A simile comes to mind,' Deb Choudhury suggested. 'It is like the fragmented, dismembered parts of a body with tremendous suspicion asking each other: Bhāi, tui āmiiy tōh?'

Brother, you're me, right?

3

Haw, maw
Scales of religion

There is a deep-rooted religious schism that has permeated Bengali history for over a hundred years, which only the most liberal in Banglasphere have ever been able to overcome.

Hindu and Mussulman. They could almost be two different species.

In my family—my mother's family, mostly temperate and multi-religious but blunt—it came down to two Bānglā alphabets, pronounced maw and haw, Bānglā equivalent for m and h. That was the code to discreetly describe if someone was a Mussulman or Hindu. The maw would be dismissed by the haw, except those relatives who were and are maw. In that case it would be justified by a simple 'Tōrā bād'—you folks are excluded.

I've seen liberal Mussulmans in Bangladesh and West Bengal, for all their talk of togetherness of language and culture, and secular ideals that are apparently ingrained in Bengali culture, in particular rural Bengali culture, appear terribly hurt that they have been traditionally, historically, looked down upon by the Bengali Hindu. They were even upset every so often by writers like the great Saratchandra Chattopadhyay—not Bankim Chandra Chattopadhyay, who was proudly a Hindu and whose seminal works like *Ānōndō Moth* came to be a beacon for both Bengali Hindu resurgence and Indian nationalism—who is largely seen as an emancipator of women, a celebrated voice for the poor and oppressed, his works transformed to instant classics.

'How could Saratchandra write such a thing?' a liberal, and elderly, society lady in Dhaka once complained to me. She meant the four-part novel *Srikāntō*. Within the first few pages there is a description, a recollection of an evening in a village where Srikāntō meets Indrōnāth; where Indrōnāth saves Srikāntō.

'Iskulér māthé Bāngāli ō Mushōlmān chhātrōdér football match. Shōndhyā hoy-hoy. Mognō hōiyā dékhitéchhi...' It was nearly evening. There was a football match on in the school grounds between Bengali and Mussulman students. I watched, transfixed...

And soon, in the same paragraph, a fight breaks out, the playing field empties but Srikāntō is confused, rooted to the spot, unable to escape, surrounded by several Mussulman boys: '...pānch-shātjon Mushōlman-chhōkrā tokhōn āmār chāridiké byuhō rochōnā kōriāchhé...'

◆

For all the disappointment with Saratchandra, a mincing sort of religious righteousness is evident to this day in a number of ways especially among the generations in Bangladesh that have known a life before Partition. And it is not always in literature, or words that are little more than pamphleteering. I was quite taken aback while reading the memoirs in Bānglā of a well-known Bangladeshi journalist, now deceased, who was variously in his youth involved in politics, agitated for a separate homeland for the Mussulman, worked in media including at the influential Dhaka daily, *Ittefaq*, and during Liberation was actively engaged in getting the voice of the 'Mujibnagar government'—yet-to-be Bangladesh's government in exile—operational in Kolkata. (The information and radio wing of this government in exile operated for a time at 1, Ballygunge Circular Road.)

Out to lunch in September 1971 with a senior journalist from *The Statesman*, whom he names, our narrator was amazed when that gentleman ordered whisky—while he opted for lassi. From this slim thread of morality he expressed surprise at the condition of 'Bengali Hindu society', which he acknowledged as having progressed somewhat from 'religious malpractices' and being somewhat better endowed with 'generosity of mind', nevertheless dissolute with drink and a certain hopelessness of spirit. And this, he assumed, caused the Naxalbari movement to spread in West Bengal. He then reeled off some examples of famous Bengali Hindu journalists travelling to famous watering holes, soirées by famous Bengali Hindu personalities, and the general alcoholic haze that seemed to envelope certain well-to-do Bengali Hindus.

And what of that story of a Bengali Hindu editor of a newspaper who was too drunk to be present at the wedding of his daughter? Or the 'highly respected' Bengali Hindu poet and Bengali Hindu novelist of the modern era who visited Bangladesh in 1972 and who—as our intrepid memoirist claimed—were issued passports of a month's validity on account of being alcoholics. And did we hear of that poet being discovered one morning, asleep by the elevator of Hotel Purbani (where I've eaten outstanding ilish and crème caramel)? What of a famous Bengali Hindu film director who visited Bangladesh, and whom our narrator never saw 'healthy'.

The narrator would have been aghast at my stories of Dhaka, Kolkata, New Delhi and Bonn variously in the company of Bengali Hindu and Bengali Mussulman journalists, writers, poets, musicians, politicians, bureaucrats and diplomats, where truths arrived with progressively boisterous talk, and the only god in attendance appeared to be Bacchus and his branded products, all quite premium, and primarily from Scotland, Russia, France, Germany, and South Africa. Among Bacchus's ambassadors there was always curiously an Old Monk from India, present even in Bonn.

We are all, Bengali Hindus and Bengali Mussulmans, guilty as charged.

What then of Bengali Christians, Buddhists and Brahmos, any other denominational variety, including atheists? Guilty, guilty, guilty. Of everything.

It's probably easier that way.

◆

Religion, as a matter of intense dislike, or as a matter of victimhood, came to me in a manner I least expected—from my father. He waited until I was at university, for me a time of runaway existentialist angst and rebelliousness and for him a time when he felt comfortable enough to speak of an uncomfortable legacy. It seemed to me so strange, how a man so liberal in his outlook and in the manner he had attempted to provide my sister and I every opportunity to fly and open our eyes and minds and hearts to the world, could in a heartbeat seem to be so determinedly against a religion. Thinking about it some years later, when I emerged from a fog of self-pity and consequent anger, Father's behaviour appeared as logical as it was disturbing, but more of this a little later.

Religion is manifold in a family such as ours. As a young boy I did not pay much attention to matters of religion. People worshipped different gods, and I went to see these different gods and ways of worship, including what was traditionally ours—a Bengali-Hindu-Brahmin family of a certain socio-economic standing.

We never worshipped idols at home in Kolkata. The family deity, Nārāyon, which my father arranged to have smuggled out of the temple in the old family estate in Kushtia before East Pakistan died and was reborn as Bangladesh, was given over to the family guru's seat in Bero, a small village in Purulia district of West Bengal, for safekeeping. My sister and I weren't once compelled to visit either the ashram or the deity. We visited a neighbour's home for pro-forma worship of Pārbōti and Shib's overachiever child, Shorōshhōti, perhaps less out of love for the goddess of learning and more out of Mother's concern over our slipping grades. We weren't ever the ideal Bengali children, studiously engaged in the pursuit of academic brilliance and worldly advance, unless the subjects fascinated us, or our teachers did. But Shorōshhōti-débi always smiled beningnly, even encouragingly to our hopeful minds, her exquisite clay features and electric colours constructed in Kumartuli, the kumōr—potters—of this north Kolkata enclave of godmakers always at hand for every manner of god, goddess and deliverance.

At thirteen, I declined the thread ceremony, passing up formal ordination as a Brahmin, citing historical and ongoing wrongs in which I saw Brahmins as having greatly exploited other castes, and offered up as example, greedy, loud-mouthed priests I saw presiding at numerous religious ceremonies for family and elsewhere. These aggressive, money-minded middlemen for the gods had existed in almost every temple of note we visited in eastern India—Bengal, Odisha and Bihar—where peace for my grandfather's soul was aggressively brokered at Vishnupad Mandir in Gaya, the pindō-dān at a nearby spot by the dry riverbed of the Falgu River, considered to be among the most auspicious ways for a soul to quickly, seamlessly reach heaven. After all, Lord Ram of legend had done so here for his father Doshōroth, and it did seem relatively cleaner, filth and all, than attempting it by the much filthier ghats of the Hooghly in Kolkata. Mother sulked for some weeks and wondered who had filled my head with dangerous thoughts. Father, a formally ordained Brahmin who delighted in a plump beef steak at Calcutta's better restaurants—Mother forbade such profanity at home—had merely smiled. (He hosted my first adventure in eating beef steak at Mocambo, a Kolkata institution, in the early 1970s; it was a Chateaubriand, done well. I burnt my tongue in my eagerness to eat this forbidden food. Mother thought it was divine retribution.)

Visiting the pandāls during Durga Pujō was more cultural sightseeing than worship. I attempted dhunuchi-nāch a couple of times at a pandāl near the home of an uncle. It's the propitiating dance to Durga usually with two earthen bowls of kindling and incense—as a pre-teen I was permitted the risk-diminished use of one. I lost myself in the mesmeric rhythm of dhāk and by the equally mesmeric swaying of dhāki, the players. Perhaps as I only carried with me curiosity, not faith, the spirit of Ma Durga did not visit my being. She was always impressive though, and even quirky at times, as in 1972, when I saw a face of Durga transposed with the likeness of Indira Gandhi, India's prime minister at the time. She had earned that honour for her part in defeating Pakistan's army during the Bangladesh war the previous year. The ōshur—demon—at her feet was the likeness of a dying Pakistani soldier with a spear through his chest; he managed to look awestruck.

As a folksy mother goddess Durga has few equals—she is a stupendous eastern Indian phenomenon, and for the Bengali a point of abiding love, devotion and annual worship that is the excuse for the grandest festivities. New clothes for those who can afford these, feasts, folk theatre, cultural functions—our world revolves around Ma Durga for close to a week. It won't be an exaggeration to say that, for so many worshippers and revellers, there is even an emotional void when we let her go, floating her likeness in clay in countless rivers, streams and ponds.

My parents would take my sister and me to St Paul's Cathedral in Kolkata. We often went there for the stained glass and the peace Mother seemed to derive from the great vault-like space. Alongside absorbing regular recitation and explanation of the Mohābhārōt and Rāmāyon by Grandmother Nirupama, my father's mother, I had before the age of ten my personal copy of the Bible for children, a large-print, dramatically illustrated chatty retelling that the publishers, Hamlyn seemed to specialize in, with Abraham, Moses and Jesus all seemingly manicured and in impeccable robes. For the voice of god, Mother directed us to the voiceover of god in *The Ten Commandments*, a syrupy movie which we saw as a family during a re-run at Metro, at the time a thriving art deco cinema on Chowringhee. Mother was infatuated with the character of Moses, especially in the Egyptian prince episodes played by Charlton Heston. (So we went to see a re-run of *Ben-Hur* too, which highlighted a dashing Heston besides the agony of Christ.)

The Quran—Kōrān to us—was a more complicated exercise, as conservative Islam largely frowns on folksy interpretation, sometimes even in the accessible manner as preached by Sufis and many pirs, even though several such saints themselves were greatly revered.

Even as children we knew this. On my way to boarding school in Ajmer, a city with the grave and shrine to the Sufi philosopher-saint Moinuddin Chishti, among the holiest places for Muslims in the subcontinent, my father had laughed delightedly when a caretaker of the shrine pulled out a dusty ledger with my grandfather and father's name and address in it—the old joint-family home in north Kolkata. Father and I were replicating a journey he had undertaken with his father several decades earlier. We discovered a similar ancestral imprint at the shrine of Nizamuddin Auliya in New Delhi.

I expressed surprise then, but do so no longer. My grandfather Debiprasad, or Kānu-babu as he was better known, was a patron of the shrine of Lālōn Shah, the legendary Sufi, and Baul composer-singer who is part of the folk pantheon of both Bengals. The shrine to Lālōn—it is almost always 'Lālōn', the first-name familiarity both a charming affectation and proof of his vast popularity—is in Kushtia, a short walk from Mohini Mills, the family textiles concern that for several decades sustained this still low-key town in western Bangladesh, not far from the border with India. Kānu-babu built a proper road from town to Lālōn's resting place, provided electricity drawn from the mills' supply, and renovated the shrine. This is still part of local lore.

◆

I last visited Kushtia a few short years ago, at the end of 2015, to refresh memories, as part of a connection with Bangladesh I like to maintain from time to time, to better understand this ancestral homeland. I visited the Mohini Mills compound and the large mansion where Kānu-babu died, where Dulāl—which is Father's dāk-nām—lived for part of his life, and where my mother, Bellie—from béli, Bānglā for a particular variety of jasmine—my sister Sumangali and I stayed to visit Father in jail.

The mills were shut, and guarded by Bangladesh Ansar, a paramilitary organization. They let me in after my cousin Bibi's husband, Joy, interceded on my behalf, saying I was a descendant of the founders. The Ansar troopers were friendly enough as they escorted me around the still-impressive grounds of the textile mill, its red brickwork—I'm told these were made by the local brick-making legend Kumbhu Majhi—and stone buildings overrun by lush green vine—lotā-pātā. They even insisted on taking photographs with me, with their senior officer saying without a trace of irony that I should tell others my family's property was being well looked after.

Shortly a group of elderly folk gathered outside, mostly those who had at one time or another worked at the mill, had known Grandfather and Father. Among them was Mohan Bahadur, a Nepali gardener at the family home—who now drove a rickshaw; and Mohammad Badshah Khan, who worked at the mill and was now a guard at a local secondary school Father had established. Together we walked along to the house, Gongā Shriti, Memories of Ganga, now a police station—too many wanted squatter's rights, so it was safer for the police to squat. After visiting the ghosts of my past, room after room of family lore and memories transformed into grimy barracks, we walked along the vast estate, collectively known as Mill-pārā, past the former manager's house where the ranking bureaucrat now lived, past other staff bungalows, former gardens now a makeshift football field, the Pujō grounds which Grandfather threw open to people of all religions in times of trouble and which still hosted an annual Durga Pujō, a large cinema house now a squatter's dormitory, the school and a 'junior college'. And on to the mājār of Lālōn, fronted by a parking lot—'Lālōn Parking' proclaimed a sign in Bānglā—and numerous shops selling tacky souvenirs—even ektārā and dōtārā, the single- and two-stringed instruments like a keepsake key chain.

The ground of the shrine where Lālōn is interred was quite well kept, through donations from some small businesses and support from the government. Lessons were in progress on the top floor of a nondescript four-storey building behind the mājār—the Lalon Academy. A student in her twenties gently argued with the teacher about her need to sing both the lesser known and better known of Lālōn's songs. 'Shomōshyā tōh nāi,' she urged. I can sing both. No problem.

There was an auditorium of sorts at a tangent to the mājār and academy, its front open on two sides where visitors and Bauls could gather. There were some knots of musicians who broke into song now and again, and gathered some tākā in thanks—Sufi busking. One such group invited us to listen and, once again when Joy had done the introductions two of them literally dragged me to their little island of Lālōn on the worn phorāsh decorated with instruments, a harmonium, toblā, ektāra, khonjōni, and begin to talk about Grandfather, whom they called Borō kortā, and Father, Chhōtō kortā, big or elder patron and small or young patron. They were a mix of former mill workers and children of mill workers who, now unemployed, had turned Baul. The most insistent of the lot was Salam Shah, an elderly former worker. There was the relatively young Mohammad Shamshuddin Sheikh, whose father was a chef at the mill's guesthouse.

I was soon assailed by a cacophony of voices in a mix of dialect and formal Bānglā:

> ...*Mill thékya line tāina kārent disilō*... *Tār-i tōh obōdān shob*... *Mohini mill silō, āmār bābā, borō bhāi shobāi sākri kōrtō, tār under-é*... *Borō kortā, Chhōtō kortā, shobāiré dékhsi tōh, ōnārā khūb kōrtén āmadér jōnyé*... *Shob-i tōh ōnār...étā shob āpnādér*...
>
> ...They extended a line from the mill to bring 'current' here... It was all his doing... My father, elder brother, they all worked at Mohini Mills, 'under' him... I remember Borō kortā and Chhōtō kortā, they did a lot for us... What you see is all theirs, all this is yours...

It was overwhelming, this paean to my forebears in a shrine of forbearance.

Thank you—is all I could say, now close to tears, but this is all yours, we're all just bits of history.

'Would you like to hear a song?' Salam asked then. 'Shāhéb-ér choice-ér jōdi kichhu thāké?...'

Nā, nā, dékhun, I responded, a little embarrassed. It's not about my choice, sing what is in your heart, it is better that way. I used the word mōn—mind—but it was really as if the heart was in play. Heavy, choked, but still in play.

So they did, Salam and Shamshuddin, who also played the harmonium:

Shorbō shādhōn shiddhō hoy tār... they began and it was as if they were singing the praise of my ancestors: All comes to those who respect humanity, those who remain with the people...

For several minutes I was transported as they sang with the power of pain and longing. It was all I could do to not be in tears as a lifetime of memory, dislocation, restlessness, and unanswered and brutally answered questions appeared to coalesce as I sat on a ragged slice of fabric by Lālōn's shrine, eyes closed, heart and mind in turmoil, and yet, wrapped in a kind of peace that sometimes follows a cathartic moment. After nearly five decades there was a little closure.

'Another song?' Salam asked.

No, I said. Your affection is enough.

◆

Islam was always close to home, literally so. I have first cousins who are Mussulmans. Two of my mother's sisters married Mussulman gentlemen, converted to Islam at the time of marriage, and chose to stay in Dhaka. As Hindu and Mussulman, we were literally blood brothers and sisters. As a child I knew the mannerisms, some portions of the religion, particular foods that differed from the way they were prepared in Hindu households, particular linguistic usage that favoured Urdu and Arabic root words. When I wanted water I asked for jol. My cousins asked for pāni. My aunt was māshi, their aunt was khālā.

In 1992, when I spent several days during curfew in the Old City of Delhi to write about the experience from the perspective of Mussulman citizens barricaded behind ancient walls, as the destruction of the Babri mosque by politically energized Hindu fundamentalists in the central Indian town of Ayodhya triggered riots in several places across India, I had to assume a Mussulman identity. It was for my own safety, my hosts told me. In the supercharged atmosphere of the time even the credentials of being an editor with one of India's largest media organizations wouldn't be enough. So to explain the colour of my skin, features and Bānglā-accented Hindi, for several days I assumed the identity of a Mussulman from Bangladesh—Azam Khan.

Azam Khan is the name of my cousin Bāpi, the son of my mother's younger sister. He lives in his family's old farmhouse in Savar, a once-pristine northern suburb of Dhaka, now a rage of traffic and a hub of Bangladesh's flourishing garments export business.

◆

The last realization of the region's wilful depravity over matters of religion would come years after the end of my childhood.

Father and I were alone at home in Kolkata during one of my infrequent visits from university in Delhi. We weren't talking much those days but through the awkward dynamic of emotionally estranged people living in the same house, one day we found ourselves together in the living room.

'Please try to keep a request of mine,' said the man who had never asked anything of me. I nodded. He patted my arm, and switched to English. 'Promise me you will never marry a Mushōlmān. Whatever else you do is fine, but that would be too much. Promise me.'

I did not make that promise, but the reason for his request, an accumulation of hurt and disappointment that had gradually turned to great dislike was now plain to see.

◆

One was, of course, the loss of the family estate and business in Kushtia. For that, blame lay with the government of Pakistan, which ultimately nationalized the family's textile mill. It was established by my great-great-grandfather Mohini Mohan Chakravarti in 1908, and subsequently a township, and a family mansion, all part of a vast estate, grew up around it. Mohini Mohan was born in Kumarkhali in Nadia district of undivided Bengal, of which Kushtia was also a part (a reason why the family didn't move initially—they thought Kushtia, a subdivision of Nadia, would be awarded to India after Partition. Cyril Radcliffe had other ideas.) Mohini Mohan served as a magistrate at various levels, being posted at Noakhali and Bhagalpur among other places and after retirement settled in Kushtia. Here he used his pension and savings to start a tiny mill several decades after retiring. The mill gradually grew into an impressive business, and spawned a cousin in Belgharia, north of Kolkata, and the Sri Annapurna Cotton Mills in Shyamnagar—the last two major victims of West Bengal's labour troubles and family disputes. (Sri Annapurna was some years ago acquired by Marwari businessmen and their associates.)

Mohini Mohan died in November 1922, well into his eighties. His death anniversary became an occasion of celebration for the family and for Kushtia, with my great-grandfather Girija Prasanna's generation and, later, Grandfather, inviting eminent people—singers, actors and historians—from Kolkata and Dhaka, to recall Mohini Mohan and his legacy. In this context, I came by a fascinating, hyperbolic and quite amusing commentary by the dignified but plain-talking historian Sir Jadunath Sarkar who was invited to speak at one such function, on 7 November 1941. Mohini Mohan's hagiography records Sarkar's speech. He praised Mohini Mohan's initiative to challenge the monopoly of western Indian mills that sent inferior cloth east at great margins of profit—especially before pujōs and Eid, a time for buying new clothes. It was an ironical reality in Bengal which at one time had supplied fabric of every quality to the subcontinent and beyond—it had become an importer of fabric, at the mercy of suppliers and prices they quoted. But the speech was also an opportunity to hit back at those who were seen as taking advantage of the Bengali, and played to a delighted gallery.

'But these non-Bengali tycoons of Bombay'—Sarkar used Kūbér-gon for tycoon, after Kūbér, the Hindu god of wealth—'did not agree, they insisted they would auction cloth and sell at the highest possible price that demand dictated. "Can we forego such an opportunity? Let the Bengali die, but business is business."' (Mōrūk shālā Bāngāli lōk kintū business is business.)

◆

Father's hurt had gone deeper than just being denied a part of heritage, let alone inheritance, as I was to learn over the years. Father held a trusted Mussulman manager responsible for collaborating with Pakistani authorities. Part of the conspiracy, as I was given to understand, was a plan to arrest Grandfather as an enemy of the state.

That was in 1965. Grandfather ran Mohini Mills from Kushtia, and lived in the family home a five-minute walk from the main gate of the textile mill. The board of directors, as it happened, included his brothers based in India, and his name featured in some family businesses in India. Unlike with West Pakistan and Indian regions of the Punjab where there was a quicker hardening of the border, in the east it stayed quite porous despite several bouts of rioting even after 1947. But now, what had remained unthreatening for several years after Partition finally began to assume sinister overtones.

Jyotirindra Roy, who is married to my father's youngest sister, Bansari, recalls phoning Grandfather and urging him to leave for Kolkata, a not infrequent destination for him to be treated for high blood pressure. Something was building up between India and Pakistan, Jyoti-pishémoshāi, as I call him, had heard from a friend in a senior position with the Indian government. And, in the general atmosphere of martial law in Pakistan that frequently harassed both Bengali Hindus and Mussulmans in East Pakistan he felt it might be better for Grandfather to leave. He says Grandfather wanted to know the reason for his being asked to advance his date of travel, but my uncle, knowing the possibility of phone lines being tapped, could only speak in generalities.

Of course Father urged him too, but Grandfather wouldn't budge. He stuck to his travel plans for August, and kept insisting nothing would happen to him. To every bit of wisdom that family and friends offered him about moving to Kolkata as nearly everyone in his family had done, Grandfather would resolutely maintain with a naïveté that had far outlived its usefulness, that no one would do him harm. The days of Partition were over. These weren't any longer times that required his younger brother, Taraprasad, a proficient martial artist, to teach the boys and girls of the house traditional Bengali lāthi-khelā, to defend themselves with bamboo sticks even against those wielding a machete or axe. And, anyway, Grandfather insisted, hadn't he just led abroad a business delegation of East Pakistan's best and brightest?

Grandfather made his way to Kushtia station, in August, when skirmishing had already begun in Kashmir between India and Pakistan, but pitched battles across the border in Punjab and Rajasthan were yet to ignite. He was prevented by local police from boarding the train to the border with West Bengal. He was told he was being arrested on orders of the military for being an enemy of Pakistan. He would be jailed. Intervention by a government-appointed doctor, that Grandfather would not survive jail, led to his being placed under house arrest.

But someone would need to be jailed in his place. That would be Father, in Kushtia at the time.

I'm told the experience killed Grandfather. Already weakened by a heart condition that necessitated frequent visits to Kolkata this latest humiliation as a political pawn proved too much. He died the following year, in 1966. I was three at the time, my sister was a year from being born.

It broke Father. I don't think he ever mended. I'm told he

was allowed to visit Grandfather on his deathbed, perform the funeral rites and return to jail. Mother and I were permitted to visit him—a journey my parents' contemporaries would know about, now mostly passed on or with fading memories. The mechanics was never fully explained to us children, then or later. 'Friends on both sides of the border helped you all,' was as far as I got from an aunt, with reluctant talk about connections, and the remaining vestiges of influence the family had in East Pakistan among those who felt the family had been wronged, and traded in the family's rapidly depleting stack of goodwill chips to help. We remained in Kushtia for a while, Father returned from jail to his old family home for some months, and during those days of hazy history my sister was born. Then Father was jailed again. Mother, my infant sister and I evidently made another escape from Kushtia with the help of some friends in the East.

We returned to Kushtia sometime later, when Father was finally released. I've seen a black-and-white photograph of my father outside the jail, my sister and I by his side. Mother is not in the photograph. I don't know who took the photograph, nobody would say. Mother, my sister and I could leave, but Father wasn't permitted to. The political situation that would inexorably change East Pakistan to Bangladesh had begun. Father was now an enemy of the state twice over. Meanwhile, there was talk of the government taking over Mohini Mills.

Family helped again. One of my mother's younger sisters, Chhondā-māshi to us, was at the time cabin crew with Pakistan International Airlines (PIA), and married to a Mussulman colleague, Farooq. I am told she would sometimes be rostered to fly a helicopter service from Dhaka to Kushtia, and was hosted by Grandfather at the mill's guest house. By using a contact at a travel agency she arranged to have a ticket issued for Father in Karachi in West Pakistan, far from prying government eyes in Kushtia, for a passage from Dhaka to Kathmandu, and had the ticket sent to her in Dhaka. The authorities expected Father to make a run for it overland to the Indian border just hours away. He was never a Dhaka habitué, his face was not well known there. He made a run for it from Dhaka, I'm told, using excellent credentials for a visit to Kathmandu—paperwork made possible with the help of a Nepali diplomat—and support provided by my aunt, well-known and unsuspected at Dhaka airport, who says she walked him right to the gate as if Father was a friend, which he was. He escaped in plain sight.

Father ditched his papers after arriving in Kathmandu on PIA, and was driven south to the Indian border. He handed over his favourite camera to a Nepali border official in thanks before crossing over to Bihar, and was driven to Kolkata by family and friends.

Father changed from a jolly businessman with a future of prosperity and peer adulation ordained by his birth, to a depressive uncertain of people, of the future. It would not be an exaggeration to say his spirit died in 1966, though he lived till 2001, when cancer finished what ethno-religious discord, notions of nationhood, and politics had begun. The cancer was surely aided by his other rogue cells—an inability to deal with changed realities.

◆

His wasn't the only family history of changed realities, of altered states.

Maulana Mohammad Akram Khan traversed a life of belief and attitudes that would befuddle anyone not from the subcontinent, or, perhaps, not from Bengal or Bangladesh. Born in 1868 in Hakimpur in present-day West Bengal—it is right up by the border with Bangladesh—the Maulana in his youth went about a stolidly Islamic education, studying in a madrasa. He stayed within this system for several decades, emerging as a conservative Islamic scholar and teacher and was, from available evidence, perennially upset with the manner in which Bengali Mussulmans were ignored or kept at arms' length by Bengali Hindus.

There's a telling recap of the Maulana's persuasion by his younger son, Quamrul Anam, in a preface to one of the Maulana's books, *Mōslém Bongér Shāmājik Itihāsh—The Social History of Muslim Bengal* that he had reprinted in 2002, more than thirty years after the Maulana's death in 1969. The anger rolled off easily, hardly held back by the Sanskrit-infused High Bānglā that is the official, educational and literary standard in Bangladesh. I have translated it here in simpler English:

> As Bengali Mussulmans had fallen far behind [Bengali] Hindus in education and other aspects in pre-Partition India, they were placed at a disadvantage in several areas. At the time newspapers and journals would not publish news that provided a Mussulman perspective. On the other hand, the contemporary educated Hindu society would offer news and views by either treating Mussulmans with utter contempt or would completely ignore them.

That 'unbearable situation' led the Maulana, with the assistance of some Mussulman journalist friends to publish the daily newspaper *Azad*, in 1936, in Bānglā. The Maulana was also the editor. 'We are told that in 1940s, a time of much turmoil over the division of India', observes his son, 'communalist Hindus had a name for *Azad*: Ojāt.' It's a pun, and a translation in English lacks the flavour the pronunciation of the letter z in Bānglā, which is written and frequently pronounced as j. But the slur is unmistakable. Ojāt translates as outcaste. Not of our religion. Not like us. His son avers: 'He attempted through his writing to inform Bengali Mussulman of their own history. He attempted to write the real history. His spent his life in the pursuit of helping to establish the Bengali Mussulman as an educated, self-confident, self-reliant people.'

I know for a fact that Quamrul Anam, who many years later would assume the editorship of *Azad*, long after it moved to East Pakistan from Kolkata along with the Maulana and his family—a result of Partition and the Maulana throwing in his lot with a country specifically created for his jāt—worshipped and loved his father. There is little doubt, either, that the Maulana was a devout Mussulman and sought for the emancipation and progress of the Bengali Mussulman. But his journey was far from liberal, much like many from those times who played religion and politics with the lives of others, these fathers of nations and defenders of various faiths whose way of inseminating nationalism and defending their faith came through the killing of innocent children, women and men. If dignity of life was to be secured through death, so be it.

Azad wrote passionately about the issues and rights of the Bengali Mussulman. Meanwhile the Maulana had entered politics, and gradually moved from the left to the absolute right. He was an integral part of the Fazlul Huq-led Krishak Praja Party. When his colleague travelled to the Muslim League, joining the formidable soon-to-be tested power of the Bengali Mussulman peasantry to the political bloodlust of League supremo Muhammad Ali Jinnah, those like the Maulana would urge him along.

After Partition, as he resettled in Dhaka, the capital of East Pakistan, the Maulana would, like Huq (and Mujibur Rahman), turn from a battle for the Bengali Mussulman to what would become a battle for the Bengali fought mainly through the crucible of Bānglā. The conservative *Azad* now advocated liberalism of language as a sense of identity; and, though many language advocates subsequently decried the stance of *Azad* as being pro-Pakistan, not least on account of the Maulana's continuing association with the Muslim League even after it had ceased to be the favour of choice in the East, it did in later years carry news that drew the ire of the East Pakistani administration, especially during the dictatorship of Ayub Khan and in the days leading up to Liberation.

This language-liberalism evidently had little to do with the Maulana's religious beliefs. His book *Mōslēm Bongér Shāmājik Itihāsh* is a near-constant rant against what he saw as the ills of Hinduism or, more specifically, the ill that is Hinduism—as a deconstruction of a religion to a level far inferior to the assumed purity of Islam. So, he compared the similarity of Sanskrit root words, the anchoring

Sudeep Chakravarti

language of Hinduism, to Arabic. Hindu holy texts were portrayed as man-made, constructed over several hundred years as they claimed to convey the word of the gods (naturally, there is no reference to any similar transference with regard to holy Islamic texts). The Vaishnav tradition and its worship of Krishna came in for special mention, especially his dalliance with several thousand gōpis, and the worship of this god-in-the-guise-of-man was held up as proof of the denigration of core Hinduism. So were tantric rituals and other cult forms of worship that involved the imbibing of liquor and licentious behaviour. The Maulana also expressed extreme regret that the people of 'Muslim Bāngla' were also affected by such accursed influences of the Vaishnavs and other sects like the Shakti worshippers for several hundred years.

The book also rants against what many Muslim liberals, indeed, even conservative Hindus, see as progressive behaviour: the Maulana was brutal about Sufis and what he described as the totally unacceptable sexually loaded initiation rites and practices of the Bauls, their all-encompassing outlook to life and, in particular, the Baul practice of drawing from Hinduism and Islam and folk traditions to meld composite lyrics—an unacceptable impurity. Evidently the time for irony was long past—acknowledgement of the fact that the very appeal of Sufi proselytizers and their practice of permitting the people to continue with a meld of their old relgion's folk practices is what perhaps led to the widespread appeal of Islam in eastern and deltaic Bengal in the first place. But now it was time for that to be converted to a more focused, hard-edged Islam that would move people, move nations.

◆

The Maulana quoted an early twentieth-century monograph by U. N. Mukherjee, *A Dying Race*, published in 1909, to bolster his claim that the Bengali Mussulman had come into his own, flung off the imbalance of society and impurities of a peculiarly subcontinental and mixed-up religion to adopt the path of pure Islam.

The Maulana's biases apart, the emergent Bengali Mussulman thesis in *A Dying* Race—the dying race being Hindu and, specifically, Bengali Hindu—makes for fascinating reading. Even though the Maulana and Mukherjee came from opposite sides of the spectrum, Mukherjee to hold up the spectre of the Bengali Mussulman swamping the Bengali Hindu, writing at a time of discord after the first partition of Bengal; and the Maulana to hold up a flag that the Bengali Mussulman had broken away from the Bengali Hindu after first being mistreated, and then having his new religion tainted with the vices and imperfections of the old.

Mukherjee referred extensively to the *Imperial Gazetteer of India* (Volume I published in 1881) put together by W. W. Hunter, who was director general of statistics to the British Indian government. The second volume, which alphabetically discussed places from *Bengal to Cutwa* (Katwa, a town in Bardhaman district in West Bengal) colourfully described the socio-cultural break between the Bengali Hindu and Bengali Mussulman. It first set up the past by offering, for instance, the situation among Mussulmans in Bengal by a 'local writer' with familiarity of the place and people. This writer is quoted as saying with some outrage that Bengali Mussulmans were largely people of whom 'not one in ten can recite the brief and simple kalma or creed' and that they were basically a 'sect which observes none of the ceremonies of its faith, which is ignorant of the simplest formulas of its creed, which worships at the shrine of a rival religion, and tenaciously adheres to practices which were denounced as the foulest abominations by its founder.'

The *Gazetteer* (quoted by Mukherjee and in turn quoted by the Maulana, and I cross-checked this with a copy of the *Gazetteer* just to be sure) heaped its own outrage on that of the 'writer' by maintaining that, while in the cities 'or amid the serene palace life' of Mussulman nobility and their 'religious foundations' some maulvi held on to piety and proper religious practices, 'the masses of rural *Musalmāns* had relapsed into something little better than a mongrel breed of circumcised low-caste Hindus'.

Sudeep Chakravarti

◆

But that could be said to be true until early nineteenth century, observed the *Gazetteer*. There was a remarkable telling of the shift, the transformation of a vast Mussulman group in Bengal from being a farce in the minds of many to emerging as a force that could be moved, swayed, leveraged. Any which way it was a gradual but sure massing that would, in a few decades, completely transform the politics and future of Bengal.

Even accounting for a post-1857, post-'Sepoy Mutiny' bias when the engineers of the empire of India increasingly realized the divergent motive force of the Hindu and Mussulman of India as a gigantic political leverage, the *Gazetteer* pointed out some stark realities. Among these—that there was 'another of those religious awakenings so characteristic of India', in this case of the Bengali Mussulman. It related the cause to itinerant preachers who roamed the country urging a return to the true faith and 'denouncing God's wrath on the indifferent and unrepentant'. And so, vast numbers 'purged themselves of the taint of Hinduism' and idolatry. The revival directly affected religious, social and political aspects of Bengal. It offered an engaging thesis, and I can understand why it gladdened the Maulana's heart.

> The stern rejection of ancient superstitions has widened the gulf between the Muhammadans and the Hindus. Fifty years ago the Bengali Musalmāns were simply a recognised caste, less widely separated from the lower orders of the Hindus than the latter were from the Kulin Brahmāns. There were certain essential points of difference, of a doctrinal sort, between the Hindu and Muhammadan villager; but they had a great many rural customs and even religious rites in common. The Muhammadan husbandman theoretically recognised the one Semitic God; but in a country subject to floods, famines, the devastation of banditti, and the ravages of wild beasts, he would have deemed it a simple policy to not neglect the Hindu

festivals in honour of Krishná and Durgá. Now, however, the peasantry no longer look to their gods, but to the officer in charge of the District, for protection; and when he fails them, instead of offering expiatory sacrifices to Kálí, they petition Government, or write violent letters to the vernacular press. The reformed Muhammadan husbandmen, therefore, can now stand aloof from the rites of the Hindus. They have ceased to be merely a separate caste in the rural organization, and have become a distinct community, keeping as much apart from the nominal co-religionists of the old unreformed faith as from the idolatrous Hindus. This social isolation from the surrounding Hindus is the second effect of the Musalmán revival in Bengal.

◆

And so it came to pass that, when those unbelieving of the Bengali Mussulman, as it were—not the Bengali Hindu, but the not-Bengali Mussulman, characterized by the state of Pakistan—came to impose on the Bengali Mussulman the shackles of another language and other system of governance, the Maulana chose language over religion. The Maulana stayed true, so his family tells me, to his ideals of the betterment of the Bengali Mussulman. In that project, Bānglā, and Bengalis came ahead of the not-Bengali Mussulman.

I can hardly disagree. Because Maulana Mohammad Akram Khan, the great advocate of purity of Islam and identity of the Bengali Mussulman, was also first president who was not from the ranks of government of the Bangla Academy in Dhaka, the institution that, from its very inception, has remained fiercely proud of Bānglā. (It has as motto: Mōdér Gorōb Mōdér Āshà, Ā Mōri Bānglā Bhāshā. Our Pride Our Hope: Our Language, Bānglā. This is taken from a song by the lyricist-composer Atulprasad Sen.)

Bangla Academy was a liberal institution by design; the years of turmoil and Islamic revivalism haven't washed that off. As you walk past the old Academy building, the well-maintained, colonnaded and profusely arched Bardhaman House, acknowledging the time Bardhaman was a princely state and Bengal was one, to the new building and its large auditorium by an often-filthy pond, four Bengali greats are quoted on the wall—in Bānglā, naturally. There is Michael Madhusudan Dutt proclaiming, 'If he who is not adept with his Mother Tongue insists he is educated, then I despise his pretension.' Kazi Nazrul Islam lyrically contributes to gender equality with a gem that equally credits woman and man for everything that is great in the world, whatever has ever helped the world:

Bishhé jā kichhu mohān srishti chiro kolyankor
Ordhék tār koriyachhe nāri ordhék tār nor

Rabindranath urges the mind to search and accept the truth, whatever good or bad life may bring:

Monébor āj kohé jé bhalomondo jāhāi
āshūk shotyoré lowo shohojé

And Lālon, with a delightfully cynical twist about mankind and life, urges the mind and heart to do as they wish.

The Maulana had a soft corner too? Well, it helps to think so. After a fashion the Maulana is family.

◆

As you know, his son Quamrul Anam married my mother's younger sister, Tolly. The Maulana welcomed her, and he and his son never imposed on her to practice Islam even as she adopted a Muslim name, Fatima, after marriage. Indeed, she continued to be a disciple of an ascetic, Brojanondo, the guru to my mother's family even after he escaped to India as a result of the Bangladesh war. Quamrul-mésho, Tolly-māshi and their two children, Azam and Nasreen, would frequently visit my grandfather's estate in Kushtia. As with other members of my mother's family Quamrul and Tolly—Fatima—looked out for my father when he ran into trouble with the authorities in East Pakistan.

An editor himself, till family squabbles and the fallout of Bangladesh's war cost him his job and fortune, Quamrul-méshō was inordinately proud that I became a journalist instead of a 'boxwallah', the blue-chip executive avenue for so many Bengalis of my background. He told me so when I visited Dhaka for a conference of South Asian countries in the early 1990s. He died soon after. His daughter Nasreen (who is an elder sister in letter and spirit to my sister and me) gifted me the Maulana's book several years after Quamrul-méshō passed on, during one of my visits to Bangladesh. It is now a part of my family's history, in letter and spirit.

4

Shéi shōmoy
Gandhi, the brief Bengali

Bengal is a place of spectacular, savage death from storm, flood, hunger and the rage of revolution and religion. Sometimes it seems like a conspiracy to perpetuate a permanent state of victimhood, but as I mentioned earlier in the book, death has come to us from nature, as well as the nature of man, and more than once that man is one of us—Bengali killing Bengali. The Partition years were like that. Things got so bad that Mohandas Gandhi came to East Bengal in November 1946 by way of Kolkata to cool the fires long after a way of life had burnt to ashes. Retaliatory riots were sparking off in Bihar even as he wound his way to Noakhali at the eastern edge of the delta. It was the sordid second chapter to a sordid first chapter in communal violence that was scripted in August of that year with a burst of mayhem that some history books still call, capital letters blaring, the Great Calcutta Killings.

Between four and five thousand are estimated to have died in Kolkata after a call to 'Direct Action' proclaimed for the Muslim League by Muhammad Ali Jinnah on 16 August 1946. Shorn of emotion, the 'action' was born of a desire to ensure a British blueprint—the so-called Cabinet Mission Plan—for a Hindu majority India and a Mussulman majority Pakistan went through, a plan the Congress resisted. Direct Action was pitched as essentially a hortāl, a sort-of shutdown protest that Bengal knows well. But in Kolkata, a vast gathering of Muslim League loyalitsts soon turned to arson, and then to Mussulman killing Hindu, and then Hindu killing Mussulman in retaliation, an orgy of violence that lasted for days before some semblance of government intervention brought a controlled disorder.

Many historians hold Jinnah and the head of the Muslim League government of Bengal, Huseyn Shaheed Suhrawardy, who also held the home portfolio, which controlled police, responsible. Even some apologists for Suhrawardy (who hold Jawaharlal Nehru responsible for rejecting the Cabinet Mission's suggestion, and thus forcing Jinnah's hand) maintain the chief minister's 'tacit support' to rioters, as part of a larger game plan. It was inevitable that attacking Hindus and Hindu-owned businesses and homes in Hindu-majority Kolkata would bring overwhelming response. And, when violence spread, as it did in a seemingly seamlessly structured way in East Bengal's Noakhali among other places in that Mussulman majority region, now inevitably killing more Hindus, it would seal more than just expedient religious enmity. The deaths and fearful displacement of people in their hundreds of thousands, even millions, would seal the deal of Partition. And it would begin in Bengal, a pivotal province over which the Muslim League had control in both nuance and numbers.

Gandhi is among the few not-Bengali who waded into our garbage, our filth of flailing faiths that insist to this day that man must be cruel, must kill, in the name of god.

At one stage he even declared himself to be a Bengali—though I'm not sure how far that went to assuage the entrenched ill will that many Bengalis maintained towards him. Hindu communalists accused him of giving away too much to the Mussulmans. Mussulman communalists saw him as pro-Hindu. And many Bengalis loathed him for humiliating Subhas Bose in the Congress Party, a mix of undeniable history and untiring folk legend even holding him responsible for sabotaging Bose's tenure as president ultimately in favour of the person they view as Gandhi's pet, Jawaharlal Nehru; and eventually tipping Bose into a radical side-street that turned out to be a dead end. Handsome traces of that dislike exist to this day.

Gandhi openly shared his dislike and disdain when Bose won presidency of the Congress Party for the second time, in early 1939, defeating Gandhi's nominee Bhogaraju Pattabhi Sitaramayya. He made comments many Bengalis interpret as self-pitying and churlish as he wished Bose well ('...the defeat is more mine than his'—meaning Sitaramayya's; and 'After all Subhas-babu is not an enemy of his country, he has suffered for it'). Bose's nephew, Sisir, the son of his older brother Sarat, maintains in a book that 'Uncle Subhas responded with great dignity to Gandhiji's most unfortunate and unkind remarks on the result of the election.' He writes in *Subhas and Sarat: An Intimate Memoir of the Bose Brothers*, that Bose 'viewed the result as a vindication of his political line of "no compromise with imperialism" and tried his level best to restore unity in the party. But sulking in defeat, Gandhiji and his supporters were simply not interested.'

Gandhi simply went cold on Bose and his coterie with him. Meanwhile Bose had taken ill, and when he encountered an attempt to weaken his authority in the name of the Mahatma at the March 1939 Congress session at Tripuri near Jabalpur, with Bose as president, he was greatly taken aback. A resolution was moved by Govind Ballabh Pant to have the Congress president appoint a working committee 'in consultation with and according to the wishes of Mahatma Gandhi'.

The war continued. It reached a peak in May that year at the Congress's All-India Committee meeting in Kolkata. Gandhi arrived a few days before the meeting, evidently to work out a rapprochement with Bose—a way requested by several Congress leaders including Bose. Though Sisir views it as a done deal, as it were, weighed in Gandhi's favour, the course already decided between Tripuri and Gandhi's arrival in Sodepur, north of Kolkata; and evident in the tone of the correspondence between the two leaders in the interim. 'It is absolutely clear from the correspondence that Gandhiji was bent on driving Uncle Subhas to the wall and destroying him politically. Pandit (Jawaharlal) Nehru did visit

Uncle...and they talked, but no progress could be made given Gandhiji's extraordinary obduracy.'

After one such interaction with Gandhi, Sisir, nineteen at the time, tells of Nehru and Bose standing 'grim and silent' in Sisir's home at Woodburn Park where Nehru was a guest—and where Bose would drop by each morning from his residence on nearby Elgin Road, to collect Nehru for their meetings in Sodepur with Gandhi, riding in a Wanderer sedan. (The German car was registered in Sisir's name, and it was the same one in which he would, in less than two years, drive Bose to Gomoh Station in present-day Jharkhand for his uncle's eventual 'great escape' to Berlin via Afghanistan and the Soviet Union.) The two leaders, recalls Sisir, had returned from 'another round of fruitless talks'. Bose broke the silence after a while. 'You should freshen up and have lunch,' he told Nehru. 'After all, man must live!'

'Jawaharlal replied, "Yes, man must live!" The two men then parted.'

At the Kolkata meeting of the Congress, held in a pandāl at Wellington Square (now Raja Subodh Mullick Square) in central Kolkata, a calm Bose read a statement that concluded with his resignation as president. As word quickly spread after the meeting was called to a close by Rajendra Prasad, there was some chaos as local Congress volunteers turned angry, and Sisir writes of how Bose personally escorted Congress leaders one at a time to their cars to save them from irate crowds.

'Gandhiji regained his absolute control of the Congress,' writes Sisir. 'For Uncle Subhas, the search for an alternative path to India's liberation began.'

◆

But Gandhi arrived in Bengal, for Bengal, when so many others in India would not, even though for a while, perhaps for the first time in his life, Gandhi was ready to give up. There is no exact record of how many people died in Noakhali and in adjoining

Tipperah district from October 1946. Estimates range from 500 (Muslim League sources) to 50,000 (other sources). Jharna Dhara Chowdhury, a resolute lady who for years ran the Gandhi Ashram in Noakhali, related it with chilling simplicity when I visited the ashram in 1997: 'More Muslims died in Kolkata, more Hindus died in Noakhali.'

Violence caught up with the ageing Gandhi like nothing else. Even before he reached Noakhali on his way from Kolkata, Gandhi was emotionally battered. The fires of Kolkata had spread to Noakhali and then on to Bihar, where in revenge for Noakhali, Hindus butchered Mussulmans. Gandhi was fasting, as he said in an appeal issued to the people of Bihar on 6 November 1946, 'as a penance after the knowledge of the Bihar tragedy'. The 'low diet' he had placed upon himself after reaching Kolkata 'will become a fast unto death, if the erring Biharis had not turned over a new leaf'. He was particularly conscious of how 'the misdeeds of Bihari Hindus may justify Quaid-i-Azam Jinnah's taunt that the Congress is a Hindu organization in spite of its boast that it has in its ranks a few Sikhs, Muslims, Christians, Parsis and others. Bihari Hindus are honour bound to regard minority Muslims as their brethren requiring protection, equal with the vast majority of Hindus.'

But even in his distress over the magnitude of killings in Bihar (the number of dead, mostly Mussulmans range from two to thirty thousand, if one believes the Congress or the Muslim League) in response to the magnitude of killing in East Bengal, and though he confessed he hadn't fully realized just how far things had gone in Noakhali, Gandhi sensed it was as bad as it could get. 'Is counter-communalism any answer to the communalism of which Congressmen have accused the Muslim League?' he asked of his colleagues. 'Is it Nationalism to seek barbarously to crush the fourteen per cent of the Muslims in Bihar?'

Yes—seemed to be the answer on either side, quite what the Muslim League's extraordinary scheme for nationhood had signalled and anticipated. Even as it leached humanity from Bengal, this nightmarish cut of the coldest politics crushed Gandhi. On 5 November Gandhi had written to Nehru: 'My inner voice tells me "You may not live to be a witness to this senseless slaughter. If people refuse to see what is clear as daylight and pay no heed to what you say, does it not mean that your day is over?"'

At nearly every point of his whistle-stop journey into Bengal's darker side—at Kushtia, Srirampur, Dattapara, and a string of places where he collectively spent more than a month—the man who found his way out of numerous problems with fasting and steadfastness gave in to feelings of helplessness. 'There is terrible mutual distrust. Oldest friendships had snapped,' he wrote in a dispatch. 'Truth and ahimsa by which I swear and which have to my knowledge sustained me for sixty years, seem to fail to show the attributes I ascribed to them.' His chronicler at the time, Nirmal Kumar Bose, wrote later of seeing the Mahatma mutter to himself in Hindi: 'Main kya karun?' What can I possibly do?

From Sodepur near Kolkata, Gandhi embarked on a train to Kushtia where he addressed crowds before moving on to Goalundo Ghat on the Padma. He then boarded the steamer SS *Kiwi* to another jump-off point before reaching Noakhali district.

'Let us pray,' he addressed crowds from the deck of the steamer, 'that the Hindus and Mussulmans of Bengal should become one in heart. But to be of one in heart does not mean that all of them should be converted to a common religion.'

Several years ago, I read a paraphrased Gandhi in a book by Nirmal Bose, *My Days with Gandhi*, in a passage breathtaking in naïveté, staggering in its ignorance of just how rent society in Bengal had become at the time, and remained so for several years afterwards before the fires stoked by Direct Action and fed by the cycle of response finally cooled to embers. 'His object in coming to Noakhali was to ask the Hindus never to run away from their homes even if they happened to be in a microscopic minority,' Bose wrote of Gandhi's speech in Goalundo. 'They should try to live with the Mussulmans where there were. Both had been nourished by the same corn which grew in the fields and both had quenched their thirst with water from the same river. Even if their brother came to slay them, they should refuse to run away, but make every effort to live with him in peace, without sacrificing honour.'

◆

Not many would hear this gloriously idealistic, seemingly tone deaf Gandhi, even though what he also asked for was that keeping the peace would first require the government of Bengal to reverse the nearly-absent administrative and police protection to vulnerable citizens—and the unsaid, implicit part—now that the political point about a separate nation for Mussulmans had been made. While a utilitarian peace returned with the carving of Bengal and India, blood would repeatedly be spilled in Bengal, in the east and west, for decades afterwards. Even during the grand butchery of 1971, when horrific rage was reserved for Bengalis of East Pakistan by the leadership and institutions of West Pakistan, a time when a country for Mussulmans wilfully killed Mussulman brothers and sisters in East Pakistan rather than acknowledge democratic principles and a different ethno-linguistic identity—that one could at once be Bengali and Mussulman without jeopardy to the idea of Pakistan—a special rage was reserved for the Bengali Hindu. Today's ultra-fundamentalist Islamic ire in Bangladesh retains that all-too-easy-to-execute impulse.

But Gandhi was also breathtaking. This was a man from Gujarat by way of South Africa; the charioteering of India's collective nationalism; and the sufferance of Winston Churchill's enduring hatred for him and the future country he hoped to free from empire. A frail, tired man only two years from the end of his life at the hand of a politically motivated Hindu assassin (appreciate this twist of history—had it been a Mussulman assassin there would surely remain far fewer Mussulmans in India). He won hearts and a grudging respect after arriving in Srirampur village in Noakhali, where he declared, 'I have become a Bengali to all intents and purposes.'

That was courage, not dissimilar to the courage of the angels of slim humanity among both Hindus and Mussulmans who sheltered those of the other faith from rape, torture, and the vilest death; those among Mussulmans who sheltered Hindus against conversion; or even those among Mussulmans who, in some cases of kindness married Hindu widows and orphaned young women to prevent them from being raped and slaughtered—not to gloat over their conversion but as a care.

Gandhi's presence in Kolkata reduced the flow of blood there. His presence in East Bengal did the same, though Muslim League leadership that ruled Bengal at the time, and several local Mussulman community leaders in East Bengal publicly spoke out and wrote against his presence in the east for the adverse publicity it would bring to the community. I would put my neck on the line and say this Gujarati who claimed for some weeks to be Bengali, whom many Bengalis still love to hate for his dislike of Subhas Bose—did more for Bengal and Bengalis in those darkest months in 1946 than did millions of Bengalis who let their leaders mix rationale with religion. A time when for all practical purposes there was no Bengali, just Hindus and Mussulmans who happened to speak Bānglā and related dialects. At a time when such linguistic and cultural links were being resoundingly, irrevocably broken, this man in a loincloth who had run a mutual admiration club with Rabindranath Tagore—to Tagore's 'Mahatma', great soul, Gandhi offered in response an equally enduring honorific, 'Kōbiguru', the guru of poets, the first among poets—actually sat down each day, symbolically, to lessons in Bānglā.

Gandhi would be able to do far less in India's western extremity—events of a similarly stupefying darkness would erupt in the Punjab less than a year later. In some ways it was similar to Bengal in the manner religious power-play demolished bonds of language and sense of community. It was dissimilar in that Bengal's demolition was built on exploitative, arrogant economics and stifling bars that conservative Hindu society and elites placed on interaction with those of another religion. But the butchery in Punjab and elsewhere in Pakistan and northern India would seem so familiar, so easy, so seamless with every deliberate, revengeful, resentful step. Bengal, and Bengalis, had shown the way.

◆

Fifty years later, I went looking for Gandhi, that brief Bengali, amidst the detritus of history, to understand better his presence among so much that had ruined my people, Mussulman and Hindu alike, disrupted the lives of so many millions into heartache that only the displaced and the destitute can know.

My first destination was the Gandhi Ashram in Jayag, a village deep inside Noakhali. My colleague, the photographer Saibal Das, and I found shelter there in a simple dormitory. It was by the side of a two-storey house that contained the ashram's offices, souvenirs of Gandhi's visit, the dining hall, prayer room, and Jharna-di— Jharna Dhara Chowdhury—and her handful of female colleagues. The men lived in the dormitory block.

As Jharna-di and I got talking she suggested we visit Pirjada Syed Golam Hakkani Hussaini. It was a little joke between these two protectors of faith—we weren't the first visitors curious about those times Jharna-di had sent the Pirjada's way. His father, she said by way of introduction, Golam Sarawar Hussaini, once a member from Noakhali in the undivided Bengal Assembly, was the man who started it all off in this area. I had read about the elder Hussaini, heard stories about him.

Reverses against Mussulmans in Kolkata after Direct Action did not immediately lead to a bloodbath in the east. A few Hindus had been killed, many more attacked and injured. Some temples had been desecrated by the placing of dead calves in them, some idols broken or stolen. Looting of Hindu households had begun.

Into this river of hate had waded the elder Hussaini. His family's hereditary estate centred at the Diara Sharif shrine in Shyampur, once a pilgrimage for Mussulmans and Hindus, became a platform for propaganda. The incendiary elder Hussaini was the voice. The structured killings began around mid-October 1946. The best known of the stories was about how the head of a local leader of Hindu Mahasabha and luminary at the Noakhali bar, Rajendralal Roychowdhury was presented to the elder Hussaini. The author Benoy Bhushan Ghosh wrote of how Roychowdhury's daughters were gifted to the elder Hussaini's key lieutenants as trophies. Long after Gandhi left the area in early 1947, rape, forcible conversion, killings, destroying of food stock, everyday looting and intimidation targeted at displacing the area's Hindus continued.

Along with the family estate, the younger Hussaini, as Pirjada, son of the pir—guide, teacher, spiritual master—had inherited this unlovely family history.

'Ask him about his father,' Jharna-di urged me, this five-feet-nothing lady who was all of ten when Gandhi visited Noakhali.

◆

'Jharna-di has sent you, has she?' Hakkani-shāhéb chuckled. 'She is always trying to get me into trouble.'

I had made my way to his vast estate in Shyampur village, an hour from Jayag over dirt tracks turned to slush with rain, snaking through impossibly green fields of paddy, in a part of Bangladesh so conservative that many women in burqa sometimes still carry an umbrella low over their heads to prevent strangers from looking at their covered faces. It isn't apocryphal, a twisted rural legend; I saw such ladies. The legend is about ladies carrying two umbrellas.

'I wasn't even born then, but in 1952,' the Pirjada drawled in Bānglā. Not too many years before my visit he was better known as a theatre personality in Dhaka. He often sunned himself by the pool of the local Sheraton—as he told me with a smile. 'Āmāké playboy bolā hōtō.' After the flash of confession that, in his younger days he had the reputation of a playboy, Hakkani shāhéb then switched to fluent English. 'I have inherited a pirhood, but not my father's politics.'

'The past is a fact,' he continued in a rush, staying with English, giving the impression that he rather enjoyed the opportunity to speak it, eschewing Bānglā for the language that is second nature to Bengalis touched by a certain urbanity and upbringing. We were seated in a room where Gandhi spent some hours all those years ago, come to make peace with a politician.

'It was a moment of anger. A lot of people were not even clear about why they were doing what they were doing. But I believe it was good Gandhi came. Things cooled down after that.'

'There,' he pointed to the low settee on which I sat cross-legged, it was large enough to double as a bed. 'Gandhi sat exactly where you're now sitting.'

◆

After an hour or so of talk, he sent me on my way with gifts, besides the blessing of Allah, that I treasured for the way it transformed numerous meals into fragrant enterprise—packages of cinnamon and bay leaf that carried the essence of deepest Bengal.

I gave some to my mother in Kolkata, who looked at me in a way that made me feel I had finally amounted to something. The remainder I jealously guarded and brought home to New Delhi, where I lived and worked at the time, to share with family and friends. The Bengalis among them also looked at me in a way that made me feel I had finally amounted to something. They wished for food cooked with that cinnamon and those bay leaves. Bengali food, naturally.

It helped to partly allay instant jealousy as I told them of a simple breakfast at Jayag's Gandhi ashram, a breakfast I knew many Bengalis even in Kolkata and, certainly, in the great diaspora in India and elsewhere in the world would travel great distances for, swear undying friendship and obligation to obtain: plump, fresh luchi, eaten with potato slivers basted in mustard oil, green chilli on the side, and fragrant lime to squeeze over fried roe of ilish.

History stirred with politics and hatred and displacement could wait, as could worldly matters of the day. Food made spiritual with such condiments as I carried, and stories of fine food and relived fragrances and tastes, mattered as much.

◆

I wandered through old Noakhali district, now broken up into three. The past could so often come alive here; but it was surreal, clashing as it did with a slice of modernizing Bangladesh—Hakkani-shāhéb was never far—itself created from the blood of hundreds of thousands of innocent Muslims. In places where some of the worst atrocities against Hindus took place, Karpara, Dattapara, Ramganj, Haimchar, there were remnants of buildings, many with still wary people living in them.

I visited one such in Baruipara village. It was a red brick mansion of a zamindar built around a courtyard. Clothes and shoots from insistent seedlings of banyan and peepul that so easily take root in worn buildings as do parrots and pigeons, lent colour and a certain purpose to the moss-stained bricks, kept from absolute ruin by the several families who now called it home. Mohammad Lakiutullah, a farmer who had lived in the house of the zamindar since that family fled in 1946, went quiet when I began to ask questions about the time. He withdrew and gently shut the door. The incongruity of asking questions of the old man these many years later struck me when his son, Mohammad Shahabuddin, a forest department official in Chittagong, reopened the door, welcomed me into a cluttered room and, as if it was the most natural thing to do, started to discuss Malthus with me.

Mrinal Krishna Majumdar of Dattapara, among a handful of Hindus who remained in Noakhali after 1946, still had not recovered from the horrors he had seen. But I saw his son, Jiban, whose name means life, build his electronic item repairs shop and a house—next to the destroyed one his father refuses to leave.

Not far, I got an earful from Mahbub-ur-Rahman, a former

professor, a sprightly eighty-five at the time we met, who claimed to have argued with Gandhi about unity *and* disunity. I began to speak excitedly in Bāṅglā but received a torrent of English in reply. By then I had stopped being surprised.

'I told him, if Pakistan was being created for Pakistanis, then Muslims staying in India wouldn't be safe or united. And if Muslims were so strong that they got the British to create a country for them, then how could they be weak in India?' He delighted in a prolonged cackle. 'Gandhi had no answer.'

Do you have an answer for why it happened? I asked, seated in his hut of mud, thatch and aluminium sheeting ringed with bushes of hibiscus, shrubs of chilli and a lime tree. Young children played with marbles in the courtyard, a busy hen and her chirping brood nimbly sidestepped that jolly chaos. Wasn't it easy for landless Mussulman peasantry to go after wealthy Hindu landlords, let the weight of all the years of paying to them taxes and giving up a large share of crop and yet, of being looked down upon as lesser beings, be conveyed so seamlessly into incendiary hatred, of a settlement of self-respect claimed with destruction and death?

'Yes, it was easy,' Rahman nodded, now serious again. 'But the riots were not consequential, they were created.'

As everywhere.

In Dattapara, at the site of one of the largest refugee camps in Noakhali—a school for girls when I visited—I discussed Bangladesh's movement for independence with H. B. M. Shamshul Basher, a twenty-four-year-old sociology graduate with no interest in a past beyond 1971, the year the only country he had ever known, Bangladesh, was born. We carried on our conversation in a tea shop, the walls crowded with revealing posters of local female stars Samira, Saabnoor and Mou. A tape recorder blasted the Bengali version of 'Macarena' from *Explosion,* an album of remixes by Sylvia Khan and Jewel Mahmud.

'The past is over,' Basher told me. 'I want a job. That's all that matters.'

Noakhali lived as much off the land as some of its people once killed for, but also on remittances from countries in West Asia. In my conversations with some among the relatively moderate government in Dhaka, they worried about the conservative bastion of Noakhali. Here, the need to own a cell phone stood out as much as a school to practice sword craft.

Meanwhile, there was the Gandhi Ashram. I saw Mussulman children attend a school run by the trust that managed the ashram. I saw Mussulman farmers buy fish seed from its hatchery. The trust provided for tubewells and toilets in the area. A flag of Bangladesh fluttered in front of the ashram.

I joined the indefatigable Jharna-di and her small band of ashramites as they sang Gandhi's favourite prayer-song, a bhojōn that is a collective paean to Krishna and Ram, husband-of-Sita, the saviour of the fallen—'Raghupati Raghav Raja Ram'—every morning and evening. When that was done, Jharna-di led her colleagues and visitors to intone: 'Bismillah-ir-rahman-ir-rahim'. In the name of God, the Most Gracious, the Most Merciful.

Book II
Shōbbhōtā/ Oshōbbhōtā
Culture Chronicles

5

Āmādér Rōbindrōnāth
Tagore plus

The Bengalis are a lot more than Rabindranath Tagore, our most-cited cultural icon, Subhas Chandra Bose, West Bengal's most-cited political icon, and Sheikh Mujibur Rahman, Bangladesh's most cited national icon. Although we might often seem to be striving, quite correctly, to escape the stereotype of being long-haired poets or rebels with or without a cause, that our three most famous sons—bongōshontān—have bestowed on us, we actually adore these images of us. Culture and cause, even reflected culture and cause, provide for some a core, for others a sheen with which, in our minds and through our days, we keep ordinariness at bay.

These three aside, there are several Bengalis who are known to the world outside Banglasphere. However, many not-Bengalis are unaware that a number of these worthies are Bengalis or have Bengali roots. Some of our greatest are not known outside Banglasphere but that's fine too. It's enough if we laud our own, if others do too, that's a bonus.

Let me name a few here (numerous others appear elsewhere in the book), those whose names and influence have transcended our chauvinistic borders or, even if they haven't, have enriched or enervated our lives in Banglasphere and outside it, shaped us for better and worse. If these judgement calls invite energetic and emotional debate—so be it.

Let's begin with Satyajit Ray. In the 1950s, he marked the beginning of a certain global acclaim for Indian cinema and moved generations with a mix of realism and class. My former colleague and Ray aficionado Sumit Mitra recalls that time in Calcutta:

> During the release of the Apu trilogy, between 1955 and 1959, his apotheosis was complete. The coffee-house crowds began to referring to him by his pet name, 'Manik-da'.
>
> Gatecrashing into his home on Lake Temple Road in Ballygunj on flimsy excuses became so common a cultural pastime that Sandip, his schoolgoing son, always full of pranks, posted a notice on the front door demanding an admission fee of eight annas. By the '60s, he was too famous a figure to visit his favourite haunt, the corner room of the Chowringhee coffee house, which was called—still is—the House of Lords.

Lord Satyajit, marquis of the magic moment, arrived with *Pather* (or *Pothér*) *Pānchāli* and its poignant, occasionally joyous journey of Apu (Ōpu) on this 'song of the road' from the lushness and concurrent destitution of rural Bengal in the first film, imbuing a work, shot in black-and-white with superlative colour and mood, to the journey of fortitude in *Oporājitō*, with its Cartier Bresson-like framing of the ghats and lanes of Varanasi in the tale of the 'unvanquished, to the pathos-imbued joy of love and its reclamation in *Ōpur Shonghshār*, a study in exuberance, self-pity and deliverance of 'the world of Ōpu'. The first movie in the trilogy debuted one of Banglasphere's most versatile and loved actors, Soumitra Chatterjee, Ray's leading man in fourteen films.

Ray launched himself into the eye of his admirers through movies based on the books of Bibhutibhushan Bandopadhyay, a writer of such brilliance and nuanced observation that he is revered as much as loved in Bengal. No literary reading of Bānglā would be complete without him. Ray took Bandopadhyay with him to the world, as he did Tagore in a manner that Tagore himself and several of his early translators could not, bringing a layering of mood and his own sensibilities with several masterworks: *Teen Kōnya*, a meld of three short stories; *Chārulotā*, which drew from the novel

Nāstōnirh, Broken Nest; and *Ghoré Bāiré*, Home and the World.

Ray conveyed modern literary maestros like Sunil Gangopadhyay and Shankar beyond the formidable reputations both writers enjoy in Banglasphere. Gangopadhyay's novels *Prōtidwōndi* (which travelled the world as *The Adversary*) and *Orōnyer Din Rātri* (*Days and Nights in the Forest*) are two such. Shankar is the pseudonym of Mani Shankar Mukherjee, an unassuming gentleman who for years worked a day job at an office; and in his literary avatar wrote gritty books on the urban condition. As a journalist and devourer of his works, I have encountered both incarnations, one as the public relations face of Calcutta Electric Supply Corporation! Ray filmed his *Jonō Orōnyō* and *Sheemāboddhō*.

(For many Bengalis Shankar's masterwork and translation into cinema continues to be *Chōwrōngi*, a book that gained cult status with its stunning depiction of layered relationships, infidelity and craven business. As a movie directed by Pinaki Bhushan Mukherjee, with a star cast of enduring legends—Uttam Kumar, Supriya Devi and Utpal Dutt—it also gained cult status. A translation into English of the book by Arunava Sinha brought him crossover fame among Western audiences.)

In the absence of extensive, quality translations of works from Bānglā to English and other languages—a situation that has only begun to be remedied with some velocity in this century with some superb translations—auteurs like Ray were for the longest time conduits beyond Banglasphere of their own art and that of others. It may have seemed an exaggeration to a Bengali but hardly to a not-Bengali when film historian and critic Penelope Houston wrote that Ray's Bengal would conceivably remain 'Cinema's India' for a time.

Formidable directors like Mrinal Sen, whose gritty tellings of a time of churn, destitution, and rebellion (*Bhuvan Shome, Podātik, Calcutta 1971, Interview, Okālér Shondhāné...*) and Ritwik Ghatak, a fiercely left-of-centre theatrist and film-maker, a master of tragic romanticism driven by his experiences of famine, Partition and displacement (his best known work *Méghé Dhaka Tara* is cult-

coursework for Indian students of film-making; his other major works are *Shubornōrékhā, Titāsh Ékti Nōdir Nām*—technically a Bangladeshi film, based on the novel by Adwaita Mallabarman—and *Ojāntrik*) were both contemporaries of Ray. But they had less universal cachet than Ray, although their work is immensely respected and, for many aficionados, counted above that of Ray's for its sheer energy, political content and humanism.

But none of his peers could touch Ray for the elegance of his work. In several ways, of those who succeeded the golden generation of Bengali film-makers, Ray's natural inheritor is Rituparno Ghosh. He was surely the most luminous of our latter-day directors, wearing his art as fiercely as he did his sexuality, his talent freely acknowledged by colleagues of his generation like Goutam Ghose. From his breakout *Unishé April,* and *Bāriwāli* to *Shob Choritrō Kālpōnik* and *Chōkhér Bāli* and *Raincoat* to *The Last Lear,* Ghosh's work melded classes, languages, and commercial and art house in nearly a couple of dozen movies in Bānglā, Hindi and English which he directed and for which he wrote the screenplay. Few would flaunt androgyny in their art and person as publicly as he did, chide Bengalis for their 'moral panic', and yet, when he died in 2013, receive as close to a state funeral as possible, with an honour guard from West Bengal police and mourners filling Nandan, the government-sponsored film festival hub in central Kolkata in tribute.

For all the distance, we haven't remained far from Mumbai. Bengal's advent in India's film industry hub of Mumbai had its moments, though far from the art house sheen we stereotypically carry. There have been several significant clan and individual contributions in everything from acting and direction to set and light design, but the standouts have to be the Gangulys, of a prōbāshi family from Madhya Pradesh. For four decades, till the late 1980s, the Ganguly brothers, Ashok Kumar (born Kumudlal), Anoop Kumar (Kalyan) and Kishore Kumar (Abhas) were fixtures as actors, directors and producers—and Kishore achieved stratospheric fame as a playback singer. The only other Bengali singer spoken of in the same breath and with similar adulation as Kishore Kumar is his senior colleague Manna (Prabodh Chandra) Dey. Across our movie-crazed subcontinent, and wherever in the world such subcontinentals live, there are till today arguments about which of these singers was more sublime, or better suited for which genre of songs, or left behind a more enduring legacy—an ādā-like pastime beloved of both the Bengali and not-Bengali.

And who can ignore Rahul Dev Burman, the half-Bengali composer who helped transform modern Hindi and Bengali film music. A runaway success for three decades till his death in 1994, he bridged the gentle era of his father, the Tripuri genius and composer-singer, Sachin Dev Burman—a hugely respected person in Bengal and 'Bollywood' alike—with the more raucous, flashy surface demanded of his own era. The cult of this father and son were associated with the career of so many holy spirits of song, including Kishore Kumar.

◆

Away from Subhas we have a brace of remarkable Boses, even more if it were to be extended to the less-Anglicized Basu—all of it Bōshu to the Bengali.

There is no finessing required with what the world of science knows as boson. That is derived from a Bose, Satyendra Nath, who like so many Bengalis achieved phenomenal successes at a time when Indians were colonial subjects.

The particle boson, an important part of quantum mechanics, was discovered by Sateyndra Nath in collaboration with that other physicist, Albert Einstein. A photon is a boson. Photons make lasers. In an Einsteinian world of relativity married to quantum mechanics, a particle is either a boson or a fermion, named after the Italian physicist Enrico Fermi.

I do not understand the beauty of the Bose-Einstein equation and its child, the Bose-Einstein condensate, that required cooling what are called bosonic atoms close to absolute zero at minus 273.15 °C, a state that some scientists subsequently termed the new state of matter, the fifth such state. But I respect its significance, the evidence of genius.

'Respected sir,' Satyendra Nath wrote disarmingly to Einstein. 'I have ventured to send you the accompanying article for perusal and opinion. I am anxious to know what you think of it... Though a complete stranger to you I do not feel any hesitation in making such a request. Because we are all your pupils though profiting only by your teaching through your writings... I don't know whether you remember that somebody from Calcutta asked your permission to translate your papers on relativity in English. You acceded to the request. The book has since been published. I was the one who translated your paper on Generalised Relativity.'

Einstein accepted the paper from Satyendra Nath, 'Planck's Law and the Hypothesis of Light Quanta', when some major Western academic institutions and journals ignored his submission, and personally translated it into German—Satyendra Nath had pleaded that his German was insufficient—and submitted it to the peer-reviewed German scientific journal *Zeitschrift für Physik*, which Satyendra Nath had requested Einstein to do. It was published later in 1924. Satyendra Nath was at the time a reader in physics at the University of Dacca, as it was then known. (He would remain in Dhaka till 1945—he was made professor and head of the department of physics in 1927—before moving to Calcutta University as professor, where he remained into the 1950s till his retirement. But University College of Science in Calcutta, established in 1917 and where he was before moving to Dhaka, appeared to have been the crucible that helped his genius flower. It was at this research institution for postgraduate studies that Satyendra Nath encountered the latest European texts on quantum theory and relativity.)

Satyendra Nath finally met Einstein in 1925 in Berlin (it was the year he also met and worked with the legendary physicist and chemist Marie Curie). They continued to collaborate. The particles obeying their postulates were finally called boson by the English physicist Paul Dirac, who received the Nobel Prize in Physics in 1933. The boson transformed into Higgs boson in the 1960s after the work of physicist Peter Higgs, who would win a Nobel in 2013. In 2012, a new particle was discovered that showed the characteristics of a Higgs boson. Some called it the God Particle.

Satyendra Nath, whose work the *Encylopedia Britannica* lists as having contributed to 'statistical mechanics, electromagnetic properties of the Ionosphere, theories of X-ray crystallography and thermoluminescence [even used in archaeology for dating finds], and unified field theory [rooted in electromagnetism—work in this area has led to several Nobel awards]', is today considered a missed Nobel by many. But his greatest contribution, as my former colleague, the science writer Subhadra Menon put it, was perhaps the amount of time he 'ungrudgingly spent with students and researchers, and on taking science to the masses'.

◆

Here, even at the cost of interrupting the Bose series, I would be remiss to not mention Meghnad Saha, who is also considered by some to be a 'missed Nobel' several times over, as selection committees repeatedly judged Saha's work as fine application more than discovery. A classmate of Satyendra Nath at Presidency College, and like his peer an untiring teacher and mentor, he rose above his roots of poverty to emerge as a leading astrophysicist. His best-known contribution is the Saha Equation, a tool for understanding stellar spectra that has contributed to key work in this field. The British astronomer Harold Spencer Jones was effusive in Saha's praise. 'I well remember how,' recalled Spencer Jones, 'on the publication of his early and important paper on ionisation in stellar atmosphere, the late Professor Alfred Fowler drew my attention to it and emphasized its fundamental importance. And so it proved, for this paper was the stimulus to the work of [Edward Arthur] Milne, R. H. Fowler, and others in subsequent years. In fact, almost all work on stellar atmosphere has been based on it, either directly or indirectly.'

Saha was a prime mover in establishing academic centres in India for the study of, and research in, nuclear physics. In 1943, he became the founder-director of the Saha Institute of Nuclear Physics in Kolkata. The institute is now overseen by the Indian government's department of atomic energy.

◆

Another Bose, Jagadish Chandra, predates both Saha and Satyendra Nath—indeed, Jagadish Chandra was among Satyendra Nath's teachers—and is sometimes seen as the co-parent of the development of the radio and microwave communication as a contemporary of Guglielmo Marconi, who got the credit. But this Bose too wasn't driven by the desire for credit or riches, it appears, and freely shared his knowledge and research. The physicist who journeyed by way of Kolkata's St Xavier's College and the universities of London and Cambridge, and returned to Kolkata to become the pride of the Presidency College faculty, was a biophysicist who established that plants react to stimuli—that they had a nervous system. He died a legend in 1937 in Giridih, a charming town at the eastern edge of the Chota Nagpur Plateau. The honorific we reserve for him is āchārjyō, an exceptional teacher and mentor, far more precious to us in posterity than the knighthood he received while he was alive.

Satyajit Ray, whom generations of Bengali children since the 1960s also know of as a writer of unfailingly engaging detective novels for teenagers (Félu-dā is the young fan's socially conscious Sherlock, his unfiltered Charminar replacing the upper-class clenched pipe) and short stories, immortalized the spirit of Jagadish Chandra in his Professor Shōnku stories. Professor Shōnku, who shows the influence of Arthur Conan Doyle on the writing of Ray, in this case Professor Challenger—lived in Giridih before mysteriously disappearing. We then come to know of him from retrieved diaries of indestructible paper, that chronicle his adventures across the world—Switzerland, Greece, Sweden, Germany, Egypt, Iraq,

Austria, England, Spain, Hong Kong, Japan, Brazil, Italy and even jungles of the Congo, a cave in Cochabamba, Bolivia, Valparaiso in Chile, and the planets Mars and 'Tafa'. We adore his several dozen inventions—among them are the Miracureall tablet that can cure anything except the common cold, stand in awe of Annihilin, the handgun that can vapourize anything, the Microsonograph that detects subsonic sounds like the distress of roses, his experiments with floral phospholuminescence, and Marjarin, which increases the lifespan of cats—the professor had a cat, Newton. It's a witty multilingual pun. Marjari is Sanskrit for cat, also used in formal Bāṅglā (as a child I wondered if Ray mixed it in with Coldarin, a popular medicine for colds). Professor Shōnku is also a tribute to Jagadish Chandra's talent as a writer—he is credited with writing the first science fiction story in Bāṅglā.

Ray also had a hand in first bringing to cinematic life one of Bengal's best-loved detectives—not one of his own, but that created by the much-loved author and screenplay writer Saradindu Bandopadhyay—the stylish, vulnerable, humane, astute and very real Byōmkésh Bōkshi who made first made his appearance in 1932. The writer and editor Sandipan Deb, a Saradindu and Byōmkésh fanatic, writes about how Ray made *Chiriākhānā* reluctantly, 'his lousiest film' that brought to life what many consider India's real foil to Sherlock. Ray's was only the first of several and quite fine adaptations of Byōmkésh mysteries in film, each one scrutinized by Byōmkésh connoisseurs for its respect to the original minds—the detective's and his creator's.

'For 80 years, Byōmkésh has been Bengal's favourite literary character, his only competition coming from Satyajit Ray's Félu-dā, who made his debut in 1965,' writes Deb. 'However, there is a crucial difference between the two. The Félu-dā stories were written for teenagers; so Ray had to work within a set bandwidth—no crime could have a sexual angle to it. (Ray even complained that this significantly restricted his freedom to plot the stories.) Saradindu-babu wrote for adults. The mysteries that confront Byōmkésh quite often hinge around lust, adultery, promiscuity, even incest.'

Deb, who few would fault for his love and knowledge of detective fiction in several languages, goes a step further to praise the art of Saradindu and Byōmkésh gradually being made available to the world through translation, as books and movies, in languages other than Bānglā. He freely compares Byōmkésh to Sherlock Holmes and Raymond Chandler's creation, Philip Marlowe: 'At his best, Saradindu-babu was as good as anyone in the world working this genre.'

Not many in Banglasphere would disagree. And besides, Saradindu-babu was a kinder man, they may tell you, echoing Deb. Conan Doyle killed off Sherlock, and was then compelled to bring him back to life upon the outrage of his readers. Saradindu actually married off his hero, nearly unheard of for fictional detectives, made him age, and pursue the stolidly middle-class dream of buying an apartment in south Kolkata; Byōmkésh even 'ponders buying a car' for his wife Shōttōbōti, practitioner of truth, spouse to the pursuer of truth.

Some of us may also tell you Byōmkésh would be too guileless for our times, too simple. Perhaps that is why we love him, the private eye so like us and yet so unlike us.

◆

As far as the world outside Banglasphere is concerned the best known Bose today is probably the one synonymous with sound, revolutionizing the perception of speakers and headphones in a stylish marriage of form and function. Bose Corporation was founded by Amar Gopal Bose, born in Philadelphia to a Bengali father and an American mother. He was only half-Bengali, but we are an avaricious lot: our glories come from viewing a glass as half-full, even if for so much of our landmark existentialist cinema and literature and poetry and plays, glory arrives from viewing glasses as half-empty.

Why shouldn't we celebrate Sal—Salman Amin—Khan who

has revolutionized the teaching of mathematics and the sciences through the internet portal Khan Academy, a contribution that is almost immeasurable. The fans of this child of a Bangladeshi father and 'West Bengali' mother include Microsoft co-founder Bill Gates, and several million who have downloaded Khan Academy's free lessons nearly a billion times.

Like Sal, Jhumpa Lahiri is an American, though born in Great Britain of Bengali parents. She is less well known as Nilanjana Sudeshna, her birth name, and more as the successful author of short stories and novels, a writing queen of hyphenated ethnicity who is at home at Pulitzer prize ceremonies and the White House. As a storyteller, she has brought Bengal and Bengaliness to the world through English and numerous languages that translate her work. And now she has chosen to learn Italian and write in it. That is about as restlessly, eccentrically Bengali as it can get, and easily trumps several of her set-piece, monotonal characters.

There is her senior and more accomplished colleague, Amitav Ghosh, who moves as seamlessly between Kolkata, Brooklyn and a village in Goa as he does between anthropology, history and literature, perhaps the only Bengali prospect at this time for the world's greatest literary prize. As far as Banglasphere is concerned, if a Vidia Naipaul can receive a Nobel, why not our Amitav, who writes engagingly and movingly of his people, lets his work embrace cultures and civilizations and histories other than his own and does so without bigotry and superciliousness; an anthropologist who teases nuance from a landscape and character—rather than consciously bolster his own.

Ghosh's much younger colleagues, Monica Ali and Tahmima Anam, have become quite the flavour of literary festivals and smart applause, bringing a Bangladesh and diaspora Bangladesh to Britain and, through the lanes and imaginations of East London and similar communities, to the world. A list of other notable writers of Bengali origin who write primarily in English could count among them the understated and quite sublime essayist and novelist Amit

Chaudhuri, who journeys easily between Bengal and Britain; another crystal voice that has only just begun an ambitious journey, Neel Mukherjee, and Upamanyu Chatterjee, that master of satire and black humour. Like Ghosh and Lahiri, they bring Bengal to the consideration of the world in English, ready for global reading and further translation, not hobbled by the need for translation from Bānglā that has lamentably prevented greater recognition for so many of our superb writers.

(Not that writing in English is a guarantee of travel. Sudhin Ghose, a contemporary of R. K. Narayan, Mulk Raj Anand and Raja Rao found critical recognition in Europe and North America for his work drawing on village and small-town Bengal with a tetralogy (*And Gazelles Leaping, Cradle of the Clouds, Vermilion Boat,* and *The Flame of the Forest*). Once praised as 'things of stylized beauty', the work of this émigré who some critics praised as the best representation of Indian writing in English in the 1940s and 1950s has almost entirely been written out of literary or academic acknowledgement in India.)

Even with their established and emergent fame our 'global' writers are far from larger than life, and, as ever, even the greatest awards will leave the future to judge the greatness of their work. And, for all the adulation they receive in Banglasphere and the world they will not be counted among the Bengali greats by our chauvinists and literary conservatives until they win over, through primary writing or translation, the Bengali multitude that is still vastly more comfortable in Bānglā; for whom English largely remains a language of commercial application or aspiration, not always the language of thought, joy, love, sorrow, anger and hope. But, of course, our writers in English are of Bengal, they are indubitably us. To make the language they use a barrier would be such irony, a diminishing of their talent, success, and our collective pride not just as Bengalis but as citizens of a world of letters.

As to the greatness of Bengali writers in Bengali, not many languages can boast such a collection of fine writers, available so numerously, so casually, without fuss—not just in their novels, poems or plays—but also in annual literary collections that remain the staple of Bānglā readership. The oldest such collection I possess is *Tērōshō-bāhānnōr Shērā Golpō*, edited by Sarojkumar Raychaudhuri, himself a well-known writer. It was published in early 1946 towards the end of the Bengali year 1352, just months before bloodletting began in undivided-yet-deeply-divided Bengal still reeling from famine and war.

The collection contains thirteen stories including one by Raychaudhuri. The other dozen writers are counted among the greatest names in modern Bānglā writing—Achintya Kumar Sengupta; Ashapurna Debi; Tarasankar Bandyopadhyay; Narayan Gangopadhyay (also creator of the sassy teen-staple character, Tēni-dā); Nabendu Ghosh; Prabodh Kumar Sanyal, who was also an inveterate traveller—and glōbtrotār, as Bengalis appropriate the English word—and probably the writer of the best-known travelogue in Bānglā, *Mohāprōsthānér Pothé*; Premendra Mitra (who also created Tēni-dā's fictional competitor Ghonā-dā); Bibhutibhushan Mukhopadhyay; Manik Bandopadhyay; Subodh Ghosh; and the maestro, Bibhutibhushan Bandopadhyay, who helped shape world views, and 'make' Satyajit Ray even as Ray took him to the world.

I treasure the book as I do so many such collections over the decades and of the present day—showcases of a mix of established and emerging talent.

I remain in thrall of our Bānglā greats, the way I am still in thrall from an experience in 2008, during the Kolkata launch of my book *Red Sun: Travels in Naxalite Country*. Two of my spirit-gurus of Bānglā writing were in attendance, the inimitable, blunt-talking Samaresh Majumdar, and the gentle, professorial Nabarun Bhattacharya, who is sometimes unkindly referred to as the son of Mahasweta Devi, our literary goddess of conscience, care and fire, but carries an impressive fiery literary oeuvre of his own. I was flanked by these two gentlemen at a bookstore on Elgin Road, and they did me the honour of attending and discussing my work written in English, displaying the easy humility that writers of great accomplishment sometimes fail to; but the trait is commonplace in Banglasphere.

Here was Nobārun-dā, a greatly respected radical writer of nuance. Here was Shomōrésh-babu, whose classic trilogy set in the times of the Naxal movement and its aftermath of the marriage of māstān and politics, *Uttōrādhikār, Kālbelā* and *Kālpurush*, I had devoured as a young journalist.

Here they were, in easy camaraderie with a roomful of students, writers, activists, police officers and luminaries which also included a former chief of India's army, General Shankar Roy Chowdhury, the second Bengali to hold the post after General Jayanto Nath Chaudhuri, a legend of sorts who had seen action in Burma, Malaya, and who was also the military governor of Hyderabad after Partition. (It may astound not-Bengalis subsumed by stereotypes attached to Bengalis, but we have numerous warriors of both pen and sword, as it were. The first Indian Air Force Chief was Air Marshal Subroto Mukerjee; in this millennium there was Air Chief Marshal Arup Raha. Admiral Adhar Kumar Chatterji was Chief of India's Naval Staff. Bangladesh, of course, has an advantage—by default almost all their warriors and service chiefs are Bengali!)

Someday, I hope to be able to translate the work of some of our formidable, incisive, humorous, satirical writers in Bānglā, join the club of translators of our classics like William Radice, or that of my contemporaries like Arunava Sinha, and his colleagues in such enterprise, Sudeep Sen, the accomplished poet whose choice of language for his own work remains English, and the poet and novelist Sampurna Chattarji with her irrepressible eye for humour and dark satire—who all take Bengal's treasures to the world in a different way than Robert Clive did.

◆

Before we move on to Tagore, let me reflect a little on a couple of other aspects. One is our musical genius. Just as it is silly to criticize

English language writers of Bengali origin as being deracinated and their work as not being as true as those who write in Bāṅglā, it would be intemperate to dismiss Ravi Shankar's brilliance as a sitar player just because he showed us the way to the world by evolving a style of presentation alien to purists. Before him his elder brother Uday Shankar was another pioneer—he toured Europe with a dance troupe in the 1930s and mesmerized a slice of the world for a time with India's cultural exotica beyond maharajas and snake charmers and poverty. Ravi Shankar or Rabindra Shankar Choudhury was a pupil of the legendary Ustad Allauddin Khan, from Brahmanbaria in eastern Bangladesh, an acknowledged, exacting mega-guru of the sitar, sarod and shehnai. Ravindra would later change his name, move on from his first wife, his guru's daughter, Annapurna—provider of nourishment, the very avatar of Pārbōti, and consort to the eccentric Shib-thākur. He would exhibit his supreme craft in a manner that would charm Yehudi Menuhin and George Harrison, help him settle into America and the world, contribute to the sitar being showcased in The Beatles track 'Norwegian Wood' and by The Rolling Stones in 'Jumpin' Jack Flash'—'pop' for certain, but global peaks that an Indian musical instrument, an extension of Indian culture, hasn't since scaled.

Some call it showbiz. The musicologist and art critic S. Kalidas once quoted a person whom he described as a 'fan' of 'rival sitarist' and co-legend Vilayat Khan: 'Everything about Ravi Shankar, from his elaborately stitched dhutis to his music is tailored with an eye on the audience and the media.' Kalidas tends to agree—that the maestro sported a 'designer look' to create his persona and bolster his art.

Others swear Nikhil Banerjee, a giant who followed Ravi Shankar's footsteps to his teacher of the Maihar Gharana, immensely respected in Banglasphere, in India, and in the world of 'world music', was a truer musician. Less flash, more art, a musician who would seek spiritual depth in his craft and himself in a twinning of souls. Banerjee travelled the world as well. Much of his music has come to us today on account of aficionados from the West. The purist with flair is seen by some as a musician done out of due fame.

They will say at least Ustad Allauddin's other stellar student, his own son the shorōd—sarod—maestro Ali Akbar Khan, also a favourite of Menuhin's, who found great fame at home and abroad, and founded schools of music in North America and Europe, didn't have to contend with a shadow on account of his mastery of a different instrument, quite a different universe. And yet, of course, there was magic whether the three played solo, or in duet as Ravi Shankar and Ali Akbar sometimes did, with Ravi Shankar's frequent accompanist, the tabla maestro Alla Rakha—a Dogra from Jammu but whom any Bengali music lover would in the blink of an eye appropriate as one of ours. And who could say where the flautist Pannalal Ghosh, another of Ustad Allauddin's stellar students, would have travelled had his life not been cut short in 1960, before his colleagues had begun to take their giant strides. But he lives on, through his music and his own legacy of stellar students in eastern and western India, who ensure the bamboo flute—the bansuri (bānshōri to us)—remains an integral part of India's classical music tradition.

Perception is a tricky trade. But Ravi Shankar, as Kalidas explains, maintained that all persona and format was to 'enable him' to present classical Indian music to a 'modern, international audience'. 'There lies his essential contribution,' as Kalidas put it. 'Even in India, it is largely after Ravi Shankar's example that the present day format of an instrumental concert evolved. Especially in the opening *Ālāp-Jōr* sequences his contribution stands unrivalled.'

Other credits are due Ravi Shankar. Giving accompanists their due. Imparting a 'structural sophistication' to northern Indian instrumental music. Superb musical expression with public appeal. Being father to the sitarist Anoushka Shankar and the outstanding singer-songwriter Norah Jones.

We can live with that.

◆

Sudeep Chakravarti

We appear to be so immersed in culture that we sometimes tend to ignore the aspect of commerce and business. We do have a few legends here. There is the seventeenth-century trader Gouri Sen. There is 'Prince' Dwarkanath Tagore, grandfather to Rabindranath, the zamindar-entrepreneur who straddled commercial might in eastern India as founder of the Union Bank, co-founder of Carr, Tagore and Company which traded opium and held vast interests in jute, mining and tea, and was co-sponsor of the Bengal Renaissance. So familiar was Dwarkanath in European circles that John Palmer, the founder of the 'Agency House' Palmer & Co. called him Dwarky. There have been a few localized textile barons, including Mohini Mohan Chakravarti, my great-great-grandfather, and, later, Surya Kumar Bose, founder of the Dhakeshwari Cotton Mills—spectacular for the time but now largely forgotten, businesses destroyed by a combination of one or more of these—Partition, geopolitics, labour trouble, inefficiency and venality of the inheritors.

Pre- and post-independent India—and West Bengal—has seen a few remarkable success stories of Bengali entrepreneurship that have endured and flourished in their own way, such as the Roys of finance major Peerless Group, Mazumders of equipment specialists Tractors India, the Burmans of healthcare house Dabur (which had roots in East Bengal), the Roy Burmans of leather and retailing brand Khadim's, and the Nags of consumer durables success story IFB Industries, which has held its own in India in the face of the some of the biggest consumer brands in the world. We have a family of tea specialists from Assam, the Chatterjis, who run an impressive clutch of gardens in Assam, have helped to rescue Darjeeling's Makaibari Estate from ruin, and plan a major foray to grow tea in Rwanda, Africa, which many consider to be the next big thing in tea.

We have the Roys of Sahara Group, whose soaring but shaky empire of finance, real estate and power-broking has now been brought to earth primarily on the charge of misleading investors— an accusation by the Securities and Exchange Board of India and upheld by India's Supreme Court. The Bengali promoters and co-promoters of several fly-by-night finance operations and pyramid schemes are on the run, in jail, or remain accused—some of them senior politicians of West Bengal with close ties to perversions of power—leading to Bengal's contribution to that New Age breed of South Asian entrepreneurs—the politician-businessman, businessman-politician, and the relatives of politicians in power who suddenly come into great wealth and flourishing businesses. Indeed, they appear to be as Mérō in such dedicated application as the Mérō Bengalis so reviled and accused of committing the vilest economic cons and crimes.

◆

It is good if the world knows us for more than Tagore, the lyrical alchemist we share with it. It is good if the world knows us to not be fixated with Tagore, although a visit to West Bengal and some parts of Bangladesh might make it appear otherwise—a worshipful temple housing an infinite number of his statues and likenesses in paint, automatic mention in text books, his briskly selling books that must grace a literary-minded Bengali home, besides his name on buildings and auditoria, and even as a lake and an underground railway station.

Although Tagore worship is mostly evident in Banglasphere, it is certainly pleasing that in the Berlin locality of Grünau there is a Rabindranath-Tagore Strasse; and a little Tagore Avenue in Singapore, and a nearby Tagore Drive and Tagore Lane.

Our Tagore fixation is today tempered with reassessment, looking anew at the work of the person and the legend.

That is as it should be, insist many who love his work and yet wish to see it break free of its time, reassessed and even reinterpreted as Shakespeare is today, in theatre and film, to great accolade even as the purity and sensuality of the original remains. Even as purists baulk at it, insisting on copybook templating, a pleasant deviation was actually commissioned by a government agency. I was reminded of it by an observation of Nondon Bagchi, among the best and most respected drummers in India for several decades. In 2011, the Indian Council for Cultural Relations approached Kolkata jazz legend, guitarist Carlton Kitto, to mark the 150th birth anniversary of Tagore with a jazz twist to some of Tagore's songs. Bagchi was part of Kitto's ensemble that performed the instrumental version of two of Tagore's immensely popular songs, *Tōmār hōlō shuru* and *Purōnō shéi dinér kothā*. The ensemble sang a third, *Phulé phulé*. The crowd, much of it Bengali, was very appreciative. But the 'gig' was in Shillong, the capital of Meghalaya, stereotypically known to be welcoming to both traditional and modern music.

One would think that slot belonged also to Kolkata. Indeed, but not always, and so ecstatically, for reinterpreted Tagore. In the world, but not so much at home. Only recently has that shackle begun to loosen. And that is appropriate, maintains Bagchi, because 'the man himself was a true free thinker, an epitome of courage and a Bohemian in many ways, loved and respected across all divisions of race, religion, class or creed.'

He insists Tagore is about the essence of Tagore.

◆

Tagore evidently moved the poet William B. Yeats to offer an introduction to his breakout work, the translation in English of *Gitanjali*, Song Offerings, which won Tagore the Nobel Prize for Literature in 1913. Yeats described it as being of 'supreme culture'. Yeats wrote:

> These verses will not lie in little well-printed books upon ladies' tables, who turn the pages with indolent hands that they may sigh over a life without meaning, which is yet all they can know of life, or be carried by students at the university to be laid aside when the work of life begins, but, as the generations pass, travellers will hum them on the highway and men rowing upon the rivers. Lovers, while they await one another, shall find, in murmuring them, this love of God a

magic gulf wherein their own more bitter passion may bathe and renew its youth.

They do, even today, and certainly where there are Bengalis. They will do so for years more, because Tagore is so much more than *Gitanjali*. They have, with ever newer, ever better translations that bring Tagore to more Indians and others, a vast not-Bengali world that appreciates this Bengali who saw and thought past Bengal and the Bengalis. They have put behind them the bashing Tagore's works took in the United Kingdom only years after more of his works were published there in English, criticized, as it turned out, more for their quality of translation by Tagore himself, and the high pitch that Yeats had provided of a sombre mystic, a fateful combination of an Atlas and a Buddha. Rabindranath—some of us call him that in cosy familiarity, the more fawning prefer Kōbiguru, the guru of poetry—had a habit of transcreation over translation, which may have led to far lesser expertise in a language other than Bānglā—*Gitanjali* was different; Yeats had a hand in preparing the manuscript in English. 'As for Rabindranath Tagore,' Graham Greene exclaimed in 1937, 'I cannot believe that anyone but Mr Yeats can still take his poems very seriously.' Ezra Pound, an early Tagore sponsor, also turned fiercely critical. Deeply sensitive to criticism, Tagore was evidently quite crushed. William Radice, among the best-known Tagore scholars in the world (Radice's other area of professed expertise is the work of the brilliantly eccentric and tragic Bengali poet Michael Madhusudan Dutt), wrote of how towards the end of his life Tagore 'often expressed regret that he had done the English versions'. In a letter to a close associate, the critic and poet Amiya Chandra Chakravarty, he described these as 'self-mockery'; to others he wrote of how his fame in the West had been 'an accident'. 'The image that those translations had projected, reinforced so indelibly by W. B. Yeats in his well-intentioned but deeply ignorant Introduction to *Gitanjali*, became a terrible burden,' writes Radice. 'It cramped the free poetic spirit in him, the Rabindranath whose Bengali writings in prose and verse could be deft and witty and charming in a way that his western admirers could never imagine.'

Others have put it less kindly. The British writer Ian Jack wrote a sharp essay to mark Tagore's 150th birth anniversary, in which he wondered about the general absence of Tagore's recognition in the world even as for people in Bengal, in Banglasphere, even in India, it remained quite the opposite. 'His western enthusiasts, however, saw what they wanted to see,' Jack wrote. 'First, he was an exotic fashion and then he was not. "Damn Tagore," wrote Yeats in 1935, blaming the "sentimental rubbish" of his later books for ruining his reputation.' Jack then gives the example of the dour poet, novelist and critic Philip Larkin who wrote to a friend, Robert Conquest, in 1956: 'An Indian has written to ask what I think of Rabindrum [sic] Tagore. Feel like sending him a telegram: "Fuck all. Larkin".'

◆

And yet we freely admire Tagore—Thākur, in Bānglā—because we Bengalis know him better than Greene ever did: we know him in Bānglā, the language of his love, hope, and despair. And, away from Banglasphere, undoubtedly because the translations of his works have vastly improved over the years. (Even early translations in languages like French by André Gide and Russian by Boris Pasternak are considered by some as superior to many of the English ones.)

If others in the Indian subcontinent deride us saying Bengalis haven't moved beyond Tagore we can claim it to be a lie, because we have moved *with* Tagore, the same as the world has moved with Shakespeare, ever better translated, read, his plays varyingly performed, edgily interpreted, made our own in our hearts and minds. We don't grudge such belittling because even Tagore knew his literature and poetry and theatre were always much more than he, even as he knew it was no sin to be free with his feelings and prolific in his art.

What is the sin in these words (and what would Graham Greene, my spirit-guru in so many ways, know of their profound effect in a place where hundreds of millions of the dominated and the dispossessed lived, once run by Greene's countrymen), words written by this resolutely unquiet Bengali, this resolutely unquiet Indian that gather force and fortitude with each repetition, a hundred years after they were written:

> Where the mind is without fear and the head is held high;
> Where knowledge is free;
> Where the world has not been broken up into fragments by narrow domestic walls;
> Where words come out from the depth of truth;
> Where tireless striving stretches its arms towards perfection;
> Where the clear stream of reason has not lost its way into the dreary desert sand of dead habit;
> Where the mind is led forward by Thee into everwidening thought and action—
> Into that heaven of freedom, my Father, let my country awake.

What is the sin in having two national anthems from your oeuvre, Jana-gana-mana adhināyaka jaya hé/ Bhārata Bhāgya Vidhātā for India and Āmār Shōnār Bānglā for Bangladesh?

India chose it for its inclusive vision for a country born of blood and guts.

> You are the ruler of the minds of the people
> the god of India's destiny.

Bangladesh chose it over work by its national poet, Kazi Nazrul Islam, a literary colossus in his own right, revered in Bangladesh as he is in all Banglasphere, because it best described the aspiration of that country, like India born of blood and guts, three decades after Tagore's death in 1941, a region in which his abiding contribution was that of a benevolent zamindar, in Shilaidaha, near Kushtia, his zamindari home there impeccably maintained by the government of Bangladesh as a national institution?

> My golden Bengal, I love you.

It has the simplicity of a love—and the greatest irony. It was written of a longing and set to tune by Tagore when Bengal was divided in 1905. And then to be adopted by Bangladesh in 1971, after carnage that ghoulishly diminished even the horrors of Partition—that near-irreconciliable event which divided Bengal for the second time.

Tagore wasn't unaware of the place he held in Banglasphere, or outside of it for that matter. Radice translated a short poem which he believes reflected this view:

How easy it is
To mock the sun:
The light by which
it is caught
Is its own.

◆

Tagore gave us something to be proud of, a humanity that we Bengalis so dearly cherish even as we've repeatedly proven ourselves to be purveyors and practitioners of the bleakest inhumanity.

'The profoundly original writer, whose elegant prose and magical poetry Bengali readers know well, is not the sermonizing spiritual guru admired—and then rejected—in London,' wrote Amartya Sen in an essay for the *New York Review*, neatly summing up our admiration of this man. 'Tagore was not only an immensely versatile poet; he was also a great short story writer, novelist, playwright, essayist, and composer of songs, as well as a talented painter...'

Sen's admiration for the man goes beyond his childhood association with Santiniketan, a home for peace and reflection that Rabindranath built. Consider how Sen connects with Tagore politically, as a corollary of his own world view and work that earned him a Nobel in 1998 for economic sciences. Were he alive today 'Tagore would have been happy...to see that the one governmental attempt to dispense generally with basic liberties and political and civil rights in India...' writes Sen. This is when Prime Minister Indira Gandhi—'ironically, herself a former student at Santiniketan'—

declared the Emergency in 1975, a complete suspension of citizens' rights. In a remarkable statement by the citizens of India, she lost the general elections in 1977.

'Rabindranath would also see that the changes in policy that have eliminated famine since independence had much to do with the freedom to be heard in a democratic India.'

Deprivation was the marquee event in Tagore's play *Raja O Rani*, The King and the Queen, Sen reminds us: '[T]he sympathetic Queen eventually rebels against the callousness of state policy toward the hungry. She begins by inquiring about the ugly sounds outside the palace, only to be told that the noise is coming from "the coarse, clamorous crowd who howl unashamedly for food and disturb the sweet peace of the palace." The Viceregal office in India could have taken a similarly callous view of Indian famines, right up to the easily preventable Bengal famine of 1943, just before independence, which killed between two and three million people. But a government in a multi-party democracy, with elections and free newspapers, cannot any longer dismiss the noise from "the coarse, clamorous crowd".'

This is the man who wrote, in parts of *Gitanjali* not usually excerpted:

Give me the strength never to disown the poor or bend my knees before insolent might.

Rabindranath extended his engagement with the public good with a deep interest in the environment, Sen retells us, addressing in his own way a concern about deforestation by initiating a festival of tree-planting as far back as 1928. In what is a mirror-image of his own beliefs, Sen insists Rabindranath would be a great votary of environmentalism without broad-brushing industry and technology with taint or resentment.

Here, maintains Sen, Rabindranath differed from Mohandas Gandhi. 'The mastery over the machine,' he wrote in *The Crisis in Civilization*, 'by which the British have consolidated their sovereignty over their vast empire, has been kept a sealed book, to which due access has been denied to this helpless country.'

Sen's Tagore reflex extends to his own work and writing, a deeply fused composite that is development economics, urging an end to the blindsiding of ills in the justifiably seductive pursuit of prosperity in a cradle of mankind that is inching closer to two billion people, among the densest gatherings of aspiration as well as the densest gathering of the poor in the world. '...Yet even a hundred Bangalores and Hyderabads will not, on their own, solve India's tenacious poverty and deep-seated inequality. The very poor in India get a small—and basically indirect—share of the cake that information technology and related developments generate,' Sen wrote in *The Argumentative Indian: Writings on Indian History, Culture and Identity*, in 2005. Sen's panacea was disarmingly simple—the removal of poverty with participatory growth, one that would need to address matters of illiteracy, poor health and land reforms, among other issues that contribute to inequality.

When we turn to look at Sen's spirit-guru, as it were, surely Rabindranath's poem *The Question* would be taken to heart by every thinking citizen of the subcontinent and anywhere people earn their rule in the name of the people and then jettison that trust, where public servants make servants of the public. Radice offers this translation of *Prōshnō*, which he maintains is one of Tagore's greatest Bengali poems:

My voice is choked today;
I have no music in my flute
Black moonless night
Has imprisoned my world, plunged it into nightmare.
And this is why,
With tears in my eyes, I ask:
Those who have poisoned your air, those who have
extinguished your light,
Can it be that you have forgiven them?
Can it be that you love them?

6

Obāngāli
A complex and much else

A great part of being Bengali is to be aware of what we are not. That is an irony in the wonderfully hybrid Bengali nation trying to classify itself as something pure—pure of spirit and pure of intent, even pure of blood, certainly pure of language—about the one cultural unifier across our religions and borders.

'Pure' would perhaps be misleading in this context. 'Superior' would be more apt. This irony too is reflected as much in West Bengal as in Bangladesh where two sets of blends combat the other's perception of who is the truer Bengali. All together it would count among the world's great ethno-cultural perversions. Racism may be a simpler word.

(Here I was drawn to a penetrating essay by the young poet and academician Manash Firaq Bhattacharjee who refers to Tagore as having 'exasperatedly' written in a poem titled 'Mother Bengal':

Shāt kōti shontānér, hé mugdhō jonōni
Rékéhchhō Bāngāli kōré, mānush korō ni
Your seven crore children, O' bewitched mother
you have kept alive as Bengalis, not human beings.

'Apart from being a cultural and moral indictment' of the 70 million Bengalis at the time Tagore wrote it, Bhattacharjee holds the lines up 'in the context of Tagore's idea of the "universal man", a person of *dharma* or righteousness, living under social obligations, working unselfishly for others.')

The generation from the 1980s or so, born around that time as well as those born earlier but from the diaspora of the time—the great wave of corporate and creative professionals who left a chaotic and economically stunted Kolkata and West Bengal in search of a better work life—seems to be less obsessed with supra-Bengaliness. They seem far more confident of their Bengaliness, partly jettisoning the conceit their forebears had, a certain insecure, paranoid construct of being on top of the intellectual and ethnic heap.

That generational modernization may be a more honest, truer reflection of the liberal Bengali soul. A certain Sufi soul, if you will, the ability to mingle with various people and various points of view, the ability to accept various points of view, that may be a more khnāti Bāngāliyānā than anything else, the spirit of true Bengaliness, the liberal ideal that educated Bengalis lay claim to. But there is several generations-worth of baggage, a great disparaging of other people and other cultures in an almost institutional manner that was used—is still used—by so many of us to underscore Bengali self-worth. So that even some Bengalis are simply not Bengali enough, or other Bengalis are merely chāshā—no more than peasants; good to see in watercolours of village life in the odd gallery and displays by sidewalk artists, words of a pastoralist poet or novelist. Any closer would be so deconstructionist, such a bore.

Those in the vicinity of Bengal are simply lesser beings, as if Bengalis more than anything need to ensure their position among such proximate unworthies, a churlish vaccination to ensure superior-than-thou. It is as if the colonial Bengal Presidency, of which Bihar, Odisha and Assam were once a part before they departed that unwieldy structure that also injected a degree of parallel Bengali cultural colonialism with clerks, administrators, judges and teachers, was alive and still kicking. Bengal Raj. Bengali Raj. I can't deny it has a grandiose feel to it.

Nearly all peoples and cultures have derogatory references for people other than they, but that does not mean it makes the ones your own people have for others any less damning. An earthy north Indian will easily call out 'Oye Bangāli!' to a Bengali or anyone from nearby cultures in eastern India, Odia or Assamese, many of whom would pass as Bengali; 'Oye Madrāsi!' for anyone from southern India. In comparison, my being called 'Sandeep' in northern India—those ears don't hear some names well—or listening to redneck Americans and their somewhat paler British counterparts enjoy pun-induced laughter with 'So deep' is like being showered by rose petals.

◆

The cultural conceit of the Bengali is in a class of its own and it holds steady in the face of nearly all disparagement. I've heard, for instance, a widely respected publisher of Tamil literature, Kannan Sundaram, lament at a major literary gathering that he could not understand why Bānglā had so little in translation of other languages except from English—and other Western languages via English—and relatively little or nothing from Indian languages, let alone excellent works in Tamil—when Tamil and other southern languages translated so freely from Bānglā and so many other languages in India and the world. He meant it, quite correctly, and in some wonderment as a disparaging comment, but I didn't have the heart to tell him of our traditional cultural conceit of looking to the West, even to the extent of ignoring valid criticism from our subcontinental peers (here, I can hear some harrumphing among our crème de la chauvin: what peers?).

Sundaram obviously doesn't know Bengalis as well as the British did, who disparaged us utterly, the one race that vilified us even as we culturally venerated them, who pillaged and steamrolled Bengal so completely so as to dismiss the educated, aspiring Bengali, the very class they had helped to create—the bhodrōlōk—with just one word: 'Baboo'.

It was a case of the honorific babu reduced to a 'native' clerk, a paper-pusher, an incompetent, a buffoon, closer to a primate than human—a mark so deep that well into the twenty-first century, the term babu, particularly when used in English is a pejorative for all manner of bureaucrat. The British had fun with it.

◆

> Venerable and ludicrous Sir.—Permit me most respectfully to bring beneath your notice a proposal which I serenely anticipate will turn up trumps under the fructifying sunshine of your esteemed approbation.

In 1870, Hurry Bungsho Jabberjee, B. A., made a spectacular entry into the satirical annals of the Raj by writing to 'The Hon'ble–*Punch*'.

He was a caricature of the dark, doltish, slick-haired Bengali babu—a polite honorific turned into an insulting hoot. Such a 'baboo' often followed the path of Macaulay all the way to Bilét and was ridiculed for it in 'Blighty'. Baboo Jabberjee was the precursor of the eventual 'Oh *yes*' and 'My *gudd*ness' and 'Birdie num num' sort of Indian caricature made famous by the actor Peter Sellers in *The Party* a hundred years later, a movie that globally elevated him, and with it Hollywood's stereotypical Indian accent. The 'baboo' worshipped purple prose and archaic formality of address; he usually remained 'desirous' of things small or big, and acknowledgement by the master was apparently like holding Excalibur. *Baboo Jabberjee B. A.* by F. Anstey, the pen name of novelist and staffer of the conservative satirical journal *Punch*, Thomas Anstey Guthrie, cut to the quick.

'Sir,' Baboo Jabberjee (in sketches depicted as usually being attired in top hat and frock coat, pin-striped trousers, sometimes in an overcoat as furry as a bear, shod in patent leather shoes, an elaborate cane handy, sometimes clutching a satchel or bits of clothing or accessories monogrammed *HBJ*) continued. 'I am an able B. A. of a respectable Indian University, now in this country for purposes of being crammed through Inns of Court and Law Exam, and rendering myself a completely fledged Pleader or Barrister in the Native Bar of the High Court.

'Since my sojourn here, I have accomplished the laborious perusal of your transcendent and tip-top periodical, and, hoity toity! I am like a duck in thunder with admiring wonderment at the drollishness...'

Baboo Jabberjee got his own back from time to time. He was occasionally used to brilliantly lampoon the shāhéb and his wits, like the poet laureate Alfred Austin, about whom it can be said that he was as worshipful of nature as he was of some conservative politicians. Rumours of the time had him being appointed at the quid pro quo pleasure of Lord Salisbury, who was prime minister of England several times. Baboo Jabberjee wrote a 'congratulatory ode' to 'The Hon'ble Poet-Laureate Alfred Austin, Esq.':

Hail! You full-blown tulip!
Oh! when the wheezing zephyr brought
glad news
Of your judicious appointment, no hearts
who did peruse,
Such a long-desiderated slice of good luck
were sorry at,
To a most prolific and polacious Poet-
Laureate!
For no poeta nascitur who is fitter
To greet Royal progeny with melodious
twitter...

Baboo Jabberjee was soon so accomplished in and of Bilét—foreign lands to us, particularly Great Britain—that he was in a few years portrayed as a writer who introduced to the world another baboo, in *A Bayard from Bengal: Being Some Account of the Magnificent and Spanking Career of Chunder Bindabun Bhosh, Esq., B. A., Cambridge*. The first chapter of the opus published in 1902, 'From Calcutta to Cambridge', begins with a 'Stanza written at sea (unpublished) by H. B. J.':

At sea the stoutest stomach jerks,
Far, far away from native soil,
When Ocean's heaving waterworks
Burst out in Brobdingnagian boil!

Indeed, as the good ship *Rohilkund* 'lurched through the vasty deep as though overtaken by the drop too much,' a kindly Commissioner returning home on leave asked after Chunder Bindabun's well-being.

'What is the matter, Baboo,' began the Commissioner in paternal tones. 'Why are you kicking up the shindy of such a deuce's own hullabaloo?'

'Because, hon'ble Sir,' responded Mr Bhosh, 'I am in lively expectation that waters will rush in and extinguish my vital spark.'

'Pooh,' said Mr Commissioner, genially. 'This is only the moiety of a gale, and there is not the slightest danger.'

'Having received this assurance, Mr Bhosh's natural courage revived, and, coming up on deck, he braved the tempest with the cool composure of a cucumber...'

◆

Beyond the absolute conceit of labelling others 'non-Bengali', used conversationally in Bāngla and English alike, there are ethnic specifics employed by the well-bred Bengali lout. Much of it is too abhorrent to be repeated here, but there are specific epithets for the Odia, the Bihari and the Northeasterners, especially the Assamese. Their achievements and their greatest sons and daughters are sometimes dismissed out of hand.

Some of this racism and discrimination is sparked off by the presence of considerable numbers of not-Bengalis in Kolkata and other cities and towns in the vast Bengal hinterland—Howrah, Siliguri, Bardhaman, Asansol, Durgapur and so on. Particularly Kolkata, self-professedly cosmopolitan, houses in central and southwestern parts of the city great concentrations of the not-Bengali, Bihari, Punjabi, Gujarati, Marwari, who live in a range of homes from squalid tenements, middle-class apartment blocks to elegant mansions, areas with relatively few Bengalis in evidence by circumstance of economic history and social choices; but instead Bengali Kolkata that surrounds these Obāngāli islands—where Bāngāli beggars are more in evidence than Bāngāli business persons and Bāngāli executives—so often appears to be the ghetto.

But of course we cherish the city without which there can apparently be no Bengali: what was once Kalikata that became Calcutta with British phonetics and was reclaimed as Kolkata. Dominique Lapierre, the Frenchman who chose to carry our infinite burdens in his attempt to locate *Les Misérables* in Kolkata also called it the *City of Joy*, the name of his eponymous book. Lapierre 'conned us', as the actor Victor Banerjee puts it, by his 'simple translation' of the word anōndō, to make Kolkata and its environs a city of joy—'the most disgraceful slum in the world', in the words of Lapierre.

The French conned us another time—and it wasn't when they put about that French colonialism was egalitarian, fraternal, liberating, and considerably more elegant than British colonialism. In my youth we were much taken by the fact that a famous musical staged in London and New York was called *Oh! Calcutta!* It was fêted as one of the longest running shows on Broadway. Known most for its celebration of nudity, it had nothing to do with Calcutta, as I was both mildly shocked and greatly amused to learn later. The title was inspired by a work of the anarchist-surrealist French painter Camille Clovis Trouille, *O quel cul t'as!* What a lovely ass you have!

The poet, novelist, biographer and writer of conscience Vikram Seth was more forthright in dealing with Kolkata, where he was born (and, as he confessed to an audience at a literary gathering in the city, his mother had initially named him Amit, after a 'rather wimpish character in Tagore's novel, *Shéshér Kōbitā*', the luminous Final Poem—his father overruled it). In 'A Morning Walk' Seth writes:

To wander through the streets of Calcutta is
To force the whole world's misery on the heart—
Children on broken stumps, staring with eyes
White and opaque, begging with hardened art.
Far from those eyes, blinded in my stead, I wander
Among these affluent trees, and stop and ponder

How fine it is to share the world and not
Its need when there are those who weep for food...

◆

A substantial part of the crude snobbishness against Obāngāli are
rooted in the days when Bengal was the spearhead of modern
subcontinental aspiration, and Kolkata the colonial capital.

The Odia, to the average Bengali, is a dismissive Uré, who
speaks a language that is a comical version of Bānglā. The Uré were
once quite grand, had the civilization to even build the Sun Temple
in Konark and the magnificent temples at Puri and Bhubaneswar,
and the astounding ancient rock caves of Jain monks at Udayagiri
and Khandagiri. Now, on a good day they are basically cooks,
Mohārāj if they are Brahmin and plain old cooks if they are not;
and Nuliā who are always ready to save our vacationing children,
these primitive but effective lifeguards, when they are at sea in Puri
and Konark and Gopalpur.

The Assamese typically receive a two-fold dismissal. One is about
the Assamese language being inferior to Bangla for all the similarties.
The other is jokes about being Āshāmi, what we call the Assamese;
it is also one of our words that means convict. For generations of
the average post-1947 Bengali the only Assamese worthy of respect
was the singer Bhupen Hazarika, whose mesmeric voice entranced
generations of us bred on the superiority of Bengali musicality.

From the time I was a child I've heard that the Bihari is a
khōttā or, with an East Bengali inflection, khātuā. It's a pejorative
that has its roots in the word for labour, so the Bihari is universally

a labourer, the fellow who, when he leaves his native Bihar to live and work across western Bengal to transport goods by handcart, pulls the rickshaws—even hand-pulled rickshaws—and a couple of times a day settles down to a meal of chhātu, dough made with ground gram and water and eaten with a little salt, maybe a green chilli and some onion.

◆

As a teenager, I devoured stories of Samaresh Basu, a prolific writer in Bengali, a modern-day literary giant with several hundred novels and short stories, provocative, reflective, grittily suburban, with many transformed into engaging, commercially successful cinema. His death in 1988 has hardly stemmed the reprinting, reach and appreciation of his work. His oeuvre and influence extended to a successful run as a writer of books for children.

The child-detective Gogol (an unusual but cherished dāk-nām, after the nineteenth century Ukrainian-born writer Nikolai Vasilievich Gogol) is your regular Bengali boy-star, charmingly solving mysteries. The adventure series was also Basu's way of showing children glimpses of Bengal and India. But to my distress, even this wonderful writer fell prey to the racism that is common in Bengal. One of his books is about Gogol's trip to Nagaland. He visits the capital Kohima deep in the Naga Hills, with his family and his beloved Lhasa apso puppy, Chikkush (an endearing dāk nām for Bengali Homo sapiens, too).

There isn't much of Nagaland in the book, its people, culture, even the sinikbewty—scenic wonders—so beloved of the Bengali traveller. Rather, it mainly purveys racist stoking about how the Nagas love eating dogs, sometimes even pets. The plot has mainly to do with whether our hero's puppy Chikkush will survive the holiday in Nagaland.

◆

The roots of Bengali racism and discrimination are watered by the stupendous sense of self of the Bengali cultural elite and their applauding, aspirational fan club of the Bengali middle classes, one feeding off the other in a congratulatory loop. Of course this is an ultimately fragile imagining where, by diminishing others the Bengali diminishes himself—herself too, certainly—in obtuse xenophobia our women are frequently out there with the men.

But of all the not-Bengali who live around us and among us, special ill will is reserved for the Marwari, the transplanted trading and compound-interest wizards who have travelled the subcontinent and beyond from a patch of the western Indian state of Rajasthan. This relationship is more complicated, the Bengali arguably less gratuitous with rudeness. Indeed, disdain and a sense of superiority may actually flow the other way—from the Marwari to the Bengali. The flow from the Bengali to the Marwari could even be a feeling of hatred drizzled with envy.

The East Bengali will usually say Māurā, the West Bengali Mérō, with a hard rolling 'r' closer to a 'd', but both mean the Marwari, ubiquitous in Kolkata and other cities of Bengal, the traditional business community that in so many ways controls Bengal's economics and has played a prominent part in it for several hundred years. Māurā or Mérō is a self-contained curse.

I would hazard a guess that the hatred of the Marwari probably goes back to the time of the boy-king Siraj-ud-Daulah and his run-in with the legendary bankers, the Jagat Seths, and their collusion with the East India Company representatives to undermine the influence of that nawab of Bengal. As always with 'John Company' there was commercial reasoning: the young nawab had, after a series of disputes, withdrawn concessions given to the Company, limited its sphere of activity, attacked its eastern bastion of Fort William in Kolkata and had several Britons locked up in a small, suffocating room—leading to their death, and the dramatic birth of the 'Black Hole of Calcutta'. The nawab had to go. The Jagat Seth at the time, Madhab Rai, with a cousin, Swaroop Chand, who held the title of maharaja, evidently threw his lot in with the eventual rulers of Bengal. Jagat Seth—banker to the world, a title given by the fading line of Mughal emperors in Delhi, but here was grandeur backed by acumen, by flourishing practice.

As much as the bitterness that exists in contemporary and subsequent Bengali sources, mostly Hindu, about the petulant nawab and his mistreatment of people, in the Bengali imagination, Shirāj, as we sometimes familiarly refer to him, is seen in popular imagination as the last hold out against depredations of John Company, and its subsequent humiliation and domination of Bengal and the Bengali. This was a gigantic step in the embellishment of the British East India Company and the British Indian empire that would follow a hundred years later, in 1857, after the great mutiny (if you're a textbook Indian nationalist feel free to call it the First War of Independence), when the Company's administration was taken over by the British government.

The Company's general, Robert Clive, conspired with—indeed, partnered—the Jagat Seth, effectively treasurers to several nawabs of Bengal, to sway Siraj-ud-Daulah's traitorous general Mir Jafar, and had Polāshi—Plassey—go against the nawab. Ergo: for the Bengali it marked the end of Bengal, all because of a greedy Mérō to whom poyshā, coin, will always ring truer than morjādā, pride, and honour.

This oral and written history of stigma has passed down to generations of Bengalis since Clive's victory at Plassey in 1757. It was repeatedly reinforced in times of crisis. 'The Marwaris were the ones to make the most out of the disruption of normal trading channels during wartime,' the journalist and economic historian Harish Damodaran writes of Marwari acumen during both World War I and World War II. In the Bengali scheme of things this is a gentle estimation. The 'speculative profits' Damodaran writes of were made in commodities like jute and cotton. But none probably hurt the Bengali mind, body and soul like the speculation and hoarding of rice during World War II, precipitated by British policies to stave off a possible Japanese invasion. Along with a few stalwarts of the ruling

Muslim League in Bengal, the Marwari is implicated, historically and, perhaps more damagingly, in the public imagination, in denying vast swathes of the Bengal countryside of grain. Up to 3 million dead is a fair number for complicity, and Marwari heroes, visibly and invisibly close to Mohandas Gandhi, providing moral support, underwriting parts of the freedom movement in a delicate balance of Crown and conscience, haven't quite been able to escape Bengal's Nuremberg of the mind. The famine of 1943 was our Holocaust till the war for Bangladesh twenty-eight years later. And then we had two.

◆

In a Bānglā short story, 'Bostrong Déhi', Nabendu Ghosh, a prolific author and noted screenplay writer in Bombay's film industry, captured the anti-colonial, anti-capitalist rage and revolutionary tonality of the times, the prayer in Sanskrit (Vastram Dehi) an invocation for being blessed with cloth, to be covered, in this context, to cover one's shame. Even more sharply in this context: Please donate cloth (with which to cover the dead).

I read it in a collection of short stories published in early 1946, just months before Direct Action Day, in a Bengal already charged with religious tinder, and starved, ragged after the deprivations of war and induced famine, a time when basic cloth, even shāri, was rationed, sold against a permit. The poor wore the generally coarse cloth when they could get it; the better-off used it to cover quilts and cushions. A black market thrived even for such low quality cloth.

The villain in the story is Chhaganlal Marwari, who after arriving from 'faraway Rajasthan' to 'this forgotten village' to trade in cloth, worked hard for years to arrive at his station. Now he lives in a two-storey house in the middle of the bazaar, lording over the village, 'in the same way English merchants arrived with just one ship full of goods to trade and slowly built fortresses along the coast'. Chhaganlal—Shéth-ji—meets the impoverished farmer Teenkōri, who is desperate to replace the one worn shāri his wife

Hōrimōti has, which she wears all day and then removes at night to cover herself with a short cloth so the shāri lasts a little longer. As the plot unwinds, the Shéth-ji implacably exploits Teenkōri's situation, denying him cloth for his wife, until, driven to desperation by his wife's condition and his own helplessness and shame, he steals cloth from the businessman. Teenkōri is caught, jailed— and ultimately released as villagers beg the Sheth-ji's benevolence. Meanwhile, tormented by guilt, the farmer's wife Hōrimōti kills herself. Nabendu Ghosh ends the story in this way:

> Are a people in shackles to be treated like animals, so weak, so helpless—so very helpless? Mōnish (a local angry young man) wonders as he looks at Hōrimōti. Such tragedy for just a piece of cloth? Mōnish averts his gaze. The crying, the wailing, Hōrimōti's half-naked corpse, makes him ashamed to even be called a man.
>
> And Teenkōri? A terrible wildness comes to his eyes, a rage and hatred a soldier feels when he confronts the enemy. It is as if enemies beyond counting have gathered around him, invisible and yet visible. He wants to tear them apart with his bare hands. He stands there, his bloodlust, his rage at the tip of his fingers, ready to leap, ready to destroy.
>
> He won't cry.

◆

The Birlas, Goenkas, Poddars, Bajorias, Khaitans, Sekhsarias, Somanys and Jhunjhunwalas and several thousand of their blood brothers in Bengal may today own much of the state and vast areas of commercial India to which they spread with their capital nurtured and expanded in Bengal—even as they employed Bengal, paid Bengal salaries and perquisites. With their wealth they may own enormous political reach. They and their kind may even be among the greatest patrons of art and culture in West Bengal, in India; Marwaris even funded Satyajit Ray's breakout movies, and his more successful ones. Some may even dress like a Bengali jōmidār with all the social nuances of the perfect bhodrōlōk, sleeves of the pānjābi perfectly crinkled—gili kora, as we say it—the dhuti exquisitely woven and worn with panache, with its front sharply pleated, like an accordion, and the end of it either folded elegantly over a wrist, or discreetly tucked into the pocket of the pānjābi. All this could happen in grand mansions owned by the Marwari in Kolkata, or spacious bāgān-bāri in the suburbs, or villas by the Hooghly—country houses and 'garden estates', former accoutrements of colonial and Bengali grandees.

But for most Bengalis they remain Mérō. Māurā. Whatever, as long as it's derogatory.

◆

But it is not just not-Bengalis who are at the receiving end of Bengali racism and discrimination. To the urbane Bengali from Kolkata (or any such Bengali in any city), the lady from Medinipur (or any stereotypical outland that is out there, somewhere, away from the city or just away from the urbane Bengali's house) is at best a maid, born and cultivated to serve on account of poverty, the same way the finest ilish or cātlā or chingri is born or cultivated to serve their bounty onto the refined Bengali palate. Her husband is a no-good drunk, her son probably a thief, and the daughter on her way to being a maid or prostitute—or both. They live in the slums by the railway tracks, where else will they stay? But at least with the money we pay them they can eat two meals a day. And what do we feed Nilu-r-mā when she comes to work? That's the same food we eat—prāye āmādér pāt-ér khābār, from our very plates, so what if it is leftovers, and she eats it from a dented aluminium plate while seated on the kitchen floor, don't we also give her some tea when the weather turns cold? And she still complains about her salary in that korkōsh, crude Bānglā, mōné hoy ōnnō kōnō jogōt-é jōnméchhé.

The maid from Medinipur, who seems so alien that she may

be from another planet, may have had a name once. Maybe it was Shundōri, the beautiful one, or Māloti, jasmine. But here she is, and will remain, the mother of Nilu, Nilu-r-mā. At least it's not an insult from the ginni, or the man of the house who might sip overly-steeped tea further destroyed by milk and sugar, and exclaim to the ginni in spousal agreement: 'Only the chhōtōlōk, the gōrib, give such names to their children. Ekdōm mānāye nā. Ki mōné kōré jé nāmgulō dyay.' The ginni may have a name, Shōkuntolā, after the heroine of Kalidasa's play *Abhigyan Shakuntalam*, of the humble yet bewitching lady who won over a king—or did the king win her over? The man of the house may be called Shomōrendrō, the victor. He may be a middle-aged manager of a modest branch of a state-run bank. Shomōrendrō-babu, what were your parents thinking when they named you? Hope, pride, vicarious fantasy and ambition, some love?

But the maid from Medinipur cannot have her name.

Maybe because she is chhōtōlōk.

◆

That brings us to bhodrōlōk.

There is an interesting and revealing description of the bhodrōlōk by the sociologist Rabindra Ray, for several years a faculty member with a cult following in Delhi University. In his excellent study of the Naxalite movement, *The Naxalites and their Ideology*, Ray writes how the idea of bhodrōlōk is rooted in the emergence of a Bengali cultural identity 'based on the ideas, values and outlook of the so-called Bengali Renaissance', which had its impulses in British rule. From it came a certain categorization, 'popular terms in which a person's social standing is typified'.

At the top of that heap is the bhodrōlōk (and the female adjunct, bhodrōmōhilā). It is rooted in the Sanskrit 'bhadra', but that 'Sanskrit sense of fortunate or privileged' shifted into polite, and its 'abstract noun' bhodrōtā, politeness in the Bengali context. From there it travelled the short distance to the nuance of 'civilized', all together taken to mean 'gentleman'. The 'lōk' suffix, also rooted in the Sanskrit 'loka' or 'lokam', denotes a plane of existence, mostly driven by a prefix (swargalok for heaven, for example), and 'people' (the modern usage of loktantra, to signify a government of the people).

The peculiarity of the bhodrōlōk is that it requires a chhōtōlōk, literally small people, but lesser or inferior people would do. Ray adds gōrib lōk, the poor, leading to my minor disagreement with him: there are enough penurious bhodrōlōk about, using a diminished social tag as insurance against being utterly adrift among the gōrib. Indeed, as Ray himself says, bhodrōlōk is really a 'status group'.

There can be little disagreement with Ray's observation that the chhōtōlōk (or the gōrib lōk) 'do not in fact constitute such classes, for they refer not to an internal principle of coherence' but to a difference from the bhodrōlōk 'in terms of which they define themselves'—the bhodrōlōk, that is. To add a touch of facetiousness, while there is a subspecies, bhodrōmōhilā, there is no such thing as a chhōtōmōhilā: the lower, uncultured classes, in Bengal as elsewhere, appear to be gender-neutral in their lowness though it hardly arrives from a politically correct perspective! Chhōtōlōk being the 'labouring' or 'serving' classes is identity enough.

Chhōtōlōk is also a handy perjorative. It is hardly unknown for cadet bhodrōlōk and bhodrōmōhilā to be kept in fighting trim by adepts and elders, with admonitions such as chhōtōlōkér motō kotha bōlbé nā (Don't speak like a chhōtōlōk); or prodded towards the correct dining etiquette with chhōtōlōkér motō kyanō khāchho? (Why are you eating like a chhōtōlōk?). There could be a comment about unbecoming behaviour, Étā ekdom chhōtōlōkāmi which even the most elegant and forgiving translation will render as: this is so chhotolokesque.

Even not-Bengalis have been taken with the bhodrōlōk on-high, as it were. I read in the abstract of a paper for a seminar at the University of Bremen that, in his *Final Report on the Surveys and Settlement Operation in the District of Bakharganj, 1900–1908*,

J. C. Jack, a British officer of the colonial Indian Civil Service, who was district magistrate of Faridpur district for some years, located the bhodrōlōk as 'all who by birth, education or occupation consider themselves above the manual lot but is almost exclusively confined to Hindus of the Brahman, Kayasth and Vaidya caste…'

'Almost exclusively' is a fair qualifier. The Bengali Mussulman wore a bhodrōlōk habit too. Many of the upper echelon of Mussulman society in Bengal, who would rail against Hindu ascendancy after the arrival of the British and the consequent diminishing of the Mussulman power structure in Bengal, were often quite particular about declaring their ashraf lineage. This landed gentry, even nobility, largely looked down upon those who lacked their Afghan or Turki heritage, who were born of the soil of Bengal, and who were largely chāshā; the peasantry is even today used as a collective, not only for a farmer, but the rustic—a form of chhōtōlōk. Over time, as sections of Bengali Mussulman society became more educated and aspirational, the rise towards the elite, towards being sharif, being bhodrōlōk.

There is stratification among bhodrōlōk, Ray encapsulates for us, as bhodrōlōk have largely come to mean mōddhōbittō, or the middle income class. As there is an uchchō-mōddhōbittō, upper middle class (but not an uchchō-bhodrōlōk!), the creamy layer is then buniyādi—a Persian root adjective that means 'having a good foundation' or 'fundamental'—which we use as bōnédi. Then there is shāhébi—the anglicized bhodrōlōk, Bengal's well-known and much-heralded export to the 'professional' white-collar and academic universe in the subcontinent and the world. (Chhōtōlōk exports, far greater than bhodrōlōk exports though far less acknowledged, toil as labourers and household help across much the subcontinent, West Asia and Southeast Asian countries like Malaysia and Indonesia.)

Here, it would be remiss to ignore the bedrock of the bhodrōlōk, the lowest bhodrōlōk in the pyramid, the nimnō-mōddhōbittō—lower-middle class—the kérāni; the clerk, the pejoratively dismissed evolutionary animal from baboo to babu of the modern day, the hero of his home to his spouse's heroine of the hearth, and anti-hero of several angst-ridden Bengali movies. Rabindra Ray dwells upon this at some length, and I was (delightedly) intrigued to see an updated and detailed (and very Bengali) approach by his younger colleague, the author of the paper at Bremen, the academic Sumit Chakrabarti of Presidency University—as Kolkata's Presidency College is now known. Chakrabarti's paper intellectualizes the clerk and seeks to explore 'The "space" that the colonial clerk inhabits', which is 'almost carcerally conditioned by time, and the lack of sovereignty over his body'. He refers to 'Clock time', the nine-to-five pattern of professional work, was introduced in Bengal by the imperial government, for the first time in the nineteenth century, and that the 'body' that was most affected by this socio-cultural change (the discipline of 'time') was that of the clerk, who was immensely fettered by the pattern of work. Low salary, lack of opportunities for improvement, little scope for social interaction confined the clerk to a limited representational 'space'.

Such a substratum of bhodrōlōk received short shrift, according to Chakrabarti, in general discussions on the mass of middle-class bhodrōlōk especially in the time of genesis of the bhodrōlōk—nineteenth-century Bengal.

Chakrabarti also seeks to explore whether the clerk-bhodrōlōk was breaking out of his imposed confines; as he puts it, 'to see if the clerk was secretly discovering a heterotopia of his own'. This is a Foucauldian premise—what bhodrōlōk can resist the tug of a French philosopher, in this case Michel Foucault, who theorized 'other places', away from the everyday, which the left-leaning love to call 'non-hegemonic'.

But that doesn't dilute the premise of bhodrōlōk-utopia, a hegemonic world quite of its own.

◆

Bhodrōlōk even curse differently, Ray wryly notes. Among shāhébi bhodrōlōk 'abuse is customarily showered in English', and 'vernacular abuse' other than shālā (literally, wife's brother, but encompassing the English 'shit' or the more modern 'shithead') or hārāmjādā (from the Arabic haramzada, meaning scoundrel or bastard), is rare. Other bhodrōlōk males, though, 'both in their talk amongst themselves and with lower orders,' and among chhōtōlōk, 'the most common abusive word as also the most insulting is bōkā chōdā.' Idiot fucker. The slur is not about a sexual act but a sexual act being performed with a person with low intelligence, a fool, the lowest of the low in the intellectual food chain; arguably even worse than 'illiterate', which is already a terrible state of non-being. Among friends bōkā chōdā can even be a term of endearment.

The curious and pervasive creature that is the bhodrōlōk is in many ways the defining species of Bengali, with its distinguishing features and a system of values, as Ray puts it:

> And that is the inordinately high status accorded to purely intellectual occupations, and this is despite the relatively weak incidence of Brahmanism in the orthodox sense. To anyone acquainted in any degree with the culture, the strikingly high status occupied by the 'intellectual' is a commonplace and constitutes an element of the effeminacy ascribed to Bengalis by non-Bengalis. This high status and an intellectual tradition that is often invoked as its origin and legitimation is, indeed a matter of pride to the [bhodrōlōk].

As ever.

7

Dāpōt, domōn
Domination

If the maid from Medinipur, who speaks Bāngla though with a loud, well, Medinipur accent and peculiarities of pronunciation— as peculiar as those employed by middle-class grandees from Kolkata: that is blasphemy to suggest, while Medinipur's linguistic meridian is plain boorish—imagine the plight of those who are firmly of the territory of West Bengal but whose first language is not Bāngla. Those who are today a part of the territory because of political draughtsmanship. The Santal, Oraon, Munda to the west of the state in Birbhum, Purulia, Bankura, and those transplanted to the Dooars in the north to work in tea gardens as coolies and tea-pluckers. The Rabha and Koch-Rajbongshi who lead lives of slow socio-economic and political oblivion near Jalpaiguri and in Cooch Behar (also known as Koch Bihar), and like the former, have found little political expression except in intermittent rebellion against the state. Here illiteracy, ill health, and joblessness remain among the highest in West Bengal.

Then there are the Lepchas and Bhutias who are subsumed by the Bengalis and Nepalis alike in the Darjeeling hills.

Nearly forty tribes call West Bengal home. It's largely a home of impoverishment, and ignorance of their ways and means by the Bengali. A home of indifference.

◆

In a way there was no escape possible for the province of Tripura in far-eastern India. It was not long ago the kingdom of Tripura, bound by Bengal to its north, west and south; to the east a slice of Cachar, the southernmost tip of Assam, and a slice of the Lushai Hills district (later to become the state of Mizoram). The Manikya kings ruled in a nearly unbroken line since the fifteenth century—the thirteenth century, if you consider the semi-mythical Ratna Fa—until 1949. The current titular king, Pradyot Manikya, told me he identifies himself as Tiprasa, as the province's indigenous collective of peoples, mostly of Tibeto-Burman stock, call themselves. Tiprasa as an identity is more inclusive than Borok, insists Pradyot, because it includes people beyond the Tripuri tribes who have immigrated over the past several centuries. It's an important nuance because this identity is distinct from Tripura's overwhelming Bengali identity.

In 1949, the queen regent, Kanchan Prava Devi, Pradyot's grandmother, signed a treaty of accession to India. For all practical purposes it stopped being Twipra, the land by the water, jettisoned the British-colonial Hill Tipperah, and emerged fully as Tripura, the Sanskritized, and mythical triple city-realm of earth, sky and heaven to which the original conjoining of 'tui' and 'pra' in the Kokborok language was as different as earth and sky.

The name wasn't all that would change. Nearby Bengal had become East Pakistan. Tripura went from being majority indigenous Borok people—mainly Tripuri, Reang, Noatia, Halam, besides other tribes—and some Meitei (Manipuri) to being majority Bengali. Between 1941 and 1951, years of the decadal census, the percentage of tribal folk in Tripura dropped from a little over 53 per cent to a little over 37 per cent. By 1981, it had dropped below 30 per cent. The census of 2011 shows the tribal population hovering above 30 per cent. Today, instead of East Pakistan it is Bangladesh to its north, west and south. The region is almost-Myanmar, or almost-Southeast Asia. It is also an intimate part of Banglasphere.

'The final Partition of India was a disaster for Tripura,' as journalist and longtime analyst of Northeast India and Bangladesh affairs Subir Bhaumik puts it. Tripura, he maintains, became an 'insignificant little pariah in India's backyard'. Bhaumik, who has East Bengal roots and passionately calls Tripura home, meant this largely as Partition robbing Tripura of a direct link with what is sometimes known as mainland India, with residents of Tripura required to either fly to Kolkata, or to travel several days by bus and train to reach places beyond Guwahati—Kolkata, New Delhi and elsewhere. Contact with East Pakistan eventually petered out, including flights from Agartala to East Pakistan. (It's true—these existed for several years after Partition. Not many recall, for instance, that Indian Airlines used to fly from Agartala to Dhaka's old airport at Tejgaon and to Khulna. In fact a Fokker F-27 Friendship aircraft that had taken off on a scheduled flight on April 1969 from Agartala to Khulna crashed while landing, killing all forty passengers and four crew members.)

Trade and industry remained basic. Agriculture was for decades the primary activity. Only in this millennium would Tripura's resources like natural gas really come of age, and new geopolitical realities would spark growth and hope and links leveraging Banglasphere, and Bangladesh—but that is for a little later.

Meanwhile, Bengalis swamped Tripura, arriving as refugees from East Pakistan as a result of communal violence even in the years after 1946 and 1947, and wars with India, in varying annual waves of hundreds, thousands, tens of thousands and, sometimes, hundreds of thousands. In 1952, close to a quarter of a million refugees poured in, dwarfing even the near two hundred thousand of a year earlier. Pakistan's piecemeal, drawn-out conflict with India over 1964–1965 drew more than a hundred thousand. Pakistan's butchery in 1971 opened the floodgates. Tripura's population of about 1.5 million at the time—already majority Bengali—swelled by a third, according to a US State Department memo to President John F. Kennedy. *Dōinik Shongbād*, a daily newspaper in Agartala, in mid-1971, estimated refugees at nearly 1.3 million. Nearly all were Bengalis.

Some were Meiteis, seeking sanctuary in Tripura instead of

Manipur further to the east for the most curious of reasons. In a way it was home. Besides forming alliances with other royal houses of the subcontinent, the kings of Tripura had for centuries married princesses of the royal houses of Manipur, from its nobility, and, quite frequently, even Meitei 'commoners'.

To be fair, the Bengali influx wasn't always a case of an invitation taken beyond every bound of expectation—even if caused by political and communal chaos beyond its borders. Tripura's kings encouraged, for entirely practical reasons, the arrival of Bengali administrators, some of whom rose to prominence in the service of monarchs as key secretaries and advisers, for instance, and teachers, even cultivators. They helped the kingdom. The kings welcomed the arts and culture from elsewhere, and were partial in several ways to Bengali influence, including the language. Indeed, the *Rajmala*, a chronicle of the kings of Tripura, begun in the mid-fifteenth century during the rule of Dharma Manikya I, was commissioned to be written in Bānglā in 1431 CE. This is perhaps the earliest instance of a formal history of Tripura written in Bānglā.

Rabindranath Tagore was an honoured and beloved guest of three generations of Tripura's royals. They were fans of his work, beginning with Bir Chandra Manikya. A story goes like this: The king was desolate after the death of his queen, Bhanumati, in 1881, and found solace, a certain understanding of his state of mind, in the young Tagore's poem 'Bhognō Hridoy'—A Broken Heart. He sent word of appreciation to the Tagore mansion in Kolkata's Jorasanko and offered to print his works, on hearing that the poet was being sneered at by established Bengali littérateurs. They met several times in Kolkata and elsewhere. His successor, Radhakishore Manikya, invited Tagore to Tripura and he went there several times. Two kings who followed, Birendra Kishore Manikya, and the last ruler of Tripura, Bir Bikram Kishore Mankiya treated Tagore with the greatest respect. Indeed, the Tripura treasury helped Visva-Bharati, Tagore's dream university take shape, and budgeted expenses for it. Tagore gushed, as numerous Tripura government information sources delightedly proclaimed: 'When the woodlands of Tripura have sent out invitations to their floral feast through their courier of the south wind, I have come as a friend.'

Not all Bengalis did.

◆

In any case, Bengalis or Meiteis, these were people fleeing the destruction of their lives and livelihoods. Tripura took them all in for several decades, during what is called the Regency Period, when Kanchan Prava Devi ran affairs on behalf her minor son after the death of her husband, a period that lasted from 1947 to Tripura's formal accession to India in 1949; and after.

Now Bengalis control everything—politics, administration, trade, political and socio-cultural discourse, even the language of office and official communication and education. The official languages of Tripura are Bānglā and Kok Borok—the latter is a matter of form more than substance; majoritarian Bānglā decides its linguistic and parochial weight gain or loss. For a Bengali travelling through the capital Agartala and the larger towns of Tripura is in some ways like passing through a cleaner and less crowded urban Bengal. The signs are everywhere, literally and in other ways. It is easier to find Bengali food in Agartala, even north Indian food, than Borok or other tribal specialities.

All that is away, out of sight of Banglasphere, in reservation-like areas, where tribal-administered autonomous councils with short strings to the Bengali-heavy polity run limited functions. In the late 1970s, an article in *India Today* magazine estimated that a staggering 90 per cent of land that did not belong to government was owned or controlled by non-tribals. Some land that was deeded to Tripuri communities by their former kings, a prescient intervention, was given over to settle refugees—and more was encroached upon. Mainstream Tripura is mainstream Bengali.

Protest was a given. As early as 1967 an indigenous youths' organization, Tripura Upajati Juba Samiti, was formed, with the intention of official recognition for Kok Borok and autonomous tribal councils as encouraged by the Constitution of India. As importantly, perhaps, there was demand for the restoration of traditional tribal lands that successive non-monarchical governments had either given to non-tribal settlers or kept silent about as these were appropriated. In the early 1970s, an angry but half-hearted effort of Tripuri reclamation took root with the Tripura Sena. It took until 1978 with the formation of the armed group, Tripura National Volunteers, or TNV, for the largely Bengali government to pay attention.

Some observers, including Bhaumik, maintain trouble could have been averted had the incoming Left Front Communist government, which took over from the electorally overwhelmed Congress, had nominated a tribal person as chief minister instead of a Bengali. At any rate the communists did try to make amends. In early 1979, they moved to restore to tribals land grabbed by non-tribals, and moved the Tripura Autonomous District Council Bill in the state assembly.

It had the opposite effect. Several hundred Bengalis, grouped under the radical Āmrā Bāngāli, or We are Bengalis, which many felt was a front for another radical Bengali-dominated sect, the secretive Anand Marg—a prominent Bengali journalist termed it 'its own variation of the Ku Klux Klan'—ran riot. By mid-1979, nineteen people had died in altercations with Āmrā Bāngāli members. The movement began by defacing signs not in Bānglā, in Kolkata, and Bengal's larger cities Asansol and Siliguri, even Guwahati. (I recall numerous such defaced signs from my childhood, on storefronts, billboards and even the names of railway stations.) Āmrā Bāngāli once 'raided' Kolkata's airport, as an article put it, to demand announcements be made in Bānglā. This was relatively vanilla chauvinism, as it were. Matters escalated when this so-called Bengali KKK barged into the Communist Party of India (Marxist)'s regional headquarters in Kolkata to protest what they interpreted as the party and the government it led going up against Bengalis in Tripura. And then violence followed in Tripura.

There appeared to be a lot at stake in the minds of the Bengalis. An article in *India Today* by an appalled Sumit Mitra described those times evocatively and colourfully, when Agartala was not the ambitious centre of trade and regional hub of energy resources it positions itself as today:

> Agartala, though seedy in its exterior, is actually flourishing. There are big traders galore, and moneybags, who would finance smuggling operations across the international border, a bare 10 miles away. They are a part of the Bengali gentry, who look upon themselves as 'colonisers' of Tripura. They own large tracts of land, bought from the tribals, 'often in exchange for a glass bangle, or a toy'. The present legislations, specially the autonomous tribal district plan, have naturally upset them.
>
> While (Āmrā Bāngāli) promises them the safety of 'Bangalisthan'…the Marxists face the dilemma of having to retain their base both among the tribals and the non-tribals. But, alleges Nagendra Jamatia, himself a tribal and MLA of the TUJS, 'the Marxists have turned into jelly. They've been so terrorised by the Bengalis that they won't raise a little finger against them'.

Political manoeuvring, police action and the rage of the tribals sorted out that fracas in a while. Anger had taken deep root among the tribals and this spurred them on to speak up and fight. Eighteen hundred people ultimately lost their lives in clashes between tribals and non-tribals—mostly Bengalis. Several thousand homes were destroyed. India's army had to intervene. Even as this fire abated, TNV was up and running, targeting government and Bengali civilians. It would be nearly a decade before TNV entered peace negotiations for a better deal for tribal folk, which some analysts have dismissed as counter-productive. Bhaumik, in his blunt manner, describes it as 'ridiculous', because it provided three more seats to tribals in Tripura's assembly, 'and little else'.

A slew of militant groups sprang up subsequently—and, in an irony that marks see-sawing relations between India and Bangladesh with nearly every change of government in that country—found shelter mainly in the Chittagong Hill Tracts of Bangladesh and sometimes in the plains, in the heartland of the Bengalis. The lessening of militancy and outright attacks against Bengali settlers has taken a mixture of governance and surgical strikes in Tripura and a change of geopolitical equations—the more India-friendly government of Sheikh Hasina, Mujib's daughter, for much of this millennium severely reduced the sanctuary for all manner of rebels against India. (There is persistent enmity between Sheikh Hasina and Khaleda Zia, the widow of General Ziaur Rahman. The two have alternated as premier nearly without a break since the 1990s. Khaleda has made no effort to conceal the tilt towards a purist, radical Islam of her Bangladesh Nationalist Party (BNP), and has quite often taken positions seen as being against India.)

An insider to Tripura's government told me of an incident as we chatted in Agartala in mid-2014, after the end of a seminar seeking to increase Tripura's transit and trade with Bangladesh as well as other nearby countries.

Exasperated by the increasingly vicious incursions of tribal rebels, a top minister reportedly advised the state's security chief to enter Bangladesh and eliminate a particular rebel leader and his base. The direction was adequate.

'Shāirā fyalāō,' he suggested in East Bengali dialect.

Finish it.

But disappointment is far from over for the Tripuri. There is still the matter of being aliens in their own land.

◆

While in these places the Bengali is basically the B-word of domination in nearly every way possible, the Bānglā script is a matter of particular resentment among nationalists in some places—it is seen as a symbol of domination, cultural and otherwise, by outsiders. Take for example, the situation in Manipur. Many Manipuris deeply resent the cultural colonialism they have had to contend with for several hundred years.

I recall a conversation in late 2009 with the Manipuri historian and theatre director Arambam Lokendra at his home in Imphal, the capital of trouble-torn Manipur. Oja, or teacher as he is respectfully called, made clear distinctions between control and contribution when it came to the Bengali influence in Manipur—specifically as it related to the Meitei community that today forms the largest ethnic group in the state of Manipur. He shared his gentle-voiced but definite contempt for how Bengalis had gradually come to dominate the socio-political landscape.

Early arrivals from Bengal (with a generous sprinkling of those from areas of present-day Assam) are thought to date back to the fifteenth century—the history is somewhat vague. They arrived in several waves. An ethnic offshoot, the Bishnupriyas, were and are looked down upon in Manipur by the chauvinists among the majority Meitei as being inferior, born of intermarriage, and such. They were mayang, the reviled foreigner. Here the Manipuri—the Meitei—is ethno-agnostic, *any* outsider is an outsider. The notion of racial and cultural purity is at a premium, and it is surely among the greatest karmic cuts that a people obsessed with racial and cultural purity feel done in by another people obsessed with racial and cultural purity.

This feeds into the inexplicable embrace of Bengali mayang by a Meitei king, and confounds Meitei nationalists like Professor Lokendra. Later arrivals from Bengal gradually worked their way up the power structure because of their knowledge of rituals, of their larger world religion, as it were, compared to the indigenous Sanamahi religion. The capstone arrived with the state's need—the king's need, the professor told me—for a 'much more heightened ritual to theatricalize the authority of the body of the king as representative of the cosmos'. The Brahmins from Bengal provided the theatre and the script.

Conversion to a Vaishnav and caste-ridden Hinduism from the traditional Manipuri practice of Sanamahi followed rapidly when King Pamheiba, who later took on the name Garib Nawaz, declared Hinduism as the state religion in 1720. Those who resisted were punished. Tantric priests then arrived from Sylhet in the 1730s, and enforced a connection with Hinduism over time with claims such as one that Manipur was in fact tied to the Mahabharata. This became an essential component of the new mythology. The priests and other cultural arrivistes propagated the notion that the Pandava warrior Arjuna had a child here, Babrubahan, by marriage to a local princess, Chitrangada. This narrative of Arjuna marrying a local girl was accepted by the early converts, the professor told me, and it later became part of the 'Indian discourse'. The first 'civil society' movement in 1934, the Nikhil Hindu Manipuri Mahasabha, even encouraged prizes for writing such history—using the Bānglā script, which had over several centuries become the script of application. In later years, Meitei radicals and Sanamahi practitioners—often the same—went to Odisha to photograph and document a village called Manipur, which records a legend of Arjuna's visit, in an attempt to discredit the Bengali-Indian whitewashing of their history.

Professor Lokendra's disdain of Bengali doesn't extend to Bengalis who had, in his mind, something to offer Manipur—theatre, for example, perhaps his deepest love. He has produced thirty-five plays, favouring an experimental approach. Here he freely acknowledges the impact Bengali avant-garde playwright and theatre guru Badal Sircar had on him and his colleagues, fellow playwrights and directors, actors in Manipur—indeed, across India.

'Badal-dada was such an influence in our lives; we had a workshop here with him in 1972,' the professor's eyes lit up as he spoke of those times. 'He told us about the clogging nature of the proscenium, he denied the proscenium'—the professor spoke of Sircar's dislike of the stylized arch that separates a typical modern stage from the audience, preferring instead free-flowing, interactive theatre spaces. '"We have to go to the people," he said. He chose *Spartacus* as our production; I played a part. Kanhailal (Heisnam Kanhailal, a theatre legend in Manipur), my friend and peer, interacted with him. He discovered the artistic exploration of the body of the Manipuri actor; and humanistic concerns of oppressed people—that was where he began his creative expressions. I was interested in political expression: I did Bertolt Brecht, for example, various things against the discourse of the state.'

The professor and I could have been seated in a smoke-filled cafe in Kolkata, so carried away with our ideas that we ignored the terrible tea and coffee, milky and sweet with a film on the surface that would prevent a fly from sinking and often did, with slowly turning ceiling fans helping waft thoughts of a new world order through a cloud of cigarette smoke.

As it was, for some of our conversation we were at Aryan Theatre, the professor's stomping ground for several years. A troupe were doing a pre-final 'run through' of a play to be staged to mark the tenth anniversary of protest icon Irom Sharmila's fast to remove from Manipur the Armed Forces (Special Powers) Acts (AFSPA), a legislation that offered immunity and impunity to the armed forces. They had chosen a trans-adaptation of Mahasweta Devi's *Hājār Chūrāshīr Mā*, a story set in the times of the Naxalite movement. The Mother of Prisoner Number 1084. This is just one work from her jaw-dropping repertoire of over a hundred published works, novels, short stories and journals—a writer who lived the life of an activist, and is considered by many to be among the greatest pro-tribal writers in the world besides a literary giant of Bengal, of India, in her own right. Mahasweta Devi inspired several generations of women and men to adopt socially conscious lives and professions—from researching the lives of Ādibāshīs with a view to affirmative action (as their guru did), to chronicling depredations of the state and its handmaidens in business against often-powerless citizens at the margins of society.

Sircar, and Mahasweta—whom Professor Lokendra called Ma

Mahasweta, mother Mahasweta, a gesture of the greatest respect in Manipur—would have loved the basic nature of Aryan Theatre. The way to it was wedged between two shops, the entrance to it through a rickety wooden door that opened onto the centre of a hall the size of a modest house. The hall was rundown, mostly empty. Plastic and steel folding chairs were scattered across the packed-earth floor. The stage was to our right as we walked in. Onstage, microphones were suspended from rafters. A large speaker faced the audience. The walls were blackened. Everything wore a dilapidated look.

Professor Lokendra, who was effusively greeted by the director, S. Rajen, explained that the theatre burnt down in 1996, and hadn't really recovered. But it seemed adequate, and the crew made it resolutely pure in the starkness of its poverty.

The three of us were shown to a front row of chairs. Before the lights were dimmed we were offered plates of kachori—'Made by the Marwaris,' the professor said with a smile—and roshōgōlla—another smile. 'Brought by the Bengalis,' we said in unison.

The rehearsal began for *Lalhouba Amagee Mama*. Stage right—from the perspective of the audience—was the wall of a living room. There was a shelf with a few books, bric-à-brac, a phone. Simple cane furniture completed the minimalist ensemble. Stage left was free space. At the back was a tiered platform.

The phone rang; a recorded crackle. A lady rushed in to take the call. She was lit with a spotlight as she mostly listened, occasionally responding with halting questions until she was suddenly quietened. An elderly gentleman entered, followed by a younger man. The older man queried her in a garrulous tone until she, without turning, numbly delivered the news. The mood changed. Fade out.

The scene shifted to the back of the stage. Four men came in and lay down side by side on the stage, and were covered by the stage crew with white sheets. The lady from the first scene was present, standing mutely to one side. A man in a police uniform standing on the top tier spoke loudly in a harsh, emphatic voice, ordering her to identify a body. She passed by two wailing women to a body at the end of the line. An orderly whipped the cloth off the bodies. She touched the face of the corpse nearest to her and started to weep, then she slowly moved centre stage and kneeled down, sobbing. Then she let out a prolonged wail that transformed into a scream. Fade out.

We could be in Kolkata.

◆

Just as in Tripura, the Bengali script is today seen as one of domination in Manipur, conflated with the sense of nationalism against dominion by the Republic of India since 1949. That year nationalistic Meiteis were deeply angered by India's formal absorption of the kingdom of Manipur by a treaty of accession, which they felt was done under pressure against the wishes of many Manipuris. Their wish was autonomy after several decades of domination by the British. This perception of denial of due respect of Manipur's identity transformed over the years into non-violent nationalistic movements of protest and, later, in the 1980s into vicious rebellion, kept alive by brutal reprisals by the government, intense militarization, and the mistreatment, torture, rape and killing of civilians and suspected rebels alike.

Alongside demands of autonomy and outright freedom from India, and a revival of Sanamahi which draws greatly from nature worship and animism, Manipuri nationalists have fought in some cases to recreate history to a suitable self-image, and jettison the script— Bānglā—with which much of the history was written. This move to formally have the local government accept Meitei Mayek as the official script for writing Meiteilon—or Manipuri, as it is now commonly known—came about in 2005 in a violent manner. In April that year protesters of a pro-Meitei Mayek group backed, according to widespread local assumption, by an influential and quite puritanical rebel outfit, Kangleipak Communist Party, set fire to the Central Library in Imphal. An estimated 1,45,000 books and manuscripts, mostly using Bānglā script, were lost.

A month later, Manipur's legislature formally voted in Mayek as an official script of communication and instruction. School curriculum began to change over the following year, beginning with junior school, and working their way up. Newspapers using Bānglā script began to include articles written in Mayek. Signage and advertising have since used Mayek and English—as with the rest of India, this language of colonialism has survived as a link language: media, government, schools, writers and rebels freely use it.

The abhorrent act of book-burning—some moderate Meitei intellectuals called it 'Taliban-like'—was accepted by several prominent ultranationalist intellectuals and writers as a necessary act of sacrifice, including of their own works, written in Bānglā script, that would gradually face extinction unless re-written in Mayek. Several media persons blandly conveyed the view of language activists that it was right to seek revenge, in a way, for righting the wrong of the Manipuri script being abused and banished in the eighteenth century. Nobody suggested the less cynical alternative of actually transcripting books into Mayek before burning them but, as ever, when scripted hatred and nationalistic pride takes root there is little room for civilized behaviour. Anger and angry purpose take over.

And domination, of course. Today, the non-Meitei people of Manipur, who mostly live in the hilly regions, a world away from the nearby plains the Meiteis call homeland, have to put up with Meitei domination. These tribes, who have little cultural or linguistic connect with Meiteis, have to kowtow to Meiteilon being the official language of the state, and being included as Manipuri, with Meitei culture, history and myths being given the status of the apex culture, history and myths.

This is something the Bengalis know all about.

◆

There must be a reason why the Bengali is so aggressively Bengali, so eager to prove his or her self-worth, so determined to dismiss others as lesser beings. If an individual in therapy were to display such behaviour, it is likely he or she would be diagnosed as suffering from an inferiority complex. Perhaps this is a trait that springs from having been at a disadvantage or powerless for a while. Call it a sort of Versailles Syndrome, the pushback that birthed National Socialism in Weimar Germany, and gave rise, eventually, to Hitler. The Bengali Hindu revival certainly began as a reaction to several hundred years of Islamic domination after Bengali kingdoms were over-run by Islamic invaders, the consequent creamy layer being resolutely Islamic. As we have seen, this then segued almost seamlessly to the British, who rapidly emerged as the inheritors of the Mughals.

Kolkata, the quintessentially Bengali metropolis, is a creation of the British. It must have been an uneasy legacy living in those times of apartheid, Bengalis segregated from their rulers' race in their own land, viewed as little more than providers of commodities and taxes and clerical services to the British empire. Being officially reviled as troublemakers and being emasculated as martial wimps after the mutiny of 1857, when the British, using a continuing and brilliantly executed policy of divide-and-rule, began to play up certain races as possessing martial prowess—the Punjabis, Gurkhas, Kumaonis, for instance, who helped them quell the mutiny and the combustion it triggered in several areas of central and northern India. Other races—notably the Bengali—were now redesignated for all practical purposes as pen-pushers, barely a step-up from the reviled 'half-caste' Anglo-Indian, kept subjugated and at a distance by the British (unlike, say, the Portuguese colonials in India, who actively practised assimilation) and 'natives' alike.

The groundwork for the new typecasting of the Bengali was done by those like the erudite Macaulay who, as you have read, glorified Bengal while vilifying the Bengalis at the same time. Take, for instance, this takedown of the Bengalis:

The Castilians have a proverb, that in Valencia the earth is water and the men women; and the description is at least equally applicable to the vast plain of the Lower Ganges. Whatever the Bengalee does he does languidly. His favourite pursuits are sedentary. He shrinks from bodily exertion; and, though voluble in dispute, and singularly pertinacious in the war of chicane, he seldom engages in a personal conflict, and scarcely ever enlists as a soldier. We doubt whether there be a hundred genuine Bengalees in the whole army of the East India Company. There never, perhaps, existed a people so thoroughly fitted by nature and by habit for a foreign yoke.

It couldn't have been easy learning of it, being vilified for belonging to the very place Bengalis had built for hundred of years with and against the flow of nature, and the sweat of millions of farmers and artisans. It couldn't have been easy being educated, on your way to becoming one of a growing mass of bhodrōlōk only to have the very system that facilitated the move do you in.

◆

And several decades later, it must not have been pleasant receiving a series of masterclasses on ruling and ruling races from George Nathaniel Curzon, Lord Curzon of Kedleston (later the Earl Curzon of Kedleston), viceroy and governor general of India for nearly seven years until November 1905.

It isn't much of a surprise that the sometimes garrulous Curzon would choose to tear into the Bengalis, as he notably did at the convocation of Calcutta University on 11 February 1905. To be fair to him this Borōlāt never held back his disdain of the natives. Subjects of the British Indian empire were repeatedly lectured on the wise ways of empire bitingly laced with references to the supremacy of the race of the overlords, and the fact that viceroy, Lord Curzon, was the biggest 'lord'—lāt—in India. Some critics might say this obsessive behaviour, this continual need to place himself above all—even though he had arguably the most coveted post in the empire after the monarch, the prime minister and the secretary of state for India—stemmed from childhood experiences. As the historian Niall Ferguson writes in *Empire: How Britain Made the Modern World*, young George's governess appeared to have treated him quite brutally, and occasionally forced him to parade around his home village wearing a dunce cap. On it were variously inscribed the words *sneak*, *liar* and *coward*. All this, and an indifferent father, evidently affected young George deeply.

At any rate, between all his lectures, being an active player in the Great Game, supervising the management of a famine, shooting tigers and such at the invitation of various pliant maharajas, commissioning the restoration of Taj Mahal, and establishing the Archaeological Survey of India—even the most cynical must thank him for the last two—as we know, Curzon found time to sign off on the first partition of Bengal, between July 1905, when he announced it, and October 1905, when it took place. The religious template for future strife was set—even the reuniting of Bengal in 1911 after consistent public furore would not be able to prevent the subsequent, second division of Bengal along religious lines.

But before that was the convocation. Some observers maintain Curzon, no stranger to lighting fires, lit a fire with a direct challenge to Kolkata's intellectuals and student body—by extension, to that of greater Bengal and India. It hit home, as it was probably meant to, though it did not quite achieve the further subjugation that Curzon may have hoped for.

Curzon had already set the bar for condescension quite high in his 1902 convocation speech: 'Neither can it be India for the Indians alone,' the viceroy offered his worldview about growing nationalism—and increasing militancy of that nationalism. 'The last two centuries during which the British have been in this country cannot be wiped out. They have profoundly affected the whole structure of national thought and existence. They have quickened the atrophied veins of the East with the life-blood of the West.'

As enraged as many of Calcutta's best and brightest (in a chain reaction of condescension in those days taken as Bengal's best and brightest) had been at this, Curzon's 1905 speech is believed to have tipped things over for many, firmly pointed them to the direction of making the British insecure and seeking to boot them out with any method at hand.

Keeping the colonial project firmly in his heads-up-display, as it were, Curzon warmed up by arriving at a segment on truthfulness and falsehoods, the simple and complex, and criticized those 'who encourage this tendency end by becoming two human beings in the same form, like the Doctor Jekyll and Mr. Hyde of Stevenson's story.' He then inflicted his first salvo of arrogance during that lecture. 'I hope I am making no false or arrogant claim when I say that the highest ideal of truth is to a large extent a Western conception.' He tried to qualify matters a bit. 'I do not thereby mean to claim that Europeans are universally or even generally truthful, still less do I mean that Asiatics deliberately or habitually deviate from the truth. The one proposition would be absurd, and the other insulting.' He qualified things further, to bring matters back to just being plain insulting: 'But undoubtedly truth took a high place in the moral codes of the West before it had been similarly honoured in the East, where craftiness and diplomatic wile have always been held in much repute. We may prove it by the common innuendo that lurks in the words "Oriental diplomacy", by which is meant something rather tortuous and hypersubtle. The same may be seen in Oriental literature. In your epics truth will often be extolled as a virtue; but quite as often it is attended with some qualification, and very often praise is given to successful deception practised with honest aim.'

While this was a bit rich coming from the viceroy of an empire crafted with wiles, deception and force, and a culture that thought up the orientalist phrase 'oriental diplomacy' in the first place, Curzon had barely begun. He launched into a diatribe against nationalist thought and meetings of the time, with a compliment to Bengali erudition and intellect that somehow felt like a slap. (Thāsh kōré, to use a Bānglā description for application of a sound slap.)

Now in India there are two sets of people, the reticent and the eloquent. I daresay you know to which class the people in this part of the country belong. I am sometimes lost in admiration at the facility with which they speak in a foreign language, and I envy the accomplishment. All I say to you is, do not presume upon this talent. Do not believe that the man who can make a speech is necessarily a statesman; do not let your fluency run away with your powers of thought. Above all, do not think that speech is ever a substitute for action. The man who in his village or his town devotes himself to the interests of his fellow countrymen, and by example and by effort improves their lot, is a greater benefactor than the hero of a hundred platforms.

He spoke of the importance of the 'native element' and 'native sentiment' as being a stimulus and check to government, but belittled 'manufactured public opinion in India', which was 'barren and ineffective because it merely represented the partisan views of a clique, and was little more than noise and foam.'

After this seemingly liberal paean to balance, even if from the point of view of the Crown, it was time to set up the coup de grâce. Curzon spoke in a seemingly conciliatory manner with undercurrents of conceit strong enough to pull the unwary into the Bay of Blandishment, as he referred to suggestions that 'India is a conquered nation and that Indians are condemned to be hewers of wood and drawers of water. I smile at the extravagance.' The viceroy allowed silkily:

> ...but I am also pained at the imputation. When I see High Court Judges—some of them in this hall—Ministers of Native States wielding immense powers, high executive and judicial officers in our own service, leaders of thought and ornaments of the Bar, professors and men of science, poets and novelists, the nobility of birth and the nobility of learning, I do not say that every Indian corporal carries a Field Marshal's baton in

his knapsack, for the prizes come to few, but I say that none need complain that the doors are shut. To all of you who have the ambition to rise I would say—Use your student days to study the history and circumstances of your race. Study its literature and the literature of Europe, and particularly of the country whose fate is bound up with your own. Compare the two; see what are their lessons or their warnings.

Then, this near-demagogue offered a paternal suggestion of immense chutzpah, not for 'perfervid nationalism of the platform, but the self-sacrificing ardour of the true patriot'. This man who would in a few months push through the division of Bengal along religious lines urged students and Bengal's elite alike to 'avoid the tyranny of faction and the poison of racial bitterness', to not arm against 'phantasms', but fight against 'the real enemies to the welfare of your people, which are backwardness, and ignorance, and antiquated social prescriptions.'

'Look up,' Curzon urged, not down. 'Look forward, not backward. Look to your own country first and foremost, and do not waste time in whistling for the moon. Be true Indians—that is the prompting of nationality.'

Then came caveat imperium.

'But while doing so strive also to be true citizens of the Empire; for circumstances have thrown you into a larger mould than that of race, and have swept you into the tides that direct the world,' Curzon began his conclusion.

As nationality is larger than race, so is Empire larger than nationality. Race weakens and gets overlaid in the passage of time and gives place to broader conceptions.

After effectively placing the English—the British—as a race above the Indian, and here particularly, the Bengali, he moved to dismiss a sense of emergent, even thriving, nationalism.

For instance, in India I see the claim constantly made that a man is not merely a Bengali, or an Uriya, or a Mahratta, or a Sikh, but a member of the Indian nation. I do not think it can yet be said that there is any Indian nation, though in the distant future some approach to it may be evolved.

Outrage was truly lit with Curzon's last words:

> However that may be, the Indian is most certainly a citizen of the British Empire. To that latter unit he already belongs. How to adjust race to nationality, and how to reconcile nationality with Empire—that is the work which will occupy the British rulers of this country for many a long year to come. I am one of those who believe that it can be accomplished without detriment to race or nationality, and with safety to the Empire. I want the Indian people to play their part in this great achievement and to share the results.

Curzon would soon return home. Meanwhile Bengal lay divided, and angry. Some say what is often called Bengal's Age of Fire, Ōgni Jūg, began then.

◆

If West Bengal's treatment of those not of Bengali origin has remained less than salutary, Bangladesh hasn't done that much better. Lost in the enormity of data that suggests 98 per cent of those in Bangladesh speak Bānglā as their mother tongue, those who do not, the 2 per cent that translates to nearly 3 million people are adrift ethnically and politically—more adrift than the socially and economically disadvantaged primary speakers of Bānglā. As in West Bengal, the forever project of inclusion and respect to those not-Bengali touches a number of ethnic groups. (Except, of course, the tiny robust handful of Marwaris who have a canny ability to survive and thrive in any circumstance—their ability to go with the flow, sometimes engineer a flow, and their enterprise and money have for long spoken as meaningfully as any language of nationalism in Bengal since the time of the Jagat Seths and earlier. An estimated

700 remain, after surviving the riots and wars of 1964, 1965 and 1971, led by families like Tularam and Dugar.)

Being not-Bengali is as much a socio-political disadvantage in Bangladesh as it is in West Bengal, but among these the worst off non-persons are surely of the 'Bihari' community, as the Urdu-speaking group of an estimated 3,00,000 are known, stranded in Bangladesh since 1971. Bangladesh does not want them; and neither evidently does Pakistan. They generally hold down minor jobs, as barbers, small-time butchers, motor mechanics, labourers and maids—at the very fringe of society. The tag of 'killers of 1971' hangs over them, and follows them through their lives in squalid camps in Dhaka and elsewhere. Dhaka's Mohammadpur area houses the largest such group. Ironically it is named Geneva Camp, a reminder of the horrors of 1971 that made a mockery of the Geneva Convention. Since then the community has not escaped the taint of being 'collaborators'.

After a couple of generations, many of them have learned to speak Bānglā as fluently as the native-born, and blend in with the Bengali mainstream and derive the benefits due citizens. Some have escaped, on the strength of Bangladeshi passports, to West Asia from where they send home money to alleviate the lives of bare subsistence of those left behind.

There are the Garos in northern Mymensingh—they and their various dialects are collectively referred to as Mandi. There are the Khasias in Sylhet, resident from before the time the British drew borders; these mirror the inhabitants of the state of Meghalaya immediately to the north where they are called Khasi. These Bangladeshi not-Bengalis eke out lives of barebones sustenance, living on government handouts if things are good and, in places, the benevolence of forest rangers who control their immediate fate. Shillong, the capital of Meghalaya and cradle of the Khasis, seems light years away if you visit the Khasia enclaves in Sreemangal, a little over 80 'kilo'—a charming Bangladeshi diminution of kilometre—south of Sylhet.

In India, they have a state—Meghalaya, a very Sanskrit 'abode of the clouds', not Hynniewtrep, for instance, the seven huts of Khasi genesis mythology, as it may have upset the Garo and other indigenous inhabitants of that abode. Meghalaya is a geographical entity in the constitutionally united states of India, earned through right of ethnicity and language but mostly, to carve itself away from the callousness and snobbery of the Assamese. (Ah, the infinite loops of karma: the Assamese dislike the Bengalis, the Khasis and Garos dislike the Assamese and Bengalis and everyone not them, and so on, in an endless play of majoritarianism, of a sense of identity that so quickly turns to ethnic machismo. Meghalaya, for instance, has seen brutal rioting reduce the numbers of the non-indigenous Assamese, Bengalis and Nepalis.)

Anyway, in Bangladesh, the Khasias, like most minorities, are a curiosity. At the Lawachara Forest Reserve in Sreemangal, a short distance from tea gardens and a golf resort frequented on weekends by yuppies and businessmen from Dhaka, the handful of Khasias who live in bamboo, thatch and tin-roof huts suffer tourists tramping through the forest, photographing their little church, children, and piles of betel leaf, the men and women, like their brethren to the north in Meghalaya, chewing kwai—lime spread on betel leaf and topped with betel nut wrapped into a mildly soporific, warming pancake.

There are Dalui, Koch and Rajbongshi in Mymensingh and Dinajpur—as there are in West Bengal. The Santal tribes are among the largest not-Bengali groups in Bangladesh, brought into this region as labourers, and as taken-for-granted with their lives and livelihoods as in West Bengal. There are the Mundas who live in the northwest and southwest of the country, brought over by zamindars and landlords from the region of the Chhota Nagpur plateau in India from the nineteenth century on to clear forests, work the land. Some Mundas to the south are even called bunō by Bengali inhabitants. 'Wild' is a charming word if you're obnoxious and racist. Few would accuse the average Bengali of not being so.

The Meitei, 'Mōnipuri' in Bangladesh, live quiet lives in Sylhet and the Sreemangal area, making a living from handloom weaves, temples unobtrusively deep inside the hamlets, far from the ultra-political majoritarian mojo across the international border, in Manipur, (where the Meiteis are frequently accused of discrimination against minorities such as the Nagas and Kukis).

The furthest I've seen a 'Tripuri' in Bangladesh go to assert an identity is a discreetly placed postcard or calendar showing the Ujjayanta Palace in Agartala, where the royal family of Tripura, proudly of the Borok people, lived until the government of India nationalized it and several other palaces after Tripura acceded to the Indian union in 1949. You already know what the Bengali migrations since 1946 did to the Borok and other not-Bengali folk in Tripura, their home of several hundred years before 'Bengali' was even a collective.

And, of course, the oriental face in Bangladesh (not the Chinese, who strut around in packs in the major construction sites and ports of Bangladesh, clear as to who really is regionally superior) is to the average Bangladeshi, a Chakma. There are others: the Mro or Murung, Khumi, Pankho, Bawn or Bom, Marma and Rakhain—with their origin in the Rakhine area further south in Myanmar. To all but the anthropologist, historian and socio-political analyst they may as well be Chakma. In Bangladesh, I've even heard the handful of Nepalis, whose forbears came over as soldiers and guards, referred to as the Chakma. (In West Bengal, an oriental face is 'Nepali', which dialect can distort to 'Nyapāli'. Either way, a lesser being.)

The Chakmas and their counterparts who live in what was for long known as the Chittagong Hill Tracts—administratively, now the districts of Rangamati, Khagrachari and Bandarban—abutting Tripura and Mizoram in India, and Myanmar, have hardly had it easy. The government of Bangladesh has done everything in its power to subsume the indigenous with its own definition of what is indigenous in order to ensure that the Bengali in Bangladesh remain indubitably indigenous everywhere in the country. In a way it is a paranoid, controlling anti-secessionist reaction to even the slimmest risk that, were they to acknowledge inhabitants other than the Bengalis in any place in Bangladesh, they would run the risk of losing control over this ethnic—and ethno-territorial entity, as it were—at some point. Bangladesh even amended its constitution to bolster its claim. (India has freely permitted states and administrative units on linguistic and ethnic lines, but brutally dealt with ideas of secession. Interesingly, various Indian states have perpetuated a Bangladesh-like strategy of domination and finessing of law and rhetoric to ensure the primacy of the largest ethnic group.)

As I read in a journal, the Press Information Department of the government of Bangladesh issued a release in mid-2014 specifically asking media to avoid using the word Ādibāshī—the advisory was later removed from its website, but a major Dhaka-based newspaper tracked the development. Media managers basically gave a nudge to correct what, through the accurate use of language—Ādibāshī are, after all, 'the early inhabitants' or 'original inhabitants', earlier than the Bengalis at any rate—and a streak of political correctness and conscience, many among the country's media used routinely. The government had made the awkwardness of Ādibāshī disappear by a sleight of wordplay. Apparently, this is what the government now wanted—politely worded, but emphatic in its Orwellian, even China-like, intent:

> Although according to the 15th amendment of the constitution of Bangladesh there is no existence of Ādibāshīs in the country at present, at various times, especially on the International Ādibāshī Day declared by the United Nations [this is the United Nations' International Day of the World's Indigenous Peoples, marked each 9 August] the word Ādibāshī continues to be used repeatedly. To note: in the 15th amendment, the khudrō nrigōshthi—minor ethnic sects—dwelling in Bangladesh have been designated as upōjāti—tribe. The request has been made for eschewing the use of the term Ādibāshī in various functions, discussions, and talk shows on the occasion

of the International Ādibāshī Day on the coming 9th of August. The request is being conveyed already beforehand to the other members of civil society, including university teachers, experts and newspaper editors, participating in all these discussions and talk shows to be alert with regard to the avoidance of the use of the term Ādibāshī in the context of Bangladesh.

To the credit of the Bangladesh media, several organizations have not kowtowed to official diktat and, at least thus far, have continued to freely use the words 'Ādibāshī', 'Adivasi' and indigenous. But as in West Bengal and any place where pureness of ethnicity and language and identity is a political project, majoritarian bias is not preserved by the enlightened and liberal, but by the less knowledgeable, presumptuous and those engaged in the expediency of creating myths of nation building.

There is a fascinating bit of history to the Bengali appropriation of the Chakma homelands—in general, lands in the Chittagong Hill Tracts. It isn't discussed much nowadays, but the Chakma Raja Tridiv Roy, who was made Chakma Raja by Pakistan after the death of his father, in 1953, changed his status from neutral to pro-Pakistan during the Bangladesh Liberation War in 1971. It was, according to the historian Willem van Schendel, who has extensively researched and written on the history of Bangladesh and the Bengal Delta, 'largely because he thought the autonomy of the Chittagong Hill Tracts would be more threatened in an independent Bangladesh than in Pakistan.' The newly formed Bangladesh government promptly declared Tridiv a traitor and he left for Pakistan after the war, abdicating in favour of his son Devasish Roy. Tridiv then led a Pakistani delegation to oppose Bangladesh's entry to the United Nations, with Bangladesh countering the move by having Tridiv's mother, Benita Roy, lead the Bangladeshi delegation.

Tridiv's concerns about the Chakma homeland would come good, though, and there would be little or nothing the diplomat—he was

Pakistan's ambassador to Argentina for several years from the early 1980s—could do. The thing is, Tridiv couldn't do much either when the Kaptai Dam project in the 1960s displaced an estimated 1,00,000 Chakmas and other indigenous inhabitants. It is known as the Great Exodus—boro porong. It was done with as much callousness and brutality with regard to resettlement and rehabilitation as similar projects in neighbouring India. As in India, it was done with as much disregard to equity of any manner, even the humiliation of the Kaptai project feeding hydroelectricity to the cities of East Pakistan—Bengali East Pakistan—with the locals, indigenous locals, if I may add, as a provocateur, deprived of this resource as well. But one could argue Tridiv's hands were tied, the situation near-impossible.

Several tens of thousands of those who made up the Kaptai exodus moved to Myanmar and India. Several thousands live in the Rakhine state in Myanmar. Tripura and Mizoram house several thousands, the remainder were resettled in Arunachal Pradesh. They remained even after the birth of Bangladesh, affected by the eruption of conflict in Chittagong Hill Tracts. It hasn't been an easy transition in India as they have always been seen as outsiders living on the benevolence of the government of India. India's Supreme Court offered redress in 2015, when it ordered that the Kaptai émigrés—mostly Chakma and some Hajong who came over to India during 1964–1969 and resettled in Arunachal Pradesh—and their descendants be given Indian citizenship.

In the 1970s, Tridiv's estranged people protested the imposition of Bengaliness and the subsuming of Buddhist and Hindu cultures and ethnic identities in the Chittagong Hill Tracts at the altar of the Bengali. Resettlement of Bengalis in the region tipped a civilian protest over into outright rebellion. Bangladesh's response has been described by some observers as akin to genocide, with horrors reminiscent of Bangladesh's suffering at the hands of Pakistan scant years earlier, reminiscent too of how India treated the Nagas and Mizos—a steady diet of torture, maim, rape, kill, burn—when they rebelled in the 1950s and 1960s.

It took twenty years for the rebels of the Shanti Bahini, the armed wing of Parbatya Chattagram Jana Samhati Samiti (or United Peoples' Party of the Chittagong Hills), to sign off on peace in 1997. But locals—not-Bengali locals, that is—still hold grievances, chief among these being the partial implementation of the Chittagong Hill Tracts Peace Accord. Deep into the second decade of this century, locals are still evicted for national projects with the full complicity of the local administration and state security. Visitors from overseas cannot visit all areas, and what they can visit, a beautiful lake here, an adventure trail there, a charming tribal hamlet elsewhere, to soak in tourism delights mandated by the state, they must do with permission of the state.

Bengali settlers and their nationalist patrons in turn claim not enough has been done to protect their interests. In a Bengali nation, they have the voice, the ears.

Official Bangladesh has the upper hand, and dictates a sort of nationalistic Who's Who. So much so that some years ago a senior government representative actually came out and declared it. In 2011, the foreign minister of Bangladesh at the time, the very articulate Dipu Moni, was quoted by the Bangladeshi media as saying at a gathering of foreign diplomats in Dhaka: 'They [the not-Bengali groups in Chittagong Hill Tracts] came here as asylum seekers and economic migrants[...] The ethnic Bengalees are not colonial settlers, neither are they foreigners or non-indigenous to their own native land and never will be.'

The scholar Carmen Brandt, a commentator on matters of identity and language in South Asia with an ability to see several perspectives at once, maintains that it was a way of saying: Even though the ancestors of some not-Bengali groups may certainly be more indigenous to some regions of present-day Bangladesh than 'ancestors of the people known today as Bengalis, in other regions it might be the other way around'. She explains the minister's aggressive nationalism as revolving around the central thesis of a country born to be resolutely Bengali, paid for in the blood and broken lives of millions of Bengalis: 'if ethnic minorities were indeed recognised as "indigenous", then what would the Bengalis in Bangladesh be?' Indigenous in the Bengali parts of Bangladesh—could be an answer. But it doesn't make for good politics. Besides, this argument would also introduce tricky aspects such as what to do with the Santals, who are not indigenous to Bangladesh but have for the longest time been residents here for no fault of their own. (Indeed, some scholars go as far as to maintain that with all the infusion of ethnicities over the centuries there are no parts of Bangladesh that are entirely, unadulterated Bengali. That is an incendiary but sobering perspective.)

To find answers to all these questions, much blood has been spilled in the Chittagong Hill Tracts, mostly of the not-Bengali—no match for the volume of Bengali blood spilled for Bangladesh, but proportionately not negligible either. As the pressure of population and politics, both ethnic and religious, increases, there is a strong likelihood of more blood being spilled. For Bangladesh, formally becoming Bengali was a costly project. Now being not-Bengali is a costly project, too.

So, too, is being a Hindu Bengali. Or, a liberal Mussulman Bengali. Or, an atheistic Bengali—born Mussulman or Hindu. Or merely an expressive Bengali on, say, a blog preaching freedom of expression, religion and gender.

In the second decade of this millennium, it has brought death and destruction by extreme believers of the faith that today makes Bangladesh a constitutionally mandated Islamic country. State married church in the 1980s.

The caring, sensitive Bengali? That too.

8

Kichhū bōlchhén?
Do you wish to say something?
(You talkin' to me?)

Wordsmithy is a time-honoured Bengali pastime as in any culture with a sophisticated language. And what is Bānglā—language and person—without English? If Bānglā is soul, Ingréji is surely soul food.

The urbanized and institutionally educated Bengali's umbilical need to be regarded as a citizen of the world is impressive. Communication is the key, and if English can be the locomotor, all the better for that communication.

At one end of this spectrum is the example of Swami Vivekananda's speech at the Parliament of the World's Religions in Chicago in 1893, where he brilliantly and with remarkable gender-equality addressed the audience as 'Sisters and brothers of America', thereby setting the mark for Bengal's star turns, and sealing his status as a perennial legend among the Bengalis. Chicago native Barack Obama (the 44th president of the United States) returned the favour in 2015, when he correctly pronounced the Swami's name, and then addressed a town-hall meeting at New Delhi with 'Sisters and brothers of India' to sustained applause. You're welcome.

(Meanwhile, the ultra-nationalist Hindu right wing in India have for some years appropriated the Swami as one of their own. Even their critics would submit there is a certain logic to that move; the Swami's universalism and humanitarian outlook did not preclude untrammelled pride in the Hindu nation and certainly heralded the arrival of the educated, urbane and networked Hindu nationalist—there are many such in large areas of Banglasphere.)

At the other end is the deadpan humour that is a staple, in particular, of daily-passénjári, a verb for the daily commute that is firmly a part of the Bānglā lexicon. The noun, daily-passénjār is sometimes reduced to 'daily', in the same way that a childhood friend of mine commiserated me when I had contracted chicken pox, with a solicitous 'Heard you've got chicken.' (Shūnlām tōr nāki chícken hōyéchhé?)

Even the legend of the Swami is sometimes humanized by the middle-aged, the supremely confident, or the supremely āntel, singularly or as collective traits within a single person, by referring to him as 'Norén'. This derived dāk-nām is from the Swami's full name, the anglicized version of which is Narendranath Dutta. Otherwise, he is Bibékanondō to the Bengali—as in the Thus-spake-Vivekananda gravitas of Bibékanondō-bōléchhilén that sets up a sermon on positive thinking and positive living. The Norén diminutive is roughly equivalent to, say, calling Mohandas Gandhi Mōhōn or cosily referring to Gautama the Buddha as Shiddhārthō— Siddhartha to the average not-Bengali. Even 'Sid', as I have heard him being called within the scrum of an alcohol-fuelled party of America-worshipping youngsters in India who call each other 'dood' or 'bruh' and have difficulty deciphering the tone of a sentence— anger, irritation, denial, bargaining, sadness, depression, hope, joy, acceptance, birthday greetings, sarcasm—or a joke, unaided by a cell phone or a social network's dictionary of emoticons. But these louts weren't all Bengali, they included the attitudinally hobbled of other stock too.

Anyway, Norén is our own—the Bengali Hindus' own—many conservative Mussulmans expectedly, if ironically, shy away from his evangelical overtones as it competes with their own sense of mission. He remains among our brightest stars of spirituality, confidence and communication. See his fearless eyes, unlined brow below a perfectly lined up saffron turban, the firm set of his chin, arms resolutely folded across his chest clad in saffron fōtua, in countless examples of calendar art, schoolbooks and statuary, way past a hundred years since his death in 1902, just shy of forty.

◆

Another dimension to the garden variety bhodrōlōk, somewhat more than the bhodrōmōhila, is his irrepressible urge to engage with the world at large in English. A corollary is the urge to be cosmopolitan and to be seen to be so, never mind that often the bhodrōlōk's behaviour is at odds with what he is trying to pass himself off as.

A dear friend, a Bengali, told me a story of his time at St. Paul's School in Darjeeling, a Macaulayesque boarding school at which for a time the more oriental, as it were—the local Lepchas, Bhutias, Nepalis and generally anyone from Northeast India, and Bhutan—were referred to as 'Barbs' for barbarians. (Such breathtaking arrogance isn't unusual. At the boarding school I attended, Mayo College in Ajmer, Rajasthan, established some years after the mutiny of 1857, to school princes and princelings in the ways of the ruling British, we referred to such 'orientals' as 'Chinks' or 'Chinky'. As a Bengali I was 'Bong'. As a brown-skinned Bong I was also sometimes 'Blackie'. But I had inalienable rights to dismissively refer to a local resident as 'loku'.) This friend never tired of telling stories of his encounters with visiting Bengalis from the plains promenading along Mall Road. These were on days the school permitted students to go walkabout, clad in school blazer, tie, 'togs', and an umbrella for rain to round off the school's image.

A portly gentleman once purposefully waddled up to this pride of young brown shāhébs after passing a quick memo to his family (Éi dyakhō, édér shongé theek é-bhābé kothā bōlté hoy), on how to converse correctly with such people (this memo naturally delivered sotto voce—to a Bengali this means speaking quite loudly on the assumption that nobody else in the vicinity understands Bānglā—unless it is specifically spoken to alert nearby Bengalis that an event of significance is imminent). This is characteristic of a people who firmly believe in the concept of verbal plumage as necessary to life as breathing.

'Khould you plij thell me da thime,' the gentleman asked my friend's group, attempting to enunciate the sentence in what he assumed was the proper English way, handsomely leavening it with Bānglā overtones. His entourage of portly wife, a boy and a girl on emaciated ponies (like the gentleman, clad in bracing spring weather as if for an Arctic storm—at this point you could reflexively say, Thāndā légé jābé, cautionary Bānglā for 'you will catch a cold'— bulky pulōbhāı, glābh, mankicap and all, looked on awestruck).

My friend and his fellow upper-class animals with their inoculation of smooth English and blessed by the spirit-guides of nineteenth-century Englishmen, seized upon the opportunity of entertainment with people other than Barbs.

'Ah, da thime,' the schoolboys swirled that around. 'Do we have da thime?' The time was delivered after a minute or so of entertainment with accents and snobbery. It ended with the gentleman offering a short bow to the boys, followed by a cheery 'goodbāi' (goodbye); he then resumed his promenade along the mall as a cosmopolitan conquering hero in the eyes of his adoring family.

This urge to be counted in English is a common affliction among Bengali urban folk of broadly the lower-middle class upwards. Commentary in āddā, among friends or family at home, or for that matter a speech to larger audiences, which may contain queries about the insufferably escalating price of fish, the human condition, West Bengal being short-changed by India, and Bangladesh being short-changed by the world, is hardly ever complete without the eternal Bengali query—kyanō?

This is frequently followed up by an underscoring of the thought in English, without which no query can be complete, worthy of serious consideration—hōāi? Why?

It follows in holistic logic that deeper enquiries may follow with where the solution is, hōyéār? (As in 'Sholiushān-tā kōthāy?

Hōyéār?'); when might it arrive, or hōyén? ('Sholiushān-tā kobé āshbé? Hōyén?'); how would it arrive, or hāu? (Sholiushān-tā ki bhābé āshbé? Hāu?'); and of course the criticality of what exactly is the solution, or hōāt? (Sholiushān-tā ki? Hōāt?'), without which there is little point to existential blather.

It is quite common for cosmopolitan Bengali youngsters of the club class in Kolkata, following the example of their parents who too travel club class, to converse with one another in English, Bānglā being reserved for traditional occasions like a marriage or family gathering, for conversation with parents or siblings, or to talk to the help. Many youngsters not of the club class are also aspirationally motivated—the accent is hardly the issue. A quite recently overheard conversation in English by Bengalis deep into this new millennium, in a franchised glass-and-neon-glare Kolkata pizzeria, brought on a flash of memory. It was of those neo-yuppie days of the late-1980s in India, at that time I was an editor with the Kolkata-based newsmagazine, *Sunday*. A game of Pictionary in the plush Alipore locality of the city (lesser beings call it 'Ālipur') was called to a close one beer-laden evening when my teammate, a copybook Bengali beauty replete with luminous duskiness, large kohl-lined eyes, dense, flowing hair, T-shirt and denims-du-jour stretched languorously and announced, 'I'm feeling sleefy.'

This should hardly be an occasion for Bangladeshis to snigger at the transposition by Bengalis of the letter p with the letter f. During an early foray into Chittagong, pronounced Seetāgāng by many locals, a further corruption of the original Chottōgrām the British ruined, I was driven to consult a tourist map, after my host insisted that the teeming city had a huge fort. It took me a while to realize he was referring to the port. Several hundred kilometres to the north in Sylhet, it is not unusual to hear that the nearby rolling tea gardens are 'farfect' for viewing at sunrise or sunset. They are indeed quite perfect at such times and even 'frittier' in winter when the sarong of mist arrives.

We wouldn't stoop so low as to allow a foreign accent conquer us. Indeed, tired of conquest by all manner of not-Bengalis for close to 2,000 years, we blithely conquer foreign accents and languages at will. In Kolkata, I've heard passionate renderings of the song *Guitar Man* by the 1970s soft rock group Bread, melodiously softened with Bānglā accent: '…Who's gonno still the show?/ Baybee eet's tha geetur m-a-a-n.'

◆

The incursions of foreign languages into Bānglā, as with several subcontinental languages, aren't new. Take Portuguese, the language of the once-despised firingi. They left us more than their DNA. It is evident as the borō-babu, after a bath with fragrant shābān (sabáo: soap), scrubs dry with a tōālé (toalha: towel) and, dressed in fresh clothes leans back with relish on his kédārā (cadeira: chair) in the front kamrā (câmara: room) of the house and looks out of the jānalā (janela: window) wondering if the view and weather would suit a tune on his béhalā (viola: violin), a puff of fine tāmāk (tabaco: tobacco), or both. Meanwhile, the lady of the house, who must work even on weekends, perhaps harder on weekends as she facilitates borō-babu's simple pleasures, checks to see if she has properly locked the all-important almari (armário: almirah) in the bedroom containing the family's valuables, tucks the chābi (chave: key) into the fold of her shāri at her waist—pinches the shāyā (saia: underskirt) and gently tugs it downward to settle it, and then goes off to the kitchen to scold the maid for again having left the bālti (balde: bucket) in the bārāndā (veranda: veranda) instead of the store room after mopping the floor.

But the greatest incursions into the language were by the Persian and Arabic, driven by invasions, proselytization and the courts of sultans and nawabs; in some cases this resulted in the creation of a composite sub language. Reverend William Goldsack, an Australian baptist missionary who spent several years in eastern Bengal in the early twentieth century, and even attempted a successful, if somewhat, controversial translation of the Quran into Bānglā—

evidently the reverend's agenda of scholarship was mixed with observations in his interpretation of the Quran to draw Bengal's Mussulmans to Christ—compiled a dictionary of what he called 'Mussulmani Bengali' to English. In it he recorded nearly 6,000 words in Bānglā usage of mostly Persian and Arabic roots, besides a smattering of Turkish and Hindi; some scholars estimate these words as comprising less than a tenth of 'Bengali' words, but it is a substantial number nevertheless.

A majority of these words have become part of the standard vocabulary of the mōlla (mullah), madrasa student, proselytizers and the ultra-conservative lay Mussulmans—sometimes a sermon sounds like Bānglā-accented Arabic or Persian strung together with unavoidable Bānglā conjunctions and verbs. Numerous words have also slipped into daily usage by the Bengali population at large. By the early part of the reverend's dictionary on Bānglā vowels, ā (or aa), I found two words were now used liberally, in modern Bānglā literature, journalism and conversations: ākhér (the end; the future) and ājōb (strange; wonderful). When a person becomes incensed, khépé gyachhé, as we say colloquially, is derived from the Persian khafā—angry, enraged, excited. The most delightful derivative is reserved for our beloved obsessives and eccentrics who live in the own world, 'do their own thing'—the khyapā. Even the 'bad word' khānki, grandly relegated to slang and chhōtōlōk usage for 'prostitute' or 'harlot' is of Persian origin. (The bhodrōlōk naturally prefer the Sanskritized béshyā.) To call a Bengali a fool or stupid or the English easyspeak of 'idiot' (usually pronouced as idiyét in Bānglā) is to invite trouble—you might be setting yourself up for verbal altercation, physical altercation, and the possibility of some or much injury. You could also use the homegrown bōkā to admonish a child. But if you employed the more elegant békūb or béōkūf you would be drawing from the Arabian well—bewakoof (foolish, ignorant, thoughtless).

We have our regional and religious linguistic borrowings too. When speaking to our granny or her siblings, my mother would use the very East Bengali/ Mussulman pāni, for water, sometimes even rain—instead of the formal brishti. This Hindi-root word for water would be smoothly transformed to jol, with a Sanskrit root, when speaking to her husband or children. Lobōn, salt of her roots, would for us be transformed to noon. Another crucial accompaniment to a Bengali meal is the green chilli pepper. That would be mōrich, derived from the Urdu-Hindi mirch, if Mother stayed true to her roots, and lonkā, when she spoke to her children and those of her husband's family.

(If she really wanted to annoy our quite arrogant and purely West Bengali—or ghōti—relatives among our extended family, she would use the very ghōti pronunciation 'nonkā', and discreetly look around to see if we got the joke, and were trying to suppress our laughter, approving such small rebellions of hers in revenge for the humiliation she sometimes encountered on account of the colour of her skin, or for the fact that she wasn't born at the altar of wealth and pedigree. Such tiny victories or even grand ones could sometimes lead to the exultation of kéllā-fotéh!—from the Arabic root kila-fateh, literally 'we have won the fort' for 'victory is ours!')

A Bengali Hindu will say māshi to mean mother's-younger-sister. A Bengali Mussulman will almost always refer to her as khālā, with an Arabic root. In West Bengal or among Bengali Hindus you will receive a Sanskritized nimontron—or, colloquially, némontōnnō to a meal or social function; in Bangladesh or among Bengali Mussulmans you will reveive a dāoāt, from the Urdu dawat (and the Arabic daa'wah). In the western or Hindu arc this invitation could be to a person's home, or bāri; the other arc prefers bāshā.

Crossing our various borders, geographical, political and of the mind can be interesting or confounding, depending on your attitude. I love the variety—more words for us to use.

◆

Millennial incursions have perhaps been more rapid. A few pujōs ago, while visiting Kolkata on the day of Shōshthi, the sixth day of

Durga Pujō, and the first day that the idol is publicly worshipped in tens of thousands of homes, pandāls and community centres across Bengal, Bangladesh, Tripura, Assam and nearly everywhere Bengali Hindus live, I watched a young boy, between six and eight years old, being interviewed for a Bengali television channel. It was a 'live' programme visiting various pandāls across Kolkata and several other places in West Bengal. The goateed and bespectacled correspondent, a young man in gaudy machine-embroidered pānjābi, tight churidar and Kolhapuri sandals, indulgently addressed the similarly dressed boy: 'Bolō tōh, Mā Durgā-r bāhōn ki?'

'Lion,' the boy smartly replied to the query about Durga's familiar, her 'vehicle'. I imagine in these cosmopolitan, globally-charged times it was silly of me to expect the boy to say shinghō.

'Ār Gonésh-ér?'

'Rat,' I promptly replied along with the boy, having now been schooled in the proper response to a query about the familiar of Durga's elephant-headed son, Ganesh. The Bānglā 'indur' would be déclassé.

'Ojō,' my father might have said to it all, with his propensity for Sanskritized Bānglā. Goat.

◆

Sometimes English becomes Bānglā. I heard a cabin attendant of the slick Bangladeshi airline Novoair (Nobhōéyār to the very Bengali) herald a flight at its Dhaka hub with an announcement: 'Honourable passengers of Novoair please proceed for boarding.' Rounded as this syrupy request was in Bānglā-accented English (she had made a pre-boarding announcement a few minutes earlier that boarding would follow in 'feeftin meenits') a subsequent announcement in what amounted to Bānglā was hardly a surprise. Everyday Bānglā across Banglasphere has adopted several words from English and made these its own in a manner of accent and application that is matchless, damn the purists in both languages. Bengali-speaking travellers, evidently the entire planeload, stirred when the lady with the dulcet voice announced in businesslike Bānglā: 'Novoair boarding sturt.' Start. As in spurt.

Go on, say it aloud, dear not-Bengali readers. You may as well begin your Bānglā lesson here.

◆

Ranjon Ghoshal, who co-founded India's first Bānglā rock band, Mōhinér Ghōrāguli (Mohin's Horses, a name eccentrically sourced from a poem by Jibanananda Das) tells a story of how the Kolkata film-maker Srijit Mukherji, among a new breed of post-Ray and post-Sen directors with gritty, stylishly groundbreaking work like *Autograph* and *Chōtūshkōn* to his credit, once described a young musician's talent: 'Priyam ājkāl akkébāré nōngrā level-é keyboard bājāchché.' What translates as 'Priyam is playing keyboards at a really filthy level' is an acknowledgement, to use modern youth-slang, of the musician's talent being beyond 'awesome'. Ghoshal, an advertising and theatre person and avid tracker of colloquialisms, maintains that this is in the tradition of the late-twentieth century praise, shānghātik bhālō (horrifically good, a cousin of the very English terribly good) and, say, effusive compliments to a singer, bibhotshō nāmiyéchhō, guru, that transcends the transliteration of 'You've gruesomely brought it down, boss' to arrive at the more meaningful 'You've sung a gruesome piece, boss.' Appreciation of a joke or repartee could be greeted with 'Guru, ki dilé'—literally, 'You've really given it, boss' but more like 'You've really stuck it to him, boss' or merely 'brilliant.' Brilliant has several colloquial cousins, the most colourful being 'byapōk', in attitude light years ahead of 'widespread' or 'all-encompassing'.

There's 'ghyam', which can be translated in a range from 'terrific' to 'sexy'. 'Chāp' is usually always more than 'pressure'. A bus conductor or co-passenger might bark at you, 'Éktu chāpbén? 'Put pressure' is actually a request to move further in; it could work equally well in a commuter train or airport bus but it is almost always used in Bengal's overcrowded buses (unlovely competition to

Bangladesh's overcrowded buses). Or they may use the incomparable 'Péchhōné égōn,' move forward to the back. (I read this translation of the very witty *Jam* by the poet Sankha Ghosh in *Grand Delusions: A Short Biography of Kolkata* by the novelist and columnist Indrajit Hazra: Heads fall off from time to time/ Some of them old, some of them young/ The conductor hollers into the crowd:/ 'Keep moving forward to the back!')

Kolkata's overcrowded privately-run buses are driven by a tribe of utterly suicidal folk accompanied by a tribe of rude attendants with a curious streak of chivalry when it comes to the matter of embarking or disembarking female passengers. 'Béndhé-lédiss!' they may shout out in warning to the impatient driver, presumably meaning something on the lines of 'Take it easy, dada, we have one or more female passengers whom it wouldn't do to injure or kill'—such implied translation a step up from the literal 'Tie it up! Ladies!' Chāp nébén nā is a more straightforward 'please relax, don't stress'.

But an 'āntél', clipped from the French 'intellectuel' certainly would, as to be a proper Bengali intellectual surely requires taking on the cares of the world. In the old days of the 1960s and 1970s, such a person would be dressed in scruffy handspun cotton, somewhat unshaved, carrying some form of jhōlā, or sling bag. He would eye everything intensely while travelling the world in leather sandals and earthy feet and smoke unfiltered Indian cigarettes like Charminar or Panama, while some dreamt of smoking unfiltered Gauloises. Nearly sixty years later, the accoutrements are similar though the modern āntél may be under some chāp with cotton and jhōlā-bags having become virulently stylish among all genders, and non-āntél carrying them off looking terrifically ethnic without being scruffy, while at the same time sporting iPhones. But the then-and-now āntél would be spiritually joined in adulation of cinematic luminaries like Luis Buñuel, Jean-Luc Godard, Akira Kurosawa, Andrei Tarkovsky— though the modern āntél would naturally throw in Abbas Kiarostami and Mohsen Makhmalbaf.

And how can you even begin to top an āntél come-on, like the one I heard a fellow Bengali student employ with a fetching young not-Bengali lady at St. Stephen's College in Delhi: 'If you want to know me, read Neruda.' That relationship did not progress far. I suspect that relationship would not have progressed even to the degree it did if the lady had been a Bengali, even if the gentleman had escalated matters and instead said: 'If you want to know me, read Sartre.' Our women have for years quickly seen through our āntél men (somehow, āntél tend to be men, the āntél woman a rarity, as if women possess a sixth sense that steers them past self-defeating, delusional shoals).

Our apex contribution to linguistics, though, lies with the nearly-untranslatable word: nyakā. It could mean 'pretentious', 'mincing', 'excessively coy', 'irritating'—frankly, anything that conveys a word with all the sarcasm and irritation we can muster. For instance, I have used the word in a gender-neutral manner to deliver the full force of an internalized thought such as *Pretentious bloody drama queen, I hope a buffalo defecates on you.*

The charm lies in the feeling. I am a humble student. There are masters who can add infinite dimensions to the meaning of nyakā with a dismissive rolling of the eyes, or a hint of sneer, infinitesimal shake of the head, just that extra reorienting of the posterior while turning away.

◆

'Guru', as you have gathered, is of course far from being a teacher. To 'boss' you could add the somewhat lowbrow anglicized 'chief'. The motive isn't always praise. This standard operating word used among friends and familiars can be employed to cadge a cigarette and a lighter ('Guru, āgun-tā dāo tōh'—literally, 'Pass the fire, boss' but with more attitude, what even Hells Angels might consider worthy of respect); tea; alcoholic drink; bus or taxi fare; expressing disappointment at the refusal of another alcoholic drink before going home (or for 'cutting' into a friend's love interest) with a 'Guru, étā ki theek hōlō?' the displeasure in tone and facial expression providing further admonitory cementing of 'Boss, this is not right, is it?' In this male-oriented colloquialism that seems to rule Bānglā, close on the heels of guru is māmā. The staid translation of 'maternal uncle' is about as far as 'teacher' is from the easy-speak version of guru. If a friend turns up at his group's evening āddā at the neighbourhood 'club' or chā-stall sporting a daring hairstyle, an appropriate response could be: Kānpiyé diyéchhō, māmā . Retentive grammaticians and linguists will probably not tell you, but in this context 'māmā' is akin to 'dude'. You've really shaken it, dude.

◆

And here perhaps, something about āddā, the birthplace of much of our attitude, and so, the life force of vocabulary with attitude.

Āddā emerged not long after bhodrōlōk, as a salon-like gathering at which thoughts and persuasions of the day could be discussed in a good-natured, if sometimes vociferous, manner. Over several decades this male preserve travelled further down the pyramid of wealth and privilege to the upper middle class and greater bulge of the middle class. And over time āddā travelled from its acknowledged birthplace of Kolkata to other places, Dhaka and beyond into Greater Banglasphere, taking wing wherever there were well-to-do hosts and a ready gathering of local worthies from pundits and poets to politicians on the make.

Āddā first took wing, some maintain, in the absence of gatherings beyond weddings, during various occasions of pujō and such. 'There was very little social life among the Bengalis of Calcutta,' wrote Nirad Chaudhuri, comparing it with European society. 'No afternoon or evening parties, no dinners, no at-homes, and, of course, no dances, enlivened their existence. The heaviest social exertion in this sense that they could or would undergo was to pay formal calls.' And so, 'what the native of the city lacked in sociability he made up in gregariousness' to such an extent that 'no better connoisseur of company was to be found anywhere in the world, and no one else was more dependent on the contiguity of his fellows with the same incomprehension of his obligations towards them.' Chaudhuri was basically describing the eventual āddā adept, and addict: the āddābāj.

It has since travelled well down to the bottom of the socioeconomic pyramid. Āddā is by now function-agnostic, taking in a gathering that can range from intense discussions at the residence of a publisher or, say, young movie director to a weekend gathering of modern-minded working friends catching up over food (and, possibly to the horror of āddā purists, including women, often women who work jobs away from home, women with minds of their own supercharged by independent incomes); even an āddā triggered by the visit of an old friend; to the determined everyday āddā. This last is a place for men and boys to gather to indulge in gnyajāno, banter and blather with a sense of camaraderie, where the āddā's Alpha male (call him āddādhāri, if you will, pivot of the āddā) holds court, and moderates discussions from the fate of the world to talent-scouting for the next neighbourhood-league football tournament hosted by the pārā.

The location can be—rok-é bōshé āddā—seated on the rōāk, slip of balcony in front of a house, even on the steps to the house. But more often it is at a distance from the home, a neutral rendezvous away from both the perceived drudgery of the workplace and domesticity, at a modest coffee house or tea shop where any visitor to urban Banglasphere will see clusters of āddā—and then a sudden rush to get home to dinner and family, the unreal life. And if even that opportunity is hard to come by, a gathering at the pārā's community club (usually pronounced clāb) or a chā-shop, chā-ér dōkān a convenient walk away, rapid escape for an hour or two after a quick bath and the day's situation report about household matters, perhaps the health of a child, perhaps a firm admonition to the boy more than the girl to be first in class, or life will, as we say, deliver a horse's egg (Clāsh-é fārsht āshté hobé, nāhōlé life-é ghōrā-r dim pābé).

Naturally, the responsibility of not landing that sort of egg lies with the lady of the house, the ginni, the mā. She is sometimes shown by feminist illustrators as Mā-Durgā, with ten hands symbolically depicting elements of housework, her own work, the child's schoolwork and extracurricular activities (kārikulār). This can range from shepherding the family's prospective Nobel winner, Olympic medallist and culture-czar through tuition (tiushān) for dreaded mathematics (onkō) to swimming lessons (shnātār), perhaps even lessons in that fashionable alternative to Indian percussion instruments, the Western drums (drām). And she still needs to churn out as perfect a meal as ingredients will provide, besides rice cooked just so to ideal firmness yet ideal softness, or ruti without any blemish of scorching or it could be rejected outright as imperfection, even irresponsibility. To paraphrase 'cogito ergo sum', the existential boast of French philosopher René Descartes, she exists so many āddābāj can.

The āddābāj may claim that it is because of āddā that the Bengal Renaissance maintained its depth and longevity and birthed the cultural soul of Bengal, the amorphous entity by which they usually mean Kolkata (and, at a stretch, Dhaka) that is our cachet to this day. It typically counters the argument that 'Bengal' plummeted from its economic pinnacle because there were too many āddābāj, employed, unemployed and unemployable alike engaged in idle gossip; and too few of the industrious to worry about pursuits like productivity. At a non-empirical level—the core of much āddā—I would maintain that everyday āddā itself is on the decline in ultra-urban Banglasphere—in Kolkata, and professional clusters of Delhi, Bengaluru, Mumbai—moving back from the mass stereotype to the preserve of those who are able to indulge in it as a weekend pastime, much like a family outing or an evening at the movies; or it has morphed to the level of occasional banter with colleagues and friends over drinks at a business-district bar before heading home.

One student of āddā termed the discussions as 'long, informal and non-rigorous'. In a doctoral thesis, with āddā at its core, that

Nabamita Das presented to the University of Birmingham she put together a fascinating insight into the activity, confirming much that Chaudhuri had acerbically yet somewhat fondly described several decades earlier. A middle-aged man told Das:

> Life becomes worthless without āddā. Your Kākimā, [he customarily referred to his wife as her aunt, automatically assuming he is kāku, like a paternal uncle] complains about my everyday evening habit of going out of the home to give āddā at the local para club and not returning...in time for dinner, as I always get drowned in these āddās. But I will not compromise on āddā, which is my food for thought. Going to para club for a smoke and āddā, in fact, defines Bengali masculinity [here he 'laughed with pride,' Das informs us]. This club which is part of growing up is almost home-like and its members, brother-like friends. These days not many people can turn up for āddā because they are busy, but those of us who come, chat for hours almost every day recollecting our ceaseless āddās of...days (gone by), of lost times and lost friends.

◆

Not-Bengalis, unfamiliar with the language may believe standard Bengali is that disseminated by Tagore, the brilliant Bandopadhyays, a Sarat, a Bankim or portrayed by auteurs like Ghatak, Ray and Sen. But, in truth, the Bengali language liberally takes from the underbelly of Bānglā which is something else altogether, colourful and fetid as the underbelly of the Bengali and as representative of the Bengali as its more refined cousin. Its sophistication is the wit of the street, not an ad nauseam portrayal of a superior culture where the only unsanitary glimpses permitted are poverty, and pettiness and greed against the underclass—the underclass that may be all right for artful cinema and form of literature but naturally denied the right to attend their own premiére or literary soirée.

This theatre of life of the gōríb and the chhōtōlōk occupies a universe distinct from that of the borōlōk and the relatively less exclusive bhodrōlōk. These Poor and Lesser People below the Big People (also the synonym in this case for Wealthy People) and the Well-mannered People or Civilized People, represent the brutal morass from which the Bengalis have for nearly 200 years made the tortuous climb to bhodrōlōk and bhodrōmōhila.

In this universe, on the roadside near Ballygunge Place, opposite the raj-era watering hole of Calcutta Cricket and Football Club, CCFC to members and familiars, those who pass by a tea shop may hear the owner paraphrasing a Mithun Chakraborty 'dialogue' from the movie *MLA Phātākéshtō* (Shālā mārbō ékhāné, lāsh pōrbé shoshāné) to tick off an errant assistant in chhōtōlōk rhyme: 'Mārbō ékhāné, pōrbi shoshāné.' 'I'll hit you here and you'll land in the cremation ground' doesn't even begin to capture the lyrical brilliance of the threat. You can hear this sort of linguistic virtuosity if only you care to listen. After attending an elegant Brahmo prayer meeting for the recently-deceased father of a dear friend, in the Vivekananda Park area of South Kolkata, I walked into a clutch of bus drivers and conductors. They were on downtime, sipping milky, sweetened chā from tiny plastic cups, guffawing at a colleague-philosopher's put-down of their boss. 'Pāgōlé bnārā ki nā bolé, chhāgōlé bnārā ki nā khāye.' The earthy proverb, A-madman-will-say-anything/a-goat-will-eat-anything was judiciously tamped with bnārā: prick, dick, cock—words pervasive in brutal everyday Bānglā along with all manner of female applications.

What of those words you may hear as you pass a squabble on the bypass to Kolkata's new airport? Or as you walk along the lake Rabindra Sarobar, among the few remaining natural saving graces of the city? Or along much of Bengal's decrepit towns, these other places where our destitute, displaced, young, unemployed and restless live? Bōkāchōdā. Idiot-fucker. Bānchōt. Sister fucker. Khānki. Whore. Khānki-ir bāchchā. Whore-child. The comparatively gentle shuōrér bāchchā. Child of a sow. The almost dulcet hārāmjādā—

bastard—derived from the Arabic. In eastern Bengal, you can add all this and add some local flavour. Kāyittā dimu, you may hear as a prefix or suffix to an already violent statement. I'll cut you up, sister fucker. This too is us, emphatically imbued with Bengaliness to the last hot button.

◆

Commentary with mid-level venom is another engaging pursuit. On one of several visits to Bangladesh, I found myself in an ageing Airbus of Biman, Bangladesh's airline that is a remarkable example of Bengali attitude.

'Yatō tārā kyanō?' a lady at a Biman check-in counter had told me when I enquired how much more my flight from Dhaka to Chittagong would be delayed.

What's the hurry?

On board, as we waited into our third hour of delay, fidgeting in seats with the foam gouged out, moisture dripping from air-conditioning vents, an occasional finger or knuckle snagging in ashtrays that had the flip-top lid missing, two cabin attendants walked down the twin-aisle jet several times, counting off passengers with the click of mechanical counters. A fellow passenger, impatient to reach Doha, the destination after Chittagong, tersely offered after some time in East Bengali dialect: 'Kāgōz-kolōm lāgbō?' Do you need some paper and a pen? (Another passenger had meanwhile short-circuited, and escalated the situation. 'Traffic-ké dākén,' he barked at a stewardess. 'Tulā-dhunā dimu.' It wasn't clear if he urged the lady to bring forth Biman's operations chief or the airport's traffic controller, so he could be beaten the way raw cotton wool is beaten, and fluffed, before use as stuffing in a quilt, mattress, or pillow.)

I find these as emphatic and imbued with feeling as some of my father's bhodrōlōk curses. While stranded in a 1970s Kolkata traffic nightmare, or similar situations at way stations to so many of the pretty places in Bengal, Asansol, Malda, Siliguri, and dozens of smaller towns from Krishnanagar (superbly crafted clay statuary and bric-à-brac) to Kolaghat (to picnic by the banks of the Roopnārāyōn River), he would grip the streering wheel of our beloved Ambassador Mark 2 (and later Mark 3 and Mark 4) and snarl: 'Gordhōb'. Alas, the traffic wasn't moved by this Sanskritized invocation, applied alike to obstructing cow and lunatic bus driver. Ass.

◆

Understatement and sarcasm comes easily to us—it is class agnostic. An uncle of mine, Jyotirindra, still speaks fondly of the humour of the Dhaka rickshaw-wallah (to us variously rikshāoālā and riskāoālā—the occasional flipping of alphabet that also prevents many of us from taking undue riks or reeks). They are a part of urban folklore. My uncle's favourite anecdote is of a well-to-do gentleman whose dhuti tripped him up as he reached the porch of his house. He more or less rolled down the few steps to the waiting rickshaw, his treasured dignity and composure lost.

But not his chauffeur's. Deadpan, the rickshaw-wallah remarked: 'Babu āyilén?' Babu, you've finally arrived?

Deadpan humour is the lifeblood of daily-passénjāri, and 'cool factor', as it were, is an unshakaeble prerequisite. These are everyday comebacks, real and apocryphal, that peppered our younger years and today pepper social networks where people share what they have overheard. In these there are some legends that are often-repeated, perhaps even artfully created; either way they take on a life of their own, their original sayers, creators, in trains (especially the 'local' or commuter trains that link a sizeable portion of Bengal to Kolkata), larger-than-life for their very anonymity. I've heard and read of the daily passenger also being called daily pāshōndō, a demon; but the tone has as much fondness as fury.

A harried passenger runs up to a train and asks a daily passenger seated by a window: 'Dādā, étā ki gāri?'

A simple shorthand, querying what sort of train it is, where it's headed, and such.

The reply?

'Rail-gāri.'

Another telling is of a person hurrying on to the platform—always harried, late, at a disadvantage to make the situation crueller and the joke more enjoyable—asking a 'daily' seated by the window: 'Dādā, étā ki shob stéshōn-é thāmbé?'

Elder brother, will this train stop at every station?

Elder Brother puts aside his paper and politely asks a question in reply: 'Kyanō, āpni ki shob stéshōn-é nāmbén?'

Why, will you disembark at every station?

9

Mā
Oedipus Hex

When it comes to the worship of women, the poet Jibanananda Das was an overachiever even in the Bengali schema of the male romantic. He described to the world the beauty of our women several generations before a set-piece, plastic competitition in 1994 brought forth to the world a Bengali Miss Universe, Sushmita Sen.

For Das, beauty was always more than skin-deep. There was Shudorshōna, the pretty one. Shyāmōli, the dusky one. Shuronjōna, the charmer. Shōbita, beautiful, like sunshine. Shuchétōna, aware, of the beautiful mind. None of them, though, achieved the cult status of Bōnōlota Sen of Natore, now a quite overlooked town in northwest Bangladesh that, besides the magnificent homes of departed zamindars, is mainly remembered for this whimsical ode to a lady that Das conjured up, the lady of the jungle vine, wild, irrepressible.

Jibanananda is about the light and shade of love—prém—of a cult of love, a cult of the love-poet. Bengalis have embraced such work because it enhances our collective identity of a troubadour of the soul, an essential aspect of our curriculum vitae. Jibanananda's work is the property of every lover, lovelorn person, and communicator of love, the proxy we use as we employ the work of other writers with unbridled poetic license to express deep emotion when words fail us, even that modern man wearing jeanpant (or jins) and pānjābi in the style of the day (unmindful that this very Bengali shirt is derived from the popular dress of Punjab and other regions to its northwest). He may woo his gentle-yet-combative lady love (she wearing a shāri, shālwār-kāmiz or jins) on that rare secluded park bench in our crowded cities, discovering a hesitant togetherness among crowds like birds do as they roost on a cable. A chatter of prém birds.

In Kolkata you will find them, these migratory prém birds, by the lék, by which we mean the impressively large Rabindra Sarobar, or on benches by Victoria Memorial—a landmark Indo-Saracenic monument to a colonial queen-empress mooted by that man who evidently wanted to free us by dividing us—Lord Curzon—or by the banks of the ever-muddy Hooghly and its riverfront architectural wonders turned utterly decrepit, watching the sun set over a old-new skyline, or on a boat with its roof of latticed bamboo and thatch or perhaps even at Eden Gardens.

I do not mean the cricket stadium, but the adjacent eponymous park that Dominique Lapierre in his *The City of Joy* dramatically mislabelled as Garden of Eden (or was it his translator?). The very same Lapierre who left us French-spelled characters called Boulboul (ours are merely bulbul, from the songbird) and geckos called tchik-tchiki (tik-tiki to us, derived from the sound the creatures make), and grand assertions that on Diwali every Indian household gambles, and description of a local grocery store that may have made even the famously sexual French cringe: '…a fixed centre, like those lingam of Shiva, those symbols of fertility standing on their yoni in the temples…'

We know how such machinery works without this fevered Frenchman and stores of divine genitalia. Prém often progresses in our linear society to biyé, marriage, eschewing the tradition of the search for a shombōndhō, a connection, a relationship arranged by a ghotōk for the institution of arranged marriage in favour of what in Bānglā is often referred to as lābh-marréj. So be it. So intense is this feeling that elopement even in our modern times isn't unknown, though of course relatively rarer than marrying against the wishes of our self-professedly liberal and civilized society's strict norms of jāt—caste—and its sub-divided categories of gōtrō. (What on earth is a Brāmhon doing, marrying a Bōddi, or a Kāyōsthō a Bōnik? What is society coming to? I mean Bengali Hindu society; Bengali Mussulman society, besides often practising norms of caste in a castless religion, already carries additional default veils of conservatism.)

Then there is the matter of tottō, which in relatively liberal instances is a ritual exchange of gifts among the bride and groom's family, that of the kōné and bor. It's an assortment of fruits and sweets, clothes and accessories, materials for pujō, and among some, even a variety of carp, one of our staple fish, bizarrely decorated as a bride down to replica nose ring—noth—like a bride, *Labeo rohita* instead of mere rui.

The ritual of gift-giving doesn't stop there. Often, even among our self-professedly liberal community in these modern times there is the matter of dowry, gifts resolutely travelling one-way from the bride's family to the groom's. To put it mildly, entire wardrobes are provided here, including the wardrobe. I have personally witnessed a situation in my extended family, all very politely conducted, of course. The bride's father and a small group of accompanying relatives were taken around the groom's parents' house. The married couple would naturally live there—nuclear families are still quite the exception with us, though career increasingly calls urban young couples away from such situations. The couple's intended room was shown as bare, along with a gently delivered suggestion that even in common areas, furniture and consumer durables would face greater wear and tear with increased visitations, now that two families were to be joined as one. The tour ended with the groom's father saying in a formal yet firm tone: Éktu dékhé nébén. Please see. Please see to it.

All my fulminations came to nothing. The future of the bride had to be secured. Her father was compelled by social norm and a certain helplessness to give in, even though eventually it turned out his daughter was treated abominably, her life little more than a combination of heirmaking and housekeeping.

My parents were once asked by a distant relative whether I had accepted gifts when I got married. When they were told, not a thing—where was the need?—the incredulous lady, often given to lectures on shōbbhōtā, civilized behaviour, gave them an earful, as if the fact of a wedding without ceremony, without even a feast, wasn't bad enough: Chhéléta ki pāgōl? Ektā borō freedge-ō chāilō nā? An assertion that the boy, admittedly eccentric, and his bride already had enough to begin their life together and would along the way, accumulate the necessary capital for more household needs, was dismissed. That he didn't demand even a large refrigerator as dowry was taken as a sign of insanity as much as stupidity.

(And how could I ever have asked to be outfitted with a wardrobe? My father-in-law, a tempest in his calmest moments, had for long responded thus whenever he heard of such demands: Kyanō, bor ki nangtō hōyé ghuré byarāé? Does the groom habitually walk around naked?)

Once past that obstacle course there is the biyé—more formally, bibāhō. Modern, sparse, socialist-minded folk opt for a visit to the magistrate's and perhaps a pritibhōj, a celebratory meal, a banquet, for family and friends. If you happen to be Brahmō, typically understated clothes match understated venues and understated ceremonies—some prayer, some song, professing of care and commitment—and then on to an understated meal.

Those not, typically opt for a three-day extravaganza. There are regional variations and, of course, great religious variations on how Bengalis approach weddings or indeed any life-ritual. It begins with gāé-hōlud (common too among Bengali Mussulmans), the purification ceremony for the bride and groom with the application of turmeric paste, prayer, song, and much humour. This is followed by the wedding, and, the day after, a formal introduction of the new bride—bōu—as part of her new family, when she offers the bōu-bhāt, a ritual meal offered to elders and select guests.

Naturally, nothing exceeds the main event. The bride in

resplendent red Bénārōshi-shāri and the groom in white dhuti-pānjābi coyly arrive at the sacred fire for an hours-long ceremony (where it is not unknown for guests to nod off) repeating after the priest declarations and prayers in Sanskrit propitiating various gods and ancestors that few understand and few care to—the priest is more a prop, a stylized validation. Family and friends dressed in their finest silks and cottons and jewellery watch and gossip and catch up, warily eyeing the bride or the groom's entourage and guests for the slightest misdemeanour. The women are adorned in elaborate gold and gem creations that Bengali shōnār are invited to replicate across the subcontinent; the males are resplendent in dhuti-pānjābi or churidār-pānjābi, buttons of gold often topped with gemstones completing the pānjābi. The gathering, bibāhō-bāshōr, sometimes resembles a treasure fit for Clive.

The bride, in her exquisitely crafted tiara-like mukut of shōlā pith, her face embroidered with patterns made with sandalwood paste, and awash in gold, for these brief hours is a goddess, literally a work of art. The groom, with his own exquisite, ornately designed headdress of shōlā, the tall and conical tōpōr, like a miniature Burmese stupa which also awkwardly lends the groom a touch of a bewildered Mongol potentate or wrestler, is relatively less impressive, though he rarely looks less than impressed that the goings-on are so much about him.

As a child these were for me engaging son et lumière shows, a swirl of several generations gathered in one place, a great opportunity to mingle, feel like I belonged to a greater purpose than simply being part of an immediate family of four. There were no tears on display except when the bride left for her new home. Children were literally let loose, girls and boys. Young men were forgiven certain trespasses: the urban legend caricature of young men slightly distanced from the festivities politely facing an elder with cigarettes behind their backs, smoke curling above them, the elder glancing at it and then carrying on as if nothing at all was out of place, even mischievously prolonging the conversation, is taken from real life.

Exuberance was expected, though elegant exuberance was preferred. I found that several of the ladies relaxed, letting go a bit even during these structured social occasions. A prim cousin, a prim young aunt, even a prim elderly one I had never seen break form, would break into song, mostly folk, and sometimes a dance, also folksy. Laughter always seemed louder at such occasions. This is where family bonds deepened or weakened, where a child would make a visible social mark with perfect deportment or disgrace. As I made my way through the gathering respectfully touching the feet of my elders, women and men, and receiving either cursory or lavish blessings in return, it seemed a lot more than just the union of two people, often strangers before the wedding and sometimes, strangers long after.

Perhaps I am being somewhat cynical, having been an active practioner of the social breakaway, from leebh-een, (as a close relative once described the live-in relationship I was in, suggesting it was good I was away working in Delhi as in Kolkata it would have been entirely inappropriate); to lābh-marréj outside the bounds of prescribed compatibility; and dispensing with ceremonial trappings. After all this is an explosion of structured but undeniably saturated celebration of joy (what stereotypical Indian weddings are known to be), though ours tend to be of greatly lowered decibel than, say comparable ones in northern India that employ Bollywood tunes and choreographed dancing, far removed from our musical staple of classical shānāi—shehnai—to welcome guests to the marriage venue, and electric garishness and unfettered display of wealth and pomp that have in popular imagination emerged as the Big Fat Indian Wedding, which they are.

After witnessing so many weddings, as a grown man was I moved as I carried my sister on a piri (a polished slab of wood that serves as a seat) with the help of two male cousins, bearing her several times around the ritually sacred fire and her ritually sacred husband? Yes. Did I wish her well at this culmination of lābh-marréj that demanded ceremonial closure even though I personally do not believe in such ceremony? Undoubtedly. Did it break my heart to see her cry at the end of the ceremony, as she ritualistically sought my blessings by touching my feet, and I hugged her as if time had stopped, and our childhood flashed before my eyes? Without question. I looked up and saw faces around me, all wearing expressions of joy and sadness. And suddenly it all felt so real, this theatre of life.

◆

Where were we? Ah yes, romance and Bonōlotā Sen.

Here she is, created by Jibananada Das, and recreated by Arunava Sinha who has taken ahead the translation in a way Das, a student and teacher of English literature, could never really soar in this language of his profession.

A thousand years, and yet I walk these paths
On darkest nights from Ceylon to Malay seas
I have wandered; Bimbisar and Ashoka's grey lands
I was there; further still, in Vidarbha's dark cities
Life foams around my weary soul again
She brought me a spell of peace–Natore's Bonōlotā Sen

Her hair as dark as Vidisha's ancient nights
Her face sculpted in Sravasti. Like the lost sailor
On the distant ocean, the ship's rudder broken,
Who sees a green land in a cinnamon isle
In the dark I've seen her. 'What kept you?' she asks, and then
Raises her bird's-nest eyes–Natore's Bonōlotā Sen

Like the sound of falling dew at end of day
Evening comes; the hawk wipes the sun-smell off its wings;
The colours of the world fade, and the manuscript
Twinkles in firefly hues for all these tales
All birds come home–all streams. All transactions end
Only darkness remains. And—face to face—Bonōlotā Sen

This lyrical worshipper of women, praised by Tagore was fated, as so many writers are to have the majority of his work discovered after his death. A tragedy but then the worship of women in Bengal is saturated with passion, irony and tragedy.

◆

The worship of goddesses in Bengal is believed to have evolved into multiple forms and applications during the thousand or so years that followed the fifth and sixth centuries CE. These draw from earlier traditions, several hundred years before the start of the Common Era. The goddess presided over nature, as guardian of forests, of mountains. She unhesitatingly took on and vanquished demons. The evolution of the goddess took place quite naturally, I read in an excellent study by the historian Kumkum Chatterjee, out of the Brahmanical tradition which had goddess depictions of Shakti or Shōkti (energy), Prakriti or Prōkriti (materiality) and Maya. A fuller 'more comprehensive and systematic notion' of a great goddess, a devi/débi or mahadevi/mohādébi, emerged a little over 1,500 years ago.

The goddess travelled through several incarnations and forms, many of which are current even in today's Bengal: Durga, Chōndikā, Chāmundi, Kāli, Bōishnōbi, Nārāyōni, Mohéshhōri, Shōkti, Gōuri, Mohāmāyā (and of course Pārbōti or Umā, the gentle yet firm consort of Shib-thākur, our Shiva)... She emerged most strongly as the demon slayer, of the buffalo-demon Mōhishāshur, who was of divine origin. None of the male gods could vanquish the demon that had run rampant across the heavens and on earth, on account of a boon granted by the creator Brahma (Brōmhō), that he could only be killed by a woman. So Mōhishāshur-mōrdini, the slayer of Mōhishāshur, this Super Eve, as it were, was created from their energies and emerged as 'a great fiery splendour'. She decapitated the buffalo and, when the demon emerged from the carcass, drove a trishul through his chest.

This super goddess, mohādébi, is most widely known as Durga, and her grand victory to save the universe is the object of worship of Bengali Hindus across Banglasphere, the reason why West Bengal and large parts of southern Assam and Tripura are practically shut down for nearly a week each year in autumn in honour of Mā Durga. It's a time of celebration of victory of good over evil, renewal of hope and a joyous insanity of cultural and emotional outpouring the world has come to know as Durga Pujō.

On Bijoyā Doshōmi, the tenth day of Durga Pujō that marks the day of victory, after the women have finished with shindur-khelā, when they daub vermilion on each other's faces and fling it in the air in celebration of the goddesses's victory (and, by symbolic extension, their own), when the idol from each pārā has been escorted by tumultuous crowds for immersion at the nearest river or lake, her cyclical journey completed for another year, in the evening the worshipful and even the merely celebratory greet each other with the words 'Shubhō Bijoyā', the auspicious occasion of victory and remembrance. Even during my childhood in Kolkata it would be time to visit family and friends, touch the feet of elders and be blessed—and, always, be offered a variety of sweets from pāyésh to puli-pithé, nārkōl-ér nāru and shondésh—that was enough reason for a visit. On these days there were always sweets at home for visitors. Though the practice has waned somewhat across Banglasphere, with ever more nuclear families and younger generations moving away for study and work, a majority will still take the time for even the smallest association with Durga Pujō, from visiting friends or the nearest pandāl with a prōtimā of Durga, and if it is not possible to visit 'home' then telephone home (or use one of numerous social network message services) with greetings of love and respect—and familial remembrance (that Bijoyā Doshōmi has also come to mean).

The worship of another mohādébi, Kali, follows just a few weeks later, fierce, dark as night, wearing a garland of severed heads, eyes afire with battle lust, tongue reddened with blood, the destroyer of more demons, an incarnation of a step up from

Durga in anger and retribution, what the scholar David R. Kinsley colourfully terms Durga's 'embodied fury' as she emerges from Durga's forehead to take on the demon brothers, Shumbhō and Nishumbhō. Kāli Pujō, is among our more mysterious rituals. In darker times, it sometimes involved human sacrifice, not merely the sacrifice of a goat or buffalo; and yet Kali is a débi so endearingly and so powerfully imprinted on our psyche that there is an entire genre of songs, Shyāmā-shōngit, dedicated to her, representing a powerful sub-culture that worships and humanizes this avatar of mohādébi away from the spotlight of her spirit-sister Durga. (To be fair Durga has her range, Uma-shōngit, and Agōmōni, the songs of her arrival before Durga Pujō and, of course, songs of her as the victorious Bijoyā.)

The goddess quite naturally lent her aura to kings and chieftains in times ancient and medieval, and an entire genre of literature called mangalkavya (mongōlkābbō in Bānglā), usually associated with Chandi or Chōndi, emerged in medieval Bengal under the patronage of local rajas, especially in southwestern Bengal in the area of Medinipur and Dhalbhum. Among the best known of the genre is the sixteenth century Chandimangalkavya (or Chōndimongōlkābbō) of Mukundōrām Chokrōbōrti, who is usually referred to as kōbikonkōn—a sort of jewel of a poet—and his work, like that of poet-chroniclers of the time like Mādhōb Āchārjjō (also known as Dvija Madhav) and Mānik Dottō, offered insights into the society, culture and politics of the time.

Even before the formalization of the principal mohādébi, what many left-wing and feminist historians term as both a Brahmanization and a 'softening' of the deity into everyday lore and acceptance, goddess worship permeated—and continues to permeate—other aspects of life in Bengal, from protecting a village from predations of the forest to small pox to weaving her general benevolence over a village or town as protector. We know her by many names across Bengal—Shorbōmongōlā Débi—the goddess who brings good fortune to all; Jongōlnāshini, who protects all in the jungle, Bōn-débi, the goddess of the forest.

In places like the Sunderbans, goddess worship even transcends religions. Bōnbibi, the lady of the forests, is the patron of both Mussulman and Hindu residents of the area, especially those whose lives and livelihood are of this delta, this sea-land of forests. It matters little whether at times and places she wears a shāri (in such depictions she is the more Hindu Bōn-Durga) or she wears medieval West Asian dress. In this meld of folklore and deep veneration, honey and lac collectors, woodcutters, and even fishermen who approach land away from their homes, worship the lady of the forests with her co-protector and brother, Shah Jongōli, to keep them safe from all ills, and death that so readily stalk this land of tides. Bōnbibi is particularly sought against the wiles of the evil lord of the south, Dōkkhin Rai, who wouldn't hesitate to take on the guise of a tiger to stalk and kill those who forget an offering or prayer to him. At Rāshmela gatherings in the stretches of the Sunderbans now in Bangladesh, Bōnbibi is worshipped alongside Krishna. Bōnbibi is double indemnity.

Such cross-religion and cross-cultural worship is commonplace across Bangladesh, usually in rural areas, though there are urban examples too. At the dancer and cultural activist Lubna Mariam's school in Dhaka, prayers are offered to Saraswati each winter. Shorōshshoti Pujō is celebrated as a symbolic gesture to Saraswati, the goddess of learning and the arts (and to some, the goddess of love) as much as a gesture of a shared past and current cosmopolitanism. This is something to be cheered in these fraught times. Dhaka University celebrates it with utmost dignity, even if some Islamic conservatives might frown at the practice, as a natural gesture of shared culture. Several Bangladeshi members of parliament, Mussulmans and Hindus alike, mark the day at the Jatiyō Shongshod, parliament house. It was particularly pleasing to see an old schoolfriend, Harsh Vardhan Shringla, born in the Darjeeling hills, an accomplished linguist and India's high commissioner to Bangladesh as I write this, join the legislators in celebration.

It appears that the goddess also had her moment in colonial and pre-colonial politics. The future jōmidār and titular raja, Nabakrishna Deb of Shōbhābājār, who allied with Robert Clive against Siraj-ud-Daula—and for his efforts earned himself the title of traitor in popular Bengali lore of Hindus and Mussulmans alike—hosted a Durga Pujō in 1757, as thanksgiving for the victory that brought General Clive and East India Company the future of Bengal, and eventually, India. Clive attended the celebrations, I read in Kumkum Chatterjee's essay, and sent 'over a number of goats to be sacrificed to the devi'. The Debs' pujō evidently became quite the event in the social calendar of the shāhéb, a time for carousing with alcohol and meat at a time of some abstinence for worshippers.

Historians speak also of the Mughals being at the receiving end of the mohādébi. Some mangalkavya speak of the demon she defeated as Mongōldōittō, which for lack of any reference in earlier texts like the Puranas, is taken by some historians to be the demonic Mughal—Mōgōl in Bānglā usage. While some writers like Dvija Madhav praised the Mughal emperor Akbar, others, like Bharatchandra Ray, the court poet of the raja of Nadia, in the eighteenth century, spun an elaborate and fantastic tale of how the débi won over the Mughals. It's a fascinating tale that involves Bhavananda Majumdar, an ancestor of Raja Krishnachandra of Nadia—who commissioned the kavya. Chatterjee tells it well in *Goddess Encounters: Mughals, Monsters and the Goddess in Bengal*:

> One of Bhavananda's principal earthly missions was to propagate the worship of the goddess who had singled him out especially for her blessings. An important opportunity in this direction occurred when according to the *Annadamangala*, the Mughal mansabdar, Raja Man Singh, was sent to Bengal to suppress Raja Pratapaditya of Jessore [phonetically Joshōr in Bangla] who had displayed blatant defiance towards Mughal

authority. The goddess decided that she wanted Man Singh to become her devotee. To this end, and at her machination, the raja and his soldiers faced seriously inclement weather and an acute shortage of food. Due to the goddess's favour, Bhavananda, whose storehouse was overflowing with abundant provisions, was able to come to the rescue of the Mughal forces by offering these to the latter.

That won Man Singh over to the goddess, in the incarnation of Annada, the provider of victuals. His devotion increased when, together with Bhavananda, he defeated Pratapaditya—which the kavya insisted could not have happened without the blessing of the goddess. (Indeed, the goddess twice over—Onnōdā as well as Obhoyā-Joshōreshshōri—who withdrew her favour from Pratapaditya on account of his 'unethical deeds'.)

Pleased, Man Singh insisted that Bhavananda accompany him to Emperor Jahangir's court in Delhi. There Man Singh spoke highly of Bhavananda and asked for him a reward, and also spoke of the influence of the goddess, to much derision by the emperor (he called her a 'ghost', the kavya tells us). Jahangir had Bhavananda imprisoned.

The goddess, angered at the emperor's denunciation of herself and his ill-treatment of her protégé, Bhavananda, proceeded to take terrible revenge on the city of Delhi. Accompanied by her entourage of spirits and fearsome creatures (dakini and yogini), she began a ferocious assault (utpaat) on the city: she and her hordes terrorized the citizens and created a serious shortage of food there. Large numbers of people died of starvation. The emperor, confronted by a crisis in his own capital city, ordered Bhavananda to be released from prison and offered the latter an apology. He issued a firman bestowing the title of raja on Bhavananda as well as the right to wear honorific robes...to fly flags and to have kettle drums played. He also acknowledged the greatness of the devi and agreed to worship her. The goddess, convinced of the Mughal emperor's genuine repentance, revealed herself to him in her full divine splendour. Jahangir, now converted from his former views, ordered that all citizens of Delhi should worship the goddess in their homes.

The grand finale of this segment of the poem comprised a scene in which the Mughal darbar became the venue for Annada/Durga puja:

> The darbar is the site of the puja, its principal participant is the padshah/Mughals and Pathans [resembling] ferocious outlaws attended [the ceremony]/ The qadi gave up reading the kalima; Quran-readers stopped reading it [also]; the womenfolk of the yavanas began to ullulate [sic].

◆

It is always a matter of some surprise to me how such absolute adulation and adoration of the female, as mother, as daughter, as saviour, went so seamlessly with the abominable behaviour towards women in Bengal, whether in Hindu society or when subsumed by conservative Islam—all the while with bhodrōlōk of both groups claiming liberal attitudes towards life in general and women in particular.

In late November 2015, as I waited one morning to board a train from Howrah to Bolpur, I purchased a copy of the local edition of the *Times of India* along with Kolkata staples *The Telegraph* and *Anandabazar Patrika*. These would be companions during a quick pilgrimage to Santiniketan for the joy of once again seeing the works of the sculptor Ramkinkar Baij, and also the paying of homage to the works of other masters like the painter Nandalal Bose—handpicked by Rabindranath to start the legendary art school, Kala Bhavana—displayed in an unpretentious manner, somewhat removed from the more upscale presentations associated with of some of our latter-day art greats like Ganesh Pyne, Ganesh Haloi, Sakti Burman and Bikash Bhattacharjee. Then I planned to visit one of my favourite bookstores, Subarnarekha; walk around the Visva-Bharati campus for a while, and round off the visit with some ālu-r chop and chā at at a favourite students' āddā location a short walk away in Ratan Pally.

My reverie was cut short by an article in *Times*. The headline was disturbing, and announced one of our dirty secrets: 'West Bengal tops chart in domestic violence.'

'Married women continue to be battered in their homes in Bengal. More than one in 10 cases of crimes against women in 2014 was reported from the state,' the article, datelined Kolkata, bluntly announced. Bengal accounted for one in five cases of cruelty by the husband and relatives, far more than north Indian states like Uttar Pradesh, Rajasthan and Haryana, whose society has been typecast as brutally parochial against the more 'liberal' and 'evolved' Bengal.

I've heard similar assertions being dismissed in so-called civilized society by people who claim bhodrōlōk do not commit such crimes; abuse, verbal and physical, is the preserve of chhōtōlōk, and such a subclass is actually subhuman—sub-Bengali if you will. I have heard such data being refuted on the ground of Bengal and, in particular, Kolkata, being cosmopolitan, welcoming to 'non-Bengalis': surely it was the culture of 'non-Bengalis' to beat and kill their women. Some went to the extent, as officials of both the Left Front and Trinamool parties did in the article, to contend that such figures are actually a result of emancipation and better law enforcement— unlike elsewhere, things in West Bengal are so advanced that women 'are able to go to a police station and file a complaint', an official was quoted as saying. Better rates of complaint have therefore led to worse statistics.

Assuming such assertions to be partly true, the numbers were still horrific, and included all socio-economic groups, castes and religions. West Bengal had remained on top of the list of domestic violence for seven consecutive years. As I read, in cases of suicides related to dowry, it was at second place, and in murders related to dowry, fourth. There were 23,278 recorded cases of cruelty by husbands and relatives in West Bengal in 2014, ahead of Rajasthan with 15,956 cases and Uttar Pradesh with 10,471 cases (the conviction rate in Bengal was 2.3 per cent as against an already dismal Indian average of 15.6 per cent). Over a decade, cases of marital violence in West Bengal increased by 235 per cent, the article mentioned, against the 110 per cent for India. More than a tenth of the cases of crimes against women in India were in West Bengal, at 38,299 cases. Uttar Pradesh topped that unlovely chart, but not by much; Rajasthan was a distant third.

'Cases are registered in West Bengal but nothing happens thereafter,' Abhijit Dutta, a lawyer interviewed for the article was quoted as saying. Madhuparna Ghosh, another lawyer and founder of Sutanutir Sakhya, a non-governmental organization in Kolkata that works towards eliminating gender discrimination, was equally trenchant. 'Despite the enactment of civil and criminal laws to deal with violence against women in their homes it continues with impunity since it is condoned by society.'

◆

The stereotype of the emancipated Bengali was born in a hall of smoke and mirrors, historically a place of domination and deceit for the Bengali male, certainly the bhodrōlōk, who lived in such self-important recesses in which the Bengali woman belonged to his command and control structure. Her emancipation lay in worshipping this prescribed lord, master and better, even to the extent of sharing him with other women. These were commandments, reprinted in chōti-bōyi, pamphlets, really, but monographs after a fashion.

Shōtir-Shār-Kothā, published by Chōndichorōn Ghosh from Shimla Street in Kolkata, found eager refuge in many eighteenth- and nineteenth-century homes. On one of its pages, this effort by Ghosh-babu shows a bhodrōlōk seated on a beautifully carved chair, his arm resting on what appears to be a marble-topped table, on which rests an ornate vase. His left leg, like his body clad waist downwards in that intricately folded garment, the knōchānō-dhuti, rests on his right knee. His plump torso is bare except for a pōité of the 'twice-born' Brahmin, the sacred thread a counterpoint to his Buddha-like eyes (the word komōlnoyōn, lotus-eyed, comes to mind). All this is topped by rich black wavy hair and manicured moustache.

At his khorōm-shod feet on a marble floor sits his lady, the bhodrōmōhilā, clad in an elaborately woven shāri, and ornaments. This gentlewoman's palms are joined in prayer and submission. There lies a thālā of floral offering, as if to a god, between this gentleman and her. Should the visual depiction prove inadequate there is urging in determined verse:

Pōti āgyā, Shōti pokkhé, Béd-ér shōmān
Pōti tushtō hōlé, tushtō prōbhu bhogōbān...

The wish of the husband is as the Vedas to the wife
If the husband is pleased, then god too is pleased.

Such wisdom was imparted early in the life of the Bengali woman, especially up to the nineteenth century; this was especially true of so-called colonial era civil society or bhodrō shomāj, as also the vast multitudes of Bengalis considered by their self-appointed betters as chhōtōlōk. When the Consent Bill arrived in 1892, writes Sripānthō, a brilliant, trenchant observer of Bengali society, ruling that a bride wouldn't be permitted to take up with her husband until she turned twelve, there was outrage in bhodrōlōk (here I cannot resist a pun using the suffix 'lōk' to define a parallel universe, akin to shorgōlōk, heaven). It had been bad enough when the age of consent was raised to ten in 1860, but twelve evidently was too much. 'People came out to the streets in Kalighat,' Sripānthō writes in *Keyabāt Méyé*, a collection of essays in Bānglā on the contested arrival of the emancipated Bengali woman. Jonmōbhumi writes, 'At least ten thousand are expected to gather at the Viceroy's residence' in Kolkata. Along with the outrage the journal claimed as having spread across the country, it listed several such gatherings in and around the capital of the British Indian empire of the time—Albert Hall in Potōldāngā, the Shābitri Shobha in Janbazar, at the residence of Nandalal Basu in Bagbazar, the Star Theatre, the residence of Prasannakumar Tagore by the banks of the Bhagirathi river...

Sripāntho (a pseudonym adopted by Nikhil Sarkar, long associated with the Bānglā daily *Anandabazar Patrika*) excavated this satirical reference to another sticking point for the Bengali male of the time—education for the Bengali female. Indrōnath Bondōpadhyay wrote in *Byangō Dorshōn*, detailing a syllabus for such study:

> Dance; the art of love; ... leaving the family, leaving the home; writing plays, stories and poetry and disrespecting elders. And once they are proficient they can move on to courses related to marriage: widow remarriage, remarriage, marriage after coming of age... Progressive girls have optional subjects: mod ō mūrgi (alcohol and chicken).

Pāshkorā Māg—another satirical bhodrōlōk offering that I would translate as *The Educated Slut* or *The Graduate Whore*—was aimed at educated young ladies who were also learned in the English language, and created a stir in such circles.

◆

We hear of the opening of the first regular school for girls under the initiative of Bengalis, in the suburb of Barasat, in 1847, three years before a similar laudable venture in Maharashtra. It later came to be known as the Kalikrishna Girls' High School. Earlier efforts for girls' education in Bengal had a looming shadow of Christian missionary zeal, unpalatable to many in Bengali high society. An influential Anglo-Indian lawyer, John Elliot Drinkwater Bethune, put his thoughts and assets behind the Native Female School in 1849, in Kolkata. He was helped by gutsy visionaries like Ishwar Chandra Vidyasagar, who wrote the first easy-to-understand book of grammar in Bāngla (I learnt from it as a child; the book of grammar is still used) and Madan Mohan Tarkalankar. It gradually morphed into the Bethune School in Kolkata, and over the next few decades spawned other schools for girls, several of them notably secular.

It ought to be a matter of untramelled collective pride for Bengalis that the parents of these young ladies and those like Vidyasagar persisted with their education and pushed for change with the handful of positive laws the colonial administration brought to bear on the populace such as banning the practice of sati and raising the age of consent for girls to be married.

And it was without question a good thing that we had what is sometimes called the Bengal Renaissance visit us when it did, for a hundred odd years from the late-eighteenth century onwards. It resulted in the awakening of the modern Bengali sensibility in many ways and a refining of modern Bengali identity and purpose.

It was brought about by a curious merging of the exposure by many proto-bhodrōlōk to enlightened European thinking from the time of the French Revolution as well as the colonial emphasis on the need for education and the elimination of horrific medieval practices (an ironical balance—giving a wealth of law and educational empowerment in return for a drain on wealth and political independence!). This led directly to the creation of a class of educated, self-aware, globally aware Bengalis who would now be administrators, lawyers, scientists, writers and thinkers, a class that rapidly outgrew the limited purpose the colonial masters had initially designed for them. Indeed, in several ways, the Bengal Renaissance saw the dawn of the bhodrōlōk (and, against severe odds imposed by society in general and quite a number of bhodrōlōk in particular, the bhodrōmōhilā), as a species that displayed societal and intellectual independence; the new bhodrōlōk, so to speak, spread way beyond the zamindar class and upper echelons of Brahmanism which once comprised the zealously guarded Bengali upper class. Indeed, several bhodrōlōk-in-the-making would now begin to look for salaried tenures, being

Sudeep Chakravarti

pushed away from zamindari inheritances and incomes.

It isn't about whether renaissance is too grandiose a word, overstating the case to equate it with the Italian Renaissance, cherished across the world. It is enough that we cherish what was essentially a flowering of education and, with it, a receptivity to new ideas and an opening up of attitudes. 'What matters is that there came into being in Bengal, beginning sometime in the waning years of the eighteenth century and flowering into fullness through the nineteenth century, an awakening of the Indian mind of such nature that we can call it a revolution,' Subrata Dasgupta eloquently observes in his book *Awakening: The Story of the Bengal Renaissance*. This was a cross-cultural mentality, as he tells us—'let us call it the *Indo-Western mind*, was the ultimate and supreme product of the Bengal Renaissance.'

Dasgupta, a scholar, scientist and prolific writer with a firm foothold in both computer and cognitive sciences and humanities, and in Kolkata, Europe and North America which have for long been his academic pasture, a bit of a renaissance man himself, is quite emphatic in his belief—one quite widely held in the logical corners of Banglasphere—that 'without the West there would not have been a Bengal Renaissance'.

There is little to dispute it even in the face of the increasingly emphatic writing of 'nationalist' commentators of which Bengal, India and Bangladesh appear to currently be in thrall. Warren Hastings, first as governor of Bengal in 1772 and then as governor general of India two years later, unapologetically extended and consolidated the Company's empire in India. But he also encouraged cultural excavators and facilitators, even if, as some historians have maintained, this was done with the cynical objective of getting to know the 'natives' a little better, 'civilize' them, educate them in the ways of empire and the world—Hindus, Mussulmans, 'native-Christians', the lot of us.

Whatever their motive or brief, these early orientalists earnestly set about their business, unfurling a series of developments that would have a great impact on Bengali society well into the nineteenth century. Nudged by Hastings, the philologist Nathaniel Brassey Halhed published his work of Bānglā grammar in 1778, which is regarded as the first ever systematic effort in the language by a grammarian, imperfect though it was. It was also the year that type in Bānglā was created by Panchanan Karmakar to enable the printing of Halhed's *A Grammar of the Bengali Language*. Karmakar, who came from a family of calligraphers in Hooghly district, is credited with creating types in several South Asian (Marathi, for example), West Asian and Eastern languages.

Within three years of this landmark event, Hastings sponsored a madrasa in Kolkata. Within four, the redoubt of orientalists in the subcontinent, the Asiatic Society, was established. India's premier orientalist destination for the next several decades was established in 1800, with the College of Fort William, which became a hub for scholarship. Although, as we have seen, it was likely premised on the need for rulers to better understand the ruled it did spawn a treasure trove in translations of texts from across South Asia and elsewhere; it became a repository for old manuscripts, and a centre for languages—Sanskrit, Bānglā, West Asian languages and even Mandarin were taught there by Indian and British scholars. Also in 1800—Richard Wellesley was then two years into the governor generalship of India—the Baptist Mission was established by William Carey in Srirampur (Serampore if you have a proclivity for Ingō-Bongō tones) along the western bank of the Hooghly, across what would come to be called Barrackpore—as self-evident an etymology as any. This signalled the beginning of an organized proselytization that would transform the religious map in great swathes of the subcontinent, and also eventually facilitate the genesis of the 'mission school' and 'mission college', from which would emerge many of the eventual educated middle class and elites of Bengal, of British India. Meanwhile, the industrious Karmakar developed a type for the Bānglā translation of the New Testament by Carey, an enormously influential missionary who had arrived in India in 1793.

The socio-cultural frenzy had barely begun.

Rammohun Roy, who soaked up a variety of influences, jobs and persuasions to emerge as a cosmopolitan leading light of Kolkata's Bengali society and among its major transformative forces, published his treatise on monotheism in Persian (though with an introduction in Arabic), *Tuhfat-ul-Muwahddin*, in the first decade of the nineteenth century. It was the opening salvo of the social and intellectual tumult he would set off for the next three decades until his death in 1833 at the age of sixty-one, in a village near Bristol. He actively campaigned against the ills of sati, child marriage and polygamous practices of what is in English referred to as kulinism—and propagated a whole new way of worship that evolved into what exists to this day—the Brahmo Samaj and its Vedic-layered, monotheistic adulation of the one creator and his munificence, a full-scale attack on the hidebound Hinduism of the time and idolatry.

What I find as interesting as his public persona is his earlier life. Rammohun's arrival on Bengal's stage is somewhat shrouded in mystery. What is known is that, being born into a wealthy kulin family of Hooghly district with strong application into the arts of kulinism, he was married off at a young age and, after the demise of his wife, twice more into what would culminate in uneasy, strained relationships. This experience certainly was the catalyst for his subsequent opposition to the practice in particular, and the edifice of kulinism in general. We know that he travelled on the bidding of his father to Patna and Kashi—Varanasi—as a youngster, soaking up expertise in Arabic and Persian, absorbing the Quran and West Asian classics and philosophical texts in their original languages in Patna; and Sanskrit and the study of Hindu scripture in Kashi. Thereafter, matters remain fuzzy for a period of several years—he roamed restlessly for several years; there are even accounts that claim he visited Tibet.

We see him again during his engagement with the indefatigable Carey, when Rammohun teamed up with him and a Sanskrit scholar in the last decade of the eighteenth century to collaborate on a religious text. Among other things, the trade-off brought Rammohun expertise in English, a language to which in a few years, he would add Latin and Greek. Alongside his intellectual pursuits this utter maverick of his time led a parallel life as a moneylender. Coupled with a slice of inheritance he over time grew wealthy enough to own several properties in and around Kolkata, including one in White Town.

In 1803, he would leave this profession behind and join the employ of the East India Company as a munshi, a quixotic decision considering he was financially independent; he later suggested that he took the job because he was driven by the need to better understand the British and their system. Some claim that endeavour may have taken him too far off the Indian mean—he wrote once of England as 'the land of liberty' though his myriad fans write that off as appreciation for the colonial government reversing several social ills plaguing Bengal and India, not adoration for a regime that was systematically impoverishing Bengal—and India—even as it went about demonstrating its white man's burden as a self-proclaimed master race.

Dasgupta's *Awakening* shares rich colour about the life and times of this mysterious man, such as this description of him in a periodical of the Baptist Mission Society in Britain, from 1817: 'Rama-Mohana-Raya, a very rich…Brahmun of Calcutta, is a respectable Sanskrit scholar, and so well-versed in Persian he is called Moulvee-Rama-Mohana-Raya: he also writes English with correctness and reads with ease English, Mathematical and metaphysical works…' In another place there is a recounting of how Rammohun held his own with residents of Kolkata's White Town, as 'Europeans breakfast at his house at a separate table, in the English fashion.'

But this was not just another interaction, as I gathered from Dasgupta's fine retelling of our renaissance, and other histories of that time of churn and change. Rammohun maintained a certain distance even as he interacted closely with missionaries or became for several years an employee by extension of the East India Company. '[He] admires Jesus Christ, but knows not his need of the atonement,' recorded the Baptist Mission's journal. 'He has not renounced his caste and this enables him to visit the richest families of the Hindoos. He is said to be very moral; but is pronounced to be a most wicked man by the strict Hindoos.' I'd say it was a liberal badge of honour.

He continued his journey of intellect, translating into English Vedic texts and portions of the Upanishads; and into Bānglā as well. He continued to rail against sati and idolatry in journals and in every available public space, highlighting for instance the horrific statistic of more than 1,500 incidents of sati in and around Kolkata between 1815 and 1818. His anti-idolatry pursuit led at one time to a lawsuit to disinherit him from his ancestral properties—which appeared to have been instigated by his mother, angered by Rammohun's position and practice away from conservative Hinduism!

Awakening has this interesting description of this man of the world whom I think of rather reverentially as a civilizational 'ninja'— in the sense of his being a skilled and stealthy force. 'Rammohun was a scholar so that he could be an activist, just as William Carey was a scholar so he could be an evangelist. He wrote not so much *on* monotheism as *for* it, and *against* sati, not *about* it.' It would take until 1829 when William Bentinck, as governor general of India, finally banned sati.

His learnings from various religions and core Hinduism and his worldview meanwhile began to coalesce through his writings into what Dasgupta perceptively calls the 'no-man's land' between communities and religions, drawing from all but giving in fully to none. The result was the creation in 1828 of the Brahmo Samaj (the Tagores took to it like ducks to water and greatly helped its propagation). This monotheistic pursuit, mentions its deed, would be 'for the worship and adoration of the Eternal Unsearchable and Immutable Being who is the Author and Preserver of the Universe'.

This is a gentle quasi-religion that draws from so many. It's hardly a surprise it hasn't drawn multitudes to its fold, only an infinitesimal fraction of the major religions, with its rituals of gentle songs worshipping such a god, church-like, unpretentious wedding ceremonies, prayer meetings at death that encourage the celebration of life, no picture of a god, no image of even a guru, an icon, just some flowers, and community gatherings in simple halls and rooms that are sometimes owned but more likely rented, that end with the sharing of simple food. Among other things, it spawned a clutch of fiercely independent women in urban Bengal supported by their parents and spouses, who went about their emancipated business usually by ensuring the education and emancipation of generations of women, Brahmo and not.

Perhaps, that is why it remained the most bhodrōlōk and bhodrōmōhilā of pursuits, if I can call it that. Even with its avowed encompassing of all it remained too much like the gentile living rooms in which it took shape. It was too nurtured, too refined and cult-like to spread, not folksy enough, not loud enough, not so much of a big deal in terms of celebrations and the visible benediction and forgiveness and wrath of its god. And, of course, because by the 1880s, the Brahmo Samaj had splintered into several factions over approaches to worship—essentially offering multiple approaches to The One as well as less esoteric matters such as the running of the organization and even conflicting stands on child marriage. Sometimes civilizational matters have their speed governors.

Two years after establishing the Brahmo Samaj, Rammohun would leave for Britain on a mission as curious as his life. As a petitioner on behalf of Akbar II, the emperor of the dying Mughal empire—indeed, he was largely referred to as King of Delhi, and by the unkind as King of Red Fort. The lesser namesake of Emperor Akbar engaged Rammohun as an emissary to the king of Britain to seek more pension. He even conferred a title on Rammohun as a matter of ceremony. The newly minted Raja would die there of meningitis three years later. It's where his remains are buried.

◆

The Bengal Renaissance—the more excitable among us would call it the Indian Renaissance—continued unabated for several decades of the nineteenth century with its epicentre in British India's capital of the time, Kolkata. One significant event after another took place in a domino effect that continued to gather momentum, until the grand fracture and political reorganization of 1857.

The Hindu College was founded in 1817, the genesis of what would later become the iconic Presidency College (now Presidency University that runs on the whims of the provincial government of Bengal that funds it); the Sanskrit College in 1824, the future residence of the brilliant, resolute scholar-activist Vidyasagar. Both were backed by wealthy, famous or progressive Bengali houses of Kolkata and had the firm stamp of approval of the Company government, and the imprimatur of Rammohun during his lifetime. (Even with their progressive roots they clearly had some progressive work to do. It took until Vidyasagar's principalship in 1851 for the Sanskrit College to permit the entry of non-Brahmins. When the newly-minted Christian, Madhusudan Dutt—he would formally assume the name 'Michael'—approached Hindu College in 1843, a callow but restlessly brilliant twenty-year-old published poet, it was too much for the institution. He was turned away and had to seek entrance at a 'mission' college.)

Thomas Babington Macaulay wrote his far-reaching 'Minute on Education' in 1835, the same year as the founding of Calcutta Medical College, the first such institution in the subcontinent. A year later, La Martiniere School was established in Kolkata, a decade before its cousin in Lucknow, by the French soldier of fortune and general, Claude Martin. Then as now it remains a premier 'mission' school, and a precursor to a flood of such institutions over the next several decades in Kolkata, and elsewhere in Bengal and India.

The tenor changed after 1857 but not the momentum. More gathered education, more gathered awareness, more gathered ambition, more gradually gathered a sense of nationalism, of Bengal, and of an emerging India. This nationalism was notably absent among the worthies of the Renaissance, including several zamindari families and their descendants, and even stalwarts of the Brahmo Samaj—they generally limited their progressive behaviour when it came to matters of colonial politics.

(This would change most notably with the creation in 1876 of the Indian Association by Surendranath Banerjee and Ananda Mohan Bose. It had as its rallying cry the 'political, intellectual and material advancement of the people'. Also called the Indian National Association, among other things it directly took on matters of discrimination against Indians, a cause emphatically espoused by Banerjee. This future president of the Indian National Congress—the Association merged with the Congress in 1886—seen in the early twentieth century as a moderate leader, with radical nationalism having by then spread quite deep into the Congress, was quite the firebrand of the time when he started out. *The Bengalee*, a newspaper founded by Banerjee, was an emphatic mouthpiece of that national aspiration. Mohan Bose, a brilliant mathematician and an Oxford graduate, and a barrister by profession would be his unflinching colleague in both the Association as well as the Congress.)

The Bengal Renaissance was far from done.

Along with the flowering of Madhusudan and the publication of his best-known work, *Méghnādbodh Kābbō* (The Killing of Meghnad) in 1861, arrived a giant of Bānglā prose, Bankim Chandra Chattopadhay, who had already created a flutter by virtue of becoming, in 1858, one of the first two graduates—the other was Juddoonath Bose—of the University of Calcutta (it was created along with the universities of Bombay and Madras in 1857). *Durgéshnōndini*, his first novel in Bānglā—he had first written *Rajmohan's Wife* in English!—was published in 1865 (*Vande Mataram*, or *Bondé Mātorom* would follow in seven years). The Indian Association for the Cultivation of Science took root in the 1870s, driven by stalwarts like Mahendralal Sircar.

Then, a frenzy till the turn of the century and beyond. The emergence of Vivekananda. His association with the seer Ramakrishna and his subsequent spiritual awakening—and his landmark visit to North America. Rabindranath's first poem and, not long after, the beginning of his frenetic creativity.

The first women college graduates of India in 1883 were Kadambini Bose and Chandramukhi Basu. They would soon be followed by the first woman honours graduate, an alum of Bethune School, the eventual poet, feminist and suffragist Kamini Roy. She is sometimes held up as an inspiration for East Bengal's iconic poet Sufia Kamal, who is also revered for her untiring work as a women's rights activist and pacifist, for her work for the cause of Bānglā nationalism, and as a liberation war hero of Bangladesh who stood up, at an advanced age, to initimidation and threats to her life. (Another remarkable alum from Bethune was the educationist Sarala Ray, who established Gokhale Memorial Girls' School in Kolkata).

There was the maturing of the globally respected scientist Jagadish Chandra Bose; and on, and on, in a prolonged starburst of formative, creative, discussive, inventive energies. At this time Bengal appeared almost to be careening ahead of itself and certainly ahead of the rest of the subcontinent. A hive of empire and at once a burgeoning hive of anti-empire.

We haven't seen anything quite like it since. You'll forgive us for still being in thrall.

◆

The gender-enlightenment of the bhodrōlōk as a species was a long time coming—it's still a work in progress! Anyhow, Bethune's school, I read, began with twenty-three girls. Sixteen of them evidently left within days, driven away by the propaganda of unsettled bhodrōlōk. The charitable enticement of free education, free books and even a free pālki ride for the commute couldn't override the derision that was hurled at the first pupils. If a palanquin served those nearby, Bethune had provided a horse carriage to bring students from afar, on which Ishwar Chandra Vidyasagar is said to have got inscribed in Sanskrit a plea: *Bring up your daughter with the same love and care as you do a son, educate her.*

By the end of the year, enlightenment had clawed back a slim advantage—the school marked it with thirty-four students. But there would for long be a block, even well after the colonial government threw in its budgetary support for the education of 'native' girls: 'As soon as they reach the age of ten or eleven, school is over,' notes *Kéyabāt Méyé*. 'There is a new concern: marriage.'

And so, the battle of the enlightened bhodrōlōk with what I would unhesitatingly term the chhōtōlōk-bhodrōlōk was fought as sharply as that fought over the age of consent. The practice of child marriage, the curse of Bengali society as in societies across the subcontinent, was bitterly defended. Can you tell exactly to the day when the mango ripens in summer? went one such query in support of the marrying of children. How then can you fix an age for a girl to ripen?

The handful of voices that managed to break through was awash in despondency and trauma. 'I was married at nine,' wrote Shārōdāshundōri, born in 1819. She was the mother of the noted social reformer Keshub Chandra Sen. 'According to the Hindu tradition I remained at my father's house for a year. When I turned ten I went to my shōshurbāri... Before I arrived at my in-laws, I used to be very afraid. I used to think they might jail me, or hang me. I cried for a month thinking these things. When my father finally forcibly took me to my in-laws it felt as if he had drowned me.'

The kulin Brahmins of Bengal, who freely practised polygamy and endorsed sati, were among the apex offenders, proud of their claim as descendants of five Brahmin families invited to Bengal to perform a yagna for King Adisura in the eleventh century CE. Many of these kulin of the Bharadwaj, Shandilya, Kashyap, Vatsya and Swavarna caste groups, or gōtrō (disclosure: my family's gōtrō is shāndillō, or Shandilya) were sometimes little more than kidnappers and child molesters, writes Sripāntho. Some were like pashas, or 'marriage traders', as he terms them, and cites one Ishwar Chhattopadhyay—Chātujjé, in colloquial Bānglā—already married several dozen times when he pounced on Nistarini, a ten-year-old from a kulin family of Bardhaman.

This was the situation in urban concentrations of Bengal where a few stories showed the truth. The villages largely remained an undocumented zone of destroyed female lives. Marriage before the coming of age was only one eventuality. Destitution after the death of the husband was frequently another. Suicide by women was rampant, a matter documented from the 1870s onwards. Kolkata, with its relatively easy access to reporting and investigation, recorded the maximum. Some young girls—kishōri, to use the appropriate word in Bānglā—searched for a kind of darkness to be able to live, as Sripāntho evocatively writes in a chapter titled 'Kishōri-bhojōnā', the worship of young girls. The population of Kolkata in the middle of the eighteenth century was taken to be four 'lakhs'. Among these 4,00,000 residents, prostitutes numbered 12,419, according to a report by the Chief Presidency Magistrate of Calcutta in 1853. Of these 10,000 were Hindus, including several kulin girls. This collective of the careworn grew to 30,000 by 1867, according to government estimates. Two years later, *Amrita Bazar Patrika*, then just a year-old infant but with an already emphatic voice, estimated that Hindu widows accounted for 90 per cent of Kolkata's comfort women, most of a young age.

They exist to this day, our cast-out widows, in our villages and towns and cities. Sometimes they are worked like servants in their own homes, sometimes they are put away in charitable institutions and old-age homes where people age before their time. Varanasi, the city of the gods and death has so many of our widows, so many of them destitute, the destination of welcome charity and the subject of numerous documentaries, living out the end of their days with their cast-out sisters, in prayer—often the only thing they can still call their own.

10

Khelā-dhūlā
Games we play

Something took shape on 29 July 1911. A bit of our history, some of our pride, much of our obsession.

Mohun Bagan had begun to storm through the field at that year's tournament for the IFA shield, mostly a white-colonial preserve made up of regimental teams managed by the Indian Football Association. The team of barefoot Bengalis—unlike other teams they played without football boots—had since the 10th of the month defeated the teams of St Xavier's College, Rangers Club, and Rifle Brigade to reach the semi-finals. There they were matched evenly with Middlesex Regiment, 1–1. The replay, also at the Dalhousie ground was a no-contest, with Mohun Bagan winning 3–0. Next up was the final match against East Yorkshire Regiment.

It was an unprecedented event at the height of Empire, and in a Bengal that still seethed at being partitioned. Indian versus British would have been hype enough. This had the added hype of Bengali versus British.

Chronicles of the time—media, official club documentation, researchers who studied the game and its implications—record that large crowds had gathered for the semi-finals, but there was nothing like the crush of between eighty and a hundred thousand that flocked to the Calcutta Football Club ground to watch the finals. Much of that throng was from Kolkata and its environs, but spectators arrived in large numbers from Bihar, Assam and northern and eastern Bengal. East Indian Railway ran special trains from

Bardhaman. Steamers to the nearest docks were packed, and so were trams in the city. Kolkata witnessed its first horrifying traffic jam.

Most couldn't make their way in, about ten thousand did. Some bought a two-rupee ticket for fifteen rupees. This is probably the first recorded incident of scalping of tickets or 'blacking' in Bengal (which would in some decades emerge as a māstān cottage industry from sporting events to the cinema and confirmed reservation in trains), different from hoarding or blackmarketeering at which those who traded in Bengal had already shown their aptitude. Spectators paid outrageous prices for snacks—a small boiled potato for one paisa, a paan for the princely sum of four annas, with sixteen annas to a rupee. Some paid between three and five rupees for a box to stand on. Mohun Bagan Club chronicles mention 'babus' were on one side of the ground, the shāhéb on another, with seating provided by B. H. Smith & Co. With such arrangements, most people could only follow the progress of the match through the roars of the crowd and shouted Chinese whispers, as it were. Kites of a particular colour would be flown to signal a goal by one or the other team—black for the British, and maroon and green, the club colours of Mohun Bagan.

It was just another day for the East Yorkshires, proud to be in the finals though somewhat wary of a 'native' team on a screamer of run to the finals. But the Mohun Bagan team, it seems, went to get blessings from Kali before their match at 11 a.m.—even Sudhir Chatterjee, a practising Christian, who would in later years become the Reverend Chatterjee. He would be the only one among the eleven to play in boots. There were ten Bengalis on the team. The eleventh member, Bhuti Sukul, was from Uttar Pradesh, and with Chatterjee formed the defence.

The British team scored first in the first half, off a free kick. Black kites. Twenty minutes into the second half 'Bagan' captain and left winger, Shibdas Bhaduri, shot in the equalizer. Maroon and green kites, and pandemonium. In the eighty-seventh minute he passed the ball to centre forward Abhilas Ghosh and Ghosh slammed it into the goal. Maroon and green kites. Going by club chronicles, there was a burst of unfettered insanity when the game ended shortly after with the scoreline reading 2-1: shirts, walking sticks (chhōri), shoes, were flung on to the ground in sheer exuberance and, alongside the chanting of the club's name, there were shouts of Bondé Mātorom.

Mohun Bagan became the first Indian team to win the IFA shield. For all practical purposes they had won the world cup of our colonized, besieged and divided world.

◆

Players and management of both teams were dignified in praising the efforts of the other team, and most among the conservative colonial press played down the hysteria. The news agency Reuters cabled London: 'The absence of all racial spirit was noted. The European spectators were good humoured and the Bengalees cheered the losing team,' as a Mohun Bagan souvenir noted. *The Telegraph* of London wrote of it as 'fair contest, fairly and gallantly fought on both sides in a friendly spirit without anything like race-hatred or rancour finding any place in the hearts of the combatants.'

The club itself played it down, as I read in a retelling of the match. The club management wrote to *The Statesman* of Kolkata that it was not 'desirable to make a fuss' of the 'success'. '[T]he Club in general and the players in particular look upon it as the result of practice and study of the science of the game under the guidance and with the help of their numerous friends both European and Indian.'

This gesture of humility and sportsmanship was a bit at odds with the general public reaction. For many it wasn't just a victory. In Bengal it was seen as payback not just for the Partition of 1905 but for several decades of public, vocal diminishing of the Bengali by lāt-shāhéb and lesser shāhéb alike. Across India it was seen also as colonized brown people beating the white overlords, overturning the odds and reversing the persistent narrative of enforced inferiority.

It was also a time when most leagues and top competitions like the Durand Cup and Rovers Cup had been restricted to British regimental teams for the longest time. Nearly all commentators agree that Mohun Bagan's entry into the IFA shield, which the sports researcher Kausik Bandyopadhyay terms a so-called open shield in its early years, was 'unbelievably hard-earned'. Entry was restricted; and rare teams like Sovabazar helped to force the crack a little wider. (The maharaja of Cooch Behar—the British phonetic for the land of the Koch people—Rajendranarayan Bhup Bahadur, began the Cooch Behar Cup more or less in disgust at such football apartheid.) If ever a football match carried the flavour of revolution, this had to be it.

Bandyopadhyay, who is among several to write scholarly essays on the match, says some Bengal-based and Bengali-owned publications pitched it as a Bengali victory, while others, whether Indian-or British-owned publications spoke of it as an Indian victory, and some used it interchangeably. There was adulation from *The Mussulman* in a club souvenir about the win, seen as what Bengalis call pāltā mār, to hit back:

> Although Mohun Bagan was a team composed of Bengali Hindus, the jubilation in consequence of its success was in fact a sense of universal joy, which pervaded the feeling of the Hindus, Mohammadans and the Christians alike. The members of the Muslim Sporting Club were almost mad and rolling on the ground with joyous excitement on the victory of their Hindu brethren.

Amrita Bazar Patrika labelled the team 'Immortal XI'.

The team was given a victory parade atop horse drawn carriages. Hindus and Mussulmans alike sponsored 'band parties' in accompaniment. Hindu ladies blew on conch shells, the traditional device for war, victory and worship. Club history claims Standard Cycle Company sold 1,00,000 products on the strength of a free poster featuring the eleven with every purchase. Musical instrument dealers Messrs Hald & Chat [Halder & Chatterjee] of Kolkata offered harmoniums at a discount of 10 per cent for two months; club members received a discount of 50 per cent. Messrs S. Roy & Co., sports goods merchants, reduced the price of footballs from twelve rupees to four, to encourage the game.

◆

The obsession hasn't really let go since, even though cricket has joined football—and far exceeded the passion football generates, with clever formatting and marketing of the game into shorter formats to fully utilize television and digital media as vehicles, and the consequent morphing of players into media superstars. It probably helps that in Bengal and Banglasphere, as elsewhere in the subcontinent, cricket has brought glory and joy to the country, even though the game is only played competitively in a couple of dozen countries.

Today, football is mostly a vicarious, global pleasure for us: India and Bangladesh's FIFA rankings are so low a cricketer would have to be a star to score in such high numerals. Until nascent attempts to energize football through new professional leagues cross-fertilized with young and ageing players from across the world begin to bear results, we will perforce have to bask in the glory of other countries and their clubs and players, during World Cups or the World Cup-standard professional leagues in Europe and Latin America.

There has been little Bengali glory in sports away from football and cricket. We sparkled briefly when Monotosh Roy won the Mr Universe title in bodybuilding in a Class 3-short men category, in 1951, making a dent in the stereotype of the weak Bengali. The following year we had our 'Pocket Hercules' when the diminutive Manohar Aich brought home a Mr Universe title, also in bodybuilding. Both became icons for fitness—Roy, in particular, for yoga—but there it stayed. It took until 2016, for Banglasphere to have a notable sporting icon beyond football and cricket, when a petite Dipa Karmakar, from Agartala in Tripura, became the first person from a South Asian country to qualify for gymnastics at an Olympic games, in Rio de Janeiro. Karmakar was, at the time, among only five gymnasts to have successfully attempted the Produnova vault, named after the Russian gymnast, Yelena Produnova. It involves two front double somersaults after first vaulting with a front handspring, and carries a degree of difficulty so high it is called the vault of death. Karmakar successfully executed it in Rio, failed to land a medal, and yet emerged a star, a beacon of fortitude and success to women and achievers of any gender anywhere, having overcome a life of hardship and India's abysmal training facilities.

◆

Meanwhile, we create our own histories in cricket. Certainly in Bangladesh, where cricket is seen as a transformative sport—in an order of magnitude similar to Sri Lanka, where the national team's 1996 victory in the World Cup was a gigantic morale booster to the country as a whole, mired as it was in a long drawn-out, stunningly violent civil war. Bangladesh now dreams that sporting dream; and it is realistically fuelled by the recent impressive strides of the country's cricket team, taking on, and occasionally beating the best in the world.

I first saw a major cricket match, a test between India and West Indies in the winter of 1974–1975, at Eden Gardens in Kolkata. India won. The batting wizard G. R. Viswanath scored a century, and the charismatic Mansur Ali Khan, the captain and titular Nawab of Pataudi, struck four consecutive fours after returning with a wired jaw from an Andy Roberts 'bouncer'. All of these pleasing results, my father explained, was because he had placed a pack of cigarettes in a particular way in front of our seats. Some others around us offered the explanation that the captain's fortitude and luck had returned since he married one of our celebrated beauties, the actor Sharmila Tagore (in 1968). Father exulted along with the tens of thousands in the stands at every upswing for India and scowled or looked to the sky to silently berate the suddenly elusive gods of cricket at every downturn. Father also complained every now and then during the downturns about selectors of the Indian teams being 'hopeless' and biased against cricketers from Bengal in general and Bengalis in particular—there wasn't a single Bengali in the team that beat one of the best ever West Indian sides—even as he appreciated the art of every Indian great and every great cricketer anywhere, period.

Everyone around us joined in from time to time, and argued good naturedly and vociferously. We shared food and beverage. They chided Father each time he retrieved the pack of cigarettes and neglected to put it back exactly in the position that would enable the Indian team to take wickets. Over those five days I learned about Probir Sen, who kept wickets for India for several test matches; about Pankaj Roy, the stylish batsman who starred in an opening partnership of 413 runs with Vinoo Mankad (against New Zealand in Madras, in 1956, a test cricket record that stood until 2008); about the short shrift given to Shute Banerjee and Ambar Roy in tests. Like many in Banglasphere it would take Father until 1996 to forgive India's cricket selectors. That year they chose Sourav Ganguly to play in the test side. On his test debut at Lord's cricket ground in London in 1996, Ganguly scored a century, the tenth Indian and the first Bengali to have ever done so in the history of the game. We again had a cricketing hero. One hero over two decades, but he was still ours, among the most successful batsmen in the history of the game, in tests and the 50-overs format, the first Indian captain since Mansur Ali to wear his attitude, even a sneer, so visibly on his sleeve.

The nawab was too much of a sophisticate to remove his shirt in public view. Our Sourav took off his shirt and waved it around his head at Lord's as India's limited-overs side beat England to take the series, in mid-July of 2002. Father died before he could see this exhibition. I wonder what he would have done—probably wince at Ganguly's lack of decorum and then smile at his daredevilry.

Bengal did, because Ganguly was so much more to us than a mere cricketer.

A former colleague, Rohit Brijnath, for several decades a 'Kolkata boy' and among India's finest sportswriters, wrote an essay in 1997 that encapsulated what Ganguly meant to Bengalis. This was just a year after his spectacular debut.

> If he was born anywhere else in India, Ganguly would not have merited such genuflection; but Bengal, short of heroes, seeing in him a reflection of its once considerable glory, looking to him to restore its receding pride, has elevated him to being a literal Prince of Calcutta.
>
> Take one story. There are days, says Ganguly, when people come from neighbouring localities or towns to see him and his durwan says he's not there. So they touch the gate in reverence, smile and leave content.
>
> One thing is clear. Fly the globe, ride universal highways, sail any waters, and you won't find anyone who worships heroes like they do in Bengal. During Rabindranath Tagore's funeral procession, tufts of his beard were plucked off as mementos. In 1911, when Mohun Bagan beat a British regimental team to become the first Indian team to win soccer's IFA Shield, legend has it that Kanu Ray, the teenage right winger from Presidency College, never ate again in his hostel. He had invitations across town. For the next three years.
>
> ...In a larger context, Bengal, once the heart of India—politically the capital, culturally the centre—had been banished, some assumed, into insignificance. Ganguly, cricket bat in hand (and nowadays a cricket ball too), mouthing the words, 'I am representing India from Bengal', is seen as altering some of those assumptions.

The deification of Ganguly, wrote Brijnath, was everywhere. Fans mobbed him on a plane, thanking him for putting Bengal 'on the world map'. In his early days with the Indian team when Ganguly was dropped for a match, and Bengal papers widely reported it, an outraged reader phoned *The Telegraph* to fume: 'What is this, Bengal has been insulted.'

◆

'Eden' is still packed to capacity for major matches. So are Sher-e-Bangla stadium in Dhaka and Chittagong's cricket stadium with its changing names, where crowds cheer the home team, the Tigers, with unfettered subcontinental fervour. A loss is like a blow to all Bangladesh, a win very nearly the justification for the independence of Bangladesh. For the country's cricket premier league, when the bizarrely named Chittagong Vikings take on the Dhaka Dynamites (they were once Gladiators) or Barisal Bulls (née Burners), Khulna Titans or Comilla Victorians, or whatever names take wing as passion and team ownerships change, viewers throng stadia and remain glued to television sets and mobile phones, similar to when, across the border, Kolkata Knight Riders take on other fantastically named teams from elsewhere in India in unabashed panem et circenses displays.

And yet the effects of football, even second-hand football, vicarious football, can be overwhelming, exaggerate the Bengali to another level altogether.

There is a bit of a running joke that OWGs, or Old White Guys, in a range from political figures to pop stars find their latter-day deliverance, a last hurrah, in an increasingly prosperous developing world, a place they had little time for in their prime because such places then held for them relatively sparse crowds and frugal income. In Bengal that last hurrah is seen to best effect when it concerns legends of football. They don't even need to be 'white', just great football players.

When Pelé, the wizard sometimes known as Edson Arantes do Nascimento, visited Kolkata in 1977, he was done with Brazil, and was playing professional football for the Cosmos Club in the United States. He came by with Cosmos to play an exhibition match with Mohun Bagan. Some media reports maintain he was drawn by a letter of invitation from the club that spoke of the club's contribution to the freedom movement—that 1911 match. As soon as he landed, some of the several thousands-strong crowds at the city's then ramshackle airport broke police cordons to rush the plane. He was mobbed as he came into the terminal. A minister tried to make his way into a holding area for the star claiming he was a minister; he was booed away by a crowd that maintained, for the day, they were all ministers. When this king-emperor of football was felicitated in the city, he was given a faux crown to wear, gifted by an adoring durbar of footballers and fans, for whom the crown was as real as the one, adorned with stolen jewels, that George wore in Delhi. The exhibition match at the sold-out Eden Gardens was drawn 2-2. Eighty thousand fans watched the game. More, if you counted the crowds on the rooftop of the nearby All India Radio building. Pelé remained front-page news in West Bengal for several days.

◆

That was still the heyday of Kolkata's football league, though it was sometimes like *Animal Farm*. A win or loss could, and did, lead to violence. An uncle, my father's cousin, had taken me to see an East Bengal and Mohun Bagan match in a stadium with patchwork wooden stands, in the Maidan. East Bengal, 'our team', was almost certain to win. I don't remember the scoreline. But I do recall my uncle hurrying me out from the stands as the match ended, saying there would be trouble. By the time we were heading south on Chowringhee from Esplanade on a tram—without question my favourite mode of transport in Kolkata, to ride it along the Maidan was an absolute, quaint charm—the Mohun Bagan tsunami of outrage had reached us (it could have been the East Bengal wave, had Mohun Bagan won). Bricks and stones were being thrown at any and every vehicle on the street. The packed slow-moving tram was a target. As passengers rushed to get away from the open entrance, we found ourselves cowering behind a slim rod. Fortunately the fans—rioters now—were keener on spectacular damage. They aimed at the windows of the tram, away from us.

That was an exhibition of heartbreak as much as mastanocracy, a sign of the times. Mobs of mostly young and mostly marginalized men who, denied even the joy of watching their legally-permitted warriors in multi-coloured jerseys, shorts, stockings and cleated boots win a war of ninety minutes, took out their disappointment and anger on whatever and, sometimes, whosoever came at hand—outraging against the world. The contests between prominent Calcutta Football League clubs—East Bengal, Mohun Bagan, Mohammedan Sporting were sometimes reduced to the vilest chauvinism of regions and religions which, incredibly, didn't diminish the artistry of the players or appreciation of their artistry by the opposition's players and fans—but only after the frenzy unleashed by a loss had diminished. It almost didn't matter what these and other local teams—Wari, George Telegraph and others—did outside the local league, or how many of their players made it to the national teams. Stardom and infamy were decided on the spot, win or lose.

Time, the emergence of more leagues and, perhaps more importantly, the opening of doors to those of other religions and other nationalities has reduced the chauvinism and animal passion of fans that for decades tarnished Bengal's football. But even that was changing during my school and university years, well into the 1980s, and certainly in the 1990s, when love of the sport and sportspersons and a certain cosmopolitanism had begun to triumph over the despair and hate. If East Bengal fans worshipped the wonder of the Bengali Hindu Subhash Bhowmick and the magic of the Iranian Shia Jamshid Nassiri, Mohun Bagan adored Bhowmick (the powerful forward switched sides, and lived! in a decade-long playing career and then a coaching career) and the Nigerian Chima Ephraim Okorie (who also played for East Bengal and Mohammedan Sporting; I've heard Bengalis endearingly call him Chima-da). And Mohammedan Sporting fans came to idolize

Nassiri and the devoutly Christian Okorie.

A win for any of these teams does not any longer lead to the frenzied purchase of ilish, chingri or baré-miān (the accepted code for beef: big man) from market stalls. A loss does not lead to the instant ostracization of players or the beginning of a riot. But that hardly means there is less passion. It's just that it's a more civilized thing. Bengal's māstān have so much else to focus on and gain from than today's slickly marketed football of brand name sponsorship and televised media conferences—Bengal's real estate, Bengal's politics, and other criminal activities.

◆

When Pelé returned thirty-eight years later in 2015, leaning on a walking stick, invited for a function of a club in a new professional league, Atlético de Kolkata, he was still a huge draw. You should have seen Mamata Banerjee—'Didi' to fans and favour-seekers. As he graciously bowed low to the chief minister of West Bengal, legend to legend-in-the-making, held her hand in both of his and raised it to his lips, looking into her eyes, she blushed like a delighted schoolgirl.

On another occasion Kolkata had welcomed another of its sons of vicarious glory, a man who mixed talent with chutzpah, the Bengali holy grail—the Argentine Diego Maradona, the 'hand of God' to Pelé's king and emperor.

There is a theory that the passion with which the Trinamool Congress government of West Bengal paints public structures—state-run buildings, overpasses, bridges, water tanks, water tankers, garbage trucks, even some taxis (city authorities issue permits and so can wield a broad brush)—with white and blue, colours that marginally adorn the party's flag, is not on account of its supremo Mamata Banerjee's fondness for the colours, nor of a shared humility with Mother Teresa's order, the Missionaries of Charity that call Kolkata home and wear simple saris of white bordered in blue, but her fondness for the colours of Argentina's football team. In the Didi-era I have more than once, over Christmas and New Year week in Kolkata seen streams of blue and white lights strung across Park Street, a colour combination I hadn't noticed in pre-Didi times, a show of light and party colours to highlight the city's premier locale to celebrate Borōdin—the advent of Christ is Big Day—which brings out vast, mostly non-Christian crowds to the Park Street-Chowringhee area, as does the Nobōborshō of the Gregorian calendar.

There is quirkiness that lends credence to such fantastic tales. In mid-2014, Mamata's government pushed Kolkata's municipal corporation, which Trinamool controlled at the time, to propose that property tax would be waived for the 2014–2015 financial year if homeowners painted such structures in white and blue. So did the state's assembly, as a Bill, only for it to be held up by a petition at Calcutta High Court. Incredulous judges asked the government's counsel about 'rationale'. There is no evidence for the theory, but when football madness is aligned to Mamata's quirks—she once said she finds the combination of white and blue soothing, and the colours would help prevent Kolkata from seeming dirty—alternative facts matter.

The indisputable alternative fact to Pelé in Kolkata is that Maradona, football's enfant terrible and genius, is divinity with a human touch, a fallen angel who dallied with drugs and a man who didn't mind calling Fidel Castro a good friend. It's an irresistible mix for Bengal's rebel heart that so readily forgives an artist's artlessness away from the canvas where he wrought great art.

When Maradona visisted Kolkata in 2008, for the foundation ceremony of a football academy, media estimated crowds of 50,000 at the airport and lining his route into the city, well past midnight when his flight touched down. Several thousand police were deployed for crowd control. Maradona was welcomed by West Bengal's sports minister of the elected Left Front communist government of the time. He received a prolonged ovation at the Salt Lake Stadium, which was packed to capacity—crowds were estimated at 1,10,000. An artist presented him a sketch of Che Guevara, and received a delighted hug in return. India's foreign minister at the time, Pranab Mukherjee (who later became the 13th President of India), made sure he was there. When Maradona visited Mother House, where Mother Teresa's memorial is, residents in white and blue saris—default Argentine colours—thronged to see him. Grinning, giggling nuns.

When Maradona's inheritor, Lionel Messi, another among the greatest-football-player-ever-league, visited Kolkata in 2011 as part of a 'friendly' match between Argentina and Venezuela organized by FIFA, the crowds were equally ecstatic. Fans painted their faces in Argentine colours, carried Argentine flags, queued up in their tens of thousands for a glimpse of their idol. It was easy then to understand a Bengali wisecrack: Pele Maradona, nā-pélé Messi. It plays on the Bānglā word pélé (to get, if we get) to string together the three gods in our football-Olympus.

Utterly insane.

11

Sinikbewty
Stories of travel

We travel. We travel like an irresistible force driven by an irresistible urge. We also travel irritably, loudly and, occasionally, helpfully.

You may know of the now legendary letter of 1909 by a 'baboo', Okhil Chandra Sen, an incendiary complaint to the divisional office of the Indian railway at Sahibganj, near the tri-junction of West Bengal, Bihar and Jharkhand. Along with a poem apocryphally written by a Bengali schoolteacher going to the jungle to shoot a 'Boshtad tiger' who ate his wife, Okhil Babu's letter has achieved cult status in the internet age. The text of the letter is now displayed at the Indian Railway Museum in New Delhi, and exceeds anything that colonial English snobs could have thought up after emptying the world of gin and tonic—or absinthe, for that matter:

Dear Sir,

I am arrive by passenger train Ahmedpur station and my belly is too much swelling with jackfruit. I am therefor went to privy. Just I doing the nuisance that guard making whistle blow for train to go off and I am running with 'LOTAH' in one hand & 'DHOTI' in the next when I am fall over & expose all my shocking to man and female women on platform. I am got leaved Ahmedpur station.

This too much bad, if passenger go to make dung that dam guard not wait train five minutes for him. I am therefor pray your honour to make big fine on that guard for public sake. Otherwise I am making big report to papers.

Yours faithfully servant,
OKHIL CH. SEN.

◆

Much of India and Bangladesh continue to defecate where they can, but a Bengali baboo's outrage apparently made certain the subcontinent's trains finally got toilets.

It's a travel convenience, you see.

◆

Like many Bengali families mine too was—is—travel-mad. We never took to employing travel houses like Kundu Special, a legendary Kolkata-based agency established in 1933, which during summer and pujō holidays would book entire coaches in several trains departing Howrah or Sealdah. Kundushpéshāl, as it is mostly known, and over time the several imitators it spawned, would transport entire lots, several dozens or several hundred travellers, to practically every notable tourist spot in India. They shepherded among the most finicky and argumentative folks on the planet who, alongside the urge to see new places and absorb new experiences, had to be catered to for their primary body-and-soul functions that even the romance of travel and the purity of pilgrimage would not dim— clockwork and palatable ingestion, the volubly discussed matter of digestion, and the near-spiritual act of egestion. It was, and is, the Battle Order School of Travel.

Top draws were and remain the lower and middle Himalayan region from Kashmir in the northwest to Sikkim in the northeast; northern Himalayan pilgrimages such as Kedarnath and Badrinath (Kédār-Bōdri in short); the hill station of Shimla and its once-pristine northern neighbour, Narkanda; Nainital; Agra; all Rajasthan (driven since the 1970s by Ray's popular family film *Shōnār Kéllā*, which involves a past-life regression of a Kolkata boy that brings him to the exquisite yellow sandstone fort of Jaisalmer); and dozens of other places of tourist interest in India.

You will find Bengalis at every noteworthy 'View Point' on every noteworthy hill, from Panchmarhi in central India to a perch looking over the majestic Kangchenjunga (Kānchōnjongā to us) in the eastern Himalaya. They will be pedalling furiously on gaudily painted cockle-shell boats, or sit like born navigators on rowboats on every noteworthy tourist-lake across the subcontinent—Dal, Nainital, Kodaikanal, Ooty, Pichola, Bhimtal, Mirik, Phewa—reliving childhoods and perhaps that early romance. The craggy beauty of the sheer marble hills cut by the blue-green Narmada not far from Jabalpur will ring with their exclamations of beauty.

They will leave their footprints on the damp and impermanent sands of every 'seebitch' from Digha in West Bengal, the Indian Bengali's home beach, as it were, to the former Anglo-Indian vacation redoubt of Gopalpur-on-sea in Odisha, to the ruined beaches of one of my adoptive homes, Goa to its cousin in the far west of India, the former Portuguese outpost of Diu—absorbing the bracing air, seeking perfect sunrises and sunsets and volubly telling the world while doing so, and often running down the quality of local seafood as being too salty, too smelly, not being of freshwater or the last acceptable envelope of brackish water or not being lightly fried before being added to a curry. Not being Bengali enough. (Gentlemen of my grandfather's generation were in their exuberant youth known to add another layer of condescension to travel usually undertaken for 'change' or convalescence. In rustic lands away from Kolkata they would refer to local offerings—from seafood to wild honey—with the frequent exclamation of 'Damn cheap'. In some places that earned the visiting tribe of bhodrōlōk the moniker of 'danchi-babu'.)

We can be heard yelling at each other from one hillside to another, or at a distance of a few feet. Friends and family, Bumbā-māmā, Potōl-dā, Minku-pishi, Chhōtlu, Mungli-di, and Bublāmāshi set the Nilgiris, Shivaliks and the Lower Himalaya ringing with nicknames at a sonic level near enough to cause an avalanche. The urging will be to come by and see the opurbō, unparalleled, or phantashtik, bhew on their side, or from their spot a few feet away. They will be found chattering continuously while riding on skittish hill ponies along Camel's Back Road in Mussourie, sinikbewty of eternal snows not far to the north be damned, the male parent coaching the discomfited yet proud child and the irritated female parent as if the torrid blood of several generations of Bengal Lancers flowed through his veins.

Father and Mother dispensed with such popular travel with a snobbishness they never quite outgrew. Sometimes my parents would even poke gentle fun at family who decamped each year on Kundushpéshāl-like journeys. The way a famous barrister at Calcutta High Court who would travel with his wife, my father's eldest sister, Tilōttoma, was typical of the time before the advent of the have-carry-on-will-travel generation of the late twentieth century and of this millennium. Travel in my father's time was mostly by train and for it preparation worthy of a major expedition was employed. There would certainly be a hold-all (singularly hōldall in Lingua Bānglā) in which there would be a mattress (tōshōk), sheets (chādōr), a blanket (kombōl) or light quilt (lép—also used in the cold-proof combination lépkombōl), and a pillow or two (bālish). This would hold true in summer or winter, as the journey could entail travelling anywhere the temperature was lower than in Kolkata even by five degrees centigrade. Besides the hold-all, and a suitcase, the head of the family would sometimes even carry an attaché case (attachí) or an airline travel bag with important travel documents and a treasure trove of medicines to temper cold, cough, fever, giddiness, indigestion, constipation and blood pressure.

Then there would be large water bottles, a sure necessity for thirst, and to prevent infection from unreliable water en route. There would be vast 'tiffin-carriers' and cane baskets of food for the journey—usually bread, boiled eggs, banana and glucose biscuits, sacred Bengali travel staples, besides lightly-fried luchi and ālur-dom—potatoes in thick gravy, the correct degree of mākhā-mākhā, coating a perfectly rounded potato or permissible potato-half—not runny, you understand? The compartment would usually resemble a warehouse, and the carts that wove around railway stations with such luggage, several coolies in attendance, could have comfortably transported the material necessary for a small war. With vast improvements in trains and with the advent of affordable air travel, many Bengalis travel lighter these days, but not always lightly.

Besides the Kundushpéshāl, there was another equally flourishing Bengali school of travel to which my parents belonged—people who travelled independently or in small groups, lightly and quietly. These travellers tried to merge with the locals as much as possible. Well before our teen years my sister and I were veterans of numerous road trips across much of Bengal, Bihar, today's Jharkhand and Odisha in nearly every kind of weather. The landscape we travelled to and across ranged from the sea to dense forests to ancient and medieval archaeological sites, to significant temples, mausoleums, and churches, to the Himalaya—over an area nearly as large as Western Europe. We soaked up local sights, culture, festivals, food and friendships like a riot of eager sponges. As with the Battle Order School of Travel we too were bhrōmōn-pāgōl—travel-mad—another form of madness that so many Bengalis are gladly infected by alongside the happy insanities of being bōi-pāgōl (book mad) or futbol-pāgōl (football mad), kreeket-pāgōl (cricket mad), mishti-pāgōl (mad about sweets), gān-pāgōl (mad about songs), an infinity of lovable obsessions. 'Ki-ré pāglā?' (What's up, nutcase?) is not an unknown greeting.

Every Bengali who is not driven by it will surely know a relative or friend who is. We show off about travel experiences. A Bengali college friend of mine argued with me not long ago when I shared a near-death experience during a flight from Doha to Goa in bad weather. A United Nations bureaucrat, he dismissed it as nothing—in his million-plus miles of travel he had weathered far worse storms over the Pacific and Atlantic—mine was a mere squall. Another Bengali friend insists, without having been anywhere near my meal in Chiang Mai, that the dish of squid garnished with red peppers she also ate in that northern Thai city was far more jhāl than mine. We then got into a heated argument about which country has better street food—Laos, Thailand, Vietnam or Cambodia—an inconclusive Indo–Chinese war. A nephew in the information technology industry wants a job in Central or South Americas so he can see every major and minor Mayan, Inca and Aztec site from Mexico down to the mid-Andes. He thinks Silicon Valley is overrated. A niece wants urgently to visit the North Pole and South Pole before the polar ice melts. The urgency of reduced ice, though polar ice should be around a little longer than here, is the same reason I want to climb the depleted snows of Kilimanjaro. Meanwhile, my unbridled passion for scuba diving is the next best option to visiting another planet.

We all want to see the world, all of it, and it can begin with an outing to the Botanic Garden in Howrah, near Kolkata or a weekend at the fast-disappearing river at Jaflong, in Sylhet, slowly being killed by stone quarrying, a touch-and-go sunrise over Kangchenjunga at Sandakphu near Darjeeling, or a riveting sunset on the beaches of Cox's Bazar at the southern tip of Bangladesh—which, with the country's penchant for claiming the number one spot in whatevever available category, the government claims as being the longest beach in the world. (Vanity extends to this side of the border. The pride of West Bengal for the longest railway platform in the world at 3,519 feet, in Kharagpur, was rudely snatched away by Gorakhpur, in Uttar Pradesh in 2013 at 4,483 feet. The disgrace of it! But it still appears to have one shred of pride—the largest banyan tree in India, at Howrah's Botanic Garden. And together, across Bangladesh and West Bengal, we have the largest delta in the world! And the waters from it empty into a bay that is really a vast sea and it is named after our land! Bay of Bengal! It's the biggest bay in the world, even bigger than Hudson Bay!)

We've had some determined gypsies like Bimal Mukherjee, a well-to-do Kolkata boy who travelled the world from 1926, when he was twenty-three, to 1937, cycling across large stretches of Europe with some friends, and working variously as a sailor, dogsbody on a fishing trawler, dairy farm worker, teacher, photographer, labourer, speaker and, in his own expansive words, a pilot. His peregrinations took him across the world to countries that would make a well-heeled and well-travelled Bengali today turn deeply envious—Arabia, Persia, Syria, Turkey, Britain, Iceland, Scandinavia, the Soviet Union, nearly all of Western Europe, Greece, Egypt, the Sudan, the United States, Colombia, Ecuador, Peru, Hawaii, Tahiti, Japan, China, Hong Kong, Vietnam, Cambodia, Thailand, Malaysia and Ceylon—among others.

He wrote a travelogue several decades later, serialized, about his experiences, and later a book, which I devoured—*Du Chākāy Duniyā*. The World on Two Wheels is a heck of a story, and, at times, seemingly fantastic. Like casually chatting with Rabindranath at the Regina Hotel in London, which Mukherjee in a throwaway manner describes as a bhālō Bāngāli hotel—a good Bengali hotel, which generally means it welcomed Bengalis and catered to them. Or meeting the dancer Uday Shankar in Chicago, giving 'lantern lectures' in a couple of colleges, and providing commentary on post-prohibition Amercia. Going walkabout in Phnom Penh, he raved about the 'Oriental Museum' and its collection of Hindu gods and goddesses, the exotica of Angkor Wat—he approved of the Khmer diet, as it was akin to the Bengali: 'The people eat rice and fish.' Similar approval awaited the Thai. I read about the world from a Bengali point of view—quaint, engaging, friendly, curious, effusive with praise for the beauty of nature, art and history. All this—and, being Bengali, arrogant.

But Mukherjee's is not my favourite story about the travelling Bengali, even though it is grand.

◆

What truly made me appreciate the travel-love and travel-fortitude of the Bengali was an experience during my senior years at boarding school. Four of us went on a trek to the Pindari Glacier in the Kumaon Himalaya, one of several standard school-and-college treks that began at a place called Kapkot, a round trip of more than 100 kilometres, and steep in several stretches. Zero Point, near the base of the glacier, is at 3,660 metres—that's a touch over 12,000 feet. Warm as you trek, chilly when you don't, freezing at night—the usual. This was 1979. We were properly equipped with the top-of-the-line trekking gear available in India at the time, and very proud of ourselves for having made it to our destination without any adult supervision, at a little over sixteen. On our way back, near a stop called Dhakuri, a tiny camp with a near-180 degree view of the mountains that would surely cure a year's accumulated fatigue, we encountered a slow-moving group of more than a dozen travellers.

They were Bengalis. Except for a young man, all were middle-aged and more, a few seemed to be over seventy. A couple of them wore dhuti, with socks and simple canvas shoes, surplus army jackets—and mānkicap. There were a couple of ponies and porters and a guide to help them along. Some of them insisted on speaking to us in English and, when they discovered two of our group were Bengalis, they were delighted. They began to chatter, admire our gear, and asked us about thāndā and sinikbewty up the trail, even though they had already experienced the bitter cold of the mountain night, and had seen, only a few minutes earlier, scenery to drain a year's fatigue. But they wanted more thāndā as well as more sinikbewty, a sort of masochistic joy-to-the-world. These veterans held walking sticks, whittled young branches, with the pride of soldiers.

It was somewhat embarrassing, and my not-Bengali friends never let the two of us forget it, but I was also immensely pleased at the sense of energy and adventure of our species. It was something to look forward to. If these old folks could keep going, so could I. Perhaps in tribute, I'd even wear a balaclava some day, though

I would slash my wrists before I call it mānkicap.

◆

At the other end of charming lies awful. I met them, too, one day, as has the unwary traveller across India and several parts of the world. About fifteen years after the Pindari experience, one summer I went off by myself to Himachal Pradesh, a solo backpacker on a break from an intensely workaholic phase with a magazine in New Delhi. Eventually I found myself on a medium-sized bus from the crowded hill resort town of Manali to the Rohtang Pass, an awe-inspiring sight at over 13,000 feet with a panorama of snow-capped peaks around us. The pass had just opened after the winter freeze. With me were travellers from Bengal and Gujarat—the other subcontinental region that has spawned travel-mad, mind-numbingly noisy travellers—nearly equal in number, a cacophony of families and honeymooning couples.

For me the trip turned from pleasure to people-watching to nightmare in half an hour. Our bus finally stalled a little short of the pass—there was a traffic jam. The Bengalis ate sliced bread, banana and boiled eggs. The Gujaratis ate savouries like chivda and khakra, their travel staple. Both species vomited generously. The Gujaratis shouted jokes about being stuck, and about Bengalis. The Bengalis loudly complained about everything from the obduracy of the weather—somewhat overcast—in relation to their excursion, to traffic management at Rohtang, to the loudness of the Gujaratis; some looked at their watches. After enduring a few minutes of high decibel descriptions of snow in Bānglā and Gujarati, a language I understand better than I can speak, I got off the bus, and began to walk back to Manali, sometimes glissading down slopes of snow and damp grass wherever hairpin bends permitted such risky travel. After anger faded I actually began to enjoy the lunacy of it. It took me about five hours, walking interspersed with hitchhiking on trucks, to reach Manali. I treated myself to outstanding fresh batter-fried trout from the Beas River at a Tibetan restaurant, staggered up to the charming cottage at which I was staying, drew a bucket of hot water, placed it in front of a chair in the balcony, poured a generous measure of rum, wrapped myself in a pure wool Himachali shawl I bought for a hundred rupees at the bus stop that morning, sat on the chair, soaked my feet in hot water and experienced bliss.

I haven't been back to Manali. Someday perhaps, with quieter Bengalis (or Gujaratis). Or none at all.

But I still possess the shawl, and incurable travel madness for the next great adventure, the next great 'discovery'. Magellan in the mind. Or that deluded discoverer Christopher Columbus. Cristoforo Colombo. Cristóbal Colón. Or our Krishtōfāī Colōmbās.

Whatever, whoever, as long as it involves travel.

◆

Bengalis didn't discover continents that were already populated. But some of us did tell the world more about some.

The earliest recorded traveller of Bengali provenance is probably Atisa Dipankar Srigyan (Ātish Diponkōr Sriggan), a precursor to the bhrōmōn-pāgōl Bengali. It is generally agreed he was born in fabled Bikrampur, in the present-day Munshiganj area near Dhaka, and also the legendary home of the best kāshundi in the world (I would choose over Dijon or any grainy mustard the West can offer).

Born to nobility in the late tenth century CE, he travelled to Tibet, where he emerged, after some years, as disciple to the renowned gurus of the time, and a Buddhist scholar of repute. In the course of his accomplishments he changed from Chandragarbha, his given name, to Dipankar Srigyan, loosely translated as 'beacon of knowledge'; and, finally, Atisa—peace—this honorific accorded by the king Jangchhub Ö of Guge, an influential kingdom in Western Tibet at the time.

But before his epic journey to Tibet through Palpa in Nepal, a region where he spent a year en route, there was the schooling in aspects of major Indian religions of the time, and handsome 'minors' in Shaivism and Tantra—all this in addition to Theravada and Mahayana Buddhism. He then left for Sumatra in the company of merchants—the island a contender for the legendary Suvarnadwipa—to study an early form of the Buddhist doctrine of Sarvastivada under the Acharya Chandrakirti. It was an epic journey in its own right. He returned after twelve years to Vanga of the Pal kings, and was accorded a position of respect at the apex centre for Buddhist learning at the time under the patronage of the Pals, at Vikramshila which was competition for Nalanda in the Buddhist Ivy League, as it were. Atisa taught at Nalanda and other great viharas of the time, Somapuri and Odantapuri, among others.

According to Tibetan Buddhist lore and other histories he then journeyed to Tibet on a petition of various rulers and gurus who, so goes the assumption, believed his contribution was essential for a return to pure dharma and a belief in the sangha, of which Atisa was a great believer. Jangchhub was apparently an insistent petitioner along with his uncle, Yeshe, and sent a posse of lamas to Vikramshila to invite Atish to Tibet.

He went, and soon composed the *Bodhipathapradipa*, or *Lamp for the Path to Enlightenment*, his best-known work and considered the most influential, a clear distillate of Gautama Buddha's teachings of Dhamma. The story has it that, when he sent along a copy of this work to his mentor in Vikramshila, the Acharya Ratnakarshanti, with a request to stay on in Tibet beyond the three years leave of absence granted him, it was acceded to after the acharya and his colleagues read it and agreed such luminous work could only be achieved with the time, space and experience that Tibet could provide.

With 'Atisa' joined to his 'Dipankar Srigyan', this former noble, now considered among the greatest Mahayana and Vajrayana scholars (and perhaps the greatest 'non-resident' Bengali—prōbāshi to us in one way or another—until Subhas Chandra Bose came along 900 years later) was permitted to remain in Tibet for the sake of dhamma. That's where he died, in 1054 CE. He is revered today among the Gelugpa, or Yellow Hat sect of Vajrayana, and even the rival Red Hat and other sects, because they respect his work to preserve the purity of Buddhism, his interpretation of the teachings of the Buddha. He is a major figure wherever Buddhism is studied.

◆

It is an apt footnote that one of the people credited with bringing back to India much information about Atisa's work, along with a treasure trove in Tibetan history, information, manuscripts and artefacts was a Bengali, too, Sarat Chandra Das. This scholar and diplomat—and, as some maintain, a spy for the British government in the fast-evolving Great Game in which Tsarist Russia was a key competitor for access and influence in Central Asia, West Asia and East Asia—was also a grand traveller. Born in Chittagong in 1849, he headed out to Presidency College in Kolkata, where he became, in the words of a mentor in Das's book, *Journey to Lhasa and Central Tibet*, 'favourably known to Sir Alfred Croft', later the director of public instruction of Bengal. Croft was a dedicated 'friend and guide' in Das's 'geographical and literary work, and by whose representations to the Indian government it became possible for him to perform his important journeys into Tibet'.

By 1874, Das, who would later be a star at the Bengal Asiatic Society and the more arcane Buddhist Text Society of India, found himself as headmaster of the newly opened Bhutia Boarding School in Darjeeling, where he had moved from the department of engineering at Presidency College. It's here that Das is believed by many to have added espionage to his curriculum vitae. He learnt Tibetan with gusto, networked with 'leading lamas', made several trips to Sikkim and met the ruler, the Chogyal. In 1878, riding on the visit of his associate at the school, the Lama Ugyen-gyatso, to Lhasa and the monastery of Tashilhunpo in Shigatse (or Xigase, now Tibet's second largest city), Das wrangled an invitation from the office of the rinpoche, or abbot of Tashilhunpo to visit. To prevent much scrutiny, officials at Shigatse 'had the Babu's name entered as a student of theology in the Grand Monastery of that place'.

His half-year of travel earned a rich haul in Sanskrit and Tibetan manuscripts and information about Tibet's history, religion, culture and contemporary politics, besides goodwill; and a survey of the country 'north and north-east of Kanchanjunga, of which nothing was previously known' to the British. Das returned to Tibet in 1881 and, besides working in Shigatse and tracking the river Tsangpo—as the Brahmaputra is known in Tibet—he visited Lhasa a few times.

He was only the third 'native' visitor to Lhasa, after the legendary surveyor, cartographer and chronicler Nain Singh Rawat of Pithoragarh, in present-day Uttarakhand, who visited Lhasa in 1866, as a member of what was called the Great Trigonometrical Survey. He was disguised as a trader. His co-legend of a cousin Kishan Singh Rawat followed in Nain Singh's extensive footsteps to Tibet and beyond into Mongolia, visited Lhasa in 1880, and mapped the place. But Das's place in history remains immovable. In his *Tibet on the Imperial Chessboard*, the historian Premen Addy quotes contemporary sources:

> Finally, a new map of the Central Parts of Tibet—replete with an indefinite number of place-names, newly ascertained and with courses of rivers and mountains accurately traced on paper for the first time—was constructed, based in part on information by Babu Sarat Chandra Das.

In 1885, Das received an elevation. In the words of a 'contemporary observer' as recorded in Das's *Indian Pandits in the Land of Snow*: 'In September…Sarat Chandra, under orders of the Secretary of State, proceeded to Peking to assist the Government in diplomatic matters connected with Tibet.' There, with the intervention of the chief financial agent to the Chinese government, 'he cultivated the acquaintance of the great ministers and chief nobles of Peking, and succeeded in gaining the confidence of the Prime Minister the illustrious Li-Hung-chang.' Elsewhere, we learn Das was in Peking—Beijing—and was sometimes referred to as 'Ka-che Lama', the lama from Kashmir.

Indian Pandits also records the Peking correspondent of the London *Times* gushing about his contemporary, this incongruously Bondesque Bengali. (I've come to think of Das, who evidently had the mien of a schoolteacher with rounded face and bushy moustache as one who could smoothly introduce himself as 'My name is Das, Sarat Das'. It works equally well in Bāṅglā: 'Āmār nām Dāsh, Shorōt Dāsh.')

At any rate, *The Times* gushed as much as a native babu could be acknowledged as a superstar with the usual caveats for native inferiority.

> In using Asiatics to conciliate Asiatics the Government would be following the line of least resistance and might hit upon the true solution of the Tibetan problem. There are Bengali Pandits, not many perhaps, who combine the high qualities of the European explorer with tolerance of privations and the subtlety of address which are special characteristics of the Hindu. Their mildness disarms hostility, and when imbued with zeal for their work their quiet resolution and infinite capacity for waiting, overcome every obstacle. With a handful of rupees they appear capable of making stupendous journeys over the eternal snows, surveying the country as they go, and gaining the active good-will of the inhabitants.
>
> Such a force as that is surely an element of incalculable strength to a Government whose external affairs are all Asiatic. That at any rate is the impression which an outsider gathers from observing one specimen of the class who has come to Peking in the suite of Mr. Macaulay [Colman Macaulay, an administrator-diplomat who led the British delegation]. The Pandit Sarat Chandra Das has made two eminently successful journeys into Tibet. On the last occassion in 1882, the history of which I am now reading, the learned Pandit worked himself into the good graces of the most important personages in Tibet,

and was admitted to audience of the Dalai Lama himself.

The Pandit's narrative is written in a simple, natural and graphic style, more like that of Defoe than of our contemporary literateurs. Every detail of the journey is described, and yet the interest never flags.

There is even appreciation of Das's friendship with a Tibetan princess, the 'grande dame named Lhacham' who 'acted the good Samaritan to the travel-sore pilgrim'. More shades of Bond.

Das retired to Darjeeling, where he built a cottage, and was quite the gentleman and host to important visitors. He died in 1917. His home still endures, and the villa, Lhasa Villa, has lent its name to an entire locality.

12

Khāi-khāi
To eat, to live

The gypsy life of a journalist and writer has taken me to all regions of India, a large part of the subcontinent, Asia and several parts of the world beyond. Along with much travel it has also meant much travel-food and much destination-food. Travel-mad, Father was keen to know where I had been, how I got there, what I had seen, what I had learnt. But no telling was complete until he found out what I had eaten. It wasn't an assertion about the superiority of Bengali food—that was implicit—but it did not prevent an appreciation of other cuisines, and an intense curiosity about food of all kinds and cultures, even the often-unpalatable food on planes and trains. Over time I began to dread the conversations that would inevitably take place after I had travelled a new route, or a familiar route by a different mode of transport, or another airline. Even if our meeting took place after a year or more, or we spoke over the telephone after several weeks, after a quick exchange of 'How are you?' he would move on like a determined falcon to the next line of good-natured parental interrogation. It didn't begin with 'How was your journey?' or 'Tell me about the place.' It usually was: 'What did they give you to eat?' or 'What did you eat?'

He couldn't cook. During my early days as a journalist in Delhi, he destroyed the only utensil I possessed, a saucepan, trying to warm bread on it as the toaster wasn't working (well, all right, I didn't possess a toaster at the time). But he knew his food. It didn't surpise me much when after his death I found next to a notebook with numerous haiku, tanka, and modern Japanese poetry—a literary smörgåsbord he had translated into Bāṅglā with the help of my Japanophile sister—a notebook of fish recipes. Alongside the sparse, lyrical works of Daigaku Horiguchi, Toichiro Iwasa and Kaoru Maruyama were meticulous, beautifully handwritten recipes for pābdā-lālshāk, a reduced curry of butterfish and red spinach with ground mustard and poppy seed; a curry of pārshé and bégun, mullet with aubergine; a preparation of rui-pōstō—carp made with a paste of poppy seed; and the very Assamese, and utterly delightful, staple of māsō téngā, a light sour curry—a tangy jhōl that is a gem with rui and pābdā alike.

Now I'm Father, and I ask my daughter similar questions. As she is intensely food-curious—her soul could be yours for the duration of a fine meal—she tolerates it. When she cannot any longer, she switches to English to admonish, put me in place in a very Bengali way: 'Uff, Baba, that is *so* Bengali.'

◆

Pride of place in Mother's cooking ouevre went to a Le Cordon Bleu cookbook from the 1960s, her apex reference for European cooking which, like most of her prized possessions, she protected with the same fortitude she did during every political and financial storm visited upon our family. Like her dreams for her children and protective instinct that leads mothers of so many species to fight to the death, she wasn't to be parted from culinary accessories that centred her. She poured her entire being into her cooking activities. Offerings courtesy of such a cookbook and cook could only be served on a fine Noritake china, like the cookbooks a determined survivor of storms.

We, of course, didn't call it European cooking, or Continental. We were linguistically basted by a bāburchi who thought in terms of 'Conti'. Even after the reduction of Cordon Bleu to Conti, this was different from shāhébi khābār, British Indian cooking, Anglo-Indian cooking—Sub-Conti, if you will—roast mutton with mint chātni, roast chicken with potatoes and gravy, a hearty tomato soup touched with black pepper and cinnamon. This strand of cuisine beloved not just by my family but numerous Bengalis can often be fabulous and sometimes frightening—at a sailor-friendly hotel in the chaotic heart of Chittagong, I once ate a vast serving of Bolognaise or perhaps Chittagongaise pasta blasted with bay leaf and cinnamon; followed by cinnamon-flavoured crème caramel with its deer-tailed tuft of cream that robustly smelled of cow and chemicals and was topped by a shocking pink glazed cherry, a warning light I unfortunately ignored.

Such was the food of the shāhéb, but we would draw the line at obscenities like mulligatawny soup, which few self-respecting Bengalis will touch unless under absolute duress—this anaemic, misbegotten nightmare to warm shāhébi bellies is for us an abomination, given the several hundred methods we have for cooking a variety of lentils, from the most exotic to the simplest, cooked and presented with understated elegance. What would the shāhéb and mémshāhéb know of the joy of shōnā-moog-ér dāl on steaming bhāt with a dollop of ghee, with a slice of gondhōrāj lébu and a single, lush green lonkā? An epicurean may describe it as golden-hued mung lentils of Bengal, simmered in a bouquet of the finest oriental spices, served with long grained delta rice, accompanied by organic clarified butter, a slice of King of Fragrances lemon and piquant green country pepper. Throw in finely julienned potatoes, golden fried—jhuri-bhājā ālu—and this simple meal is enough to give the average Bengali a sense memory of paradise that Proust would envy.

Mulligatawny? An unappetizing version of rasam, that outstanding restorative lentil preparation of Tamil origin graded with nearly all the spices that drew Vasco da Gama and subsequent explorer-conquistadors to India, turned by the British into a sludge of rice and dal with some 'curry powder' thrown in to remind them of the glory of East India Company and several joys of their empire. (Alas, mulligatawny remains.)

For oriental—more oriental than ours, that is—cuisine Ma-moni used to make these lovely dishes from *Mrs Ma's Chinese Cookbook*. This Mrs Ma seemed to really know her recipes because whatever Ma cooked from Mrs Ma's cookbook, from simple fried rice to egg fu yung with crabmeat, and fried fish wrapped in lotus leaves, with ingredients procured at Kolkata's Gariahat Market (seafood) and New Market (meat, tofu, vegetables, condiments) was exquisite. We didn't require the accoutrements of red paper lanterns, fat porcelain laughing Buddhas and mournful Canto-pop to enjoy the subtle tastes of a great cuisine. Even then, although we were too young to be outraged by its explicit racism, we didn't care much for the blurb on the cover of Mrs Ma's book: 'Few persons who enjoy real Chinese cooking will fail to understand the old saying in the Far East that Chinese food, a Japanese wife and an American home would make an ideal life for a man.' But what I do remember is that we were utterly enamoured of the food—to us, Ma-moni mirrored Mrs Ma with every turn of the wok (a hefty Bengali korāi), every sprinkle of soy sauce from the Sing Cheung Sauce Factory, every dash of red chilli sauce from Pou Chong Brothers—of Kolkata, not Canton.

It was altogether different, the way we approached Bengali food. That was sacred territory, a mix of heritage and home. Food was part of our oral history. It was a matter of watch-and-learn, taste-and-learn, cook-and-learn, passed on from one generation to the next, with every mā cooking it better than méyé, every shāshuri cooking it better than bōu in an honour code of acknowledgement. The only person who could be acknowledged as having surpassed a mā's cooking was either a thākumā or didimā—paternal and maternal grandmothers who, in the Bengali Mussulman telling, would become dādi and nāni. Grand Mā. Away from this hierarchical sisterhood, it would be a brave, liberal and deeply loving man who acknowledged his bōu to be a better cook than his mā or ammi—even after mother or mother-in-law had passed on to the big kitchen in the sky. It's a burden that bōus still bear in many Bengali households where it is traditional to keep men's egos fattened and women's self-esteem flatlined. That is not an exceptional situation in Banglasphere where, obversely, goddesses are periodically worshipped with such passion, respect and fear it would make so many paternalistic religions shrink with embarrassment and paranoia.

The average Bengali man—the average urban Bengali man, that is—appears to come into his own as a hunter-gatherer of ingredients for the culinary altar of his ginni, or his bāri or bāshā. This spousal and household function is a sacred space for many, irrespective of class, and endures even with the emergence of nuclear families where chores and duties may be on occasion somewhat equitably distributed, where even women of the house head to work each day. It's a reaffirmation of being, you see; even manhood to some extent, as the Bengali man steps out to hunt-gather in the morning, before work, or hunt-gather on his way back from the āpish.

There is great ritual attached to banter with the shōbjiōālā or the female equivalent, shōbjiōāli, over the quality of produce. The quality comes first, the price always later, and of course a face-saving exit if it proves unaffordable. The seller of jaggery, even rock salt, may each time hear an earful about how quality has dipped—not sweet and pure enough; how the salt doesn't look right. The māchhōālā will be stretched to the limits of his vast reservoir of patience as the babu diligently inspects the freshness of the fish by expertly prising open the gills with a thumb to check if it is the acceptable hue of darkest-pink-bordering-on-red, or prods the flesh of the fish to check if it is acceptably firm; and, of course, the fidgety, bony kōi-māchh and kānkrā, crab, will simply not be considered unless these are demonstrably alive. The māngshōālā or koshāi will be lectured on how to properly portion the chicken or cut of goat, sheep or beef; he may be quizzed on their provenance, and if the animal were correctly slaughtered, and when. And, damn it all, if someone alongside protests if the matter could be hurried along as he has also to hunt-gather, or, heaven forbid, the butcher displays impatience—how *dare* he?

It's a habit no matter how the universe is ordered. I've actually seen Bengali men in stores that stock processed seafood and meats prod a frozen pack of clearly labelled produce and ask attendants how fresh it is, and insist on a clear answer.

It's also a matter of prestige. It wouldn't do to return home and be chided for sloppy shopping, of not hunting efficiently, not gathering surely. The hunter-gatherer could then experience an existential meltdown.

The sisterhood of personalized and delicate culinary habits, the brotherhood of bombastic and sometimes fragile shoppers, and celebratory, industrial-size meals such as at weddings cooked by mostly male chefs—a coexisting anachronism of the finest order—are charms that sustain us, the excess baggage of memories we gladly carry from the time of imbibing to the time of our dementia or death. We speak of the hāth—literally the 'hand', that provides the cook with an imprimatur as unique as his fingerprints and double helixes. So it is that we are sustained by the chicken rézālā at Kulsum-khālā's house, or shōnā-moog and ālu-potōlér dālnā at the home of Khuku-pishi, the fine turn of spice and temperature that flowered a chorchōri of pālōng-shāk and chingri at Noor-āpā's place, chhānār pāyésh the way Ma made it—makes it—the outstanding pork curry with a thick gravy of freshly made mustard paste and chilli and rock salt that Durjoy's shāshuri adapted from Odia tribal delight to seamless Bengali, the kāliā of bāghā-chingri, tiger prawn at the roadside eatery in Diamond Harbour en route to the weekend trip to Kakdwip, and the fat chunk of golden-fried rui, the skin crisp and the flesh white and steaming at that 'hotel' in Port Canning, peerless kānkrār jhōl in Bōrishal, a crab curry to rival all crab curries, the Kachchi biryani with the tenderest beef at Rahman-bhai's dāōāt, and the time Dilip-dā ate half a bālti of mutton at Shoma's wedding, and then followed it up with a kilo of mishti dōyi and a couple of dozen of the finest roshōgōlla? He didn't even need Gelusil after all that, bhābté pārō?

Can you imagine?

◆

The Bengalis have a most disconcerting habit—well, it can be disconcerting for some not-Bengalis. The more we progress into a fine meal, at home among families or a meal to which familiars and guests are invited, or as a guest to another's home, or at a restaurant, or some other location or occasion—essentially, almost everywhere—our random access memory invites itself to the table, or floor, or grassy picnic spot. Someone at the gathering will begin recounting a fine meal eaten elsewere, and elsewhen, even as accolades over the ongoing meal pour in over a second, third, even a fourth helping. That memory could be of a particular dish, its fragrance, texture, the quality of ingredients. Or the love, expertise and anecdotes with which it was served. Several other cultures would find this profoundly insulting with the probable exception of Italians (and, on their very good days, Kashmiris; and Odias and Assamese, our eastern cousins who possess food finesse and the ability to intuitively absorb and handle vast arrays of ingredients and cooking styles), who obsess over ingredients, cooking and unbridled eating.

For us it is the highest praise. What can be a greater compliment to a fine meal than to recall other fine meals? Or to plan the next one? It is done with its own civilizational protocol, one that regularly compliments the host and chefs. Oshādhārōn! Extraordinary! Opurbō! Superb! Khub bhālō khélām! I ate so well! Or formidable— Durdāntō!—which could easily morph into an appropriate name for a marvellous pasta dish by a Bengali chef with a sense of humour. And attitude; always, attitude:

And there was Spaghetti Durdanto alle vongole e funghi.

◆

Such adventurism is not far-fetched: after all, it is what makes for recipes that last generations, and builds appreciative taste-memories, a certain longing. The gourmet-gourmand-critic, unabashed eater of all manner of fine food, Sourish Bhattacharyya, once accepted my invitation to write about Bāngāli rānnā and offered an interesting twist, pairing our food with wine. It needs intense discipline—this should work well, as culinary discipline is about the only discipline most Bengalis will gladly follow.

To begin with, you would need to go slow with pānch phōrōn, a robust five-spice combination of fenugreek, nigella seeds, cumin seeds, some mustard seeds, and fennel seeds that is often used for vegetable dishes or bits of fish and seafood paired with vegetables, and eaten towards the beginning of the meal. 'Keep shuktō off the menu,' Bhattacharyya counsels. 'I wouldn't also risk my neck suggesting a wine to pair with chorchōri, chhéchki and chhānchrā. Nor would I demand that you pair a wine with your ālu-bhāté or mushurir dāl. Why kill the simple joy of having these notables with a liquid accompaniment more elevated than water?'

After wisely winning over fellow-Bengalis with gentle flattery—Bhattacharyya clearly respects his peoples' penchant for sharp knives and sharper words—he ventures to entrées. For shōrshé māchh, the recommendation is to pair it with an 'easygoing' Sauvignon Blanc, or even a relatively gentle red, like Beaujolais. For the heavenly, steamed māchhér pāturi and bhāpā chingri, stay with Reisling, which journeys well with dāb chingri too, but a fruitier (lychee-toned), crisper variety that pairs well with this dish that uses coconut milk. Mildly sweet whites would pair with ālur-dom—'this foxy little thing which walks the tightrope between mild sweetness and in-your-face pungency'.

The meats bring forth a procession of reds. A 'fruit-forward' Pinot with māngshōr cutlet and kōbirāji—but keep the sauce and kāshundi locked away. A Pinot would do nicely for koshā māngshō, but it's a Cabernet Shiraz for chitol māchhér muitthā. Dōyi māchh can take either a Pinot, or Gavi, a superior white Barolo from Italy. This latter offering is Bhattacharyya's preference for smoked hilsa—ilish—too. The poorer cousins will simply have to make do with the various grape varieties and méthode among Indian or

New World wines. Either way, this connoisseur insists there is a dish waiting to seduce a wine.

We know the feeling. There is always a dish to seduce a Bengali.

◆

Bengali friends and family gather to catch up with each other as much as to share a meal. People of other cultures most often post on social network sites photographs of friends and family meeting at home or a restaurant. Bengalis and those of Bengali persuasion (with partial DNA, or a not-Bengali with a longtime Bengali companion, or simply Bengali at heart) are frequently driven to share photographs of the meal. Animated discussions might quickly follow on the place, memorable dishes, the taste, the recipe. Among India's best-known graphic novelists, Sarnath Banerjee, who also has a twisted sense of humour (do graphic novelists have any other kind?) once shared on Facebook an image of golden gravy-flecked skeletons of hands-length pābdā, aesthetically arranged on a plate. An animated discussion followed, mixing envy with questions about the location of the laid back meal (for which there is a colloquial Bānglā phrase, lyadh khāōā), who cooked the buttery fish, and how. As a Bengali I could virtually sense sighs and warm glows emanating from friends, family and complete strangers across the subcontinent and elsewhere, Bengalis linked by the imagined taste of a meal and, to paraphrase a Tagore translation, of feeling at home in the world, all on account of an image of fish bones conveyed through a combination of ones and zeroes. Rhythm, not algorithm.

Food is such an obsession that revelling in it, immersing oneself in it is utterly unconscious. As I searched through notebooks, recordings and articles going back thirty years to reabsorb travels in Banglasphere, alongside conversations on politics, society, business, history, violence, literature there were frequent references to food. A working luncheon at a top editor's house in Dhaka, besides the animated discussion on politics recorded digitally, also featured as a menu in my notebook—mashed potato garnished with green chilli and mustard oil; lightly fried radish leaves; a mash of sheem, a broadbean turned magical with mustard seed; a delicate dāl of red split lentils with a hint of ghee and cumin, a murgir jhōl where the pièce de résitance was the gravy with overtones of onion, ginger and red chilli—I would have gladly eaten the divine jhōl without the free-range chicken, only it would have been impolite; plump, slightly smoky rice from his ancestral village; and quite possibly among the top-ten roshōgōllā I have eaten thus far.

This includes roshōgōllā made in Odisha, with near-mythical proportions of texture, fragrance, taste, aftertaste and, as crucially, afterglow—a feeling that absolutely must accompany any rating of food in the Bengali scheme of things—which I rate as being as good and often better than roshōgōllā made in Banglasphere. As this submission could invite for me the status of Bengali non grata more rapidly than many other observations in this book, let me go a little further and state that I would put the Sri Lankan version of mishti dōyi on a pedestal along with that of the undying Bengali passion, sweet curd made with date-palm jaggery—preferably the treacly nolén, or new gur. Kiri pani is yoghurt mixed with palm treacle, also a near-divine offering which makes me wonder if it did not travel to this beautiful island with folks from ancient Bengal and Odisha—a treasured genealogy in Lanka and among the dominant myths of the birth of the Sinhala nation. This myth involves Vijaya, the exiled son of the king of Vanga, Sinhabahu, who is said to have arrived in ancient Lanka in the year of Gautama Buddha's death—what is formally called parinirvana—in 544 or 543 BCE. (There you have it—we could be the Sinha in Sinhala, the race of lions, and may I now be forgiven for equating Sri Lankan mishti dōyi with that of the Bengali.)

In any case my list will always be better, more definitive than that of every other Bengali; each one of us possesses a list better and more definitive than any other Bengali's. In such a contest it is good that everybody wins, as even the perception of a loss can lead to embarrassment, estrangement and, in extreme cases, injury when action replaces words.

On another occasion, an evening at a well-known Bengali novelist and dramatist's house in Dhaka (he invited me for dinner with the equally irresistible à la carte, 'Éktu āddā hobé') our conversation began with the shredding of self-important cultural impresarios and semi-literate and uninformed critics, over wasabi-flavoured peas and robust South African Cabernet Sauvignon. By the time we arrived at the subject of self-important writers—we were too polite to include ourselves in that tribe—we had journeyed to a variety of kābābs of Bengali Mussulman provenance, a variety of spinach from sharp to creamy, shôrshé ilish, and a broadly filleted fish in light gravy that I was mortified to not be able to identify (and was therefore unable to compliment my hosts as to how impeccably cooked it was). For a Bengali guest at a Bengali meal, a compliment must be specific, a dish cannot be identified as 'étā'—merely 'this'—is incomplete, proper appreciation and respect comes from identifying the vegan and non-vegan species at hand. An escape was made possible with vague humming noises of appreciation of the dish directed towards my hostess, hoping a writer's eccentricity coupled with plentiful Cabernet earlier in the evening would suffice.

Of course, there was dāl and bhāt. Each course was given its due respect, the greens eaten first with rice, then other vegetables, then dāl, then fish. The kābābs were eaten by themselves, or at most as an accompaniment to the dāl and bhāt, the few times we mix dishes with something relatively neutral like a dāl, its gentler flavour helping its pairing with stouter flavours, like that of stir-fried or batter-fried vegetables, or, in this instance, kābāb. Otherwise the mixing of everything, the way Westerners tend to eat—by that Bengalis mean everyone to the west of them—is just uncivilized.

The only way a high commissioner of Bangladesh to India felt he could really communicate the issue of illegal Bangladeshi immigrants to me was over lunch at the designer farmhouse where he maintained his residence in a fashionable enclave of the entitled in South Delhi. This future foreign secretary of his country flatly denied any Bangladeshi was ever an illegal immigrant to India, offering polite outrage in the face of the several millions that India's government of the day claimed were living illegally in the country, including one employed as a cleaning lady at my residence, who went home twice a year across the porous border along West Bengal's Malda district. She had managed to purchase an official Indian election identity card using a Hindu name as an alias. Her status was as legal as the residence the high commissioner rented. So he and I argued politely over the finest Dhaka meal in Delhi— seasoned with gentle criticism from his elegant spouse about the inferior quality of ingredients in Delhi, as compared to Dhaka. We agreed on that point.

Reference to food is plentiful in each book I have written. How could this not be, how could one ignore this basic ingredient of life, a marker of how people live, and what they live on, the markers of their deprivation, subsistence, prosperity or celebration?

In a book published some years earlier on the convergence of business and human rights, food was sometimes a counterpoint to the institutional abuse of citizens. One reviewer, an elderly armchair specialist took great exception to the fact that, as a narrator, I was describing places, people and their ecosystem from habitation to eating habits rather than simply sticking to core facts and analysis. That I was doing so in order to take those not from a particular place and situation to that particular place and situation with words, images, information and emotion, the devices of any writer, seemed to have escaped him completely. There was this instance of depleting catches, and in the course of writing about it, I described the food I ate with protesters at Idinthakarai, a seaside village of fisherfolk, a short walk from a post-Fukushima nuclear power plant in Tamil Nadu. Or a deeply polluted industrial area, also in Tamil Nadu, a little to the south of Pondicherry near the town of Cuddalore. Local residents, whose villages had been usurped, and livelihoods affected, lived a life of intimidation by the management of factories, and local bureaucrats and police—often in concert. Their water sources were all polluted, the local rivers, their source of fish and water, choked with industrial refuse.

After a lengthy meeting, my hosts, all local residents, took me to a tiny shack nearby for lunch. We had a simple and unrefined village meal of plump rice and sambar and vegetables, cooked with heart and eaten heartily and with humour, the way meals ought to be taken, the way people ought to bond. Someone offered fried fish. I hesitated. My hosts, uniformly poor, some weakened with malnutrion and pollutants, broke into gales of laughter and assured me the fish wasn't local; it came from far away, and wouldn't kill me with the poison that daily destroyed their lives.

What is the need to write about food 'and so on'? the critic demanded. It 'detracts from the otherwise indisputable merits' of the book.

What would *you* know, you soulless coot? I wanted to rail at him. You wouldn't have maintained this if you saw beyond your sedentary life, if you cared about how others lived and died to bring you comforts; and if you had perception to complement your presumption, not merely presumption of knowledge that is really ignorance of the life of another. If you knew about these things, you would know of food and companionship, that often food *is* companionship.

If you were Bengali you would instinctively know descriptions of food and culinary companionship to have indisputable merit in a book on human rights and business.

Soulless coot.

◆

Mother was nearly six when famine came to Bengal in 1943.

As a people we know food as much as we know the lack of it. Malnutrition is one way to describe it. Generations of stunted Bengalis in rural and poorer urban Banglasphere, millions of hollow-eyed, sunken-cheeked Bengalis for decades roamed South Asia in search of food-for-work. Famine, too, is a Bengali experiential speciality. It defined us for several decades, drove movements of the poor towards the claiming of lands and livelihoods with violent means (of which more later), sustained the robust platform of religious hate that communalism built and that formally took off on gigantic wings in 1946—and sustained that flight for several decades after. The Bengal countryside is still controlled by land, food grown on it, its ownership and sustenance.

There was no famine in Kolkata, protected as the eastern holdout of empire against Japanese onslaught and adequately supplied with rice and other staples to keep the government and citizens in this citadel safe. Mother and her family lived at the time in Bhobānipur in southern Kolkata, a solidly Bengali enclave not far from Kalighat and its famous temple to Goddess Kāli. The starved and starving arrived from rural areas of southern Bengal, mostly the 'granary' regions of Medinipur and the 24 Parganas. They were everywhere. Her family, like many others, fed as many as they could, mostly skeletal men and women; there were not always children among them—long dead in the villages or recently dead in the city. Every day there were dead people in the streets. Some died because they ate too much after not eating at all for a long while—their dissolving stomachs, cannibalized by their desperate bodies, couldn't handle the food. She saw some starving people eat too quickly, and vomit everything out. She saw other starving people pick the grains of undigested rice from the vomit and eat it, sometimes fighting off crows which in any case would eat anything, and even neighbourhood stray dogs, which had been quite well fed in the city unlike those in the countryside. Driven by hunger, packs of dogs and jackals roamed the villages, eating the dead that could still be eaten, and attacking the dying, who often waited for the end where they fell, sat, and, as some chronicles tell us, stood, ankle-deep in the mud of a riverside, or pond, unable to stir. British soldiers recorded horror stories in some of Bengal's cities. Of naked, starving children outside their barracks, whom they were forbidden to help, though many did. One British soldier chronicled a story of a young girl in a rural area whose arm was bitten off by a jackal. She wasn't yet dead. The luckier ones died when their parents or loved ones simply killed them, slit their throats, drowned them in a river, pond or well.

Many lived as labourers, as whores, as servants of the less-wretched-than-they and the wealthy. There were never so many in the cities of Bengal ready to sell their bodies and souls to live as there were at this time.

In a rare moment of weakness Mother once told me that she probably lost her mind then, in Kolkata, and her childhood with it, though she desperately, resolutely, attemped to reconstruct both in later years.

Mother was fortunate. She lived, scarred as she would remain by this for the rest of her troubled life even as fresh wounds visited her. As children my sister and I learned early to not waste food. Mother would beat us severely if we wasted anything served to us; more so, if we wasted anything we had asked for ourselves. Sometimes she would beat me for nothing at all, no reason I could discern at any rate, then hug me and cry. My stubborn silence seemed to trigger in her a certain madness—the jailing of Father, dislocation of the family, the horrific birth of Bangladesh and the constant fear her mother and siblings could, at any time, be slaughtered, appeared to bring back old horrors that began with the year of the famine—the emotional, buried responses of a child would flower in her adult mind. There was no counsellor at hand to treat such horrors; Mother belonged to a generation where victims and the disturbed offered succour to each other through their understanding of shared experiences. At times I found the courage to hug her back.

To this day I cannot bear to see food wasted. Some years ago an acquaintance of Punjabi heritage came up to me during a meal at a restaurant. 'Bhookha Bāngāli,' he teased. Hungry Bengali, starving Bengali. Along with 'refugee' I've heard the slur numerous times during my time at boarding school and at university in Delhi. At school I would fight with any boy, older, bigger, stronger, to defend myself against these taunts. Mother's miasma had infected me so it was impossible to differentiate between a zoo-like provocation of an easily angered teenage boy and the impossible, ludicrous defence of an entire people and vast histories with fists, knees, elbows, feet, because nobody seemed to care about words or reason or perspective so soon after 1971. There was the visible flood of Bengali displacement and deprivation, homelessness and anger married to the anger of the ongoing Naxal movement, splashed across India's newspapers and in government documenataries shown in cinemas; so soon after stories my tormentors' parents had told them of 1943, 1946, 1947 and beyond, our chronological collective of hunger and hopelessness and hatred. To these not-Bengali scions of relatively stable histories, Bengalis were displaced, deprived, hungry, and angry, often full of bitterness.

The anger has cooled down, but memories remain. At an outdoors meal not long ago a not-Bengali acquaintance commented on my robust appetite, and commented in a somewhat inebriated state the slur I had not heard for a while—Bhookha Bāngāli. So I told this gentleman some stories about the origin of the phrase. Embarrassed, he left in a hurry; I left too, following a suddenly failing appetite that couldn't be revived after churlishly scoring a point, using information as ammunition to deliberately counter-shame someone who didn't know better. Would it have helped had I told him that, not many years before this encounter, my colleague, a fellow senior editor at a magazine where I worked at the time in New Delhi, turned to me during a fortnightly editorial meeting, at which the fate of the country, if not the world, was decided, and loudly exclaimed, 'Bhookha Bāngāli' when I took a second biscuit from a plate that was passed around. At another time, during a similar meeting when he was at the receiving end of an argument, he opted for a scorched-logic tactic reserved for Bengali colleagues: 'What would you know about Indian politics?' he exclaimed, as most others in the room had the grace to look discomfited. 'You're a refugee.'

◆

Three million from Bengal died for the Allies to resist the Axis forces, 1.5 million if you believe the colonial government's figures, 3.5 million if you believe the figure of some Western—non-British—analysts and historians. It was the Bengali war effort.

Our prime minister by default, Winston Churchill, wouldn't have it any other way. He couldn't be expected to find a soft spot for Bengal if he didn't particularly care for Indians. Besides, he was incensed by the Quit India Movement initiated by the Congress Party in August 1942. The sequence of events, the deadly domino effect that would lead to famine and later prime southern and eastern Bengal for rioting was already in play. Madhusree Mukerjee's excellent and haunting history of the famine, *Churchill's Secret War*, relates how Churchill saw things on 9 August 1942, the day the government of India arrested Mohandas Gandhi and other Congress leaders for the party's Quit India resolution of the previous day: 'I hate Indians,' he exploded. 'They are a beastly people with a beastly religion.'

A little over a year later, at a celebratory dinner to mark Lord Archibald Wavell's departure to India as viceroy, Churchill would gush over Britain's accomplishments for India where there had been 'no war for three generations'. 'Famines have passed away—until the horrors of war and the dislocations of war have given us a taste of them again—and pestilence has gone.' He called it India's 'Golden Age'. Visiting Bengal in late 1943 as viceroy of India, Lord Wavell—the former field marshal of Britain's army was elevated to a peerage as the first Earl Wavell—realized just how bad the famine was, But Churchill (and his key advisers) had ensured that his racism and disgust with India coupled with the exigencies of war had created another of Bengal's bespoke nightmares.

◆

It wasn't Bengal's first celebrated famine. We had quite a grand one in 1770, just over a decade after the Battle of Polāshi—Plassey—which as you know is another of Bengal's laments.

After the defeat at Polāshi, General Robert Clive's co-conspirator at the court of Bengal's nawab, Siraj-ud-Daula, Mir Jafar, was compelled to pay the equivalent of £3.4 million to the British East India Company as reparation and a service charge, if you will, for handing him the nawabi of Bengal, though it was really Jafar who helped with others to hand Bengal to the Company. A third of the amount went to the officers and soldiers, and began the personal enrichment of Clive. When Mir Jafar proved unsuitable for their purpose, Mir Qasim was appointed in his place, and he was made to fork out £2,00,000 worth of tribute to the Company for that privilege; and also hand over to the Company revenue control over several districts, including Medinipur and Bardhaman or Bordhōmān (or Burdwan) in Bengal's west, and Chottōgram (Chittagong) in the east. The Company auctioned revenue collection to the highest bidder.

This dismantled the revenue collection system of the zamindars, over a thousand of them, big and small that was established by Murshid Quli Khan, nawab of Bengal and later bolstered by Nawab Alivardi Khan, Siraj's grandfather. 'Let them grow rich,' he is said to have told Siraj of Bengal's farmers, textile workers and traders who formed the backbone of the economy, the zamindari system, and the nawab's treasury, 'and the state will grow rich also.' As Mukerjee reminds us, that advice was remodelled to generate maximum revenue using any device at hand. 'Thus numberless harpies were let loose to plunder,' observed a future governor of Bengal, Harry Verelst, 'whom the spoil of a miserable people enabled to complete their first year's payment.' Such sentiment was rare.

The British insisted on reduced duties. Mir Qasim was soon overthrown when he demanded British soldiers leave Bengal in exchange for trading and tax concessions. Mir Jafar returned, in exchange paying out another fortune. Less than a decade after Polāshi, the Company ran Bengal's revenue collection, giving the shaky Mughal emperor in Delhi an annual sum while the Company's profits were eight or ten times that amount—soon, even more. Such revenues paid for purchasing local goods, staunching the Company and Britain's revenue drain of the previous centuries. We learn that Bengal exported £6,311,250 worth of goods and products during 1766–1768, and imported a tenth of that—the exports were financed by Bengal's revenues the Company now controlled.

The rains failed in 1769–1770. Crop failure loomed. Traders and speculators purchased as much rice as possible—Indian and British traders alike, setting a cold, calculating mercantile template that would repeatedly revisit Bengal. And, instead of shoring up resources for the local population, Company officials shipped grain wherever else in its subcontinental domains it was required. I have read of consequent horrors in similar accounts, heard of it from family and friends who are well-known academicians, but Mukerjee's recounting of a telling by historian William Hunter, a nineteenth-century chronicler, is as chilling as any horror in Belgian Congo or any other in living memory:

> All through the stifling summer of 1770 the people went on dying... The husbandmen sold their cattle; they sold their implements of agriculture; they devoured their seed grain; they sold their sons and daughters; till at length no buyer of children could be found; they ate the leaves of trees and the grass of the field; and in June 1770 the resident at (Murshidabad) affirmed that the living were feeding on the dead.

Ten million died in Bengal. A third of the population. In those days 'Bengal' was, in terms of revenue collection, and, for all practical purpose, administratively, also much of present-day Bihar, and parts of Jharkhand and Odisha. Bengal and Bihar were brutally hit in a rolling tragedy the direct effects of which lasted for several years.

The Company's directors would later complain about the 'disappointing' revenue from some districts even as overall revenue collection was, quite amazingly, maintained at the previous year's level. Warren Hastings, governor general of India during the Company years maintained it was on account of collections being 'violently kept up to its former standard'.

◆

That came to be known in Bengali lore as Chhiāttōrér monnōntōr, as it began in the year 1176 of the Bengali calendar—1176 Bongābdō; chhiāttōr is seventy-six.

The one in 1943 had its own local appellation, Ponchāshér monnōntōr. The Great Famine of Fifty, based on the year 1350 of the Bengali calendar. It was a famine born of geopolitics, war, paranoia, callousness, greed and nature.

After their attack on Pearl Harbour in Hawaii on 7 December 1941, Japanese armed forces advanced rapidly across the South Pacific and East Asia. By the summer of 1942, they had occupied Malaya, overpowered the British there and their prized colonies and trading posts of Hong Kong and Singapore and blitzed into Burma. The British army and the British Indian army retreated at the back of several hundred thousand refugees. Northern Burma and what is called Northeast India (for me it remains far-eastern India) was within Japanese reach. The Japanese army had begun to bomb Bengal's other port of Chittagong, and British India's main eastern Indian hub, Kolkata. British—Allied—control of the Bay of Bengal was wrecked. In early April that year, Japanese dive bombers had proven their reach by sinking a British aircraft carrier, HMS *Hermes*, and several other ships off Batticaloa in eastern Ceylon (it became Sri Lanka only in 1972), which straddled the sea lanes from East and South Asia to West Asia and the Suez.

In late 1942, a cyclone shredded Medinipur and the 24 Parganas, killing nearly 15,000 people. Perhaps more tragically in this relativity of horror, it destroyed standing crops; the rice had begun to ripen. The western delta of Bengal was ravaged.

Meanwhile, spooked by the Japanese advance, the British ordered the destruction of medium and large boats across Bengal's delta, west and east. An estimated 60,000 boats that carried people and produce were within days turned to kindling to prevent them falling into Japanese hands; the British thought the Japanese army would use these boats to control the myriad rivers and waterways of the delta and tide the country.

To bolster Kolkata, which had turned into a garrison city as much as a trading city and a munitions-building city, against siege, the government ordered the stockpiling of rice and other grain—masses of food for soldiers and civilians alike. Kolkata and eastern India had become a rallying point for American troops and flyers as well, to supply Chiang Kai-shek's troops with flights over the Himalaya with the Burma Road to China cut off. Air strips and cantonments came up across Bengal—as a child I saw one such near Polāshi—displacing quite large populations even before the famine took hold. The soldiers and flyers all had to be fed, had to be protected. Even as rice was sucked out of Bengal, particularly southern Bengal, such stock was also used for export to war 'theatres' as decided by government, as supplies from Burma and other parts of Southeast Asia had been cut off by Japan's advance.

The imperial government of India funded this purchase with its network of buying agents—among them some prominent members of Bengal's Muslim League-controlled government, who like many others were advanced money by the government—which bypassed the traditional route of the middleman, and dislocated the traditional agrarian purchasing mechanism across all of southern Bengal from present-day Bangladesh to present-day West Bengal. If farmers and traders declined to sell, these buying agents had the authority to use any means in the name of the government. There was simply too little food left in the countryside and what remained was priced out of the reach for most—the price of rice had greatly risen even in the cities.

What rice stock remained in rural areas was often destroyed at the scorched-earth orders of government, by soldiers and local police—at several places these were poured into rivers and burnt where it was in silos. Meanwhile, the destruction of boats had destroyed the fishing economy as well as the major means of commuting and transport relief—although there wasn't much relief forthcoming.

People began to die. In southwestern Bengal, Medinipur and the 24 Parganas became deathscapes. Quoting several sources, the historian Willem van Schendel notes that in the southeastern districts of Faridpur, Comilla and Chittagong 'one out of ten inhabitants perished and on the large island of Bhola'—today part of an eponymous district in Bangladesh—'famine took every seventh person'.

The government sent Indian rice to Ceylon and West Asia. War requirement. Offers of aid to Bengal from other countries of the Allied cause, the United States, Australia, New Zealand, Ireland, were denied citing logistics and security. (Éamon de Valera, the future president of the Republic of Ireland, whom Subhas Bose had met in Dublin and London in the mid-1930s when de Valera was already a towering politician, led the effort for humanitarian assistance. Bose's nephew, Sisir, recalls a meeting with de Valera after Ireland's freedom from Britain in 1948, during which he mentioned that 'Uncle Subhas' had personally thanked de Valera and the Irish Red Cross in a 'wartime radio broadcast'.) Sympathetic government officials had to cajole their superiors to transport foodstock from elsewhere in the subcontinent to Bengal. Churchill and his aides, even the governor of Bengal, John Herbert, evidently remained unmoved.

An estimated 60 million people died as a result of World War II. A tenth of them were Jews. Three million is one-twentieth of 60 million, dead in months. But they were not counted in the cost of war in terms of lives lost; even if they were 'collateral damage' of that war.

Bhookha Bāngālis were nothing.

The dead in the Bengal famine are only counted when war-related famine is calculated, like many millions in China, the

Soviet Union, Southeast Asia. The famine-dead are usually beyond mourning except in occasional books and stories (that only the historian or conscience-stricken will write or read), or in the works of a Somnath Hore, whose stark, tortured paintings, sculptures and sketches haunt us decades after they entered his mind and never let go, the insanity of the times finding an outlet in the sanity of art. Like Hore, those times entered the mind of Zainul Abedin and found expression in his 'Famine series', every bold line of horror in those sketches, bent, emaciated backs, shapes eating off the street, a mother skeleton feeding a child skeleton—or so those morbid, angry, definitive lines seem to suggest—will forever shadow his other works—picture-postcard depictions of his lush Bengal countryside and its handsome, proud people.

The dead remain as nothing but fragments of our imagination.

13

Prōbāshi, bidéshi
At home in the world

In the summer of 2013, I was in Chicago with another Indian writer, the affable Amish Tripathi, who is very successful with his retelling and interpretation in racy fiction of Indian myth and legend. While my alternative realities on pressing areas of socio-political and socio-economic conflict in mall-struck India are far less eagerly sought, both young Amish and I had consecutive engagements at the charming, capacious dance centre of Columbia College. After our well-attended interactions he was whisked away by a wealthy Indian-origin businessman and Shiva- and Amish-devotee, and I travelled to a prosperous southern suburb of Chicago to interact with a group of Bengalis, to talk about my novels, non-fiction work, writing, and writerly trivia. The promise thereafter of a fine Bengali lunch at the home of one of my Bengali hosts, a leading food technologist based in Illinois, was also an incentive during this extended visit to North America.

Besides, I basked in the gentle afterglow of Swami Vivekananda as some Bengalis of a particular age consciously and subconsciously do when visiting Chicago; even though he gave his famous speech in 1893, and his original message of humanity is only dimly remembered by his increasingly belligerent modern-day acolytes in the subcontinent. Vivekanada and Chicago is part of a Bengali temporal tour package.

Only, I could have been in south Kolkata. Our interaction was fittingly at a local Bengali community centre which doubled as the Durga-bāri and the festival home of other gods and goddesses beloved of the Bengali Hindus. After my interaction with Sanjoy Roy, a fellow Bengali and one of India's leading culture impresarios, the event descended to a rude free-for-all argument led by a foul-mouthed, middle-aged Bengali gentleman in typical Bengali-style, colour-mismatched Western clothing—which is to say it was as loud and discordant as an amateur heavy metal concert. He didn't care about anything but an opportunity to hit back at an elegant, middle-aged Bengali lady—dressed impeccably in a pastel Dhākāi shāri and pearls—over the ignoring of his suggestions for pujō and other community matters. His grouse couldn't wait. He argued, trying to play things up, accusing others of insulting him. She argued, trying to play it down, even as she was plainly being insulted. He had support. So had she. A fair number of neutrals looked on shocked. Roy and I attempted to control our laughter.

It was all so familiar. Nearly 13,000 kilometres from the eccentricities of Bengal, we were home.

◆

Several million Bengalis are part of a great scattering on account of personal persuasions and insecurities, even victimization, of politics and economics. They are to be found across West Asia and the Persian Gulf Emirates, the United Kingdom, United States, Canada, Pakistan and India (if you count the vast numbers who escaped religious and political persecution in South Asia), Malaysia, Singapore, the Maldives, Myanmar...

In these other lands we live as citizens, residents who may still retain citizenship of India or Bangladesh, and a far slimmer though still impressive stream of illegal residents who jump their visitor visas or work visas to live and work in the twilight zone of survival.

Not all stories are tragic though, like the great migrations caused by Partition, subsequent riots, the war of 1971, and subsequent riots. Or the decision by the Burmese dictator Ne Win in 1962 to expel people from the subcontinent; 3,00,000 had to leave quickly, among them numerous Bengalis, who settled mostly in West Bengal. At one end of the scale lies troubled pasts and the great bulge of humdrum migrants' existence. At the other end lies great recognition in the sciences, arts, academia and, occasionally, business. Sometimes they are simply fascinating footnotes of forgotten histories, trivial to some people; but few things are trivial to the information-hungry Bengali, adepts of an obsessive, near-mystical practice that is sometimes known as 'general knowledge'.

Let me tell you the story of Cornél Bishshāsh. It's about a boy who left home, the village of Nathpur by the Māthābhāngā (Broken Head) River, not far from Kolkata, and ended up a colonel in Brazil's army. He was a full-fledged 'Non-resident Bengali', a blue riband prōbāshi.

We use the term for any Bengali who has migrated from Bengal, irrespective of the distance of that geographical separation. Even if they maintain links, the occasional visit to attend a marriage, or for marriage, to visit relatives, or make a quick pilgrimage to a temple or mājār of a pir, they remain prōbāshi, even those who live outside the subcontinent and still carry an Indian or Bangladeshi passport. In some ways it's as if 'Non-resident Indian', or NRI and the non-resident Bangladeshi are subsets of 'Non-resident Bengali', where désh is the homeland, and elsewhere is naturally bidésh.

I may be treading on dangerous ground here with such universalism—conservative Bengali Hindus who migrated from West Bengal or Greater Bengal, East Pakistan, even Bangladesh, are often loathe to have Bangladeshis, mostly Bengali Mussulmans, identified as Bengalis alongside them. In turn, many similar-minded Mussulman Bangladeshis, quite content in their Bengaliness—and, increasingly, in their Bangladeshiness—do form groups of religious exclusion. Even regional exclusion—more than 90 per cent of all Bangladeshi immigration to the United Kingdom, for instance, is from Sylhet, to the north of the country, and such migrants are bound by that root as much as the distinct Sylheti dialect that all first generation migrants speak. It's such a bond that even Bengali

Hindus of Sylheti origin, displaced by Partition or later, will identify with it. During Partition there was even a move to accord Sylhet special status! The traffic is now worthwhile enough for Biman, Bangladesh's national airline, to offer direct flights several times a week from Heathrow to Sylhet's Osmani International.

It isn't as if there isn't any interaction between religious groups. As with commonplace instances of bonhomie among Indians and Pakistanis, once they are outside the subcontinent, Bengalis from both India and Bangladesh come together for various social functions. This transcends the barriers of their various national 'associations' or 'clubs'—mostly places of simplicity, not posh. This is easier with younger migrants or second generation of migrants onwards. As Salim Lakha notes in a perceptive essay on the Indian diaspora in Australia, this camraderie among Bengali speakers is to be found several removes from generations that have seen or suffered Partition and various subsequent abominations of religion—'though to some extent,' remarks this diaspora commentator, 'this depends on their parents' predilection for interaction with people from one or the other community.' That is a polite way of saying—it's about Hindus and Mussulmans, not Indian Bengalis or East Pakistani Bengalis or Bangladeshi Bengalis. If that is what just social mixing entails, imagine acquiescing in mixed-religion marriages. And for all our stated liberalism, in some communities, especially among Bengali Hindus who are Brahmin or of other upper castes, and the Brahmin-like ashrafi Mussulmans, there is still a parent-led reluctance to let children marry someone of a different caste or lower status group.

◆

Anyway, back to the cornél—the way we write it in Bangla, and pronounce it is very close to the Portuguese coronel—I was talking about. He married restlessness to survival instinct and a sense of adventure.

Although few Bengalis remember him today, *The Telegraph* in

Kolkata acknowledged his existence with an article in 2011, to mark the sesquicentennial of his birth, and bemoaned that he was 'so thoroughly ignored and forgotten'. The only institution that preserves his name is a school named after Biswas in Nathpur, the Nathpur Cornel Bishshash Primary School, established in 1954 and now run by West Bengal's department of education.

A hagiography, *Léfténant Shurésh Bishshāsh,* written in Bāngla by a friend of the cornél and published in 1899, about the only source material for this enigmatic and quite extraordinary man, proclaims giddily that it is a '…Supernatural Incident-filled Incredible Story of His Life'. The writer quotes a fantastic observation from *The Times* (presumably of London), correctly described as a 'mouthpiece of the conservative establishment' that, if a nation has as contemporaries our cornél Biswas, (the scientist) Jagadish Bose and (the impeccably Macaulayesque Indian Civil Service officer and, later, the much-knighted diplomat for the Crown) Atul Chandra Chatterjee, then that nation cannot be ignored. Biswas was described as an antithesis of the 'bhiru, kāpurush Bongōbāshi' stereotype of the time encouraged by the government's word and deed of differentiating between martial and non-martial races, especially after the mutiny in 1857—the easily frightened, cowardly people of Bengal. That demon of description persists till today.

Hyperbole was typical of numerous hagiographies around the turn of the century (my great grandfather's being one) and this one conforms to the type. Biswas, who was born in 1861, didn't cry when as an infant at his mother's kōl, he touched a lamp's flame. He climbed a 20-feet mōyi when he was two, and was seen clapping his hands in delight atop the bamboo ladder. He rescued a squirrel from a cat when he was two and didn't cry when the cat mauled him nearly to death. When the family moved to Kolkata—his father held down a modest position at a government office—he was known to indulge in warlike games with fellow youngsters, using earthen missiles as cannonballs 'like Napoleon played with snowballs instead of cannonballs in his youth' (jérūp

Napoleon gōlar pōribortē borōfkhondō lōiya balyōkhelā khélitén).

On a trip back to the village from Kolkata and studies at 'London Mission College' he beheaded a poisonous snake. He was eleven. Later he cowed a wild boar with a blow of his hand—earning the appreciation of the Ingréj shāhéb who were hunting it. This was evidently a life-changing episode, as it led young Suresh to proximity with some admiring Britons, including a mém who turned out to be a bit of a patron, teaching him English and such. They would bring him into contact with Christianity, which he would subsequently adopt after continuous admonition and beating by an authoritarian father, who wanted his son to retain his focus on studies when all he wanted to do was wander off or be with friends. The rejection of his family followed the rejection of his religion. He was fourteen, a pariah to his family, and impoverished.

He then scrabbled around for a living. We learn that his former headmaster offered food and shelter at London Mission School. He finally found a job with Spence's Hotel, the first major hotel in Kolkata, waiting on guests that arrived at the jetty or station—an early version of a guest relations executive. Restless after several months here, he bought a ticket to Rangoon, sailed there, was unable to find satisfactory work, sailed to Madras, and, without finding work, returned to Kolkata through the charity of an elderly foreigner he met in Madras. He finally managed to convince the captain of a ship of the British India Steam Navigation Company to hire him as an assistant steward, and headed off to Britain. He was seventeen. The record of what happened next was apparently carried as notes to Biswas's family and the biographer through one of Suresh's British well-wishers; there were also some letters written to an uncle that his biographer claims he read.

Biswas found a shipmate to spend time with, described by his biographer as literally a 'Shippie White'—'jāhāji gōrā'—lowly enough to befriend a 'real black Indian' and drag him to dives around London's East End. I love the descriptions—they bring the area to life more than a hundred years before Bangladeshi-

British writer Monica Ali's debut novel *Brick Lane*, a sort of Sylhet-transplanted-to-East-End saga, was praised for doing something similar. The biography insidiously deconstructed the lordly British for the Bengali using the lowest common denominator. 'The poor of London live here; there isn't a place as filthy as this even in India. All of London's scoundrels and criminals live here; it's their āddā. At every step there are shops selling alcohol!'—the latter day equivalent of East London's infamous gin houses.

> Drunkards are everywhere; such poverty perhaps doesn't exist anywhere in the world. Here, sin rules alongside poverty. Starving children play in the sewers like dogs and pigs. Hundred of women, many made skeletal with hunger and exhaustion, roam the streets. Raucous groups of unemployed men are everywhere...

For a while Biswas lived in a small room in a house mostly occupied by prostitutes—the cheapest accommodation he could find. 'It wasn't that he was of the purest soul or virtue, he occasionally drank wine, but he had to live with coarse language, horrible acts, and hair-raising behaviour.' And one day, after engaging in drunken revelry with two women it appears young Suresh lost his virginity—the biography describes the two-day binge in some detail.

He then escaped a job as newspaper delivery boy and the amorous clutches of a landlady to roam the countryside as a travelling salesman, before chancing upon a circus in Kent. After wrestling the circus's current strongman into submission he became his successor at fifteen shillings a week, and eventually became the circus's lion tamer. His next job was of a tamer-and-trainer of wild animals. This took Biswas to Hamburg and other European cities—a visit during which he chanced upon a former sweetheart from the circus—it turned out she was a wealthy German heiress. A whirlwind romance became a scandal and, chased by the girl's relatives, Biswas left for the United States and found work with a circus in 1885, and eventually found his way to Brazil with that circus the same year. Biswas found his place in the sun in 'Raio de Jamiro', as his biographer occasionally called Brazil's largest city and its capital at the time.

Besotted by Brazil's natural beauty (and, it appears from the biography, the refreshing presence of creoles and mulattos which brought the comfort of colour), Biswas chose to stay in Rio de Janeiro and, as he wrote home, he was featured in *La Cronica*—it isn't clear whether it was the name of the paper or 'chronicles' is used collectively—for his circus acts and as a public speaker. Biswas had added Portuguese to his linguistic string of English, French, German, Spanish, Dutch and Danish. He applied for and got the job of superintendent at the local zoo. He also applied himself and won the love of 'snow white Desdemona' ('tūshār dhobōl Desdemona'). We are told Desdemona's tease about how Suresh would look smart in a soldier's uniform led him to join Brazil's army in 1887, as a corporal. By 1893 he was a first lieutenant, and had seen action in a battle to quell a naval revolt, among other skirmishes. He married his lady love. They had a son.

Then the biography pretty much wraps up. Suresh died in 1905. From another biography we learn that he had become a cornél.

◆

Fascinating as Suresh-babu's story was, there were stories about other Bengalis I would love to know more about. Take the descendants of the handful of Bengalis who reached New Zealand in the early nineteenth century as the British dominion of the subcontinent was well and truly underway. Permanent Settlement had been emphatically introduced in Bengal, changing forever the pattern of zamindari, creating new rajas and nawabs.

Some Bengali loshkōr ('lascar' to the rest of the world) from the Chittagong area appear to have jumped ship at Otago Harbour on New Zealand's Pacific coast in 1814. Three survived of a group of six deserters of a British East India Company vessel, and eventually set to work teaching the Maori 'strategies for fighting Europeans', as I read in a work on the Indian diaspora. One of them even 'took the moko', the Maori tattoo, and was heard of in 1844, living with his Maori family in the far south, on Stewart Island. There was an even earlier instance of a Bengali deserter, in 1809 (some say 1810), from the ship *City of Edinburgh*, who subsequently was a 'servant' to a Maori chief, and later took a Maori wife and lived in the Bay of Islands. He is referred to by a historian as the 'first Indian ever to set foot on New Zealand soil'.

But that precise honour, according to another historian, could actually belong to the 'Bengali lascar Nasreen', who came ashore in 1769 at Aotearoa, at the time a generally accepted reference to the country's North Island—not the Maori word for all New Zealand as it has come to be accepted now—with a colleague from Pondicherry, Mahmud Qaseem. They belonged to a party of sailors from the vessel *Saint Jean Baptiste* who had been offloaded to recuperate after they had fallen sick on board. (Ship's logs reveal that both evidently recovered, moved on, and died within sight of the Peruvian coast the following year.)

We know of some other curious early prōbāshi stories, in Scandinavia, for example. Tamils got the first cut on Scandinavia on account of Denmark's colony in Tranquebar, or Tarangampadi, a little to the south of Pondicherry. They arrived as residents (slaves, servants, sailors) and petitioners to Danish courts, a familiarly colonial activity. As far as Bengalis go, we know from tales of the intrepid cornél that he absorbed Danish while on a visit to Scandinavia in the latter part of the nineteenth century. A formal Indian diaspora history records the first Indian settler in Norway to be a Bengali, Surendranath Boral, from Hooghly. He spread Vedantic thought and spiritualism as the Swami Sri Ananda Acharya. A prolific author of several dozen books, his effort also included a Norwegian translation of the Ramayana, *Rama-Kvaedet*, a project with the writer Arne Garborg. The acharya was evidently so taken with his surroundings that he bought a house on Mount Tron in eastern Norway, in 1917; and was buried on the mountain when

Sudeep Chakravarti

he died in 1945.

(At somewhat the other end of the trail of Bengalis to Scandinavia is the story of Barun 'Bicky' Chakraborty, now married to Swedish royalty. Barun left Kolkata in the 1960s to study in Stockhom, and stumbled upon success when he took over a cooperative business that rented out empty student dormitories as hotel rooms in summer. He eventually bought out the business, and elevated it to a premium profile. He is today Sweden's biggest hotelier, and is sole owner of Elite Hotels that owns properties across Sweden, and elsewhere.)

◆

For the post-Independence generation in India, East Pakistan and Bangladesh alike, my family's situation and that of my friends is hardly unique. Most Bengalis, so-called bhodrōlōk and so-called chhōtōlōk, will know of another who made it out of the désh in search of work across a vast range from labourer to laureate, travelling shāt shōmūddōr tyarō nōdi pār, as a colloquialism goes, journey across seven seas and thirteen rivers. The experiences of my immediate family and friends are echoed everywhere in Banglasphere.

My eldest māshi, Dolly, lived for several years in Dublin after escaping the birth of Bangladesh. Her son and his family still live there. Another māshi travelled to London with her Bengali (East Paskistani) husband, Farooq. She returned to Dhaka after his death. Their son, my cousin Navid, like his father a hotel executive, lives in London, married to an English girl. His sister Nazly, frenetically rediscovering her Bengali roots for herself and her two half-German children, is a career 'infotech' person and lives at one of the quality canal addresses in Amsterdam. (Once when I visited she proudly showed me the neon sign for Biman's office and another for Air India.) Yet another māshi, Shelly, has lived on several continents with her Irish hotelier husband Colm. Their daughter Erika lives in the UK with her quarter-Bengali children. Chhōtō-māmu, my mother's youngest brother Sujit, lives with his Bangladeshi—Bengali Mussulman—wife in Arizona, in the United States.

My youngest pishi Bansari's son, Hirak, an engineer, lives with his wife Asmita, an architect and a Bengali from Tripura, in Muscat, Oman. A second cousin, Abantika, married a Bengali who lived in Johor Bahru, Malaysia; they now live in Canada. As I write this my sister has joined a branch of the Japanese government, Japan her spirit-home after a life of learning Japanese, imbibing Japanese culture and several decades working for a major Japanese transnational company.

Among my circle of Bengali friends from my schooldays, Arunava Majumdar, a highly regarded nano-technologist and energy specialist, was science adviser to the Obama administration and lives in California. My roommate, Bhaswar Mukhopadhayay, has spent a career with International Monetary Fund, shifting residences between Washington DC and wherever he was posted as resident representative, from Kyrgyzstan to Tanzania. Of my Kolkata friends, Swandip Dutt, my comrade in comprehensively rediscovering the spirit of Woodstock in Kolkata approximately ten years after the landmark musical event at Max B. Yasgur's farm in New York State, worked at business planning and insurance with major Wall Street-headquartered companies. Another Woodstockian comrade, Sreedhara Sen, commuted between Texas and Chandigarh, in northern India, to run a business process outsourcing firm after some years in academia.

Like them, other people who left for post-graduate studies and remained overseas to live and work, numerous Bengali friends from my university days in Delhi, are almost all employed with global funds and banks—a few manage their own businesses—and have lived and worked in New York, London, Paris, Frankfurt, Zurich, Geneva, Hong Kong, Tokyo and Singapore. A good number of them are economists, economics being for Bengalis both an honourable and fashionable profession!

My daughter dreams of living and working in Paris. She is

besotted with the idea, and her Bengali mother and I can hardly grudge her a romance with Paris, or France. That city, that country and that culture of seemingly poster-perfect romanticism are like a bee-to-flower for so many Bengalis. Perhaps the most famous among them, as you know, was the ninetenth century tragic-romantic writer Michael Madhusudan Dutt. There was also his younger colleague of the Bengal Renaissance, Toru Dutt—young Tarulata Dutta— of a Bengali Christian family of deeply religious persuasion who, like Michael Madhusudan, would find posthumous glory. She died in 1877 at the age of twenty-one, irrepressibly bitten by French romanticism and the language, as she was by English—she would master both during her time in England.

She wrote *A Sheaf Gleaned in French Fields*, a collection of poetry in French that she later translated into English, among her numerous poems in both languages that continue to be discussed regularly in appreciative literary and academic circles. She wrote *Le Journal de Mademoiselle D'Arvers* (The Diary of Mademoiselle D'Arvers), it is a classic coming-of-age novel that moved at least one noted European critic to describe Dutt as a 'woman whose place is with Sappho and Emily Bronte'. (She is also the author of *Bianca, or, The Young Spanish Maiden*, which is considered to be the first novel in English by an Indian woman.) Like Michael Madhusudan she returned home to Kolkata. Their graves are shrines for more than a few fans.

An intense admiration for France that continued several hundred years after the Bengal Renaissance was drip-fed by the very ideas that fed the French revolution. A well-known colourful twentieth century Bengali editor testified to that truth, in his inimitable manner. Here's the short story:

The vast Anandabazar Group of Publications of Kolkata (or ABP as it is commonly known) derives its name from the group's iconic and eponymous Bāngla newspaper. There's *The Telegraph*, a daily in English which built its reputation for being combative; a once formidably combative and now-defunct weekly newsmagazine,

Sunday (at which I worked for over two years till early 1991); a major Bānglā book publishing business; and a slew of magazines in English and Bānglā from a literary magazine to a refined *Cosmpolitan* of sorts, staples in Banglasphere. The group didn't own a television business at the time this incident took place.

In the late 1980s, the journalist Ian Buruma met the group's editor at the time, Aveek Sarkar, for a chat and an introduction to Satyajit Ray. That interaction was for an article in the *New York Review of Books*. Its publication created a little history for us, not only because it contained a review of some of Ray's recently released works in the West, a collection of stories and *The Home and the World*, by which the world knows his film *Ghare-Baire*, but for what Sarkar said.

Buruma began his article with what he claimed was an apocryphal story told by Sarkar about the sophistication of Bengali culture, and the French director Louis Malle. The maestro had spent some time in the city to film part of his famous—'and in India notorious', as Buruma put it—1969 documentary on India, *L'inde fantôme*, Phantom India. 'One day Malle was shooting a riot scene, not uncommon in Calcutta. This infuriated a Bengali policeman who ran up to Malle threatening to smash the camera. Malle objected. "Who do you think you are?" shouted the Bengali. "Louis Malle," replied the director. "Ah," said the Bengali with a sweet smile, *"Zazie dans le Métro."'*

'I was told this anecdote by a young and very successful newspaper editor called Aveek Sarkar,' Buruma wrote. 'We met in his office, housed in an old building in the centre of a commercial district where beggars and rickshaw-wallahs dodged in and out of the hopeless traffic jams, while entire families, the children naked, the adults in flimsy clothes, washed themselves by burst waterpipes. Aveek was dressed in a dhuti and smoked Montecristo cigars. He offered me a fine Scotch whisky and talked about Bengali poetry. Every Bengali is a poet, he said. There are at least 500 poetry magazines in the state of West Bengal and when Calcutta celebrates the birthday of its greatest poet, Rabindranath Tagore, poetry bulletins are published by the day, sometimes even by the hour. "We don't look to the rest of India, which is intellectually inferior," he said. "Our literature is related to French literature, not Hindi. I don't even read Hindi. Calcutta is like Paris.'"

Bengaliness in one fell swoop.

♦

Just how numerous are bidéshi Bengalis? Exact numbers aren't easy to come by, especially given the vast numbers of illegal immigrants to be found in several countries. Estimates rule this numbers game where the governments of India and Bangladesh sometimes play fast and loose with data to suit that wilfully generous term, 'national interest'—the political parties that control such governments often focus or fade numbers to suit even provincial and ultra-local political interests. 'Post-truth' and 'alternative facts', buzzwords that are all the global rage after the fractious American presidential elections of 2016, have applied to this South Asian metric for several decades. But what is indisputable by far is that bidéshi Bengalis, permanently bídéshí or, like most labour migrants temporarily so, are overwhelmingly of Bangladeshi (or East Pakistani) origin.

Bānglā and Sylheti count among the most spoken foreign languages in Britain. Of the numerous South Asian languages spoken in United States, Bānglā is among the fastest growing language and is among the most spoken. It is hardly surprising given the numbers, which will only rise.

Bangladeshi migrants to Britain are estimated at 5,00,000 according to a position paper from 2015 for the Bangladesh government prepared by the International Labour Organization (ILO) and other agencies. Focused on developed economies, the report lists such people as 'long-term Bangladeshi migrants' who look for 'permanent settlement', not those who migrate for short-term or seasonal work. An equal number is estimated for the US. Italy has 70,000 such migrants; Canada 35,000; Japan 22,000;

Australia 15,000; Greece 11,000; Spain 7,000 and Germany 5,000. The countries that harbour between 1,000 and less than 5,000 are South Africa, France, the Netherlands, Belgium and Switzerland.

Britain is really where the transcontinental flow began, as I was reminded by a fine research note by scholars Benjamin Etzold and Bishawjit Mallick for BPB, Germany's Federal Agency for Civic Education. Post-war Britain began to look to the Commonwealth states to fill labour shortages, and youngsters from Sylhet in East Pakistan of the time were among those who readily obliged. This began 'chain migrations' as initial settlers' experiences attracted more migrants; they almost all began to bring across family. The steady trickle from the 1950s to the early 1970s exploded after the Bangladesh war. The impetus of poverty, uncertain livelihood prospects in a brand new country with its rocky politics, and the oil boom in the Middle East and consequent demand for cheap labour began to snowball into a rush that is yet to stop, even as Bangladesh has since emerged as an undeniable socio-economic success story with vastly improved human development indices and a booming economy.

Six thousand Bangladeshis moved to work outside the subcontinent in 1976. During 1990–1995, the number had grown to 1.2 million, including both temporary and expatriate workers—temporary workers form the bulk of it. Between 2000 and 2005, it numbered 3 million, over half of such movement to the Middle East. That region remains the biggest destination in this roll-over migration as freshly contracted labour replaces those with expired contracts, but Southeast Asia, especially Malaysia and Singapore, have emerged as key worker destinations for Bangladesh. According to Bangladesh foreign ministry 'sources' quoted in local media, 4,00,000 workers were legally present in Malaysia in 2016, while 'some 20,000 others become undocumented', as the *Daily Star* newspaper in Dhaka put it. (This is probably a conservative estimate. A furore erupted in Malaysia where demands were put forward to 'regularize', or legalize, illegal migrants from Bangladesh instead of bringing in a fresh crop of migrants!)

And while almost 95 per cent of such migration is male, female labour migrants, more numerous than ever, are becoming a presence in the United Arab Emirates where they number over 90 per cent of the total and almost 100 per cent in Jordan.

Altogether they remitted a little shy of US$15 billion to Bangladesh for the 2015–2016 financial year, according to Bangladesh Bank (India, the world's largest recipient of foreign remittances brought approximately $70 billion during the same period). For Bangladesh the number has grown from $764 million in 1990–1991, about a twenty-fold increase. Remittances were second only to earnings from garment exports, Bangladesh's trading mainstay. Remittance is such a factor in the country's economic growth and balance of payments that global credit ratings firms like Moody's Investors Service now use it to gauge its ratings.

They can contribute in other ways too. Indeed, the ILO study strongly recommends leveraging members of Bangladesh's diaspora to help with the country's development, adding to the increasingly robust effort of local businesses, the economy and society at large. The report holds up the example of former Harvard professor Omar Rahman, who helped develop the Independent University, now a major institution in Bangladesh. Dr Sarder A. Nayeem and Dr Jonaid Shafiq returned from Japan and, in 1993, set up the Japan Bangladesh Friendship Hospital, for providing healthcare facilities to the poor. S. M. Ali and Mahfuz Anam launched the *Daily Star* in 1991. Today it is Bangladesh's leading English language daily—and to my mind among South Asia's better newspapers. Since 2013, it has a competitor in *Dhaka Tribune*, published by another 'returnee', K. Anis Ahmed.

Iqbal Z. Quadir, a former star at the Massachusetts Institute of Technology (MIT), began a telelcommunication effort with Telenor of Norway, with help from aid organizations and development banks. The result is Grameenphone, a leading telephone operator. Abul Hussam, a professor of chemistry at George Mason University in the US, has developed the SONO filter, which uses a low-tech, effective process—manufactured locally from 'cast-iron turnings, along with readily available river sand, wood charcoal, and wet brick chips' that claims to remove all but 2 per cent of arsenic content from water, addressing a massive problem of arsenic contamination in Bangladesh and West Bengal. The design won a $1 million prize, mostly channelled to a Bangladeshi non-profit to produce and distribute more than a quarter of a million filters in Bangladesh. SONO filters are now exported.

◆

There is also the greyest of grey areas that largely remains unacknowledged by Bangladesh—officially, that is. About 2 million Bangladeshis are estimated to live in Pakistan, a holdover from the time of the Bangladesh war and, subsequently, a trickle of illegal runs through any available country of transit—India, Nepal, and the Maldives. Impressive as that is, estimates for India, from the Indian perspective, are eye-popping. India's deputy home minister told that country's upper house of parliament in November 2016 that an estimated 20 million Bangladeshi immigrants were illegally in India. Even accounting for the ultra-nationalist bias of the Bharatiya Janata Party-led coalition that formed the government in mid-2014, the numbers are staggering. The estimates were enormous enough in 2004, when the Congress Party-led coalition's deputy home minister placed the number at 12 million, with 5 million in Assam and close to 6 million in West Bengal. A row erupted, mainly on account of objections by the Congress government in Assam, a province that, like many others, has for long seen migrants as 'vote banks'. The government in New Delhi withdrew the statement citing the 'unreliability' of the report.

(The politicking continues. The Bharatiya Janata Party, which won elections to Assam's assembly in 2016 in a landslide victory, snapping a three-term Congress streak, made the illegal migration of Bengali Mussulmans from Bangladesh a major campaign issue.)

Another estimate takes into account immigrants of various types. It accounts for those who now permanently live in India and have acquired various Indian identities—a driving licence, income tax registration number, even a voter ID card and an Aadhaar card—through a thoroughly corrupted system and deliberate lack of government oversight, and a seasonal push that includes farm labour and menial labour widely utilized in Northeast India, eastern India, and indeed, across much of northern and central India; the 'legalized' or 'regularized' illegals and the plain illegals add up to between 5 to 20 million Bangladeshis across a year.

In a 2016 essay for the think-tank Carnegie India, Sanjeev Tripathi, a former chief of India's curiously named foreign intelligence service, Research & Analysis Wing (RAW) of the Cabinet Secretariat, sounded plaintive as he pleaded a case for a national security issue. He admitted there were no reliable figures of exact numbers of illegal immigrants from Bangladesh in India, but maintained that 'analysis' of population growth figures and demographics for Bangladesh and India since 1981 'suggests with reasonable certainty that their number exceeds 15 million'. As with many Indian officials he blamed Bangladesh for denying the matter or preventing the flow of these mostly economic migrants. Pushing back such immigrants doesn't help—they just re-enter through another porous area along the border, or are 'pushed back into India by Bangladeshi border guards'.

Detecting illegal immigrants from Bangladesh is a daunting task. 'The subtle differences in the accents, dialect, and features between an Indian Bengali and a Bangladeshi are not easily discernible,' Tripathi correctly observed. 'The fact that most Bangladeshis already hold ration cards, voter identity cards, or even the unique-identity Aadhaar cards'—biometric identification launched by India in 2009—'further compounds the difficulty. Ironically, an illegal Bangladeshi immigrant is more likely to be equipped with an Indian identity document than an Indian Bengali who may take his or her Indian citizenship for granted.

During several visits to Bangladesh over the years, and to places in India across the Bangladesh border from West Bengal and Assam to Meghalaya and Tripura, like many chroniclers, I too have come by stories of easy migration—which border guards call infiltration—from Bangladesh to India and back; sometimes aided by border guards who have an eye to supplementing incomes. The archives of newspapers in eastern India are figuratively packed to the rafters with instances of such crossings, and arrangements for such crossings.

My favourite encounter, if you will, was not long ago in Sylhet with a border crossing habitué, a man in his mid-thirties who knew well the lie of the land in three Bengali-majority Assam districts of Karimganj, Hailakandi and Cachar. He claimed to have worked in Imphal, the capital of Manipur, had family and friends in Guwahati, and spoke Khasi fluently, the result of substantial stays in Meghalaya. Variously a truck driver, taxi driver, and delivery man in both his native Sylhet and in Northeastern India, he showed off his Indian—Silchar—driving licence, spoke to me in Khasi and told me of places in Shillong that I knew well and several others of which I had only a passing familiarity.

The man, whom I will call Abul—a name he picked—to protect his identity, related several of his journeys across the porous border to India. 'Éktū ríks āsé,' he said as we chatted over a meal in Jaintiapur not far from Sylhet's border with Meghalaya. The risk he spoke of is of an everyday sort. He responded to the urging of a mentor in Sylhet, who said an associate in Karimganj town, in Assam—which shares a 4.5-kilometre border with Bangladesh—needed some help with this small business.

'Fot kōri zā,' this mentor urged him in the Sylheti manner. Go quickly. So young Abul went to the border with Karimganj district due east from Sylhet, and stayed close to a group of village women who were washing clothes at the Kushiara River, the southern branch of the Barak, by the occasionally patrolled border. And then he just waded across the dry-season streams of this river which forms the international border for a large stretch of Karimganj and Sylhet.

India's security agencies maintain they will have fenced the stretch of border across Karimganj town by 2017, and alongside attempt to fence off nearly 100 kilometres of riverine border in what they call the Karimganj Sector. But Abul and those like him will probably find a way, helped along by the gods of wilful crossings. A little over 4,000 kilometres of border, with a myriad river systems and a myriad economic systems, have many such gods.

◆

In this somewhat bizarre situation it is easy and convenient for Bangladesh to dispute the figures. Diplomats and officials will unofficially acknowledge the issue exists—but urge leniency from the 'Big Brother'. Sometimes officials make fun of it all, as with the quite natural logic that, if people in India are provided official Indian identification by Indian officials, then surely such people are then Indian—and surely the governments of India and its states are not that incompetent or electorally and financially venal to provide illegals such privilege.

At other times, Bangladesh has simply ignored the matter. No acknowledgement of remittances from India finds any mention in data from Bangladesh Bank, for instance. In the 'Others' column— for sources other than major remitting geographies that Bangladesh freely acknowledges—I found an entry marked 'Wage Earners Remittance Inflows' that mentioned a figure of $800 million for the years 2014–2015. On the other hand, 'Migrations and Remittances' data released by the World Bank placed remittances from India to Bangladesh at $4.45 billion for the same period, and marginally less for the previous year.

At yet other times, Bangladesh officials and some in media have actually thrown the problem back at India, claiming half a million or so Indian workers from Indian states surrounding Bangladesh work in the country's booming garment export sector. And that they are mostly illegal.

An accurate tracing of migration patterns and information about Bengali migrants from India is not an easy task, as there is much that is not known especially where 'illegals' are concerned. But there are certain broad trends that can be identified, some of which I have already touched upon earlier. Bengali Hindus formed the bulk of the migration of students and professionals to Europe, North America and elsewhere largely from the 1960s onwards, a mostly bhodrōlōk migration—and Bengali Mussulmans formed the bulk of migrant labourers from West Bengal to destinations in West Asia and elsewhere, in part mimicking the Bangladeshi trend. They are part of a vast number of about 4.5 million Indians who work in Saudi Arabia and the Persian Gulf area. Their move, like migrant workers from Bangladesh and several other worker-bee countries, was triggered by the oil boom of the 1970s. And of course, there was the great migration of the colonial times, both enforced and voluntary.

India's foreign ministry recorded, at the end of 2016, just shy of 18 million people of Indian origin across the world, early immigrants as well as those who left later and took on citizenship in their adoptive homelands; and a little over 13 million of what are known as Non-Resident Indians—low-level migrant workers, mid- or senior-level information technology folk, other professionals, businesspersons—who live overseas as short-term workers or permanent residents, and retain Indian citizenship.

The latest foreign ministry data I could access listed low-level migrant workers from West Bengal as forming the fourth largest group of the nearly 8,00,000 for which it issued emigration clearances in 2015, after those from Uttar Pradesh, Bihar and Tamil Nadu. As for the professional or businessman, India's great internal migrations and growing cosmopolitanism have ensured a fuzziness. In effect it's the Indian taking a flight out to bidéshi destinations from Kolkata, New Delhi, Mumbai, Bengaluru, Chennai, Hyderabad, Pune, and so on; not the Indian Bengali or Indian Bengali Hindu or other ethnicities and religious groups from India's bewildering matrix.

Much like in an Indian city away from Banglasphere, it is only when such a Bengali of any religious persuasion or not, registers with a Bengali social club or 'association'—different from a 'Bangladeshi association'—in another country of residence; or, say, a Bengali shows up for local Durga Pujō celebrations, would even the vaguest estimate of overall numbers of Bengalis abroad register. And some of these may be Bengali Hindus who migrated directly from East Pakistan, or Bangladesh—and some may still carry Bangladeshi passports; besides, unlike India, Bangladesh permits dual citizenship in certain cases. There could be about 15,000 Bengali Hindus in Canada, around 50,000 in the United States, between 30,000 and 50,000 in the United Kingdom, a few hundred in France, several hundred in Germany.

Only they know.

◆

Their numbers will only grow—Hindus, Mussulmans, a smattering of Christians; Indians, Bangladeshis; by the second generation, half of one (or two) or the other that could arrive by a mixing of religion and race; and by the third generation... Bāpré bāp! Or, as my father-in-law would exclaim, recalling a favourite expression from his time as a student at university: Ārré father!'

Indeed, the Bengali diaspora in all its shades is now already so diverse and vast that, in 2015, Kalyani University near Kolkata started a Centre for Bengali Diaspora. It was moved by the Kashmiri vice-chancellor of the university, Rattanlal Hangloo, who described himself to the media as 'Bengali by heart'.

Were the Centre for Bengali Diaspora to take off, and I fervently hope it does, it will be notable in its intent to not only focus on the better-known names among the Bengali diaspora, but its stated purpose of reaching out to the diaspora from both West Bengal and East Pakistan/Bangladesh; and attempting to document the 'contributions of unknown but remarkable Bengalis'.

Hangloo and his colleagues felt there was a 'disconnect' between the diaspora and their désh. So the centre seeks to diminish that disconnect by offering research and study (and archiving) in literature and the arts, public affairs, governance, the sciences, technology and, eventually, the way Bānglā and its various dialects have evolved as prōbāshi tongues. It even offered as a heads-up an inaugural seminar with the dramatic title: 'Offsprings of Bengal in Distant Lands, Quest of the Disanchored'.

◆

Although there may not be much reliable data, there are numerous articles on the Bengali diaspora, and numerous studies. One that is striking is Bānglā Stories, in Britain. A project backed by the Sociology Department of the London School of Economics (LSE), the Centre for Research in the Arts, Social Sciences and Humanities at the University of Cambridge and the Runnymede Trust, which calls itself a 'race quality thinktank', it's the brainchild of one expatriate Bengali academic and three part-Bengali ones. Joya Chatterji, my contemporary at Delhi University. Claire Alexander is with the sociology department of London School of Economics; she is partly Bengali, and describes her mother as a 'Bengali Hindu from Kolkata, with family roots in Sylhet'. Shahzad Firoz arrived from Bangladesh for a doctorate in anthropology at the School of Oriental and African Studies (SOAS), University of London. And Annu Jalais endearingly describes herself as 'Franco-Bong'; she is a former student at LSE who did her doctoral thesis on life in the Sunderbans, wrote a book on it, and later moved to Yale Univesity as a post-doctoral student.

Chatterji was keen to get a sense of the 'wider processes of migration in Bengal' through several generations, backgrounds and locations in the United Kingdom, and roped in like-minded colleagues and pitched for a grant. The result was Bānglā Stories. If you take a look at its website *banglastories.org*, you will find a

Sudeep Chakravarti

buffet of histories, experiences, emotions and identities.

The interviewers chatted with one youngster who opted for the pseudonym Mad Max. Here's how part of the conversation went:

Q: Where is your désh?
Mad Max: I'd say Bangladesh.

Q: What is your bidésh?
Mad Max: My home is England...that's my bidésh.

Q: So, your désh is Bangladesh?
Mad Max: Yeah.

Q: What does désh mean? Is it home?
Mad Max: Yeah.

Q: And what does bidésh mean?
Mad Max: Bidésh means home and désh means away.

Q: Are you sure, I thought it was the other way round...I may be wrong. I thought that désh was your home and bidésh was away.
Mad Max: I dunno.

Q: Ok...let's say where is...home is England?
Mad Max: And away is Bangladesh. I got family in there that I don't really get to see... Once in a blue moon.

◆

The prolific Bengali-American writer and academic Bharati Mukherjee, who died in January 2017, movingly captured the striking mood of the immigrant in a 1996 essay in the *New York Times*. This much-quoted 'op-ed' piece was about the different directions her sister Mira and she chose after moving to America in the 1960s as students. Mira married a Bengali and chose to live and work in the United States retaining Indian citizenship, believing that permanent residency offered by her 'Green Card' offered an ideal mix of ties to the old country, which she could visit at will and then return to the place that offered her fine work that she did well. Bharati jettisoned that attachment, beginning with her marriage to an American citizen of Canadian descent, and giving up her Indian citizenship to accept an American one. The article was moved by Mira's dilemma when, on account of her need to continue to stay and work in America, she was compelled by changing local laws to accept US citizenship (citizenship of a country where Bengali is today recorded as being among the most spoken of all the South Asian languages! I've heard some snobbish immigrants from West Bengal insist it is on account of a flood of legal and illegal Bangladeshi immigrants and that, in any case, their Bānglā is not quite right).

Mira told Bharati she would eventually ditch her adoptive nationality and revert to Indian citizenship, and return to India in her autumn years. Meanwhile there remained Bharati's own realization of issues of foreignness she experienced for some time living as a person of Asian origin in the 'French' part of Canada—even though she had meanwhile so completely 'married' America and thought herself liberated from restrictive bonds of her homeland.

'By choosing a husband who was not my father's selection, I was opting for fluidity, self-invention, blue jeans and T-shirts, and renouncing 3,000 years (at least) of caste-observant, "pure culture" marriage in the Mukherjee family,' Mukherjee wrote. 'My books have often been read as unapologetic (and in some quarters overenthusiastic) texts for cultural and psychological "mongrelization." It's a word I celebrate.'

Two sisters. Two widely divergent immigrant experiences, wrote Mukherjee. 'Which of us is the freak?'

Neither, naturally.

(For the sake of argument, if we had to choose between one or the other sister for freakishness, what would we then call Nirad Chaudhuri, among Bengal's best known men of letters, and often reviled by Bengali and Indian nationalists for utterly turning his back on the country of his origin? Chaudhuri was in his fifties when he emigrated to England—I say England, not United Kingdom to mark Nirad-babu's preference of destination!—without regret at having finally found a home to his liking. For all the opprobrium he received for the apparent selling of his soul to the idea of the British empire—driven in part from a mis-reading of his 1951 opus *The Autobiography of an Unknown Indian*, which cost him his government job at All India Radio—approbation continued alongside controversy for this unapologetic creamy-layer bhodrōlōk whose political views remained closer to Naipaul than Nehru. In 1975, the Sahitya Akademi awarded Chaudhuri its annual prize for a work in English, *Scholar Extraordinary*, a biography of Max Müeller, placing Chaudhuri alongside several of India's best known novelists, poets and essayists.)

Our so-called purity is rooted in mongrelization. It has taken us a long journey to arrive where we have, with our distinct streams of culture, distinctive sub-languages and dialects with a unifying super-language that is itself mongrel.

It is through our openess to the world and cultures other than our own, that we have evolved our Bengaliness that is so distinctive, so unique. It's what makes us enduring, indolent, insular, outgoing, endearing, adventurous, gypsy-like, nesting, sentimental, adaptive, rebellious, questioning, accepting, and infuriating in turn—or all at once. To be anything else would probably be so very boring.

Book III
Ōgni Jūg
Age of Fire

14

Alōron
Turmoil

Surely the greatest etymological joke in Bengal emerged from a tribute during the charged stick-it-to-them times of the 1960s. At the time, Harrington Street in Kolkata was named after John Herbert Harrington, an East India Company employee who, among his other important appointments was for a time chief judge of the Sudder Dewanny Adawlut (to the British; Sadr or Sadar Diwani Adalat to others), the highest revenue court in British India, in the early nineteenth century. In 1969, the street held a collection of crumbling but spacious apartment blocks, a few stately mansions, just a hint of newer apartment buildings that would follow, some stores at one end. And the American consulate.

The Vietnam War reached fierce new landmarks that year. The second Tet offensive was launched by the North Vietnamese and their southern allies, the Viet Cong, against South Vietnam and their American allies. The United States carpet-bombed eastern Cambodia, a venture codenamed Operation Breakfast, to try and destroy North Vietnamese and Viet Cong transit bases and supply lines. That was the year of Hamburger Hill, the pointless capture and abandonment of a feature called Hill 937, that ground down both US infantry and North Vietnamese soldiers. And late that year, in September, North Vietnam's legendary leader, Ho Chi Minh, died.

In tribute, and reflecting both the left-of-centre and general 'Third World' outrage at what was seen as American meddling at best and an American invasion at worst, the second United

Front government of West Bengal, led by Ajoy Mukherjee, renamed Harrington Street as Ho Chi Minh Sarani. And there the American consultate resides today, 5/1, Ho Chi Minh Sarani. It's the official address. It is on cards US diplomats hand out, and formal invitations to functions.

And it remains after several decades of communist and non-communist governments in West Bengal, a shift in India's geopolitical windvane towards the US, and the US's own thaw with Vietnam. It's still odd, still funny, somewhat adolescent but provocatively apt.

And ironical—1969 was the year the Naxalbari rebellion took full flight, and those of the Left sticking it to the Americans had to deal with the breakaway extreme Left sticking it to them.

And angry, as so much of modern Bengal's history visibly is.

◆

Ōgni Jug, our Age of Fire, began in the first decade of the twentieth century, and it has had the longest run, nearly a hundred years from the comet's head to tail. The fires of rebellion against colonial Britain transferred to what rebels called 'neo-colonialists' of the Indian state and various provincial governments. The tag of the angry Bengali isn't unfounded even though it didn't—and doesn't—apply to all of us. But for so very long raging against the system had almost become a religion.

The first division of Bengal in 1905, Curzon's parting gift of poison apple, is when the fire is believed to have been truly lit. Nationalistic anger against British rule had been building for some years, and many among the educated Bengali Hindus, the growing elite, had enough of what they perceived as a clear policy shift towards the Mussulmans. They were already at odds with the Mussulman elite led by Dhaka's nawab, Khwaja Salimullah, who wanted to diminish Kolkata's domination in the politics and economic life of Bengal.

Nawab Salimullah was frank in his support for Partition.

'The Partition has given a new life to the people in the Eastern Province. They are feeling a refreshing sense and a relief from the thraldom of...Calcutta,' the nawab declared, claiming that Partition benefited 'children of the soil, both Hindus and Mohammedans... They find their rights more quickly recognized and their existence and importance more adequately appreciated than they could as mere appendages, as heretofore, of Western Bengal.' He even took the battle directly to 'our Bengali Hindu friends' in western Bengal by criticizing their opposition to Partition as also diminishing the spirit of nationalism. 'What is, pray, the real significance and import of this nationalism? Does it mean a cementing together of the Bengali Hindus within themselves and outside with all other races?' (There is a counter-criticism that the nawab was operating in a silo, more for the preservation of privileges of eastern Bengal's Mussulman elite than the emancipation of the Mussulman-at-large. And, that his stance was helped along by the leverage of a large loan from Lord Curzon's administration.)

Some historians claim the Ōnushilōn Shōmiti (Anushilan Samiti), which would soon lead militant activity, later spawning the breakaway Jugāntōr Party (Jugantar Party), was already in place by 1902. Translated as the Society for the Promotion of Culture and Training, it would in a few short years claim 500 branches and cells across Bengal. Aurobindo Ghosh, the future spiritualist, was a key member, as was his brother Barindra, or Barin. Jugāntōr was smaller, more concentrated in and around Kolkata and nearby districts. There was an eponymous revolutionary journal from which it took name and inspiration; Bhupendranath Datta, Swami Vivekananda's brother, was an editor. The revolutionary mantra of the Maharashtrian nationalist ideologue, Bal Gangadhar Tilak, was also a siren song—a not-Bengali aspect sometimes buried in breathless Bengali storytelling.

'There was a clear undercurrent of Hindu religious revivalism in these activities inspired by the teachings of Swami Vivekananda and active association of Sister Nibedita (Margaret Noble, an influential

Scots-Irish disciple of the Swami who gave her the Indian name after she followed him to Kolkata from London, and received initiation), and Aurobindo,' writes Nitish Sengupta, who provides a comprehensive and dispassionate profile of Ōgni Jug in his book, *Land of Two Rivers: A History of Bengal from the Mahabharata to Mujib*. He also quotes Barin Ghosh as saying, in defence of revolutionary terrorism—indeed, whether it could achieve freedom by killing a few British: 'No, we do not expect that.' He and his colleagues wanted to 'rouse the country from the torpor it was in with the sound of the bombs.'

Lord Curzon, in particular, pushed for the divide, which several historians claim was done to divide nationalistic fervour in the region driven primarily by Bengali Hindus of the now-flourishing bhodrōlōk class; and drive a communal wedge by splitting a Hindu majority part of Bengal from the Mussulman majority part—who would then be alienated from the 'Indian' nationalistic movement and be more focused on securing and controlling a Mussulman majority province. The move for division was announced by Curzon in July 1905. Bihar and Odisha were clubbed with western Bengal to form the Bengal province, and the vast province of Assam was administratively merged with northern and eastern Bengal to form East Bengal. There the community calculus, some historians maintain, was done to have 12 million Hindus in East Bengal outnumbered by 18 million Mussulmans; and to have 17 million Bānglā speakers in the western province outnumbered by 37 million people who did not.

Curzon wrote to an associate that Bengal's division would undermine the Bengalis' 'sense of superiority and destroy their dreams and that is why they are agitating against it'. (A major figure of the agitation was a former civil servant Surendranath Banerjee, a moderate politician who nevertheless earned the moniker 'Surrender-not'.) A government chronicle of the administration of Andrew Fraser, lieutenant governor of Bengal at the time, and published in 1908, spelled it out: 'The more highly educated classes [of Bengali Hindus] realized that their interests were affected, because the Muhammadans were now likely to exercise more influence on the administration and to obtain a fairer number of appointments.'

On 16 October, the day Bengal's first partition came into effect, much of the Bengali areas of the provinces shut down. The cry of Bandé-Mātaram—Vande Mataram, I praise thee, Mother or I bow to thee, Mother—from *Anōndōmoth*, Bankim Chandra Chattopadhyay's novel that used the metaphor of a rebellion by sadhus as a call to arms against the British and at another level, for Hindu revivalism, rang out loudest in western Bengal.

The first two stanzas of the verses written mostly in Sanskrit and partly in Bāngla were accorded the status of India's national song in 1950, the year India became a republic. These stanzas were religion-free, as it were, and I use here a translation in English by Aurobindo:

Mother, I bow to thee!
Rich with thy hurrying streams,
bright with orchard gleams,
Cool with thy winds of delight,
Dark fields waving Mother of might,
Mother free.

Glory of moonlight dreams,
Over thy branches and lordly streams,
Clad in thy blossoming trees,
Mother, giver of ease
Laughing low and sweet!
Mother I kiss thy feet,
Speaker sweet and low!
Mother, to thee I bow.

The latter stanzas have clear references to Hindu goddesses; and they also accounted for the slogan and the verse in entirety being interpreted as a rallying cry for Hindus, not India, by many influential Mussulmans; and alongside growing Mussulman assertion, contributed to that community's general distancing from anti-colonial upsurge:

> Thou art Durga, Lady and Queen,
> With her hands that strike and her
> swords of sheen,
> Thou art Lakshmi lotus-throned,
> And the Muse a hundred-toned,
> Pure and perfect without peer,
> Mother lend thine ear,
> Rich with thy hurrying streams,
> Bright with thy orchard gleems,
> Dark of hue O candid-fair
>
> In thy soul, with bejewelled hair
> And thy glorious smile divine,
> Loveliest of all earthly lands,
> Showering wealth from well-stored hands!
> Mother, mother mine!
> Mother sweet, I bow to thee,
> Mother great and free!

Bengal's British administration acknowledged Bandé-Mātaram's influence. An official record said of the protests and its symbol:

> Strenuous efforts were made to give the movement an air of national unity, and a watchword was found in the expression *Bande Mataram*. This was the refrain of a song in a Bengali novel *Ananda-math* written by one of the best Bengal novelists, Bankim Chandra Chatarji, and published in 1883. The name of the novel means 'the monastery of happiness,' and its subject was the revolt of a number of sanyasis or Hindu ascetics against the Muhammadans. The former were represented as having, in the course of the revolt, defeated some sepoys under an

Sudeep Chakravarti

English commander, and after the action the *Bande Mataram* song was sung by their leader. The meaning of the expression has formed the subject of considerable speculation, some maintaining that it is an invocation of Kali, meaning 'Hail Mother,' others that it merely means 'Hail Motherland,' and that it is an invocation of *bharatmata*, i.e. Mother India. There is no doubt that while many, accepting the latter meaning, used the phrase quite innocently as an expression of their love of country, it also came to be used in an aggressive and turbulent manner in processions and meetings. It became a common practice in certain localities to shout it in an offensive manner at Europeans—the *Firinghi*, as they were now called—much in the same way as 'foreign devil' by the Chinese. And in several instances it was so shouted when assaults were committed on Europeans or those who did not fall in line with the agitators.

◆

Some historians call it a rebellion of bhodrōlōk, with Bandé-Mātaram resembling the French revolutionary song 'La Marseillaise' (which became France's national anthem). The general disconnect of the elite with the masses, Hindus and Mussulmans alike, combined with the government's arrests and deportations of revolutionaries, and the steady growth of non-militant politics led to the winding down of the first phase of Ōgni Jug. However, it is credited with making a general sense of nationalism permeate through several socio-economic layers of Indian society. Shodéshi, or swadeshi, the battle cry against colonial goods and services as well as the need to support homegrown manufacturing devasted by British policies, grew firmer roots at that time, long before it became a Gandhian call to action. Among other things, imports from Britain of salt, cotton yarn and textiles, shoes and cigarettes were recorded by Calcutta Customs as having plummeted. Stores across Bengal's provinces sold less British goods. Historians record cobblers refusing to repair

British-made shoes.

The administration in East Bengal and West Bengal cracked down massively on the movement. Anti-Partition protests were banned and you could get into trouble for saying Bandé Mātaram out loud or even expressing it in written form, in journals and graffiti. Joseph Fuller, who was at the time lieutenant governor of East Bengal, supervised a series of brutal prosecutions and persecutions using the law, police, and Gurkha soldiers, a Britain-approved martial race that kept the peace, through assault and injury on civilians, men, women and minors alike. The district of Barisal saw some of the worst instances of such action, but it was hardly the only district to be steamrolled by Fuller.

Meanwhile, a series of attacks and assassination attempts against British targets continued, as well as robberies to fund revolutionary activities. These were undertaken by youngsters, many of them students, spurred on by older, often middle-aged ideologues. It jolted the administration. The distirct magistrate of Dhaka was shot and badly injured in December 1906; he survived. This is taken as literally the first shot. In 1907, revolutionaries twice used explosives to try and wreck the lieutenant governor's train between Mankundu—folklore has it that it was named after Raja Man Singh, one of Akbar's generals, who sent an army to subdue Mog dacoits—and the French enclave of Chandannagar. And a third time, at Narayangarh in Medinipur; the engine and the tracks were somewhat damaged.

Perhaps the most spectacular and messiest undertaking was by the Jugāntōr Party, which targetted D. H. Kingsford, the district judge of Muzaffarpur (now in Bihar), on 30 April 1908. Khudiram Bose and Prafulla Chaki lay in wait for the judge, who in an earlier avatar in Kolkata had passed harsh sentences on political activity (Andrew H. L. Fraser, lieutenant governor of Bengal at the time, later wrote of it as Kingsford convicting 'several printers of seditious newspapers').

The attack with handmade bombs failed when the two, waiting

near Kingsford's residence for him to return from the local club in a carriage, mistook a similar carriage in which the wife and daughter of a British lawyer were returning from the club. The ladies died. Chaki was chased down by a police sub-inspector, Nandalal Banerji, and shot himself (Banerji is till today portrayed in patriotic Bengali prose as a traitor; the revolutionaries killed him in six months). Khudiram was caught and sentenced to death by hanging. He was eighteen when he died, expressing remorse for the mistaken killings at his trial but not the reasoning behind it.

Aurobindo Ghosh was snared too as co-conspirator, along with dozens of others. Most were sentenced with 'transportation' to penal colonies, or jailed in the subcontinent. Aurobindo got off the hook but only after a complicated chain of events. One of the group, Barin, fingered another, Naren Goswami, because of a suspicion that he was in league with the authorities—evidently Naren had backed out of the Muzaffarpur operation. After being arrested, Naren turned approver, and among other things, named Aurobindo and his role in the group. Two arrested revolutionaries, Kanai Datta and Satyen Bose, who were also in Kolkata's Alipore Jail, took on the task of killing Naren before his day in court against Aurobindo. But it would be difficult as Naren was kept in the European ward of the jail, to keep him safe. The two pretended to fall sick and were transferred to the jail's infirmary, and managed to reach out to Naren with suggestions they wanted to confess. When Naren came to meet them on 31 August that year, the two shot him dead with revolvers that had mysteriously come into their possession. Kanai and Satyen surrendered, and were hanged in November.

On Aurobindo's day in court, the well-known barrister and future co-founder of the Swaraj Party and die-hard Bengali 'unionist', Chittaranjan Das, was his counsel. He spoke on behalf of Aurobindo in a speech that began with: 'The charge against me is that I have proclaimed the idea of freedom in the country and I admit this charge.' He went on to say: '(Aurobindo) will be looked upon by us as a poet of patriotism, as the prophet of nationalism and the lover of humanity. Long after he is dead and gone, his words will be echoed and re-echoed not only in India but across distant seas and lands.'

Chittaranjan became an instant hero, and remained so until his death from ill health in 1925—he earned a popular honorific, Déshbōndhu, friend of the nation. Aurobindo, whose journey away from armed revolution began with his arrest, is considered in Bengal more a hero and less a spiritual leader—though at the time there was scant difference between the two.

(At the time Aurobindo was still a few years from having the prefix 'Sri' appended to his name, emerging as a saint after finding sanctuary in the French-held southern Indian territory of Pondicherry to escape British pressure and persecution for his activities as a revolutionary. There he would sow the seeds of a cult of universalism and an eventual commune with an acolyte, also described as his 'spiritual collaborator', Blanche Rachel Mirra Alfassa—who came to be known as 'The Mother'. Aurobindo, whose name means lotus, also referenced for Vishnu, is of course the 'Auro' in Auroville, an hour-and-half's drive south of Chennai along the Coromandel Coast. He was evidently a changed man after his time in jail.)

Khudiram like his compatriots is also considered a hero, but perhaps more so. There is a song written about him which I've heard since I was a child, sung on radio, television, on trains by seekers of alms, at talent competitions during Durgā Pujō alongside classics by Rabindranath and Nazrul.

Ekbār bidāy dé Mā, ghuré āshi/ Hnāshi-hnāshi pōrbō phnāshi, dékhbé Bhārōtbāshi... Tokhōn jōdi nā chinté pārish/ Dékhbi golāy phnāshi.

Let me go now, Mother, I shall soon return/ I shall wear the noose with a smile as all Indians watch... If you do not recognize me/ Look for the noose around my neck.

In Bengal, cause and courage has usually triumphed over effect—as the adoration of several generations of revolutionaries since the early twentieth century show.

◆

A more lurid description of the incident, embroidered with Hindu hocus-pocus that overshadowed the simple reasoning that homework, patience and a moonless night might offer the attackers more protection—and which, possibly, led to the error—was carried in the government-sponsored volume, *The Administration of Bengal under Sir Andrew Fraser, K.C.S 1903–1908*:

> It may or may not be a coincidence that the murder was committed on *Amabasya* night, which is the auspicious night for the worship of Kali. It is, however, noticeable that that the murderers had waited twenty days in Muzaffarpur before throwing the bomb; and that some time before a speech had been delivered advocating the sacrifice to Kali of white goats—a thinly veiled allusion to Europeans. As is well known, Kali is the principal goddess worshipped by the Saktas, a prominent sect among Bengali Hindus, and one of their Tantras recommends the sacrifice of human beings as an offering pleasing in her sight. However this may be, it is at least certain this was the first day of the new (Hindu) year; and it is most probable that the conspirators waited for it in order that the murder might usher in the year.

The document also took care to stick a knife into the collective Bengali gut and give it a twist before leaving it there, while referring to some protests in places with large Bengali populations like present-day Bihar, Jharkhand, Odisha, Assam, Madhya Pradesh and Uttar Pradesh, brought there largely on the back of professionals: doctors, lawyers, teachers, administrators and engineers. Bengalis are troublemakers, the British suggested, and arrogant too. '[And] it may be added that in these large sub-Provinces there is no love lost between the native, whether Hindu, Muhammadan, or Animist, and the Bengali immigrant.'

In 1911, Bihar and Odisha were delinked from Bengal, and Assam from East Bengal the same year. It was also the year British India's capital was shifted from Kolkata to Delhi, among other things on account of political necessities born out of broadening the scope of provincial legislative councils by the so-called Morley–Minto Reforms. It was felt that the more centrally located Delhi would be better equipped to manage even this severely restricted democracy that polarized Hindu and Mussulman electorates, combined with the allure of making a statement from a former imperial capital—the Delhi Durbar to be held that December for George V to proclaim him emperor of India, was imminent.

But as a letter from Charles Hardinge—Lord Hardinge, the viceroy of India—to Robert Crewe-Milnes, or Lord Crewe, the secretary of state for India showed, the sting of revolutionary activity and heightened protests were also a factor in rolling back this Partition: Bengal's 'prevailing insecurity' caused by the kāpurush—cowardly—Bengalis, dismissed as effete by Macaulay, had demonstrated that colonial masters and self-proclaimed superior races bled too. If cause, politics and anger pushed them, the Bengali would be willing to kill, and willing to die.

(This would come back particularly horribly in 1946, when communalism became a cause, and sporadically even earlier. As Sengupta tells us, quoting official figures, between 1922 and 1927 there were 112 communal riots in Bengal that led to 450 deaths and about 5,000 instances of injury. 'There were two standard points,' Sengupta writes, mirroring provocative behaviour that has carried across the subcontinent to the present day. 'For the immersion of Durga idols… Hindu processions would insist on playing music near mosques where the Muslims would object to being disturbed while praying. Or during Bakr-Id, Muslims would make it a point to kill cows in the open, thereby hurting religious sentiments of orthodox Hindus.' It was the ideal set-up for agents provocateurs.

Unfortunately, Bengalis were also willing to kill Bengalis, and die, if the cause was projected as being right.)

Hardinge and his colleagues put chess pieces in play several months before the shifting of the capital and the reunification of Bengal were actually announced by George V, and all opposition anticipated, including one against reunification by the nawab of Dhaka. 'There is only one big Mohommedan in Eastern Bengal and he is the Nawab of Dacca,' Lord Hardinge had written to Lord Crewe on 24 August 1911. 'I intend to recommend him for an honour, and he is at the same time hopelessly in debt to the Government of India. I do not anticipate any opposition from him.'

The nawab received his knighthood, grudgingly, it appears. And the British move didn't cow the revolutionaries, as it turned out. Just a year after the Delhi Durbar, as Hardinge and his wife sat atop an elephant on a stately march through the newly minted colonial capital's Chandni Chowk area, Rash Behari Bose is believed to have thrown a bomb at the couple—some Bengali revolutionaries from Allahabad, for long a Bengali migratory redoubt, like Varanasi, are also believed to have been part of the conspiracy. Lord Hardinge was injured; his wife managed to escape; the mahout died. Within days a representative of the undersecretary of state for India made a statement about Hardinge's condition in the British parliament: 'The shock was severe and the wounds painful, but his hearing, at first injured, is returning, and he has been able to see some of the members of his household. A small piece of metal in the neck still has to be removed.' Close call.

Three of Rash Behari's associates, one Bengali and two from a group of revolutionaries from Punjab—Rash Behari was quite the networker for the two groups that made common cause—would eventually be caught and executed. Rash Behari managed to escape.

Bengal's revolutionaries would commit one more major—somewhat foolhardy and certainly grandiose—act in 1915, with World War I raging, before the first phase of Ōgni Jug came to an end. The Jugāntōr Party, with the help of Jatindranath Mukherjee,

Naren Bhattacharya and Rash Behari—who was in touch with Ghadar Party revolutionaries in Punjab—and several other associates actually planned to guide a German ship with arms, ammunition and explosives to Odisha's coast near Balasore. The materiel would be used to blow up railway bridges in Bengal to isolate the province, establish a 'liberation' army in eastern Bengal, overrun armouries, and occupy Fort William, the British Indian army's headquarters in the east!

Naren, using a pseudonym went off to the Dutch East Indies to establish operational contact with the Germans; initial contacts had been made with Europe-based Indian nationalists at the start of the war. Other associates, also using pseudonyms, went to Thailand and Japan. Jatindranath—who had earned the moniker Bāghā Jōtin after fighting off a tiger and killing it with a knife—headed off to Balasore with some colleagues. A business had been established as a cover. A German-controlled vessel, *Maverick*, was to make the delivery at the mouth of the Mahanadi.

None of it happened. The plot unravelled, some say in Europe, with Allied spies twigging to it through moles among the Central Powers led by Germany, the information then travelling back to India. The plotters were betrayed. The ship failed to arrive. Police raided the front company. 'Tiger' Jatin and four associates were tracked to the spot at which they were waiting for the ship. They fled, triggering off a series of firefights. The final showdown took place by the Buribalam River. Jatin was injured and later died in hospital. Other associates were killed or apprehended, and subsequently were either sentenced to death or transporation, almost always to the Cellular Jail in Port Blair, in the Andaman Islands—across the taboo kalapani, literally 'black water', the place where all caste was lost, along with freedom.

On the run, Naren Bhattacharya found his way to Japan, the United States and Soviet Union, and was welcomed by Lenin. He had meanwhile been transformed into Manabendra Nath Roy, or M. N. Roy, as he mostly came to be known. He returned to India in the early 1930s, propagated the concept of radical humanism, and is credited by some as being a co-founder of the Communist Party of India.

Rash Behari Bose had meanwhile escaped to East Asia, and found his way to Japan, where he would be a crucial support for Subhas Bose and the Indian National Army. He died in Tokyo in early 1945, just a few months before the death of his longtime comrade Subhas, in August.

◆

It turns out there is more to that story than merely Subhas's exhilarating but truncated run with the Axis Powers in World War II. As with the leaking of the plot during World War I, there may have been a leak during this war too, with most of this tragic hero's moves tracked by British Intelligence. *The Indian Spy* by London-based journalist and writer Mihir Bose tells of Orlando Mazzotta, the nom de plume Subhas adopted for his escape from Kabul to the Soviet Union. He may have been burned (in spy-speak), because Silver, whom Mihir Bose describes at the 'most remarkable agent of World War II' ratted on him to the British. Silver or Bhagat Ram Talwar, a Hindu Pathan and quintuple-cross spy, actually met Subhas in Peshawar to Kabul on 21 January 1941, four days after Subhas left his Kolkata home for Gomoh to catch the Kalka Mail, on the way employing the disguise of Mohammad Ziauddin, an insurance agent. On 25 January, the two left for Kabul, where they arrived on 1 February. Subhas was playing for his version of India. Talwar was playing for every side in the war, though evidently his compulsively fickle heart lay with the Communist Party of India on account of which it is speculated he was asked to escort Subhas to Kabul.

While in Kabul, Talwar used the offices of a German who was ostensibly a representative of Siemens to reach the ambassador to the Italian legation, Pietro Quaroni. Talwar arranged for funds for the cash-strapped and restless Subhas until he finally left for

Moscow and Berlin on 18 March with guides for the first part arranged by Talwar. Subhas had meanwhile gathered the support of Axis representatives in Kabul, driven in great part by Quaroni, to convince the Soviet Union to offer safe passage to Subhas, a co-warrior in the Axis fight to dislodge the British from India. These were still days the Hitler–Stalin pact was intact, Hitler was still several months from his invasion of the Soviet Union in June.

Subhas was soon ensconced in Berlin, having met Schutzstaffel or SS chief Heinrich Himmler and Adolf Hitler. There he was reunited with his Austrian companion Emilie Schenkl—they had met when Subhas visited pre-war Vienna in 1937—and the two had a daughter in 1942, Anita. Subhas with his new allies made grand plans of war and sabotage, driven by political unrest in India. The Germans shared these plans with the loyal Talwar. The loyal Talwar promptly passed the information on to the Soviets.

Subhas left Germany for Japan by submarine in February 1943, making a rendezvous with a Japanese submarine off Madagascar in April. He finally arriving in Tokyo in mid-June that year. Talwar—Silver—had been singing about Bose, among several other matters, directly to the British since late 1942, when he was tracked down and arrested by them at Nawakot in Lahore. *The Indian Spy* records the British version of what he told them during interrogation: 'He now regards Subhas Bose as a traitor to his cause and having deliberately betrayed those who helped him'—evidently Subhas's run to Berlin instead of Silver's spiritual home of Moscow, and Hitler's brazen invasion of the Soviet Union, infuriated him. 'He is thoroughly glad therefore that he has been able to pay him back in the same coin.'

◆

The fire would die down for a while. A more defining fire, spurred on as ever by a cocktail of revolutionary thinking and growing hatred against the colonial government, would erupt again in the 1920s and 1930s, creating more assassinations, more plots, martyrs, more household names that are still revered in Bengal—and many even in Bangladesh which grew its own crowded field of martyrs and freedom fighters in 1971.

Many of the rebels marched to fiery poetry of which perhaps, the greatest exponent was Kazi Nazrul Islam. He was twenty-three in 1922, just two years out of the British Indian Army's 49th Bengal Regiment he had joined in 1917 out a sense of adventure, when his poem 'Bidrōhi' was published. *The Rebel* (of which I share here a part, in Kabir Chowdhury's translation) catapulted this frenetic genius who wrote with a rough-and-ready passion (and looked to Rabindranath for inspiration), to fame as a great romantic, a rebel poet.

I am Orpheus's flute,
I bring sleep to the fevered world,
I make the heaving hells tremble in fear and die.
I carry the message of revolt to the earth and the sky!...
I am the rebel eternal
I raise my head beyond this world,
High, ever erect and alone!

Nazrul, who moved from his cantonment in Karachi into the cultural maelstrom of Kolkata, was already a published poet and novelist by this time. He excavated his experience as the son of an imam at a village near Asansol, a mining and industrial town northwest of Kolkata, writing for the travelling folk theatre group of his uncle, drip-feeding from other cultures and languages of India as an eager teenager. He scripted plays about Emperor Akbar and the poet Kalidasa and so many others, worked at a bakery and, as Nazrul-lore has it, at a tea shop, and moved to Mymensingh in eastern Bengal to learn about West Asian literature and music. All before he joined the army.

Kazi Nazrul wouldn't be done even when, in the 1940s, he began to lose his power of speech, cognitive abilities, memory and his brilliant mind to a rare form of dementia called Pick's Disease.

It confined him on and off to mental asylums as his condition remained undiagnosed for several years. As he journeyed in a dark, anxious place of his mind that few could visit, his work continued to be present, and his art practised.

His rebel-poetry and his songs inspired East Pakistan's freedom fighters. After the birth of Bangladesh the government requested the Indian government to permit him to relocate to Bangladesh, where he was welcomed with honour and given the title of National Poet. Kazi Nazrul's infirmities didn't improve, and he would die in the care of nascent Bangladesh, his old-new home, in 1976. He was given a state funeral.

(It was a year after Sheikh Mujib and most of his family were assassinated in the name of a different kind of freedom.)

◆

With the colonial administration hardly laudatory about 'native' media covering such activities, martyrs were emotively manufactured in the public mind with the death of rebels—or freedom fighters.

They often failed in their individual mission by getting jailed or killed, sometimes as we've seen, they inadvertently killed the wrong target, but their iconic status was sealed with what the Japanese call the nobility of failure, adding to the success of the collective mission of taking on the British, sometimes singeing them, sometimes infecting the empire with mortality. They set the Bengali imagination on fire in their own time, and their exploits continue to be part of our folklore a hundred years on and more.

Relatively few in Bengal would not know, for instance, of Benoy, Badal and Dinesh, the expansion of the Kolkata acronym BBD Bagh that replaced Dalhousie Square in the business and administrative heart of the city. Benoy Bose was twenty-two, Badal Gupta and Dinesh Gupta, were still in their teens when they died.

The exploits of BBD were required reading: as with so many children, among the first books my sister and I were gifted was *Benōy, Bādōl, Dinésh*, a dramatic telling of the story in Bāṅglā. Well before we turned ten we were told through these and parental sources how the British ruled over us, and how Bengal's revolutionaries were enraged by the way they were ruled. We knew of how these boys decided to kill Léftānént Cornél Norman S. Simpson who was 'jail-ér-in-charge' and who 'beat and tortured prisoners' like freedom fighters (Simpson was the local inspector general of prisons and had a reputation for brutality among political prisoners).

BBD-for-children told us how the boys purchased shoes from Cuthbertson & Harper, a shop between the Esplanade and Dalhousie Square which, when I last walked past it in the mid-2000s still had the faded sign outside, but now sold plastic suitcases. They had their tailors make fine new suits, and as trained revolutionaries they also carried handguns—peestol or rebholbhār. (Benoy was already a veteran, having killed the local inspector general of police at Dhaka's Armanitola Medical School, in August 1930. He evaded the police dragnet and made it to Kolkata where he had some narrow escapes including a raid on his hideout by Kolkata's notorious police commissioner Charles Tegart—himself a survivor of several assassination attempts by revolutionaries. Dinesh is said to have trained revolutionaries in weaponry—his 'students' would go on to assassinate three British district magistrates).

They ate well that morning on 8 December 1930—the golpér bōyi told us it was Benoy's mother who cooked choice dishes and mishti for them. Then they prayed to Kali and went to complete their job, the storybook continued, dressed in Western clothing, confidently marching into Writers' Building which then as now housed the province's secretariat. They shot at and killed Simpson, but were trapped. Badal took cyanide. Benoy and Dinesh were injured; Benoy eventually died in custody after being tortured, and Dinesh survived to be hanged the following year.

◆

It was as if there was a rush of revolutionary activity in the 1920s and 1930s, or so it appears from the way names and incidents have been etched into the Bengali telling with a near-total lack of moral ambivalence, 'good' violence for the cause of freedom at a time 'non-violence' for the cause of freedom would soon begin to make its presence felt as a political strategy. After the outrage at Jalianwalla Bagh in 1919—which, among other things, jolted a young Subhas Bose to quit probation in the Indian Civil Service in England and return home—guns and Gandhi would go their parallel ways. At times the ways would come close, as during the Congress's annual convention in Kolkata in 1928, at which both Gandhi and Bose were present. It appears Bose led a parallel life as a mentor to Bengal's revolutionaries. He even backed a volunteer corps, the Bengal Volunteers—with several thousand youngsters, many of them revolutionaries.

When today's martyr-and-icon Bhagat Singh threw a bomb inside the Central Legislative Assembly in Delhi in 1929, Batukeshwar Dutt threw one too. Kanhailal Bhattacharya, a student, killed the Alipore judge who had sentenced Dinesh to death, and then consumed cyanide. The same year, 1931, fifteen-year-old schoolgirl Shanti Ghosh and her fourteen-year-old colleague, Suniti Choudhury, entered the house of Charles Stevens, the district magistrate of Comilla, on the pretext of a request for help with a competition. They shot him dead. Another ōgnikōnyā as they were called—daughter of fire—a student, Bina Das, attempted to kill the governor of Bengal, Stanley Jackson, as he delivered a speech at the convocation of Calcutta University, in 1932. Jackson, who some credit with recognizing the talent of Indian cricketing legend and Nawanagar royal, Ranjitsinhji Vibhaji, while at Cambridge (Jackson captained England's test side for a while), escaped the several bullets Das fired at him. Like the Comilla schoolgirls, she was arrested and jailed.

John Anderson, Jackson's successor as governor of Bengal, survived an assassination attempt at the racecourse at Lebong, near Darjeeling, in 1934—the same year a seventeen-year-old girl (I was unable to trace her name) shot dead G. C. B. Stevens, the district magistrate of Tipperah. Part of the Lebong group of four was a young lady, Ujjwala Mazumdar, twenty. Pritilata Waddedar, a philosophy graduate, was twenty-one in 1932 when she led the group that attacked Pahartali European Club in Chittagong—infamous for its 'Dogs and Indians Not Allowed' sign. She and several associates attacked the club, shooting and wounding several. Police officers in the club at the time returned fire. On the run and wounded, she consumed cyanide to avoid arrest.

The incident that mesmerized Bengal and stunned British India with its audacity—as foolhardy as it was audacious, some historians have called it 'quixotic'—was surely the raid on Chittagong's armoury in 1930 by a group led by Surya Sen, or Master-dā, as textbooks and other hagiographic references in Banglasphere fondly, reverentially, refer to this schoolteacher-turned-revolutionary. When the several thousand Bengal Volunteers dispersed after the Kolkata session of the Congress, some came to Sen in Chittagong. By 1930, they had been transformed into the Indian Republican Army. Even if they differed on cause and effect, there are several tellings of what happened next.

The group decided to attack Chittagong's armoury on the night of 18 April, Good Friday, a day the British could be counted upon to be somewhat relaxed on account of a religious holiday, their military installations minimally staffed. Sen's band also planned to take over the city's communications and transport hubs, including the port. It went partly like clockwork: the armoury taken over, and the telephone exchange and some railway facilities. Pritilata was part of the team that snapped telegraph and telephone lines. Another group damaged railway tracks. The Congress tricolour—Sen, an Ōnushilon Shōmiti alum, was a Congressman too—was raised in place of the Union Jack. Sen proclaimed a Revolutioanry Republic Government in Chittagong!

'Dear Revolutionary Soldiers!' the proclamation went. 'The heavy responsibility of the Indian revolution now rests on the revolutionary army. Inspired by patriotism we have earned the glory of completing in Chittagong the revolutionary mission of fulfilling the heart-felt longing of our countrymen… This government expects and claims active cooperation and total obedience from every… young man and woman of Chittagong.'

Not much of that happened. The local majority-Mussulman residents largely kept away from the fracas. But amazingly Sen's motley crew held on for a few days by which time the government expectedly struck back in force. By the fourth day, the attackers had retreated to a series of low hills near the city. The final stand was at Jalalabad Hill, fifty-four mostly young men with Lee Enfield rifles and low on ammunition—a flaw in the armoury raid was that a meagre amount of ammunition was commandeered—ranged against the massed British Indian police and army. Several rebels died in the battle. Sen managed to escape at night with several comrades. He remained on the run for nearly three years before before being captured at Gairala village, supposedly because of the treachery of a villager. Along with a colleague, Tarakeswar Dastidar, Sen was sentenced to death, and hanged in Chittagong Jail in Janury 1934. Jailers took their revenge on Master-dā before hanging him, so goes the story: his teeth were smashed, fingernails torn out, and joints broken, before he was dragged to the gallows, unconscious. They dumped his remains in the sea.

But his glory, and that of his comrades, has not died. Many among us are still entranced by it: A few dozen men and a few women—'languid' Bengalis best suited to slavery to a foreign 'yoke'—took over Bengal's second largest port city, its second most important commercial hub, and for four days held out against the most powerful empire of its time.

15

Nokshālbāri
Your chairman, our chairman

About the spark that set a subcontinent on fire.

'Do you remember what happened that day?' I asked Punjab-dā.

Punjab Rao knew what I meant, this former Indian Army soldier from the Vidarbha region of Maharashtra who settled down in these parts after being decommissioned—and became a farmer-revolutionary.

'Twenty-fourth of May, 1967. Just up the lane from this house,' he pointed behind him, eyes alight, voice sharp. 'Landless peasants had had enough.'

The broken hut was a few yards off the road near Naxalbari—Nokshālbāri. A patchwork of mud, straw and tile covered an open veranda-like area, a couple of rooms and a tiny kitchen. A few hens and a rooster strutted around, small potatoes were laid out on a coir-strung cot. The wall facing the open area was in disrepair. It was steps from Naxalbari town, run-down, dusty, with a couple of sweet shops with fly-blown offerings, some temples, the ubiquitous chā shops. Two tin-roofed movie theatres with curtained entrances drawing large knots of youngsters to gawk at the posters of buxom women that adorned their walls. After the tiny Naxalbari station, from a fork outside town a road travelled northwest to Nepal's eastern borders; another narrow road travelled southwest towards Bihar, linking northern Bengal through forest, farmland and tea gardens. About us were vast tea estates of North Bengal's Dooars region, and a patchwork of farms still worked by the very poor, mostly tenant farmers.

The Naxalbari of revolutionary grammar extended beyond the turn to a cluster of villages and small towns with quirky names from nature and history—Hatighisa, after elephants; Phansideoa, literally, hanged; Bagdogra, derived from bāgh or tiger, which housed the region's major airport that doubled as an air force base. These points on the map of often-forgotten history were on the way to Naxalbari from the bustling commercial centre of Siliguri, and its nearby railway hub of New Jalpaiguri—the place of olives.

Anger had been brewing over issues like the scarcity of food, issues of landlessness, share-cropping and bonded labour for about a year up to May 1967, Punjab-dā told me as we sipped lāl-chā brewed by his wife; I called her bōudi, literally bride-elder sister, the honorific reserved for the wife of an elder brother of blood or respect. 'There was talk of revolution, but they just wanted to assert their rights,' he recalled. 'They had taken over land. Then the police came, called by the jōtdār. As soon as we heard about it, we set off with whatever we had—swords, bows and arrows, spears, farming implements. The people with us, as soon as they saw the group of police and landlords, they let the arrows fly. One hit the landlord, another hit someone on the leg. The police ran away. That was the beginning.'

The police came back in large numbers the following day, and destroyed houses, broke what they could, mixed rice and lentils with dirt, destroyed all other food. By then the spark had spread to Bengaijote, just beyond Naxalbari. Eleven protestors died by police firing that day. 'Naxalbari had its first martyrs,' said Punjab-dā. 'And the Naxalbari movement was born. Bas.'

◆

Charu Mazumdar, a co-founder of what has come to be known as the Naxalbari movement and its adherents as Naxal—Nokshāl—and his extremist colleagues in the left spectrum ran hard with—indeed, sprinted with—this cause handed to them on a platter, through their writings, speeches, networking and recruitment. In the June 1968 issue of *Liberation*, a journal he founded, Mazumdar exulted in an article titled 'One Year of Naxalbari Struggle':

> This is the first time that peasants have struggled not for their partial demands but the seizure of state power. If the Naxalbari peasant struggle has any lesson for us, it is this: militant struggles must be carried on not for land, crops, etc., but for the seizure of state power. It is precisely this that gives the Naxalbari struggle its uniqueness.

Mazumdar had a way with fiery words that chimed loud those years when cause of the trodden was carried by educated urban elites. 'Only by waging class struggle—the battle of annihilation—the new man will be created, the new man who will defy death and will be free from all thoughts of self-interest,' Mazumdar said in May 1970 in his address to the First Congress of the Communist Party of India (Marxist-Leninist), or CPI (M-L), a breakaway of the extremist faction of CPI (M) in Kolkata.

Mazumdar led this break along with disenchanted party members from West Bengal, Andhra Pradesh, Odisha, Punjab, Kerala, Uttar Pradesh and Bihar. M-L, as it came to be known, was formed in 1969, and capped that year by holding a massive public rally at Shahid Minar—Martyr's Column, renamed from the earlier, colonial Ochterlony Monument—in Kolkata. The faction took shape after the initial Naxalbari incident of farmers' protest and police retaliation in May 1967, as the conflagration spread to revolutionary hubs like Ekwari and Mushahary in Bihar; Lakhimpur Kheri in Uttar Pradesh; parts of Punjab and Srikakulam in Andhra Pradesh—areas of stark rural poverty and caste discrimination. These provinces would quickly become among the most affected by the message spread by the raging ultra-left, many of its leaders and even cadres, like Mazumdar, from the educated and socio-economic elite, bhodrōlōk besotted with the idea of radical social and political change. In radical left-wing circles, the images of Mazumdar and his colleague Kanhai Chatterjee, who at one stage disagreed with Mazumdar's hell-for-leather approach and advocated a more deliberate, graded one, (but with the same end result of the 'annihilation of the class enemy'), are still propaganda ornamentation on pamphlets and as portraits alongside those of Marx, Engels, Lenin and Mao.

'And with this death defying spirit he will go close to the enemy, snatch his rifle, avenge the martyrs and the people's army will emerge,' Mazumdar further counselled the would-be revolutionary. 'To go close to the enemy it is necessary to conquer all thought of self. And this can be achieved only by the blood of martyrs. That inspires and creates new men out of the fighters, fills them with class hatred and makes them go close to the enemy and snatch his rifle with bare hands.'

This approach was inspired by the early years of Mao Zedong's generalship, before Chinese communists finally took over control of China in 1949. As the Naxalite movement grew in strength, Mazumdar's rhetoric became disconcerting even for some believers—some of whom took it as a sign of utter impracticality bordering on derangement. For example, the November 1969 issues of the revolutionary publications *Déshobrōti* and *Liberation* published an essay by Mazumdar in which he maintained that 'Mao Tsetung Thought' had established deep roots 'in the soil of India', and a People's Democratic Republic was a possibility. 'The first rays of the red sun have already lit up the coasts of Andhra and will tinge the others states also before long. A India bathed in the rays of this red sun will continue to shine brightly for ever.' And then Mazumdar made the statement that perhaps brought the movement as much discredit as anything else—he had crossed a line, especially with India's humiliating defeat in a border skirmish with China in 1962. 'Victory certainly belongs to us because China's Chairman is our Chairman and China's path is our path.'

Apart from extreme sloganeering, though, there was enough

real passion among the stalwarts of the movement about standing up for the dispossessed and destitute. Revolutionaries spoke of it in glowing terms: 'Spring thunder has struck all over India,' echoing a message of approval from Maoist China's official radio station. There was a flowering of revolutionary poetry, a mix of fire and storm and unabashed romanticism. One by Murari Mukhopadhay went like this:

When in love,
Do not become the moon.
If you can,
Come as the sun.
I'll take its heat
And light up the dark forest.
When in love,
Do not become a flower,
If you can,
Come as the thunder.
I'll lift its sound
And pass the message of battles to every corner.
The moon, the river, the flowers, the stars, the birds—
They can be watched at leisure
Sometime later.
But today
In this darkness,
The last battle is yet to be fought.
What we need now is
The fire in our hovel.

◆

The first eleven dead Naxalbari have a memorial not far from Punjab-da's home, at the village of Bengaijote. I took a rattle-trap bus there with Abhijit—Abhi—the son of Charu Mazumdar, the father who disappeared from his life and that of his sister when they were still children in Siliguri.

The beautiful Tukuria forest loomed to our left. It was a little after three in the afternoon, and the sun was gentle. There was a cool breeze blowing from the direction of the hills. Paddy fields shone a liquid green. A few huts could be glimpsed through coconut and plantain groves.

'Tukuria was really dense once,' Abhi said as we crossed the road on to a bund between fields. 'A good hiding place. There were so many stories from that time—legends, really. There was talk that Charu Mazumdar would walk about on stilts.' He used here the Bānglā ron-pā, literally, battle legs, used to cover great distances at speed. 'That Kanu Sanyal would ride a horse with a sword in each hand, cutting down enemies.' He laughed.

The imagery was absurd. The two were never known to be more than frail. Fiercely determined, but frail. The hamlet of Bengaijote was mostly a scattering of mud huts, a handful of brick houses. Inhabitants were a mix. Some Rajbōngshi tribal folk, indigenous to this area, some ladies in traditional sarongs, snot-nosed children in rubber chappals; a half day's ride to the east, militant representatives of this trodden and forgotten group were fighting for their independent homeland of Kamtapur. Independent of West Bengal, really, which had treated them poorly—it was a statement being made for more development as much as identity. There were some Santal tribals, brought in generations earlier from parts of present-day West Bengal, Bihar and Jharkhand as labour for the tea gardens. A radio somewhere behind us on the narrow winding lane crackled with Nepali pop music. The eastern border of Nepal lay less than an hour away by bus and rickshaw.

A turn to the right of the lane, and we came to a small school. It was by a small clearing that had a great expanse of paddy as backdrop. At the far end was a makeshift flagstaff with a small red flag, and four pedestals painted blood red with busts on each. Marx, Lenin, Mao and Mazumdar. The Naxalbari pantheon. To the right, appreciably away from the pantheon, was another memorial, to the eleven killed on 'Historic 25th May 1967', all unarmed protestors, men and women, all now co-opted as 'Comrades'. Dhaneshwari Devi, Seemaswari Mallick, Nayaneswari Mallick, Surubala Burman, Sonamati Singh, Phoolmati Devi, Samsari Saibani, Gaudrau Saibani, Kharsing Mallick, 'and two children'.

Abhi was quiet.

I was taken aback yet again with the realization that places associated with historical events of great significance can be so ordinary. Plassey—Polāshi—where Robert Clive defeated Siraj-ud-Daulah was a cluster of mango trees, a modest museum and, nearby, an abandoned airstrip from World War II, at least that's how it was when I last visited it as a child.

'So this is it,' I said.

'Yes, this is it.'

'How do you feel being here? Do you think of your father?'

'Yes.' Abhi looked everywhere but at me.

'Do you hate the state for what happened? Why it all began?' I asked after several minutes, as we began walking back.

'Yes, of course, I hate the state.' We could have been discussing the weather.

'I hate the state a lot.'

'The state? Or the state of affairs?'

'The state is responsible for the state of affairs.'

◆

His father had thought so too. In Abhi's compact, walk-up apartment in Siliguri, pride of place on the wall of the small living room belonged to a black-and-white photograph of Mazumdar. It showed a handsome, delicate-featured bhodrōlōk in Western clothing, circa 1953. Very different from the emaciated, grimacing man in the iconic photograph taken at Lalbazar Police Station in Kolkata, of the revolutionary surrounded by policemen, before his incarceration between 16 and 28 July 1972, during which he died. It is still not clear if he died from ill-health or the rough prison handling that became the hallmark of West Bengal's anti-Naxal operations. It was a time when custodial beatings and torture and fake 'encounter' killings were popularized by the police as an important secondary method of dealing with extremism—the primary method being shootouts during real encounters. This happened in rural Bengal, but mostly in towns and cities—Kolkata was like the second epicentre of the movement. Counterattacking remained the norm through bewilderingly rapid changes of government—seven changes of administration from March 1967 to March 1972, a shuffle between two left-leaning United Front governments, a short-lived coalition of the Progressive Democratic Front, and three bouts of President's Rule—direct rule from New Delhi. But it began to peak even before the Congress government of Chief Minister Siddhartha Shankar Ray took office in March 1972, and exploded thereafter.

There was a reason for the brutal counterattack by the state—the Naxals had escalated the viciousness. The Naxals went truly 'urban' only in West Bengal, and particularly so in Kolkata, even as in terms of the general movement, matters went far beyond Bengal. The threat by the extreme left-wing movement, Maoist rebels of the present day, to launch in urban areas continues. However, although the media from time to time plays up this aspect, what is not taken into account is how logistically difficult it would be to pursue such a course in cities with their intrusive surveillance, massed police and, quite often, nearby bases of army and paramilitary forces. This was as true in the late 1960s and early 1970s as it is now. But Bengal's incendiary hell-or-high-water movement, stoked by Mazumdar's nihilism, flouted the Maoist strategy of first conquering rural areas before reaching for the 'citadel'. In Kolkata it was pure mayhem at the time. Naxals would attack even the slimmest example of a 'class enemy', like traffic policemen in Kolkata.

As a child in Kolkata in the late 1960s and early 1970s, Naxals for me were young men in jeans and batik kurtas who threw Molotov cocktails and soda bottles at the police, and fought battles with knives and handguns. We were caught on numerous occasions on the sidelines of such pitched battles between groups of Naxals and the police—while shopping for someone's wedding or visiting family, or while out to Sunday lunch. One day in central Kolkata we actually saw a traffic policeman get shot, and another, whose only weapon was a whistle, have his throat cut, all this observed from the relative comfort of the family Ambassador, which Father quickly pulled to the side of the road. We were asked to roll up the windows, as if this would keep the world out.

Shielded by our parents, my sister and I looked out at an urban jungle we couldn't understand, with boys falling on their faces on the street, and sometimes, policemen. Screaming, sirens, explosions, blood.

Walls, especially near colleges and university campuses, were covered in graffiti—angry letters shouted about exhortations against 'oppressors'. There were depictions of police firing and torture in lurid blood-red. Red flags. Schools and colleges would be shut for days, even after the Bangladesh war of 1971, the euphoria of victory forgotten as violence peaked in the streets.

For me, personally, the climax came with an overnight operation by the Indian army against a university residence right across our home at the time, an apartment in Jodhpur Park. The residence housed students of Jadavpur University, established, ironically, with American money. Using a work-in-progress drainage ditch that had eaten up the road as cover, late one night the army launched a massed attack with automatic weapons. Their rifles were trained on windows that during the evenings had been full of students, looking at the world go by. Some of these students were visitors to our home, they would call Mother 'māshi-mā' and my father 'méshōmoshāi', play cricket with us. My sister and I saw soldiers marching in through the gates. Seeing our open window, some of them shouted at us to shut it. We did, and discreetly opened another one further along. Then we heard machine guns firing, what sounded to us like pistol shots, and what sounded like bombs—we knew it from the movies and war documentaries.

Then we heard screams. This went on through the night.

It was quiet the next morning. We watched students being marched away, hands above their heads and several being kicked and beaten with sticks and rifle butts. Some were taken into the adjacent police station, others were herded into trucks. For close to a week, we heard the frequent sound of screaming from the police station. It confused and frightened us. The Government of India and the prime minister at the time, Indira Gandhi—depicted in West Bengal as the goddess Durga after the 1971 war (whom we were taught to revere by the family and at school), appeared to us to do a lot of killing. Father, a mild-mannered businessman more comfortable with theatre and languages, and already traumatized by his experiences in East Pakistan, was shocked at the extent of it. He had no answer when I innocently asked him why some people were picking up guns and why they were being killed when there wasn't any colonial power ruling us any more. Why were they fighting? To gain freedom from what?

◆

By 1972, this edition of the revolution would be pretty much over in Bengal and elsewhere, steamrolled by the state. One of the worst massacres took place in August of that year in Kashipur and Baranagar areas near Kolkata, when police literally dragged out and killed known and suspected Naxals. There is no credible estimate of the numbers killed in that episode, beyond 'hundreds'. Dozens disappeared, including some well-known Naxal leaders (decades later, when the sewage system in that area was cleaned up it yielded many skeletal remains). Some, like Saroj Dutta and Sushital Roychoudhary, suave well-to-do intellectuals who looked like kindly uncles or indulgent grandfathers—as ever, revolutionaries were difficult to discern till they spoke, acted, or wore battle garb—disappeared and reappeared in different ways. Dutta was found dead in the Maidan in Kolkata; Roychoudhary managed a rarity—natural death. Skirmishes continued well into 1973, a year when the number of Naxals in jails across India exceeded 30,000.

Little remained thereafter, barring sentimental outpourings by urban remnants of the movement before they were also killed or had revolution squeezed out of them. Some continued to hold true to their beliefs. The journalist and Naxal chronicler, Sumanta Banerjee writes of the time, on 3 May 1975, when five Naxal prisoners were killed by the police in Howrah Jail. Prabir Roy Choudhury, whose dāk-nām was Pākhi—bird—a twenty-two-year-old student, was among them. Hearing of it, Pākhi's comrades in Presidency Jail, across the river in Kolkata, used stone and bits of rubble (Banerjee writes that they were not allowed the use of paper and pens) to gouge out a poem on the wall of their cell, a poem that is unadulterated Ōgni Jūg:

> Silence!
> Here sleeps my brother.
> Don't stand by him
> With a pale face and a sad heart.
> For, he is laughter!
> Don't cover his body with flowers.
> What's the use of adding flowers to a flower?
> If you can,
> Bury him in your heart.
> You will find
> At the twitterings of the bird of the heart
> Your sleeping soul has woken up.
> If you can,
> Shed some tears,
> And—
> All the blood of your body.

◆

Rabindra Ray, the scholar, has in his work *The Naxalites and their Ideology*, somewhat sneeringly termed this call to revolution a 'utopian one, rhetorical and plaintive'. But, while the 'Naxal' movement (its first phase, really, what I like to term Maoism Mark I, a doff of the cap to a model of the iconic Ambassador car that was manufactured for decades at Uttarpara, near Kolkata), was indeed utopian, rhetorical and plaintive, it was also a lot more. As if to echo Mazumdar's boast in an article, 'Long live the heroic peasants in Naxalbari!' in the July 1971–January 1972 edition of *Liberation*—'Naxalbari has not died and it will never die'—over the years the Naxalbari movement spawned several off-shoots that continued to thrive even with all the factionalism and mergers and more factionalism, through Marks II and III, each time re-merging with more gusto. Maoism Mark IV came to be in September 2004, when two major extreme left-wing groups, the Communist Part of India (People's War) merged with the Maoist Communist Centre of India to birth the Communist Party of India (Maoist). Over the next four years, this would influence what has since been called the Red Corridor, a swathe from southern India to India's borders with Nepal. From three villages in one district of West Bengal, the rebellion had, to some degree or another, spread to a third of India's districts across several states, including core areas in Andhra Pradesh, Odisha, Bihar, Jharkhand, Chhattisgarh and Maharashtra.

The ideological focus of left-wing rebellion had firmly moved away from Bengal to Andhra Pradesh and Bihar, but the Bengal imprint still remained. Two Naxal veterans were part of it. Sushil Roy, who brought the Communist Centre to the merger table, became its number two and member of its politburo. He had with him a senior colleague, Narayan Sanyal. India's ongoing failures in governance, justice and development ensured these two old men, and others like them, were still rebels with an enduring cause, ebbing and flowing with the tide of the times.

Naxalbari lives.

◆

I wanted to get a sense of the times from one of the leaders of the Naxal movement, Mark I. Kanu Sanyal was a rare one—alive, over ground, and talkative. I met him on a warm summer day in April 2006, at his home, a fifteen-minute walk from Hatighisa post office near Naxalbari.

I arrived as Nepal's monarchy was visibly collapsing, and Nepal's Maoist and democratic parties were in the thick of what came to known as Jan Andolan II, a people's movement reminiscent of the pro-democracy agitation in 1990—this second edition ultimately ended the monarchy. Tea gardens in this part of the world, in the Dooars region, were destitute and in ferment. Several had gone bankrupt and labourers who worked in some cases been simply left to starve. The recent suicide of an elderly worker, driven to desperation by poverty, had the gardens on edge. Meanwhile, rebellion was brewing in West Bengal's tribal areas. Elections to West Bengal's assembly were due in some weeks, and the fires from a land acquisition programme gone wrong were already lit.

It seemed like a perfect time to visit one of the leaders of the Naxalbari movement. It would give me a quick course in Revolution 101 from the old guard of the CPI (M-L).

The walk to Sanyal's house took me through a neat village with houses mostly made of bamboo, thatch and mud bricks—some with stunning, twisting columns of mud at the entrance, in the Ādibāshī fashion. The inhabitants of the village were mostly tribals from Bihar, Jharkhand and southwest Bengal, brought to the tea estates as labour. Children played in the rivulet of Mānjā Nōdi—the main stream diverted to irrigate the tea gardens. Women bathed and washed clothes a little distance away. There were clusters of bamboo groves, animals out to forage.

Home for Kanu Sanyal was a two-room mud hut, its floor gleaming with a recent coat of freshly plastered mud. The single door to the hut was open, and I could look straight in at the pantheon displayed on the wall: Marx, Engels, Lenin, Stalin and Mao. On the floor, covered with reed mats and plain handwoven local rugs, lay an old manual typewriter. Files were scattered on the floor, some newspapers; a mattress, pillow and hint of mosquito netting.

He was seated on a wrought iron stool on the veranda, leaning back on a wooden roof-support, dressed in pyjamas and a once-white sleeveless sweater. I looked for the frayed shirt collar of the I-don't-give-a-damn-about-such-things communist. It was there. As were basic sandals, thick-lensed spectacles.

I began to take off my shoes.

'Why are you taking your shoes off?' he snapped, in Bānglā. 'This is not a temple.'

'I don't want to dirty your floor. I can see it's been freshly layered.'

'It's mud. It can always get another layer.'

He resumed a conversation he was having with another visitor, which I joined in. Sanyal spoke of the time in 1964 when his colleague Charu Mazumdar had published an article in *Amrita Bazar Patrika*. Sanyal spoke of 'Charu-dā's' vision—'there should be small armed groups and these groups should kill class enemies—finish them off.' Sanyal employed English here, and then resumed in Bānglā. 'Me and others disagreed with this suggestion. The party'—Communist Party of India (Marxist) or CPI (M)—'was also upset. They wanted to expel [him]. The party secretary came to Siliguri. We stood by Charu-dā. We said, "How can you expel him without a show cause [notice]." They agreed. Charu-dā also withdrew from his stand and promised in future he would show his writing to the party before publication.

'So while we disagreed with him, we supported him in this regard. But he wanted revolution. Instant revolution. I didn't believe in that.' This was an important distinction, a matter of nuance. 'He wanted small guerrilla groups to go and kill, take over land.'

Sanyal and some of his colleagues thought it was going too far, too fast. 'We felt that was wrong. I…we…felt that farmers and workers should first take over land'—he used the Bānglā dokhōl to express it—'and then defend it.'

Revolution couldn't be forced. Conditions, what revolutionaries call 'objective conditions' needed to be there. In Sanyal's telling, the Paris Commune, which Marx described as 'storming heaven', lasted for only seventy-two days after the spring of 1871 because objective conditions were not right. It was ultimately too ambitious, too rushed, too disorganized, underpowered—under-armed and under-supported. This laboratory experiment, as it were, led to the big success of the Russian Revolution but the latter succeeded because the objective conditions were exactly right in 1917. 'Not before. Not after.'

'So the Naxalite Movement...' I waded in, trying to extend the argument that it was premature.

'The media called it that,' Sanyal barked. 'We did not. People just added another "ism". For us, it was Communism, not Naxalism.' He took a breath, and continued. 'We were back in jail. Meanwhile, conditions had built up in north Bengal. Things moved very quickly—too quickly to even keep track. That's how it was in '67 ... I was either in jail or underground. Then, almost suddenly, the party was formed. CPI (M-L). Many of us didn't agree with the charter of armed revolution by just cold-blooded killing, but we joined up. We were for armed revolution but not in this manner.'

Sanyal and his colleagues went underground from 1969 to 1972. During this time he also visited China. 'Mao-ér shongé āmār dyakhā hōlō,' he stated blandly. I met Mao.

After talking to Mao, discussing the situation in India, Sanyal said he became 'even more convinced' that the so-called Naxal way was not correct. Part of it was Mao's lecture to him about how the movement began in China, of times the Reds had only 150 muzzle-loaded rifles. Success arrived only after the communists in China worked among the people and built up popular support. 'He told me, "You won't need help from anyone outside if you have popular support."'

In the end, it wasn't enough, even though then as now left-wing extremism exists as a mirror of the nation's failings.

How can you tell when the time for revolution, armed or

otherwise, is right? I asked Sanyal.

'There are four stages,' he replied, as if lecturing a student. 'In the first stage, you talk and they listen to you but they will forget what you say as soon as you leave. At the next stage, they will listen to you, but there won't be any understanding. In the third stage, they realize something needs to be done, and they might want to do it, but something holds them back. In the last stage, they are ready to move—do anything. They are completely convinced.'

He stopped to change position, limber up a bit. 'Charu-da moved too early,' Sanyal said, repeating what was a familiar refrain with him. 'He said, "Bring everything, anything—farm implements, swords, bows, arrows, snatch guns from police…"'

Still, I insisted, how do you really know when the objective conditions are right?

He smiled, and for the first time in the past hour, he was patient, calm. 'When you light a fire under a pan of water, it gives out a bit of steam—but that doesn't mean the water is very hot. It needs more time to boil. Different people have different boiling points. In a people's movement, individual feeling, individual anger, must first become crystallized for a people's movement to succeed.

'Take the case of this farmer,' he continued, eyes pinning me to the chair. 'This is from half-a-year ago. He lives about 8 miles from here. He came to me, complaining that his land was being grabbed by a local landlord through encroachment, and by using local village authorities. I told him what to do but he didn't listen. Then they came to break his house down, claiming that too did not belong to him. So he went along with his entire family and killed the landlord. That was his boiling point.' Kanu-babu was now trying to get the man out of jail.

He paused to sip tea. 'There is a situation in the gardens. Thousands of workers are being discriminated against and ill treated. We have to assist the motivation of the people.'

Is that why you stay here, I asked, preparing to leave. Why don't you stay in Kolkata, motivate students and intellectuals like they do in Hyderabad, in Delhi?

'You need to be with the people to know what they feel, what they think, how they live. They need to see you. You need to see them.'

I thought of my meeting with Sanyal the day he was found hanging in his home, about four years after our meeting. He had been depressed from a persistent illness. It may have finally proved too much.

◆

Before Naxalbari there was the Tebhaga movement, which contributed participants and experience in some volume to the 'Naxal' movement. Tebhaga is literally 'three parts'—to share by thirds. Sharecroppers of unpartitioned Bengal in the 1940s demanded that two-thirds of the crop belonged to them, not to zamindars and other landlords—who ought to receive no more than one-third. The farmers protested that they were the ones who tilled the land but received less than subsistence in return. The initial protest coalesced into an organized movement from 1945, helped along by the Kisan Sabha, the Communist Party of India's front organization for farmers. It became active in Jalpaiguri district, not far from Naxalbari, in the 24 Parganas area to the north and south of Kolkata, and in several areas of present-day Bangladesh. A law enacted by the provincial administration of the time, the Bargadar Act, wasn't effective in lowering temperatures, owing to pressure from the powerful landlords' lobby.

After India's independence in 1947, the protests turned belligerent, especially in West Bengal. The administration and police waded into protestors, beatings and torture was commonplace. Several dozen protestors were shot in 1947. Several latter-day communist (and even some Naxal) leaders were affected by the Tebhaga movement, among them a future home minister of India, the Communist Party of India stalwart, Indrajit Gupta. He was typical of numerous bhodrōlōk drawn to the Tebhaga cause.

'In 1948, the area around Kakdwip [an estuarine area south

of Kolkata] used to be called Lal Ganj—the Red Borough, people used to quake,' my father-in-law Deepankar Roy told me during one of our less volatile chats.

Deepankar, who retained an incendiary, unifocal persona until his death in 2013, would know. He was part of the movement, this member of the elite tier of Calcutta society like his cousin Indrajit, the future minister, a graduate of St Xavier's School, holder of an engineering degree from Jadavpur University he deliberately spurned the legacy of a father who attended Cambridge. (Deepankar later left the movement to look after a widowed mother and younger brother, working first with Burmah Shell, which he quickly found to be elitist, and then doing a much longer stint as an engineer with Hindustan Aeronautics Limited, supervising engine assembly for MiG fighters.)

Like many of his time his anger was not just founded in injustices he was protesting but was part of a long and continuous tradition of anger and protest that was integral to a certain strand of Bengali society, and which was reflected in its literature and culture.

One of the first such revolts dated back to the years immediately after the Sepoy Mutiny of 1857. Known as the Indigo Mutiny, it comprised widespread disturbances and protest against a brutal regime of indigo cultivation. It raged between 1859 and 1862, when farmers of indigo in what was called Lower Bengal refused any longer to farm indigo, a cash crop that enriched European estate owners (mostly British, with some French and 'Eurasians') who were noted for their rapaciousness. Even in the late eighteenth century there were recorded instances of indigo farmers forcing landowners—and so, their ryōts—to plant indigo, sometimes by uprooting fields already planted with other crops. The depredations of indigo captured the imagination of the Bengali peasantry and nascent intelligentsia alike, and continues to find reference and study in Bengal of the present day.

The lucrative but volatile indigo market had led to an over-leveraged situation for this British-dominated enterprise in India by the 1840s. As I read in *The Blue Mutiny*, a work from 1966 by the American scholar Blair B. Kling, besides several other works of economic history and a few of plain outrage, indigo was a top export from Bengal. In the three decades before the troubles, only opium—the trade of which was a government monopoly—surpassed indigo. Soon other exports from Bengal, like foodgrains, took over. Some historians say that indigo's declining importance in the overall scheme of things actually led the government to ignore the plight of indigo cultivators.

The burden to squeeze the last rupee of profit went down the food chain from traders to planters, their supervisors and down to the ryōt, the cultivator. Often the local jōmidār, as rent-seeker, was an important part of the food chain. First the government run by the East India Company looked away, and then for some years the British Crown. When it counted the government came down on the side of the planters. The few administrators who raised a red flag, reporting unfairness and warning of potential unrest were largely ignored. And unrest began to flare up among cultivators across vast tracts of Bengal that formed part of the indigo tracts, in Nadia, Jessore, Bakarganj, Pabna, Rajshahi, Faridpur, Malda, Murshidabad, Birbhum, Burdwan, Hugli, the 24 Parganas...

Proverbs like this one (the translation is from the unpublished works of the academic Mazharul Islam) with an east Bengali flavour gained currency:

Tākā tākā tākā!
Gāér roktō pāni korāō
hātér muthi phnākā.

Money, money, money!
Even if you work till your
body sweats blood,
your fist remains empty.

The report of the Indigo Commission, which the government

was driven by unrest to constitute in 1860—in part because it was fearful of another conflagration like 1857—finally exposed the depradations of indigo cultivation. These included the forcible cultivaton of indigo, a cycle of debt repayment at very high rates of interest and, upon refusal or default, severe beatings, occasional rape of family members, destitution of the household, calling in of mortgages, and sometimes, death.

'In 1860 the Lieutenant Governor of Bengal,' writes Kling, 'calculated that the ryot lost 7 rupees per bigha (a third of an acre in Bengal; bigha measures vary across India) when he cultivated indigo in place of another crop. Along with the ryot's expenses of cultivation must be placed the various bribes which he was obliged to give to every factory servant with whom he came into contact, to the head ryot who arranged with the planter for cultivation in his village, and later, contributions for lawsuits and other expenses incurred extricating himself from the Indigo contract.' This last usually went the way of the planter, a near-inevitability in cases ruled by European magistrates.

In September the same year, a play by Dinabandhu Mitra, *Neel Dorpōn*, began to make waves after it was published in Dhaka. Word of Indigo Mirror—some call it The Mirror of Indigo—and the injustice committed by its two principal villains, the planters J. J. Wood and P. P. Rogue, spread quickly. The play recorded the inevitable fightback. It involved a few public trials and execution of planters, destruction of several factories and depots, but largely a refusal by indigo farmers to sow the crop or pay rent, and demand clear tenures; and massive reprisals by government forces and toughs in the pay of landlords. Within weeks news of the play reached the highest levels of colonial government. W. S. Seaton-Karr, secretary to the government of Bengal, is said to have read the play in Bānglā. There is some confusion about the provenance of its translation into English, but the generally accepted version is that the Reverend James Long, an Anglican missionary who was greatly sympathetic to the plight of indigo farmers, commissioned Michael Madshusudan

Dutt to translate it. Seaton-Karr is said to have printed several hundred copies at the expense of government—with Reverend Long as the go-between—and subsequently ensured a couple of hundred reached members of parliament in London, old India hands, and major media in both Great Britain and India.

An important sideshow unfurled in the general furore and publicity that followed. Long was actually tried for libel in the Calcutta Supreme Court in July 1861—a suit brought against him by planters (formally the Landholders and Commercial Association). The judge, Sir Mordaunt Wells, known for his anti-Indian stand, primed the jury: he maintained that Reverend Long had been swayed by 'other than pure motives' to publish the translation. Reverend Long was found guilty, fined a thousand rupees and sentenced to a month's jail. There was an outpouring of support for him among Bengal's notables; Kali Prasanna Sinha, among Kolkata's more prominent jōmidār and a patron of the arts and literature, paid the fine. (Sinha wasn't easily impressed by the British—in 1845, the Bengal Club took over a residence he owned at 33 Chowringhee, for some years) By the end of the decade, indigo plantations in Bengal were largely history.

Neel Dorpōn, which I was given to read as a child, is available in Bānglā and English, and is even occasionally performed to this day, a beacon of protest and rebellion more than 150 years after it was written and first performed, when it took Kolkata and much of Bengal by storm.

◆

Two experiences of his time as a revolutionary that my father-in-law Deepankar shared have stayed with me.

'A group of us went to the house of a jōtdār called Akrur Das,' he began—the simplicity of his tale making it more chilling. 'We killed the guards and went in, and found nearly 100 tōlā of gold ornaments stuffed inside pillows, and about 1.5 lakh rupees in cash. Can you imagine the value of it those days?'

After looting the landlord, Deepankar and his associates escaped and went in different directions. He was soon doing a steady, shuffling semi-trot through the clayey soil of the paddies. 'Kodōmchāl,' he said in Bānglā. 'That way, you don't sink into the mud. The momentum keeps you going.'

Then he heard someone calling out to him. 'What is it?' he asked, without stopping. A villager pointed out four armed policemen in the distance. 'They were after me in the same half-trot.' They went on like that through the night. He said he 'had the edge on them' and made his way to the station, just in time to catch a train to Ballygunje—then, as now, a posh part of Kolkata. But the policemen had made it too—he saw when he looked out. He jumped off the train, on the other side away from the platform, and made his way to a vendors' coach and hid himself among the sacks of vegetables and baskets of fish. 'They couldn't imagine someone would hide there, in all the muck and the smell.' He got off at Ballygunje station and walked down Rash Behari Avenue to the upper-middle class neighbourhood of Hindustan Park where the family then lived.

'When I walked into the living room, my mother and uncle and some house guests jumped up screaming!' He guffawed. 'Relax,' I told them, 'It's me, Deepankar—Khōkōn.' He was sunburnt, had a beard, and was wearing a dhuti in the way farmers still do, wrapped tight about the waist and hiked above the knee; his hands and feet were caked with mud.

◆

He lit a cigarette and carried on talking about his past. 'You know, it's difficult to explain the romance of the times, for a just cause. There was a famine.'

One of the things the Tebhaga movement fed off was the anger created by a famine in 1943. In the Bengal countryside, in the west and east, the fortunate ate roots. The unfortunate, as you know, didn't eat at all—it was another sordid chapter in the history of Bengal, subsumed by the greater immediate histories of India's freedom struggle, Partition, and World War II.

Food scarcity, and rebellion, didn't end with the war. Deepankar told me another story, from 1949, two years into India's Independence, a brave new world. 'People were starving in these three villages in Sandeshkhali. We led a raid.'

The jōtdār there, like all wealthy landlords, lived off tenant farming and squeezed the tenants. He had thirteen large stores of paddy. 'There was a stream around his property, and barbed-wire fencing. There was a Muslim fellow in the group. He went ahead, a short sword clasped between his teeth, crawled under the fencing and got rid of the guard by slashing his throat.' Deepankar was matter of fact as he related it. 'Then we went in and opened the doors to others. There were thirty maunds of paddy.' Well over a ton. 'A group of starving villagers were with us, about two hundred, but many more were waiting. We formed a chain gang and managed to roughly distribute the paddy.'

The police caught him while he was trying to make his escape. Deepankar was first taken to the nearby Basirhat Jail, he says, where he was tied to a tree and beaten for eight to nine hours with a thick rope. His eyes were never quite right after that and he would get blinding headaches every few days until the time he died, just one legacy of an angry life.

He said the judge threw his case out because he simply wouldn't believe the police version that a bunch of bhodrōlōk revolutionaries and scrawny villagers would have the strength to spirit away so much grain in a few hours. Fortunately for Deepankar, the judge didn't seem to realize the motivation and strength hunger and anger could instil in people.

'Even now, I think it was absolutely justified. We were determined to bring justice to the poor—at any cost. And for that we were willing to give up our families, wealth, our lives, everything.'

'Would you do it all over again?' I asked.

'Yes.'

16

Māstān
Mastanocracy

The meek, cultured Bengali a thug? We've been that way for decades. This is an evolutionary step up, from the point of view of such matters, from the complicated cult of the thuggee that gave birth to word 'thug'. Those medieval highway robbers used deceit and cunning to rob and often kill their victims. Bengal's thugs of the present day have no time for such subtlety.

Our thugs are māstāns, a word that has also outgrown its Hindustani root, of being mast, intoxicated by spirituality, with god. In Banglasphere, māstāni, the act of being a māstān is about intoxication with violence and power as a way of life and livelihood. It has proved to be quite infectious. It has certainly infected the state, which has travelled from using māstāns to being māstān, evolution that has come to define much of the politics of West Bengal and to a great extent, Bangladesh.

♦

The thuggish nature of Kolkata, a corollary to the communal nature of Kolkata on which thugs fed and their puppet masters were happy to let them, by most accounts became set in stone during the second United Front, or UF, government, a coalition of major and minor left-wing parties between February 1969 and July 1970. The political scientist Atul Kohli wrote in his forthright work, *Democracy and Discontent: India's Growing Crisis of Governability*, that it was similar to the first run of the UF government between

March and November 1967 (coincidentally the period when the Naxalbari agitation sparked off). Kohli's work exposes the organized chaos and manipulation that brought on the attitudinal eclipse from which West Bengal is yet to fully emerge.

There is another word from those times, as much as from the lexicon of protest as the lexicon of intimidation—ghérāō. To surround; and, effectively, to smother.

The word came to be so frequently employed that it was eventually included in the Oxford English Dictionary. It lists the word's origin as Hindi. It matters little. Perhaps there has not been in recent times a word made so powerfully Bengali and ultimately so debilitating for West Bengal. Ghérāō made the cut to the *Cambridge Essential English Dictionary* too, as an Indian-English word describing 'an occasion when people show that they disagree with something by standing around a person in authority and not letting them leave until they agree to do what the people want.'

'And again chaos resulted,' Kohli writes. 'Gheraoes, forced distribution of land, internecine fighting among political parties, riots and political murders once again became the order of the day.' Things got so bad that President's Rule, in which the government in New Delhi assumed direct control of the governance of West Bengal, was imposed in 1970. Ajoy Mukherjee was chief minister of both United Front governments. (Jyoti Basu, the future communist overlord and chief minister of West Bengal before he was eased out towards the end of an incredible fifth term, served as both home minister and deputy chief minister in Mukherjee's government.) Mukherjee would return as chief minister for a third chaotic time, between April and June 1971, as head of a Congress government after having earlier led coalitions against it. This stint would again end with President's Rule. Through the years 1967 to 1972, West Bengal politics resembled the notoriously unstable and operatically vicious politics of Italy. It was as if bhodrōlōk had finally come of age as the Borgias.

This was far from the latter-day communist government in West

Bengal in the early 2000s which, in a desperate move to attract investment, sent word out that ghérāō was no longer welcome, and labour militancy must diminish. It used the party organization to also enforce the primacy of left labour unions in businesses and in matters of land acquisition, seen in Singur and Nandigram in the mid-2000s, and numerous business projects across big and small towns of the state—the most intense is surely the Rajarhat New Town in northeast Kolkata, where land was acquired on the back of māstāns. But this embodiment of māstān in the CPI (M)-led government and party structure that spectacularly collapsed after 2008, was passed off as being for a good cause—prosperity.

◆

The UF government had its own take on prosperity. It ordered the police to not 'interfere' in matters where management and labour went head-to-head. According to government sources, in the initial months of UF rule there were about a thousand instances of ghérāō in and around Kolkata. Geoffrey Moorehouse's *Calcutta* records a bizarre statement by the state's labour minister, Subodh Banerjee, that was like a micro-sized replay of Stalinist fervour—brutal put-downs posturing as purity of that high pursuit for the greater good. 'I have allowed a duel between the employees and employers in West Bengal, and the police have been taken out of the picture so that the strength of each other may be known.' Police could not intervene in any labour-rooted incident of lawlessness and disorder without the express permission of the labour minister. Kohli correctly concludes: 'The UF, as a result, may have improved its political standing with labour, but industrial production plummeted, and capital flew to other parts of India.'

I was reminded of this truth in an evocative essay by Sumit Mitra, among the more perceptive political observers of post-industrial West Bengal. Sumit-dā wrote of the times that rode anger upon anger, an expression of public rage that 'came to the people like a flash flood in mountain streams'. He reminds us that public anarchy was hardly restricted to matters of religion. 'In the 1950s, a one-paisa rise in second-class tram fare led to a bonfire of the cars; it paralysed normal life for weeks on end...' In the 1960s, workers of the French Motor Car Company shot the owner. 'Soon afterwards, the general manager of Ludlow Jute Company was thrown into a furnace.'

With the Naxalite movement by then in full flow, even under President's rule in Kolkata, there could be 'as many as 60 political murders committed in a single day', Kohli recorded a reference in Biplab Dasgupta's *The Naxalite Movement* from 1975. Add those across Bengal, and we have a nightmare in bloom. 'Politics became a dangerous profession,' writes Kohli, and then gently adds the most chilling of twists. 'Those who entered politics in that atmosphere generally were people with an outlook that would allow them to continue to function amid urban terrorism.'

The run-up and aftermath of the war in Bangladesh had massed armed forces in West Bengal. When President's rule was imposed between June 1971 and March 1972, Indira Gandhi was prime minister. After the crushing military defeat of Pakistan in its eastern arm, military reverses along its western border with India, and Pakistan's general humiliation by global opinion, Indira could do no wrong and she took full advantage of the fact: 'Indira saw to it that many of the Naxalites...were jailed and eliminated,' Kohli writes. 'With the extreme left thus reduced in significance and Indira's popularity soaring, the massive 1972 Congress win in West Bengal may well have seemed for the moment like a restoration of "politics as usual".'

Meanwhile, the seeds of further political thuggery had been bountifully sown. And although obduracy of the leftists was seemingly the only cause for it, the reality is that the Congress, which had generally taken a vicious turn after Indira's elevation to prime minister in 1966 and her firm defeat of dissenters, permitted its organization in West Bengal to literally run riot. The māstān was both hammer and chisel in this evolving political situation in which the Congress wanted to wrest power at any cost.

Several researchers and chroniclers of those times, including Kohli and the 1974 work *The Great Gherao of 1969: Campus Violence and Protest Methods* by Sugata Dasgupta and his colleagues Ronen Bhattacharjee and Surendra Singh, claim it extended to Congress tacitly supporting Naxalites, who were eager to attack former comrades in both the CPI and CPI (M). The youth wing of the Congress, the Chhātrō Pōrishod, a product of this pipeline, assumed significance. The other key approach was the patronage to māstāns—some of the Chhātrō Pōrishod had māstān roots and practised māstān behaviour. They thrived in the chaos. In *The Great Gherao* we learn that the Pōrishod had decided to 'take on a fighting role'. It extended to massive participation in the 1972 elections by physically dominating left-wing supporters, and the rigging of votes; the students' body of the Congress took over West Bengal's Congress. The māstān and the youthful neo-māstān of politics were effectively the 'next-gen' leadership, willing to use violence to take ahead their own interests and that of the party, and, as there was a power vacuum of sorts in leadership, the Congress let them lead the way. Kohli states: '…(B)ecause they could mobilize force to meet the political challenges of the day… Because of the new cast of characters in the old fight over positions and patronage, there was a rapidly developing tendency to resort to violence, including political murders.'

Kohli quotes a politically neutral Kolkata scholar, an anonymous source whom he describes as 'a Gandhian socialist who supported neither the CPM nor Congress', to highlight that such domination and murders were aimed at opponents such as the Naxalites; the Naxals, too, were responsible for unbridled terror attacks on those who could only by a stretch be described as class enemies. The Congress government employed tactics like tasking local police, paramilitaries of the Congress and occasionally the Indian Army to kill known and randomly suspected Naxal cadres, and even the garden variety of less incendiary left-wing cadres. Sometimes they would literally be dragged out into the streets before being killed. And even earlier, as we learn in an essay on the police's perspective by Ashok Kumar Mukhopadhyay in a July 2006 issue of *Economic and Political Weekly* which refers to eyewitnesses' claim that 'the armed police in those days used to raid Naxalite hideouts in north Calcutta or east Calcutta, select some young boys (who were suspected to be Naxalites), make them stand in a single file and then riddle them with bullets. This scene was enacted in the city over and over again in 1970-71.' Between March 1970 and August 1971, a time of a short-lived Congress government followed by President's Rule controlled by a Congress government in New Delhi, nearly 1,800 Naxal 'supporters/ members' were killed in Kolkata and its suburbs, Mukhopadhyay writes, which subsequent investigations placed at double that number. 'Between May and December 1971, the police opened fire on Naxalite prisoners in at least six jails in West Bengal.'

The saturated violence spilled over even to political infighting. The scholar Kohli quoted earlier, the 'Gandhian socialist' suggested that between 1972 and 1975, clashes within the Congress led to '102 murders of Congressites'. It was a time before the advent of the Emergency in June 1975, which unleashed further political grotesquerie in West Bengal—with the full complicity of newly-blooded Bengalis in politics who readily discovered support in Indira, her son Sanjay, who led the Youth Congress and by default controlled Chhātrō Pōrishod, and their satrap, the Congress chief minister, Siddhartha Shankar Ray. Kohli didn't hesitate to call the spade a hydraulic excavator. 'Bengalis take pride in the fact that "what happens in Bengal today happens in India tomorrow". There is little reason for pride in the fact that the early emergence of the goonda-politician-police nexus in Calcutta politics foreshadowed similar developments in other parts of India.'

This mix of labour conflicts, untrammelled student violence that included urban Naxalism, the splenetic reaction to it and general repression by the state, and the overlay of māstāns continued for nearly a decade until 1977.

As the subsequent three decades of Communist rule and that of the Trinamool Congress since 2011 have showed, the mingling of democracy and māstān continues. The chronicler Sajal Basu wrote colourfully and presciently of it in one of his several studies on the violence of those years: 'Political dependence on these rowdy cadres has precipitated a situation of Mastanocracy.'

The māstān moved steadily from pawn to power broker in what Basu termed the chessboard of politics.

Kasba, an area near Ballygunge (or Bāligonj, in Bangla) was the legendary heart of the kingdom of māstāns. (As children we were warned against going anywhere near Kasba—Koshbā; the millennial real estate development of high-rise apartment blocks and markets for the middle- and upper middle-classes of Kolkata was then not even a mote in the exuberant futurist's eye.) As Basu wrote in another study on the politics of violence in West Bengal, Kasba had since the mid-1960s become 'famous…for its concentration of mastans. A group of mastans ran a boxing club here whose main source of income was black marketing in local cinema houses and theft from railway wagons… When factionalism developed within the club over issues of appropriate share of the booty, the rival groups sought out support of politicians and police. That's how a number of them joined the Congress. Some of these māstāns are now local leaders of the Congress in Kasba.'

Congress leaders like Priya Ranjan Dasmunsi and Somen Mitra emerged from that scrum, writes Kohli among others. And those who led them, like Subrato Mukherjee, who was minister of state for home in the Congress-led West Bengal government for two years from 1972, was unapologetic about the politics of this time. In an interview with Kohli, Mukherjee, who oversaw the police and law and order, was matter-of-fact: 'I played an important role in Youth Congress since 1969. There was no (Congress) party left. All fell apart under the struggle with the left forces.' The Chhātrō Pōrishod, he said, became 'de facto Congress'. 'The left terrorism created tremendous disillusionment,' Mukherjee said. 'We confronted this… Dasmunsi and myself. There was tremendous violence throughout the state.'

Mastanocracy, as Banglasphere now knows well, truly arrives when the state turns māstān.

◆

Some would say mastanocracy evolved into a different degree of viciousness during the reign of the next bhodrōlōk to assume the reigns of West Bengal, Jyoti Basu. He took office on 21 June 1977 at the head of a CPI (M)-led Left Front government after Congress was decimated at the assembly elections earlier that month. He finally demitted office on 5 November 2000, leaving behind what critics say was a de-industrialized, economically chaotic wasteland that pushed several generations of the state's vast professional talent-pool to seek work and life elsewhere in India and across the world. However, what even several of his detractors maintain is that, for all the calumny heaped upon Basu, he oversaw perhaps the most significant change—and boost—in the state's rural fabric, an act that earned his party and him a firm political base that would last more than three decades.

Basu would earn much hate for what many saw as his duplicitous Jekyll and Hyde persona, a communist who saw no ill in his son Subhabrata (more commonly known as Chandan) score visibly easy business success under his reign, as pointed out in an article by Sumit Mitra in *India Today* in December 1982 titled 'Comrade papa's capitalist son'. 'With only three years in full-time business, Chandan now headed three separate companies,' Mitra observed, noting too how mysteriously accessible bank loans came his way to expand his biscuit business, and how 'startling success' came to Chandan's trucking business with some of India's biggest companies contracting this newly-minted entrepreneur who preferred *Fortune* over *Das Kapital*. Meanwhile the elder Basu was a man who loved his whisky in the evening and, as religiously, summered in England.

At home his party's māstāns ran amok, ruthlessly enforcing his will, repeating what Basu as a minister in the United Front government had presided over and greatly encouraged. He was Bengal's mafia don, his critics still rage. A man who utterly destroyed whatever remained of the legacy of the statesmanlike, peaceable Bidhan Chandra Roy, West Bengal's first chief minister, who knit together a state devastated by Partition, and, till he died in office on 1 July 1962, after twelve-and-a-half years in office (for two years prior to that he was the second premier of the post-Partition state that had yet to form an Assembly) attempted to maintain Bengal's place in industry and industriousness, and blue-printed the planned growth of what is now Kolkata's vast suburb and technology and back-office hub of Bidhannagar. (It is often commonly called Salt Lake City or Saltlék). During Basu's tenure the area saw the emergence of communist leaders and cadres who extended mastanocracy to things like the forcible resettlement of the local population, destruction of the area's natural drainage mechanism, the business of contracting labour, and the procurement of material and other services for construction.

Basu was also called the Marichjhapi Man by his critics, a reference to the massacre of Bengalis in mid-May 1979 on an island of that name in the Sunderbans (Mōrichjnāpi in Bangla). His government first blockaded, then had the police and party thugs participate in beating, rape and the killing of refugees—more than 1,000, some accounts maintain more than 1,500. They had first poured in from East Pakistan in great waves, mostly low-caste Bengali Hindus; several tens of thousands of them relocated to refugee settlements in central India, in what is known as the Dandakaranya region. From the 1960s and even earlier Bengal's Communists had worked among them, invited them to return to Bengal.

'During the B. C. Roy government, in the 1950s and early 1960s, Jyoti Basu, then the leader of the opposition, had presented their case in the legislative assembly,' I read the academician Annu

Jalais in the left-leaning journal *Economic and Political Weekly.* 'As late as 1974 he had demanded in a public meeting that the Dandakaranya refugees be allowed to settle in the Sundarbans. In 1974-75 leading members of the subsequent Left Front government, including Ram Chatterjee, the minister of state for home (civil defence), had assured the refugees that if the Left Front came to power they would arrange their resettlement in West Bengal and at a meeting of the eight Left Front parties in 1975 it was resolved that the refugees would be settled in the Sundarbans.'

When they arrived, encouraged by the formation of an elected communist government—several tens of thousands 'poured in', according to one account, to West Bengal from nearly all points of the compass—they found the political tides had changed; they were simply too many for Bengal to handle.

Bengal, Basu's Bengal, no longer wanted Bengalis, had no more room for refugees, and began to forcibly deport them to wherever they came from, including central India. It saw in their streaming in to Marichjhapi, a slip of land in the Sunderbans that had by then attracted several tens of thousands of refugees and local settlers alike, a crime against the state.

Blockading began in January that year, of water supplies, food, medicine, of all essential items. Nearly forty protesters were killed by police firing on 31 January when they resisted resettlement. Matters snowballed. Most settlers refused to leave, some fought back, giving the government the justification it needed. Boats packed with police and cadres moved in. 'Prohibitory' orders were issued to prevent the outside world looking in. Media was barred, especially, as I read in one account, after photographs of the refugee-plight at Marichjhapi were published that February in *Amrita Bazar Patrika.* Newspapers were threatened with withdrawal of government advertising if they published news of Marichjhapi. Still news emerged of the atrocities, provided by a handful of doughty chroniclers like Pannalal Dasgupta, and the near-legendary journalists Sukharanjan Sengupta of *Anandabazar Patrika* and Jyotirmoy Dutta who worked with

The Statesman. Then the May massacre happened.

Outrage eventually faded, scattered much like the Marichjhapi refugees, some of whom returned to central India; the descendants of many others continue to live in utter destitution in and around Kolkata. In all its years Basu and his government, and the Left Front government after Basu, declined any neutral investigation into the incident, any judicial oversight. He, his party and some of West Bengal's best-known left-leaning public intellectuals and supporters of CPI (M) who have since long weighed in, quite correctly, on all manner of communal and human rights violations across India perpetrated by political parties of shades other than communist, buried Marichjhapi.

They also buried several other atrocities, alleged and proven, of the Basu regime. One such took place in end-April 1982, widely reported in local and national media at the time. Seventeen members of the secretive Kolkata-based sect, Ananda Marg—the organization calls itself the path of bliss—sixteen monks and a nun, were attacked and burnt after being dragged out of taxis. Several others were badly injured. They had been on their way to attend a conference at Marg headquarters in Tiljala in southeast Kolkata, north of the once-infamous māstān redoubt of Kasba.

The sect's founder, a former railway employee, Prabhat Ranjan Sarkar or Sri Sri Anandamurti as he was known by his acolytes, had journeyed quickly from being a social worker to a proponent of 'neo-humanism', the love-all bedrock for 'Prout'—Progressive Utilization Theory that debunked both communism and capitalism for a 'humanistic social order'. He peddled esoteric concepts like Microvita, which the organization claims as having 'captured the interest of scientists around the world' as Sarkar 'struck at the heart of conventional physics and biology, pointing out that the basic buildings blocks of life are Microvita—emanations of pure consciousness.' This Kolkatafornian guru, if you will, and his order were ideologically opposed to CPI (M), and were even seen as threats to the party's activities of outreach and indoctrination.

Five Margis were thought to have been killed by CPI (M) cadres in an attack in Purulia as early as 1967. Before the 1982 incident word had been about that Margis were abducting children under the guise of their schools. According to several media accounts, including in the *Times of India*, *Indian Express* and *India Today*, CPI (M) leaders of the Kasba-Jadvapur area let loose their hounds, the early avatar—obōtār—of Hārmād in a premeditated attack.

Basu later appeared nonchalant, when asked about the murders of the Margis. 'Emon tōh hōyéi thāké,' he said, a statement that became his hallmark, a man who was a monolith in a monolithic party. Such things happen.

Then there is Basu the benevolent dictator, the provider for the masses as fawning obituaries announced. His government provided legal protection for sharecroppers from eviction, securing their tenure in a massive exercise that came to be known as Operation Barga (after sharecroppers) that fine-tuned land reforms undertaken in the mid-1950s. At the time of his death, the number of recorded sharecroppers had increased from 1 to 1.5 million, and 'registered' sharecroppers accounted for a fifth of households that depended on agriculture. More than a third of these were Ādibāshīs, and those of low-caste. All this had taken place in as little as two decades.

Basu's Bengal led too in the redistribution of land that was surplus to government-mandated ceilings on landholding, an exercise that was ongoing until his death in 2010. 'What this means is that West Bengal, which accounts for only 3.5 per cent of agricultural land in the country, accounts [in 2008] for 22.6 per cent of ceiling-surplus lands distributed in the entire country,' claimed an essay in the left-leaning magazine *Frontline*. Again, it overwhelmingly benefited the more marginalized sections of society. There is, however, a downside—small landholdings became smaller over time through inheritance, and there are farmers who grow reluctant to carry on farming their own uneconomical lands—as evidenced by former farmers from West Bengal even working as farm labour in the villages of faraway Tamil Nadu, including the village where I now live.

But that wasn't then part of the communist calculus.

Basu for a time even emerged as what political commentators in India adoringly term 'kingmaker', politicians and their operators who work to make or break alliances, a skill especially prized since 1977 when coalition politics came into its own after several decades of the Congress Party's majority rule. Though there have been claims of Basu declining the opportunity to become the Indian prime minister in a coalition government over 1990–1991 on the advice of his party's politburo, in 1997 there was a real chance of Basu becoming prime minister in the United Front coalition government which the CPI (M) helped to prop up in the political void of a hung parliament after India's general elections of 1996. His party's central leadership, the politburo, declined, and while Basu acquiesced, as would an ideal apparatchik, he later confessed to it being an 'historic blunder'. As the political commentator M. J. Akbar—in the 1970s and 1980s a formidable editor, and founding editor of both *Sunday* and *The Telegraph*—had it, Basu possessed 'more power in Bengal than most prime ministers have in India'. Basu was 'content' in Kolkata and 'capable of mounting an offensive from the Red Fortress that could shake the parameters of the Red Fort.'

What remained in the end was a legacy suffused with lost opportunity. The leader of the so-called New Left of the mid-1960s degenerated to being a leader of the Moribund Left. As even the perpetually mild-mannered commentator Subir Roy concluded after Basu's death, he and the Left '[are] credited with having actively worked for, not just presiding over, the de-industrialisation of West Bengal.'

◆

We have had our share of political skulduggery for the sake of anaemic gains, embracing avoidable, self-destructive situations with gusto, destroying the stereotype of the sensitive, caring, enlightened Bengali and yet again revealing the Bengali that is every so often little more than thug, a māstān—bhodrōlōk and chhōtōlōk alike.

Singur and Nandigram are two examples from West Bengal in an indelible history of democratic how-not-to. (It also helped greatly to end more than three decades of communist rule—that other Bengali stereotype.) Ironically, in this case the government of West Bengal had been attempting to attract business to Bengal. The chief minister at the time, Buddhadeb Bhattacharjee, eagerly welcomed Tata Motors to make its landmark 'people's car', Nano, with lucrative discounts in tax and cost of energy, among other incentives. Too eagerly, as it turned out.

The year 2006 will be remembered as the year when heavy-handed land acquisition, openly aided by local leaders and cadres of the ruling CPI (M), ran into opposition by farmers who found in Trinamool a willing ally. Matters spiralled out of control in Singur after 18 December 2006, when the body of Tapasi Malik, the daughter of a local farmer, who was part of the movement protesting acquisition of land for Tata Motors, part of the giant group controlled by Tata Sons, was found mutilated and burnt near the site of the factory. So confident had that business group been of the government coming through for it that it had begun construction of the main plant and those of its vendors even before land acquisition had been completed. And, as incredible as it may seem in hindsight, reassured by Bengal's government, Tata Motors continued with construction at Singur even after Malik's death escalated the furore over land acquisition for its plant. And things almost worked for them, all the hurdles notwithstanding, as I discovered while researching, through interviews, 'ground' reportage and archival material for my book *Red Sun: Travels in Naxalite Country* and, later, *Clear.Hold.Build: Hard Lessons of Business and Human Rights in India* (I have also written about these matters in the business newspaper *Mint*).

A top bureaucrat in West Bengal, who has intimate knowledge of the episode on account of the portfolios he handled and proximity to powers-that-were, told me a curious story in July 2013 over lunch at Eau Chew, his favourite Chinese restaurant in Kolkata, in the busy warren-like business and trading district in the city's centre. This gentleman mentioned a visit to Paschim (or West) Medinipur district by Chief Minister Bhattacharjee during which he requested the senior bureaucrat of the district to provide land for a 'major Tata project' because it would bring immense prestige to the state. The bureaucrat, I was told, readily agreed. Indeed, the local bureaucrat mentioned that he had the 1,200 acres requested by the chief minister readily at hand at a location near the highway that linked Kolkata and Mumbai. And this acreage was 'vested'— the land belonged to government, it was as hassle-free as it could get. Evidently, Bhattacharjee left greatly relieved and quite excited about the prospect of luring a major business house to shore up the state's long-faltering investor appeal.

'The Tata people came and saw that land,' the bureaucrat told me over a heaped plateful of steamed noodles and roast pork. 'They liked what they saw. There was no need for (land) acquisition, no problem of any sort.' A refurbished highway ensured a three-hour run to Kolkata and its port; another major port, Haldia, was nearby. The site was practically next door to the major railway hub of Kharagpur, better known as the location for a highly regarded campus of Indian Institute of Technology.

He said in the end Tata Motors opted for Singur in Hooghly district. 'We were surprised and shocked when we came to know,' the bureaucrat told me.

He offered a reason for the shift. For one thing, Tata Motors felt more comfortable with a location closer to Kolkata. For another, some among the CPI (M) saw in Singur an opportunity to show up the increasingly belligerent Trinamool, their opposition at the time. The constituency in which Singur is located had voted in a Trinamool candidate as MLA—and the Marxists, the bureaucrat told me, 'went for it as a ploy to show locals they could bring business and jobs and dent Trinamool's vote bank and influence in this key constituency'.

'But that seems like a recipe for disaster,' I offered. 'Why leave vested land for potential trouble in Singur, where they would need to buy fertile agricultural land? Why hadn't the Tatas done their political due diligence?'

They had, he told me: the government would come through. As it turned out, the state undertook to buy land for Tata Motors and its vendors. Just under 1,000 acres were marked for acquisition. The government claimed that things finally ground to a halt about 180 acres short, the owners of which were unwilling to sell.

Trinamool leaders put the acreage that farmers were unwilling to sell at 400. And, during a hearing in Calcutta High Court, the government could show consent forms for less than 300 acres. Incidents such as the death of Tapasi Malik, and repeated, brazen forays into the area by CPI (M) cadres to intimidate farmers to sell land attracted massive outrage in Kolkata. A prominent section of intellectuals openly allied with Trinamool leader Mamata Banerjee—who was repeatedly prevented by police from reaching Singur.

Acts of political violence—and Tata's construction of facilities in the face of public outrage—continued through 2007.

It all went horribly wrong. Strong-arming of land acquisition by the communist government, signalled to Mamata Banerjee that there was an opportunity to place a decisive foot in the Marxist doorway to gain political control of West Bengal.

'The government thought Singur would be over in three days!' the bureaucrat told me, referring to a meeting he says he attended in the secretariat to discuss the Singur issue. 'I was shocked but kept my peace. I couldn't believe the administration could be so out of touch with reality—it had not only misjudged the clout of CPM cadres, but entirely misjudged the mood on the ground.'

The government misjudged the mood on the ground in Nandigram too, one that would help drive an emphatic nail into the coffin of the Singur project.

Nandigram was a large patch of land dense with farms and fisheries near the coastal area of Purba (or East) Medinipur district selected for a special economic zone for Salim Group, an Indonesian conglomerate. Estimates of the area marked for this project to create a chemical hub range between 10,000 to 14,500 acres—even the lower estimate makes it a large area. Residents of several villages in the area took issue with the government's proposal to acquire land on behalf of the foreign conglomerate—their steady livelihoods being disrupted by the move. The Bhumi Uchchhed Pratirodh Committee, or the Committee to Oppose Land Acquisition ('uchchhéd' in Bengali translates more accurately as 'uprooting'), took exception to the plan as well.

By the beginning of 2007—around the time Singur had begun to peak—the standoff in Nandigram spiralled into a battle of wills between Marxist leaders and cadres of the area, backed by massed state police, and locals opposed to the project. More precisely, to the arbitrariness with which the administration approached the process of land acquisition.

Skirmishes continued, and scaled up. To prevent the police from entering, villagers dug up roads and tracks leading to villages. In January 2007, protesters torched the house of a CPI (M) leader from where they had been fired upon—two protesters died. A policeman was lynched. Finally, on 14 March 2007, several thousand police and armed Marxist cadres stormed the protesters in Nandigram.

Many of the protesters were formerly Marxist supporters, and included women and children. Fourteen people were killed, several dozen were injured, many severely. The brutalities committed against women and children over 14–16 March were subsequently recorded by human rights investigators.

A public statement issued by the governor of West Bengal at the time, Gopalkrishna Gandhi, grandson to both Mohandas Gandhi and C. Rajagopalachari, the polymath-politician and India's last governor general, counts among the more eloquent remarks in India's agonizing history of land acquisition. To the great discomfort of the CPI (M), displayed by the outrage of several of its leaders, the governor described how the incident filled him 'with a sense of cold horror'.

'The thought in my mind—and of all sensitive people now is—was this spilling of human blood not avoidable?' Gopalkrishna pointedly asked in *The Hindu*. 'What is the public purpose served by the use of force that we have witnessed today? Force against anti-national elements, terrorists, extremists, insurgents, is one thing. The receiving end of the force used today does not belong to that order.' He wasn't quite done. 'I leave it to the conscience of officials responsible to atone for the event in the manner they deem fit. But I also expect the Government to do what it thinks is necessary to mitigate the effects of this bitter March 14, and to do it visibly and fast.'

Nothing of the sort happened. Nandigram remained restive well into 2008 as skirmishes continued between groups for and against the project, and as farmers, who had chosen to give over land for Salim Group's project, attempted to return home. With the domino effect of Nandigram, besides being roiled by its own dynamic, Tata Motors formally withdrew from Singur in early October 2008. In transit at Kolkata airport, while travelling on a research trip to Northeast India, I browsed Ratan Tata's comments made at a media conference in Kolkata in a copy of the *Financial Express*, dated 3–4 October 2008. The newspaper quoted the chairman describing it as an 'extremely painful decision', that 'there was no other option', but that there was also a 'great feeling that we are doing the right thing'. This was clearly corporate spin. Tata went on to say: 'You cannot run a plant with police protection. We cannot run a plant with walls broken. We cannot run a project with bombs thrown. We cannot run a plant with people intimidated.'

Within days, Tata Motors announced relocation of the facility to manufacture its Nano car to Sanand in Gujarat. The chief minister of that state at the time, Narendra Modi, had offered clearly vested land, with no pending issues of acquisition and contestation.

And just like that, the Tata Group brushed off responsibility for the process of land acquisition and resultant chaos in Singur, because that process had been pursued by the Government of West Bengal. I studied the annual reports of Tata Motors for five years from 2006 onwards. The unsavoury developments in Singur were downplayed or buried or passed off as someone else's problem. Indeed, the Tata Group emerged from it as a corporate martyr, having undeniably lost project time and funds—several billion rupees in land, plant construction and logistics.

◆

Bengal's sustained economic doldrums continue, where even the patchy, confused, sometimes incoherent attempts at attracting investment since 2000 or so hasn't yet been able to reverse the business-unfriendly reputation of the state.

It remains a state of middling performance and promise. A few overpasses in gridlocked Kolkata, BPO or business process outsourcing operations in its eastern suburb and growth in real estate businesses are held up as examples of major economic transformation, instead of harnessing the restless energy of the non-Kolkata countryside, the ageing industrial-urban centres of Asansol and Durgapur, boosting the northern gateway city of Siliguri, creating economic hubs in a score of cities from Kharagpur in the southwest to Malda in the north. In the countryside employment and economic generation by government handout remains the motive force, the most significant exercise being the reorganization of landholdings during the rule of the Communists—a game-changing exercise in political economy that, as you know helped, along with an increasingly ruthless cadre, to keep the Left in power for over three decades.

Beyond this, it remains a Bengal of whims and fancies.

◆

I sometimes think back to a meeting with the Gujarati businessman Dhirubhai Ambani, who used foresight, energy, indefatigable networking, outright chutzpah and a clever reading of the maze of rules and regulations that govern doing business in India to lay the foundation of one of the largest corporations in the world. We met at the group's headquarters at the time, in Maker Chamber IV in Mumbai's Nariman Point, as part of a series of interviews for an eventual cover story I wrote on the group and its succession planning for *India Today* magazine. Formal interview with his sons Mukesh and Anil done, Dhirubhai and I relaxed for a few minutes over tea and chit-chat in his office suite. He suddenly stopped, and fixed me with a glare.

'Tum sala Bangali hai, na?' he snapped out in his typical expletive-filled, earthy-speak Hindi; he was equally blunt in Gujarati.

Yes, I said.

'Sala tum log itna bright hai,' he fumed. 'Lekin Bangal ka halat dekho.'

You people are so bloody bright, but look at the state of Bengal.

◆

Mastanocracy would seal the fate of the Marxists in favour of Mamata, and in this another M, Maoists, would contribute greatly.

Like his predecessor Jyoti Basu, chief minister Bhattacharjee routinely denied the existence of local Maoist cadres of various factions and, since 2004, primarily of the Communist Party of India (Maoist) conglomerate; their militias; and pro-Maoist sympathy as being imported from neighbouring Jharkhand, which bordered the three fairly-forested Bengal districts of Pōschim Medinipur, Purulia and Bankura. Bhattacharjee and his colleagues brushed aside Maoist attacks on government property and personnel as not being a consequence of weak governance and administrative dysfunction. The state chose to respond to the attacks through the Marxist party machinery as much as through policing. The situation in Bengal was, to borrow a phrase from New York-based academic Sanjib Baruah, a state of 'durable disorder'. Conflict was kept to limits considered manageable by the state.

That delusion was rudely interrupted. On 2 November 2008,

a motorcade was attacked by Maoist rebels. The motorcade carried, among others, Bhattacharjee, Ram Vilas Paswan, at the time India's minister for steel; and his deputy Jitin Prasada. The ministers were returning after attending the foundation stone-laying ceremony of a proposed steel plant of metals and mining major JSW Steel: a subsidiary, JSW Bengal Steel Ltd, wanted to set up a plant at Salboni, up the road from Medinipur. JSW Steel's chief Sajjan Jindal and his controversial cousin Naveen, who runs Jindal Steel & Power Ltd, were part of the motorcade. As the motorcade approached, the Maoists exploded a landmine at a spot just 7 kilometres north of the district headquarters town of Medinipur.

Some cars were battered, some accompanying security personnel and staff were injured. The ministers and businessmen survived.

But the Maoists had made several points with the attack. It was a protest against JSW's plant, against a prime example of a Maoist public enemy—exploitative capitalist 'roaders'. It was a hit against the Marxist-led government, at a moderate-left to the Maoists' extreme-left, a government widely perceived in the Lalgarh area as managing a reign of terror—as I discovered during a few visits, during which I conducted several interviews and travelled though large swathes of conflict-territory—through cadres that subsumed public administration and the area's largely agrarian and forest produce-based economy located in one of the poorest and underdeveloped regions of West Bengal. Besides Pōschim Medinipur this arc of poverty and neglect included Purulia and Bankura, which also contains the largest concentration of tribal folk—not-Bengali Ādibāshis, literally 'early settlers'—in the state. It was a near-perfect catchment area for the Maoists; and the attack was their most spectacular assassination attempt since the targeting, in 2003, of N. Chandrababu Naidu, Andhra Pradesh's chief minister at the time.

The attack also brought home the reality of rebel ambition, taking place as it did at a distance of about 200 kilometres west of Kolkata, even in the crush of traffic a mere three hours along a new expressway. That proximity also fed media with near-live news. OB, or outside broadcast vans, of a dozen and more television channels, print and digital media posses thought nothing of driving down from Kolkata for this conveniently located battle that escalated on 8 November.

The Marxist government's response was swift and brutal. It turned loose police and local leaders and goon squads of the CPI (M)—known locally as Hārmād Bāhini, or simply as Hārmād. (The word is believed to be a derivative of the time of Portuguese marauders and pillagers in Bengal, a corruption of armada that in mastanocracy came to be associated with thugs of the party.) It was a tactic of control by politicized māstāns of a 'mastanicized' party—as observed earlier in this chapter, and as I learned first-hand in Lalgarh and during my conversations with senior police officers of the district with intimate knowledge of the conflict—similar to those used in the enclaves of Singur and Nandigram. While those incidents remain human rights abominations in the course of conducting business and political enterprise, in Lalgarh it was overkill on overkill. Local CPI (M) party bosses were already satraps: they administered, extorted, provided instant justice in a bellicose, corrupt, and entrenched system. Rooting out Maoist sympathizers became a free-for-all of arrest, molestation, torture, killing of the area's villagers, both of tribal heritage and those of lower castes as listed by India's constitution, and destruction of homes and property in a wide radius of what came to be collectively known as Lalgarh, centred on the eponymous village.

The resistance grew spontaneously, and coalesced within weeks in the shape of what came to be known as the People's Committee against Police Atrocities. This organization (in Bangla: Pūlish Shōntrāsh Birodhi Jonōshādhārōnér Comity) worked in concert with the Maoists. And it played into the Maoist construct: a veritable war on the people, so we shall make it of the people, and by the people. Lalgarh became a 'name', in much the same way other places had: like Naxalbari, Dantewada in Chhattisgarh, Gadhchiroli in Maharashtra, and Koraput and Malkangiri in Odisha. Lalgarh yet again proved the axiom: anger and desperation make warriors of the meek. Perceptive politicians in Bengal have repeatedly 'got it'—get it—when it suits them, when they are on the make. When they arrive at their political destination they are blinded by what in some years, unseats them. The Maoists and their angry ilk pursue this axiom as a matter of course.

By the time 2008 had turned to 2009—winter to spring, and quickly to summer—Lalgarh, was declared a 'liberated zone' by the Maoists. When I visited Lalgarh at the time, in mid-June 2009, the People's Committee, almost entirely comprising the area's villagers, had gained enough strength to literally beat back CPI (M) cadres, control impressive territory, and enforce a blockade. However, Lalgarh was not yet a 'liberated zone', much as Maoist propaganda and some giddy media would have it. Such a zone could truly emerge if Maoist cadres and sympathizers were able to successfully defend it from attack, and with impunity run a de-facto administration. That wouldn't ultimately happen—but that is not the point of this story; letting things slide is.

It was nevertheless a stunning situation. The CPI (M)'s entrenched system was under attack for the first time in three decades, its seemingly invulnerable leaders assaulted, several leaders killed, their houses set on fire. The hand of Maoist leader Mallojula Koteswara Rao, the spearhead for fomenting rebellion in West Bengal, who went by the nom de guerre Kishan-ji, was seemingly everywhere. He and his comrades were diligently assisted by the web strung together by the People's Committee and its leader, Chhatradhar Mahato. The People's Committee and the Maoists set up a cordon sanitaire in the Lalgarh region with Lalgarh village as the epicentre. Mahato ordered a boycott of the police and paramilitary. Residents in the zone were warned to not sell them anything—groceries, toiletries, information.

On 17 June 2009, joint teams of the West Bengal police and paramilitaries controlled by the Indian government began to move in on the Lalgarh area in an attempt to encircle it. Kishan-ji asked media persons to leave Lalgarh by sundown the following day, maintaining that his cadres could no longer be responsible for their safety.

From a chronicler's perspective I figured it was absolutely the best time to be in Lalgarh. As all media teams departed around sunset the next day, we entered this seething area of siege, Soumitra Ghosh, a photographer-acquaintance of several years, and I. Having been warned that all access roads to Lalgarh were 'cut'—wide, deep trenches dug to prevent entry of security transports—we took a roundabout route through the town of Jhargram to the southwest of Lalgarh village, and then moved northeast towards our destination in a laborious, tense zigzag.

The road towards Lalgarh was blocked by trees, axed where they had stood by a stretch of tar. Elsewhere large branches of acacia had been cut and dragged onto the road. A few such the driver of our hired car could navigate around; others we had to request villagers to help us to move, let us carry on so we could write about the siege. Repeatedly using the cachet of being there as storytellers we negotiated passage in the only way that seemed to work: by helping blockaders replace the impediments once they let our car pass.

Past the hamlet of Phulberia, Soumitra and I joined several hundred Ādibāshīs as well as non-tribal folk on a march, women in front, men behind, children scampering alongside. These were Chhatradhar's 'people'. A few held People's Committee banners with slogans that urged people to stand firm in the face of 'elections through the police'; to evict all police from jongōlkhondō, or the forest areas. A few beat on drums to provide energy. And all— absolutely all—carried an assortment of tribal weaponry. Bows and arrows—teer; spears, or bollōm; crude swords; woodcutters' axes; the Ādibāshī battle-axe with a curved blade, the tāngi; sickles; stout bamboo staffs; knives.

Men and women broke into martial cries from time to time: a chilling wa-wa-wa-wa-wa, the back of the palm rapidly moved in front of the mouth to break up an extended howl. This was the Maoist line of defence against seasoned troopers and the Hārmād. The march was a display of intent, a morale booster. A few young men, their faces covered, moved alongside the marchers, keeping an eye on us.

◆

'Why?' I asked Sudhakar Mahato of Phulberia, as we joined this agitated snake of a line, and walked past the hamlets of Salpatra, Kendangri, Bandorboni, Kumeer Katra. It was a collection of dirt-poor, dark hovels mocked by nearby signs that proclaimed a rural electrification initiative under the Rajiv Gandhi Grameen Vidyutikran Yojana, named after a former Indian prime minister who was assassinated by Tamil Tiger suicide bombers in 1991.

'We have little but our pride,' Sudhakar Mahato told me. 'If the police start their shontrāsh then we will have nothing left. And what if something happens to our mothers, sisters and daughters?' He meant: if the police were to resume their shontrāsh—terror—in a bid to reclaim Lalgarh.

It seemed to be a no-win for the government. If its troopers stayed away, the state would cede territory to Maoists and rebels of their ilk. Or, there would be a bloody battle in which non-combatants too would die. Others would be made fearful, resentful, angry. And Maoists and others like them would eagerly leverage this negative energy.

Mamata, riding on the political capital provided by Nandigram and Singur, had already leveraged Lalgarh. Playing the peoples' leader to the hilt, she visited this area in early 2009 and actually shared a crowded platform with People's Committee chief Chhatradhar Mahato to hold what was effectively a press conference criticizing the Left Front government for all its ills, including the situation in Lalgarh. It played over primetime network television and in all major newspapers in West Bengal and across India.

Was Mamata pro-Maoist or even pro-People's Committee?

Hardly. It suited her to be seen that way, but more as pro-people (who at the time had the backing of Maoists, who at the time were dead set against her political opponents of the ruling CPI (M)—your enemy is my enemy).

During our visit on 18 June 2009, a combined force of the central government's paramilitary and West Bengal's police made a move to reclaim the Lalgarh area. The Maoists and People's Committee workers, having made their point, withdrew from Lalgarh town into nearby forests and village strongholds. Intead of simply reclaiming territory and trying to make good the administration's lapses in development, West Bengal's government permitted a full-scale attack reminiscent of November 2008. Within days and weeks, while several People's Committee leaders and supporters were expectedly arrested, including People's Committe leader Mahato, or killed by police, paramilitary and CPI (M) goon squads, several villagers were, as earlier, arrested, questioned, threatened, and tortured. Several of them simply disappeared. Maoists engaged in guerilla-style battles, scoring a few victories and regularly taking losses.

Meanwhile, Mamata variously voiced her support for, and criticism of, the Maoists and People's Committee—it didn't seem to matter to her that the stances she took were often contradictory. The only constant remained realpolitik considerations and her rigid animosity towards West Bengal's rulers at the time. Even after the People's Committee and their Maoist mentors lost massive popular support when, in May 2010, some rogue People's Committee leaders and cadres caused the derailment of a goods train, causing a passenger train, the Jnaneshwari Express, to crash into it, killing 150 people and injuring several hundred more, Mamata—who was at the time India's railways minister as part of the United Progressive Alliance coalition— diffused blame. She actually addressed a political meeting in Lalgarh on 9 August, barely three months after the train wreck, a guerrilla-style visit with the tacit support of the People's Committee and local Maoist leadership, and again tore into Bhattacharjee's government. That was still the main event for

Mamata: nothing mattered except to unseat the Left Front, with any play at hand.

I was back in the jungles around Lalgarh during that summer. I was alone this time, and journeying low-key. After arriving in Kolkata I made sure to travel by 'local train', the commuter transport and economic lifeline that connects the stations of Kolkata and Howrah with a web of towns and villages to nearly all points of the compasss, on some routes a link of more than 100 kilometres. Trains in the morning bring in vegetable, fruit, flower and fish-sellers and a throng of blue- and white-collar workers, students, even beggars. The evening trains take home the 3 million and more 'daily' passengers. I rode out with them, one among several thousand that stampeded cursing, wailing, across the cavernous and utterly chaotic station; railway authorites had announced a change of platform just minutes before a 'galloping local'—a relatively fast train that skipped intermediate stations—was to leave for Kharagpur. I spent the night at a seedy hotel not far from Kharagpur station.

The following morning, after a short bus ride to Medinipur, I ran the security gauntlet by blending in as a local, riding in on the rooftop of a battered, overcrowded bus to Jhargram as so many villagers did, alighting at a predetermined hamlet from where, after a tense rendezvous at a tiny chā shop, my contacts whisked me into the 'jongōl', forest. In the villages things were even worse off from a year earlier. The dirt-poor residents were even more cut off, under pressure and scared. In the absence of state-run facilities, the ragged but still-functional People's Committee had organized a few works such as building packed earth roads, minor irrigation and excavating ponds. It maintained health centres that the paramilitary and police disrupted by destroying or taking away whatever meagre stores of medicine were there.

I moved from mud hut to mud hut and village to village because residents were afraid to invite police ire for harbouring a writer—and outsider. And also because no household could afford to feed me more than once—even a battered aluminium plateful of boiled rice and smidgen of dal; or puffed rice soaked with water to trick the belly into submission—the better-off among them would add a spoonful of sugar to go with it. It was their usual economic state: when the rice harvest ran out in three to six months, villagers would try to gather sāl leaf—shāl pātā—from the forest to weave into plates. A thousand plates fetched seventy to eighty rupees.

Everywhere I went there were stories. A village woman raped by the Hārmād. A cowherd beaten to death by the jouthō bāhini, the joint force of the police and paramilitaries, beaten so severely that his bones were pulverized—tulōr mōtō, I was told, his body felt like cotton wool. A boy beaten and sodomized. A girl threatened, and then...

Horrors as usual.

◆

That, then, was the battleground for the Marxists, Mamata and the Maoists. I had absolutely no doubt how things would turn out. General elections to West Bengal's assembly were due in early 2011. With her skilful manoeuvring Mamata played into the hearts and minds of Jongōlmohōl, and at the same time her party's leaders and workers were engaged, in Jongōlmohōl, as in Left Front fortresses across West Bengal, in negotiating a transfer of power from the goon squads of the Left Front—the formally and informally recruited māstān—into the ambit of Mamata's Trinamool Congress. There could be no illusion about how this would be maintained. As I wrote in *Mint* after my second extended visit to the Lalgarh area in 2010, were Trinamool to win assembly elections in 2011, with it grabbing Jongōlmohōl from the Marxist combine, the party could be expected to be as brutal in maintaining a hold as its arch enemies had done since 1977. The Maoists would continue to remain the third force, along with the People's Committee or a new militant faction, to provide Mamata an ally—or, after her victory—an enemy to be used at will right up till her massive electoral victory against the Left Front in May 2011.

That Mamata, the chief minister of West Bengal at the time of writing that particular article, and the Maoists would turn on each other was also a given. Using the anti-CPI (M) upsurge in conjunction with organizations like the People's Committee was always an electoral ploy, not a substitute for on-ground development or salve for festering wounds. After becoming chief minister Mamata intensified operations against the Maoists, who had already become much diminished in this area. It was capped by the killing in November 2011 of Maoist leader Kishenji, the brain behind the upsurge in Lalgarh. On Mamata's watch.

The Maoist rebellion in West Bengal dwindled to nearly nothing, and the 'Bengal model' of combating India's ongoing Maoist rebellion began to be spoken of in security seminars. Most People's Committe leaders remain in jail as I write this; and there they will remain till they are again deemed as politically useful.

◆

There's more.

After her 2011 victory Mamata visited Belpahari, a former hotbed of Maoist activity now in Trinamool's bag. A bus conductor-turned-struggling farmer queried her at a political meeting about her development credentials in a long-neglected area vulnerable to poverty, anger and armed protest.

'Maoist!' Mamata raged in full view of electronic and print media. At the chief minister's prompting, West Bengal Police arrested the man.

A couple of years later, a female college student was abducted, gangraped and killed in Kamduni village, near Barasat, north of Kolkata. According to several media reports, including by *IANS* and *Business Standard*, Mamata blitzed in, and when she was heckled for her government's inability to provide security to citizens, save them from goondas, māstāns, she lost her temper.

'CPI (M) people!' Mamata raged.

As television anchors and their guests raged about rape, Mamata claimed many such incidents were linked to pornography.

There's a method to these seemingly irrational statements and actions. What Mamata did was try to deflect noise and criticism with high decibel noise of her own, in concert with high-voltage development plans for rural areas, as well as keeping 'troublemakers' and protesters in check through the iron hand of the party organization, much of it made up of former CPI (M)-affiliated thugs.

In 2015 she again won West Bengal by a landslide. The Leftist opposition was in disarray, the CPI (M) still vastly discredited. And the assiduously structured sting of the Bharatiya Janata Party, quite the political juggernaut across India, was still mild here, the violent rhetoric and aggressive displays of ultra-nationalism by Hindu grassroots organizations that typically prepare the ground for the party's political upsurge only just visible—though these activities became more cranked up, more visible, as 2017 came around.

Bengal's elected monarchs may rule, but their subjects usually do not forget their transgressions. As and when Mamata Banerjee trips up, it is a certainty she will find out the hard way.

What could follow? Bengal will find out the hard way as it always has.

17

Bānglādésh
Bengalidesh

Carmen Brandt, a professor of South Asian studies at Bonn University in Germany, once acted in a movie that was aimed at contributing to the image makeover of Bangladesh. She was in the country in 2003 as a student of South Asian studies—she had already adopted Bengal as her focus of research—when she heard that Shibly Sadik, a director, was searching for a 'foreign woman with Bengali skills' for a project. With her knowledge of Bānglā she landed the part of Lisa, an American visiting Bangladesh—the bidéshini, foreign lady, in *Bidéshini – From Bangladesh with Love*. She was aware of Bangladesh's image overseas, even in her own country, where people viewed it as a place of poverty, misery, floods, cyclones, displacement and hellish sweatshops that were known to mistreat as a norm and kill through poor safety standards—and little else.

'Thus, I had no problem in becoming an unofficial ambassador for a positive Bangladesh in which I had found many new friends and felt at home,' Brandt wrote a decade later of her experience.

Even as she participated in a project designed to make perceptions of Bangladesh more nuanced and less simplistic she found herself battling reverse stereotyping. She found a sequence in the script objectionable, a dialogue between Lisa and the character of Joy, a Bengali—Bangladeshi—journalist who finds Lisa and a female friend at a gathering at a local shrine, saves them from kidnappers, and then accompanies them on a tour of Bangladesh. After having what Brandt terms a fancy dinner, as Joy and Lisa walk home, they get around to discussing Lisa's family, and the reasons why she has left her wealthy, emotionally distant parents. On their way, Lisa stops at a makeshift shelter for the very poor. While there, Lisa and Joy chat:

Lisa: Beautiful.
Joy: They are very poor.

Lisa: Is there misery in that?
Joy: They have neither home nor house.

Lisa: They have sleep. They can sleep in peace.
Joy: When they cannot get two square meals a day.

Lisa: Nonetheless, they are happy. And I? We have luxury goods all around, we have plentiful food, we have houses in which we can go to sleep. Still...still...there is no end of our burning pain. Why? Why this distance? Why this difference? Today, hundreds of youths and young women of America are taking heroin, are taking marijuana, committing suicide. Why, why, Mr. Joy?

When Brandt flagged this reverse-stereotyping and pointed out the implausibility of such a conversation taking place in Germany, let alone the United States to the director, she claimed he snapped: 'This is my film! When you make your own film you can decide everything.'

Bangladesh's ministries of information, civil aviation and tourism, internal affairs, and culture funded the project. The plot wove in tourism magic. Lisa and Joy travel the country together (at some point they fall in love, fall out of it, and fall back in love again) for more than a month, Lisa is depicted as a rich but open-minded traveller, and Joy—how I wish I had this magical commission—is a young journalist funded by his editor to 'write an article about a rich foreigner's experiences in Bangladesh'.

That 'experience' included beautiful images of places that

quite correctly belong in any promotional material for tourism—Banderban, Comilla, Sylhet, areas around Chittagong, seaside Cox's Bazar, southernmost Teknaf, a mix of natural beauty, history and rolling tea plantations. These images were designed to balance out images of floods, slums and sweatshops. 'Additionally,' relates Brandt, there was music by Rabindranath Tagore, 'for instance "Ō gō bidéshini"—Oh foreign woman—'the showcasing of a folk theatre play in a village, and the Bengali New Year celebrations are obviously meant to represent the cultural richness of this country.'

In the course of their travel, Lisa and Joy encounter problems and misunderstandings that would make Bollywood proud. Her father arrives in Dhaka, and puts the US Embassy on the job to track them down with a mind to take her back home. Everything is finally resolved at Dhaka's chaotic airport, and ends with Lisa staying back in Dhaka with Joy—a standard Bengali dāk-nām elevated here by opportune scripting. The father had tried to buy him off with a million dollars but received in turn a sermon about how a meaningful life matters more in Bangladesh than money. The father, played by a Dutch expatriate, departs with this farewell: 'God bless you, Bangladesh!'

The movie didn't get its overseas play, but has regularly been broadcast on several television channels in Bangladesh since its release in 2005, evidently aimed at a happier, more self-confident country.

That takes a lot more than a movie.

◆

Bangladesh is a project, Bengali and otherwise, in every sense of the term. And it literally began with reshaping history.

The historian Willem van Schendel, who has written a go-to book on Bangladesh's history, places the post-1971 construction lucidly. 'The sense of history that now dominated was fiercely nationalistic. It focused on how the people of the delta had been victimized by British imperialists, Hindu landlords and West

Pakistani usurpers and how their struggles had finally led to their emancipation as a recognized and independent nation. It was a story of political activism and democratic motivation. A national narrative of the delta was constructed to give meaning and legitimacy to the new state.' ('Delta' is less wordy than 'present-day Bangladesh' or 'former East Pakistan' I am sometimes compelled to use to avoid confusion for those not familiar with Bangladesh.)

Partition was jettisoned as a 'focal narrative'. It was no longer relevant, as pre-1971 Pakistan and its birth was now the unsavoury past. It was also a break from the Indian narrative—and, perhaps, the Bengali narrative that includes West Bengal—for exactly the same reason. Indeed, even as he writes of it in his otherwise excellent primer that is recommended for the young student and the first-degree curious alike, van Schendel soft pedals the violence of those times in relation to the 'delta', even placing the onus of the split of Bengal into what would ultimately become West Bengal and East Pakistan on 'Hindu communalists' who were determined to not live in Pakistan.

van Schendel's observations on Bangladesh's creation myths and realities, though, are quite impeccable. 'In both India and Pakistan the Partition of 1947 remains the pivot of national consciousness and the bedrock of nationalist historical understanding,' he observes. 'In Bangladesh it has been resolutely displaced by the events of 1971.' Thus colonialism in the Bangladeshi context ended in 1971, not 1947 as in the Indian and Pakistani telling. As 1947 legitimizes the state for India and Pakistan, 1971 legitimizes the state for Bangladesh. And with it arrived the responsibilities for this largest homeland of the Bengalis.

◆

There are disquieting goings-on in Bangladesh, the country with which India shares its longest international border. In a manner similar to India where many observers believe self-righteous politics increased the chances of a hardline Hindu future, a wave of such politics in Bangladesh may be inviting a hardline Islamist future. This, of course, stems from the idea that such futures are divisive and hence of little good to countries overburdened with histories of divisiveness.

This assumes significance with the growing resentment in extremist and even in some moderate enclaves of opinion in Bangladesh about the pogrom-like mistreatment of the Rohingyas, who practise Islam, by ultra-nationalist elements in adjacent Myanmar—sometimes led by Buddhist clergy. It is close enough, geographically and emotionally, to singe vulnerable pockets in far-eastern India (as I have said elsewhere in the book, what I believe is a more appropriate term for Northeast India) and elsewhere. Sometimes the mistreatment of Mussulmans in India also acts as a catalyst for Islamist unhappiness in Bangladesh.

There are other reasons for concern. Since 2013, there has been an outpouring of sentiment damning schools of hardline Islamism and several of its leaders for being complicit in killings and atrocities against fellow Bengalis—in the 1971 war. For some the festering wounds from that time will only heal when these génocidaires are exposed and punished—executed if need be—after decades of roaming free through administrations that overlooked their sins because it was politically convenient. Others saw it as an attack on their religion and their leaders, because politicians, specifically of the Awami League, designed it to be so.

Massive protests broke out in Dhaka in February 2013 when Abdul Quader Mollah, a top leader of Jamaat-e-Islami Bangladesh, was sentenced to life imprisonment by a tribunal set up to judge pro-Pakistan war crimes; the anticipated sentence was death. The country's liberals, through columns and, significantly, blogs, snowballed liberal resentment into a massive public protest, called the Shahbag Movement after the place in Dhaka where it was centred, just north of Dhaka University in the old—and still, the symbolic and political—heart of capital. For them 'life' was too good for such 'war criminals'.

Militant Islamists, students and others, struck back violently. Rioting and killing resumed after another leader was given the death sentence. More radical Islamist violence erupted that year in May when Héfájat-é-Islam, a relatively new coalition of hardline organizations, led a protest of thousands in Dhaka and elsewhere, demanding stricter laws based on Shari'a. The sentencing for life that year in July of former Jamaat leader Gholam Azam, ninety years old at the time, was another trigger. A month later, Bangladesh's high court cancelled the registration of Jamaat, because of its demand to implement Shari'a law—deemed as contrary to the country's secular constitution. It only intensified protest by hardline Islamists. In September, Mollah's life sentence was converted to a sentence of death for war crimes. He was hanged that December.

Bangladesh remained on the edge of an abyss, buffeted by highly emotive positions—the extremism of liberals and the extremism of extremists.

That abyss was evident even three years later. There was a curious advisory in early January 2016, hosted on the Facebook page of a Dhaka-based security services firm, Elite Force. 'Be safe and very vigilant,' it cautioned, stressing content over grammar. 'Keep track on news, but don't let silly rumours panic you. Take care.'

Reminiscent of the upheaval during much of 2013, the country was locked down on account of a strike called by Bangladesh Jamaat-e-Islami. The radical organization was protesting the confirmation by Bangladesh's Supreme Court on 6 January 2016 of the death penalty given to a Jamaat leader, Motiur Rahman Nizami. He stood convicted of counselling the killing of several hundred innocents during the war of 1971, in particular the massacre of intellectuals towards its end. Nizami was at the time chief of the Al Badr Bāhini, a militia which variously seconded Pakistan's army in arrest, torture and genocide. Nizami had also been a minister in a BNP-led government between 2001 and 2006.

And the Jamaat was still livid in 2016; the previous November, its leader Ali Ahsan Mohammad Mojaheed was executed for war crimes. I was in Bangladesh at the time. Tension was palpable. Social networking services largely accessed through mobile phones such as Whatsapp, Viber and Facebook were for several weeks blocked by the government. Of course, citizens and visitors like me, took the cue from helpful Bangladeshis, and immediately went on to so-called rogue internet servers to bypass the stricture, but the government's communications strictures did acknowledge the threat perception of radical Islamists that citizens, some more than others, lived with daily.

Radicalism had begun a visible upward curve from 2010, when Sheikh Hasina's government constituted a war crimes tribunal for 1971. The Shahbag protests and radical Islamist reaction to it in 2013 had meanwhile unleashed a disturbing reality in Bangladesh—regular attacks on journalists, bloggers—in particular a sub-species that is endangered in Bangladesh as I write this: the 'secular' blogger—publishers, academicians, priests and foreigners as they went about their business or leisure. They were variously knifed, attacked with the machete-like dā, swords, cleavers, their throats slit, bodies hacked.

While most attacks took place in Dhaka, the terror touched Sylhet, Rajshahi, Pabna, Madaripur, Satkhira, Banderban. Even if these deaths were a relatively isolated several dozen in a country of nearly 160 million, they were each of them shocking for their brazenness, brutality and, more often than not for the prompt and righteous claim of responsibility in the name of Islam by shadowy groups that counted among them radicalized seminary students and seemingly ordinary white-collar citizenry. Occasionally, the matters were hyped when those claiming responsibility spoke on behalf of the so-called Islamic State or Daesh, or those who claim inspiration from that monstrous non-Islam that deals death with savagery reminiscent of Rwanda and Kosovo.

The apex of this cycle of violence would arrive on 1 July 2016 when six young Bangladeshi men, from a range of backgrounds from frugal to well-to-do, with great precision and calm attacked a fashionable eatery in the northern Gulshan neighbourhood of Dhaka, also a diplomatic and expatriate hub. In a saga played out over live television across much of the world, the six released hostages who they judged to be either Bangladeshi or adequately proficient in Islam, and during a stand-off with elite security forces, slaughtered twenty-one women and men hostages, most of them foreigners. Five of the six terrotists were killed.

It was the country's London, Paris, Madrid, Bali and Mumbai moment, reminiscent of terror attacks in those places that have come to define, and redefine this millennium. Dhaka had joined the club. Bangladesh, troubled as it was by attacks of the previous years that had placed it firmly into what I like to call South Asia's ring of fire, was shell-shocked.

◆

As we know, those belonging to the Awami League suffered greatly in 1971. Sheikh Hasina personally suffered, soon after, in 1975, as an army-backed coup killed her father and Bangladesh's first premier, Sheikh Mujib, and much of her family, as a reaction to administrative chaos and the absolutism of Mujib as much as anything else.

In a few short years Mujib had gone in the eyes of many from demigod to seemingly delirious with power. A country ravaged by war, poverty and still-lingering effects of natural disaster of the pre-war year and its consequences, and immediately thereafter a victim of a great disorder from scarcity and black-marketeering, appeared to be ripe for order, for control. It came in patches, subsidized by massive foreign aid—and, as Mujib's detractors had it, the overwhelming influence of India.

Governance began to be built on personal whims and loyalty. Great suspicion from the war led to freedom fighters and associates being appointed to prime civil and military positions. The post-colonial practice of the old bureaucratic, law and order and military establishment becoming the new establishment was jostled, contributing to administrative dislocation and resentment of the dispossessed. Meanwhile, Mujib commissioned what, for all purposes, became his personal guard, owing personal loyalty to him—and leveraging that power to do his will and whatever will enforced by these enforcers after the initial task of trying to bring order to social and economic chaos—the hoarding, the black-marketeering—began to to be addressed. The Jātiyō Rōkkhi Bāhini became the nation's stormtroopers—and came to be seen by many as defending Mujib more than being the national defence force. (I heard whispers in Kushtia that the cinema built by my grandfather, Kanu-babu, for the mill community and Kushtia-at-large, on some days became an interrogation centre, carrying on the tradition of their Pakistani predecessors in 1971.)

Manufacturing and trading were mostly nationalized, sapping entrepreneurial spirit that would, for all the criticism and accusations of corruption directed at them, be revived by subsequent governments.

Then in the middle of such chaos, in 1974, arrived a famine that killed tens of thousands of citizens, driven to a corner by floods and mismanagement of economic activity and faltering supplies. Meanwhile, since 1972 a left-wing insurgency had taken root, targeting Awami League members and even police. It added to the dislocation of governance.

In January 1975, a beleaguered Mujib took what would for him be the ultimate step. His government amended the constitution to grant him absolutist presidency for five years. In February, Mujib made Bangladesh a one-party state. In this dictatorship only the Bangladesh Krishok Shrōmik Awami League, a renaming of Awami League to encompass farmers and workers, was permitted. BAKSAL, as it came to be called, was a last ditch battle for control of dystopia.

By August he would be assassinated in his residence in Dhanmondi, now a national shrine, along with most of his family—many other relatives and familiars would also be killed, as would some of Awami League's remaining leadership later that year, while in jail. Sheikh Hasina was among those who escaped. She was then in Germany with her sister, Sheikh Rehana. (They were subsequently flown to India by the government of India, where Sheikh Hasina lived till 1981, when she returned to Bangladesh.)

◆

There was no doubt in anybody's mind, least of all Sheikh Hasina's that if she ever had the power to do she would find closure for 1975. Whatever else they say of her, few doubt her courage. I recall a meeting with her in mid-1994, when her political nemesis, Khaleda Zia was in government and, after the initial years of begum-bonhomie were over, had marked each other out as arch enemies. There was also that other nemesis, the Jamaat, once-collaborators with Pakistan, now partners of the BNP government. It was hardly something to make Sheikh Hasina retreat into a corner and cower. As leader of the opposition she was out there and in-their-face. We met at her residence for an interview.

What are you trying to achieve, I asked her as we chatted, mostly in Bāṅglā in preliminary conversation before switching to an easy mixture of Bāṅglā and English once the interview began. An ornate table lay between us, and a large portrait in oil of her father behind her.

'Democracy doesn't seem to have gone very far in this country,' she said, unmindful of ironies. 'We want true democracy in Bangladesh.'

She spoke for a while about nation-building before snapping back to the core of my query. 'Before the last elections, Khaleda Zia and Gholam Azam sat down and discussed seat sharing. This helped the Jamaat move ahead.'

'Do you find it ironical that the Jamaat, which was accused of betraying Bangladesh...'

'...is now accusing others of betrayal,' she shot back. 'This is our fate.'

But reviving the spectre of 1971, as morally justified as it may be, only came towards the end of a cycle of electoral tenure for the ruling Awami League government led by Sheikh Hasina. Elections were due in January 2014. The slew of verdicts by a court that some human rights and judicial observers felt was keener on a verdict than on a trial, earned radicals the propaganda leverage of a vendetta; they accused Hasina and the Awami League of using the trials to give her party an electoral boost. (She was hoping to repeat the performance in late 2008 when the Awami League swept to power, winning 230 of 300 seats in parliament. The BNP won a paltry 30, Jamaat a minuscule 2.) As it turned out the opposition boycotted the elections in 2014. Hasina went right ahead, and won practically unopposed. She and her party would now run Bangladesh until the elections of 2019.

But the Awami League's victory needs to be interpreted correctly. It cannot be assumed that the battle against religious fundamentalism had made great strides forward. Being steamrolled at elections is never a perennial guarantee against radicalism, merely an indication against incumbency. (In neighbouring India, the centre-right Bharatiya Janata Party, with all its religious excesses accumulated since the late 1980s, made great gains in the parliamentary elections of 1996, steamrolled the so-called secular opposition in a rapid series of general elections in 1998 and 1999; was steamrolled out of power in 2004, and steamrolled right back to power in 2014.)

The government of Sheikh Hasina and her supporters in media, in Bangladesh and well as a few vociferous ones in Indian Banglasphere have been quick to distance the toxic stamp of Islamic State from the attacks, claiming these to be of a toxic stamp of domestic origin—worrisome by any account—and of a provenance that brought accusations disturbingly close to the Awami League's arch foes, BNP and the Jamaat. Sheikh Hasina's government has since gone flat out to reel back the advantage and her credibility, by hunting down terrorists in the dens, sometimes in Dhaka, sometimes in Chittagong and elsewhere, small cells that fight to the death or sometimes even blow themselves up en famile, as it were. It was really a siege against all that Bangladesh and its implicit and self-professed liberal traditions that the average Bangladeshi professes, and holds dear.

◆

Some portray what is going on in Bangladesh as a fight of good against evil, in which Sheikh Hasina and her party are portrayed as being on the side of the angels, for development and progress as opposed to a more conservative Islamist conglomerate that threatens to drag Bangladesh back to the Dark Ages. I recall a meeting around that time in Dhaka—naturally, over a memorable luncheon even in stressed times—with a young Bangladeshi businessman with excellent connections to Sheikh Hasina's office, and quite often a conduit for meetings in the space of negotiations that diplomats and political analysts are fond of calling Track Two. He went as far as to tell me, 'We keep telling you (India) we need ten more years. We'll finish them off.' He meant: Islamist radicals; and it was a plea to help Bangladesh secure India. As an Awami League loyalist he also partly meant—finish off opposition to Sheikh Hasina.

But for all the talk about good versus evil, as I have maintained for some years, we may also need to recognize a shift that, for the generations radicalized since the war, sentencing their leadership for past crimes, even heinous ones, amounts today to sentencing Islam. This momentum, fed with radical overtures and investment in conservatism from West Asian autocracies, will continue to impact Bangladesh.

◆

This brings with it a bizarre mix of insistent democracy and Islam's pre-eminence over democratic norms in the same breath, a condition Bangladesh has lived with since its birth.

I recall a meeting in Dhaka with Gholam Azam in 1994 when he was the chief of the Jamaat.

It was also a time when the Jamaat was pressing its election ally BNP to give it more prominence, make it more powerful than ever; if its demand was not met, it would continue to boycott parliament as a show of anger for an alliance turned sour. The Jamaat was then part of Islami Oikyo Jote, a conglomerate of radical Islamist parties. And it was a finely-tuned pressure tactic, not a bludgeon that most would associate with people who were about as extremist as such people could be in the 1990s—in the days before the radical supremacy of Al Qaeda and its millennial, more maniacal cousin Daesh, or Islamic State of Iraq and the Levant.

What Azam—who like many associated with excesses during Liberation returned to Bangladesh after Mujib's assassination—told me then appears as revealing and portentous now.

'There is no time limit in politics, but even here the Quran provides guidance,' Azam said to me when we met in his office. 'It says: if there are people capable of bringing victory to Islam, then it will provide that strength. Only Allah can give that strength, and our orders come from Allah. The Jamaat, our student league [Islamic Chhātrō Shibir—colloquially just Shibir, and also greatly marked for pro-Pakistan excesses in 1971 as well as horrific, relatively recent attacks against "secular" bloggers] and other Islamic organizations are working towards that goal, and when we have done our work Allah will help us.'

Before I could intervene he carried on in a rush. 'See, we are in every country. In some places we are allowed to work openly, in others we are forced underground. But there is no Muslim country in the world where there isn't an Islamic movement.'

'Do you believe in democracy?' I asked.

'Yes, we do,' Azam replied. 'We are part of a democracy. But Allah's code is not under a democracy. Democracy is under Allah's code.'

His confidence was breathtaking. This was a man who just two years earlier in 1992, after a popular movement had branded Azam a war criminal for taking Pakistan's side in politics and committing genocide against his own people, had had his citizenship revoked and was placed in detention, when a pro-Islamist BNP had given in to massive public protest to avert a crisis of its government. But by July 1993 Azam was released after a bench of the Supreme Court found him not guilty. Sources close to the attorney general's office told me that government lawyers were 'not provided with enough ammunition'. This apparent going easy on an ally by the BNP merely increased the Jamaat's ambition. Jamaat was already looking to exploit the situation by trying to introduce a discussion on the Blasphemy Act which, among other things, sought to increase a two-year term of imprisonment for blaspheming to life in prison, or death.

Azam and I moved on to a discussion on the strength of the Islamists.

'We concentrate on people's hearts, minds and characters,' he explained, as if he was conducting a tutorial. 'We study these aspects and we appeal to people's logic. We focus on building sincerity. That is why our people don't change allegiance, the way it happens with other political parties.'

'Here and elsewhere people get nervous when Islamic groups start a political movement,' I interjected, 'people get nervous with strong Islamist groups—'

'Maybe it's because they don't believe in Islam's precepts,' Azam replied. 'And also because if we win, they will lose strength, they will be out of power.'

I had then asked the de rigeur Taslima question. 'Has the Taslima Nasrin issue helped you, moved your plans along a lot more quickly?'

He neatly turned it around. 'The issue is not our creation. It has been made into an issue. Anyway, the issue isn't Taslima. It's about people like her who insult Islam.'

'Surely,' I pressed, 'you have used it to further your cause?'

'No comment.'

◆

Gholam Azam didn't need to elaborate. It was all out there for anyone who cared to see it. Nasrin had greatly upset the conservative corner with *Lojjā*, her breakout book of 1993 that was a statement on minority Hindus in Bangladesh being at the receiving end of the structured ire and manufactured hatred of Islamic fundamentalists after the destruction of the Babri Masjid in India by Hindu fundamentalists—who also structured ire and manufactured hatred. Initially published in Bangla, her book was quickly banned by the Bangladesh government after an uproar. Those were times when in Bangladesh Islamism began to be equated with nationalism, quite the mirror to India, where a revivalist Hinduism—the precursor of the Hindu ultra-nationalism of present-day India—led to the Babri Masjid incident, and a series of riots in many parts of India, including West Bengal.

Much like liberals across religions and atheists in India who took a strong stand against depredations catalysed by the Babri Masjid demolition, and were thereafter marked as 'pseudo-secularist' by the Hindu religious right and subsequent ultra-nationalists, Nasrin was attacked by Islamic fundamentalists. *Lojja*—shame—was banned on the grotesquely ironical charge of disturbing communal harmony.

A year later Nasrin, a qualified doctor and practising gynaecologist for some time, and self-confessed atheist, was declared a pariah by her homeland when she questioned the validity of Shari'a, the hard-coded Islamic law which the ultra-conservative wanted imposed. In her own words:

> In 1994 a newspaper in Calcutta published an interview with me, where I said that the Shari'a should be abolished. Unfortunately, the newspaper misquoted me as saying that I thought 'the Qur'an should be revised thoroughly'. But as I do not believe in the Qur'an, there is no reason for me to say it should be revised. I think the Qur'an is, like all religious scriptures, out of place and out of time, totally irrelevant for our era. Nothing will be gained by reforming the Qur'an;

instead, what is needed is a uniform civil code of laws that is not based on religious dogmas, and that is equally applicable to men and women.

The Taslima fracas—the writer had left Bangladesh by the time Azam and I met, embarked on a life of exile aided by a global cooperative that helps writers at risk—was arguably Jamaat's most high profile success. In an in-your-face, even brilliant, move, the Jamaat managed to reverse the pro-Pakistan, anti-Bangladesh image it had been tagged with; after Taslima, those who were against Islam were anti-Bangladesh, anti-national, a difficult to refute argument as Islam has been the state religion of Bangladesh since 1978.

◆

The question is not, and never was, what Taslima Nasrin wants, though outside Bangladesh it sometimes appeared to be that way. It was more the beginning of collective soul-searching by the country as it tried to reconcile a declared liberalism with the evident conservatism that was gaining ground everywhere, in attitudes from the wrenchingly mundane to the cynically grandstanding.

◆

At the point where the city limits of Dhaka begin to give way to the wetlands that envelop much of Bangladesh, I met Maulana Azizul Haq to try and get a handle on the Islamist rage that was sweeping the country.

When I met him, Haq was leader of the Islamic Oikyo Jote. Haq's place of work and worship was at a significant madrasa in the Shāt Mōsjid or Seven Mosques area. Nearly every wall in the vicinity prominently displayed graffiti, a message from Haq and his colleagues. 'Toshlimā Nāshrin-ké phnāshi dāō.' Hang Taslima.

'We believe in the precepts of Islam, and their preservation,' Haq said after I explained the purpose of my visit. 'That is our mission.'

We conversed in Bānglā, but he used the word 'mission' in

English. He leaned back into his chair and gently delivered the punch line. 'Bangladesh is almost 90 per cent Mussulman. It should be the country's mission as well.'

He leaned forward. 'Shétā-i theek noy ki?'

I told him I wasn't sure if it was correct, but it seemed logical. Surely though, Islam should be able to coexist with other religions. Were Taslima's suggestions all bad?

'No. But she insulted Islam. Nobody has the right to do that. We have asked for her death according to Islamic law. It doesn't matter where she is, she has committed the gravest sin.'

Can't Islam forgive?

'Yes, if she repents.'

As I took my leave I couldn't resist a cheeky farewell. 'Bangladesh jindābād.'

He shot right back. 'Bangladesh jindābād.'

◆

May Bangladesh live long.

I couldn't help thinking at the time: many would say Bangladesh hadn't really had a chance to live, a mere twenty-three years on from a bloody and chaotic independence following in the unlovely footsteps of its estranged parents, first India and then Pakistan. It was still so much a land of suppressed rage and a desperate tranquillity. Every time it took a step forward it appeared as if it took more than a couple of steps back, torn apart by chicanery and circumstance rather than being driven by goals—though it had always begun with noble goals.

It wasn't uncanny logic. It married a very Bengali tendency to strain against yokes to a very Bangladeshi need to define and redefine the very purpose of breaking free twice over.

◆

'The whole point of freedom was freedom,' Asad Chowdhury put it so simply, so eloquently.

A leading poet, Chowdhury was also deputy director at Bangla Academy in Dhaka when we met; he later became its director. Bangla Academy is the country's creaky but nevertheless loved repository of Bānglā and Bengali culture. The reason why Bangladesh fought the war with Pakistan was to preserve a language, a culture, a people, an identity, focused in part through Sheikh Mujib, but almost entirely through a common desire for a land for the Bāngāli people, a shōnar or golden Bānglā, that you know as the central theme of what became the national anthem.

'We also fought for a land where everyone would be able to hold up their heads; and people from all religions and walks of life would be equal.' Chowdhury waved his hand to take in several hundred people gathered outdoors at the Academy on the occasion of Rabindranath's birth anniversary.

A land of peace. A land with a majority Mussulman population, certainly, but not a land of bigots.

Looking around, seeing people, several visibly, devout Mussulman, listening to a lecture on the relevance of Rabindranath's writings and songs in the present day and, later, seeing several of them move to the lilting tunes of Rōbindrōshōngeet—indeed, among the most revered modern-day singers of the form is Bangladesh's Rezwana Choudhury—it was difficult to disbelieve Asad-shāhéb.

Shamshul Haq, an elderly man in the flowing beard and skullcap of the conservative Mussulman, whose attention never strayed from the stage, had no time for superlatives over the bouquet of culture.

'This is life,' is all he would say to me in fluent English. 'Tagore wrote about life.' He used the anglicized 'Tagore', not the traditional Bānglā 'Thākur' as Rabindranath's surname, as we spoke in English, his language of choice after I introduced myself as an editor with an English-language publication.

There was Kamaluzzaman, a student of history at nearby Dhaka University, who lit up a Benson & Hedges cigarette and spoke about 'Rōbindrōnath Thākur'—we conversed in Bānglā. And, almost in the same breath, breezily insisted, prodded by my wisecrack about Bengal and Bangladesh being a confounding mix of the liberally fundamentalist and the fundamentally liberal, that 'liberal fundamentalism', somewhat like in Malaysia, was a viable socio-political option for Bangladesh. A country where Pohélā-Bōishākh, the Bengali New Year is celebrated each April with fervour and colour, where numerous less conservative Mussulman women dress in shāri and wear teep—the bindi associated with Hindu tradition—to spontanesouly celebrate alongside men a culturally unifying festival of harvest and renewal. And a country where their sisters are often encouraged to remain out of sight, celebrate only what is deemed by scripture.

◆

I've yet to hear of a better description for Bangladesh—liberal fundamentalism—I thought then as I did so many years later, well into the second decade of this millennium, as I wandered along the lanes by the shrine of one of Bangladesh's most revered saints, Hazrat Shah Jalal, who now also lends his name to Dhaka's international airport so that lesser mortals—well-wishers of a Zia who had claimed it for a time, and perhaps in time well-wishers of more than one Sheikh—aren't able to squabble over who should claim the name to the country's preeminent international gateway. Shah Jalal brought Islam through sword and Sufism to northern Bengal, and established its heart there, one that flourished for centuries, hidden in plain sight, and spread outwards, southwards across the delta and emerged full blown when it was time for a reckoning of religions six hundred years after his death in 1346.

The way to his shrine in Sylhet is through a crowded lane ornamented with numerous eateries, hotels, shops selling offerings to the saint—rosewater, flowers, candles—and souvenir shops that sell the region's famous teas and pickles, shawls and 'Pakistani three-piece' dress ensembles. To get to the shrine you walk past the spotlessly clean courtyard beyond the East Gate, lined with a few khéjur trees to the left, by the large mosque, and an open area to the right that leads past a spot where several hundred pigeons are fed, to the pond where the faithful wash before prayer. Onward past the mosque, up a few steps and then right, through a narrow passage, and then right again, to reach the mājār shōrif. The faithful, prayerful and the penitent crowd the grave of the saint, cover it in marigold blooms and garlands, a sprinkling of rose and hibiscus— the lush blood-red hibiscus, roktōjobā.

Some among the devout sway as they pray, some stand still with fixed stares, or eyes closed to the world around them. It's a place to open hearts and minds, to open doors. Except one that remains shut: the room that houses Shah Jalal's personal weapons, the ones the warrior saint whose ancestry is claimed by both Turkey and Yemen, used besides Islam to firmly bring Allah to Bengal.

Not far from his shrine, and not far from the Holy Gate Hotel where I stayed at the end of the lane from the dargah entrance that joins the busy Hazrat Shah Jalal Road, on the way to the Surma River, you would perhaps stop by the modest Nazrul Academy, where in the evening his songs of romance and rebellion are taught and sung by Mussulmans and Hindus alike. And to both, Nōjrul-giti exponents like Feroza Begum have exalted status, the same as she does across Banglasphere. Perhaps patrons will treat you to a cup of gurér chā as one offered me, and a discussion of the possibility of religious coexistence and the daily coexistence of peace and a violence driven by those who use religion to settle scores and expand business prospects.

Not far from here you might pass the London Mansion and Guesthouse, and a cluster of shops selling the memorabilia of football clubs of those other Sylhets: Chelsea, Manchester United, Arsenal, Liverpool. You might see a young man at a clothing store that plays old songs by the popstar Runa Laila (Sylhet's very own who once held sway in both wings of Pakistan, Bangladesh, and briefly carried her fame even to India), carrying a bag that advertises a mobile telephone company, wearing a cap of the Mussulman devout, and a T-shirt decorated with a green seven-pointed leaf that proclaims: *My Secret Is That I Am Always High.*

It's all here. All at once.

18

Pōrshu
The day after tomorrow

India has for long viewed the borderlands along Bangladesh, in West Bengal, Assam, Meghalaya, Tripura and Mizoram—and the eastern hinterlands of Manipur and Nagaland, as a troubled part of the country, politically, socially and economically. It isn't any easier for Bangladesh, this karmic loop of natural and man-made realities and fault lines.

Migration is one such—a defining characteristic.

Besides the obvious but increasingly crowded destination of West Bengal, Assam has from the time of Partition remained a migration hotspot. Vestiges of the political manoeuvering that led to its inclusion in the Republic of India instead of what was then East Pakistan (and is today Bangladesh) have remained. Indeed, ethno-religious dynamics have shaped the discourse in Assam against non-Assamese such as Bengalis in general and Bengali Mussulmans in particular, carrying as they do the implicit suspicion of being migrant, legal and illegal, from the territory that is now Bangladesh. Such discourse has spread to other areas of far-eastern India, Tripura and Meghalaya in particular, and today fuels emotion in Nagaland, Manipur and Mizoram. Whatever its ethnic and religious colouring, the issue goes beyond the realm of religion—Hinduism, Islam, Christianity, tribal animistic beliefs—to the equally real world of migration.

West Bengal has absorbed a series of enormous migratory hits of Bengalis. But, as we have seen, Tripura and parts of Assam—at the time of Partition Assam included Meghalaya, which became a separate state in 1972—were also inundated by the influx of largely Bengali Hindu migrants from across the border in two well-known waves: one around the time of the Partition and later during the Bangladesh war in 1971. There is the lesser-known wave of 1964, when riots were triggered in Bangladesh in retaliation over rumours of the loss of a hair of Prophet Muhammad at the Hazratbal shrine, in faraway Kashmir. Besides the slaughter of numerous Bengali Hindus, and the flight of tens of thousands of Bengali Hindus, these riots also led to the forced eviction of several tens of thousands of tribal people like the Garos and Hajongs from north Bengal (at the time, northern East Pakistan), who were caught up in the rage of Islamists. There have been other smaller waves of migration as well.

◆

Among other things, as we know, migration transformed Tripura from an overwhelmingly not-Bengali and tribal entity into an overwhelmingly Bengali Hindu one—about 70 per cent Bengali—bringing with it a diminishing of the indigenous populations. In Tripura, the government, administration, trade, discourse and language began to turn Bengali from 1946 onwards, irrevocably propelled by politics, pogrom and geopolitics in the Bengal delta. It surprised few when such pressure eventually spawned a string of armed movements by Tripuris that began in the late 1970s and ran well into the first decade of this millennium. As you know from an earlier reference in this book outright dislike for Bengali settlers, mostly Hindus but some extremely poor Mussulmans too, drove such movements.

In Assam, too, such migration has never sat comfortably. The Miāns, the Bengali Mussulmans, Bangladeshi (and, earlier, East Pakistani) immigrants, both legal and illegal, bear the brunt of ire in Assam's incendiary politics, but the Bengali in general isn't in any case an overly welcome ethnicity in those parts, as we saw with Bongal Kheda and language issues in Cachar.

Over the years, migration caused by religious discord has

reduced, giving way to migration for livelihood. It is a matter of record that several politicians in far-eastern India, particularly Assam, have wooed immigrant populations to ramp up electoral support, over the years transforming illegal migration into legal by applying the Indian practice of 'regularizing' an illegality by administrative and legislative fiat for a range of things from illegal construction to zoning. Resentment accruing from such political manipulation has often exploded into chaos—the Nellie Massacre in Assam in 1983 that killed several hundred Bengali Mussulman men, women and children was only the most infamous of such incidents—and has spawned emphatic student movements and armed rebellions. Trouble between indigenous Bodos and immigrant Mussulmans in the Bodo Territorial Council-administered districts of Kokrajhar, Chirang, Baksa and Udalguri in Assam, are no longer rare phenomena. Several hundred have died as a result of inter-ethnic butchery. The pressure on land and the need for protecting indigenous identities and futures means that it is unlikely to stop if long term solutions are not provided.

Those who would dismiss the issue of migration need to keep in mind that almost without exception across far-eastern India, people are wary and even frankly resentful and suspicious of migration from what is often called Mainland India, leave alone Bangladesh. Forced migration caused by the nineteenth-century colonial practice of bringing plantation workers into Assam from eastern India and the twentieth century influx of traders and low-end workers that continues to the present day causes enough local heartburn to fuel strong rhetoric and violence.

The concern is real, and goes beyond religion. Let me share just one of several examples. I was part of a panel at a gathering in New Delhi in late 2014 for what was described as the diaspora from India's eight far-eastern states to share ideas for conflict resolution and development. Senior ministers and India's national security adviser attended a few sessions. When talk came to acting upon India's so-called Look East Policy that sought better relations with

Southeast Asia using the conduit, the bridge, of far-eastern India to integrate the Asian highway system beyond mere numbers on a map to actual travel of goods and people; and the opening up of road, rail and waterway links between India and Bangladesh to enable the movement of goods, services and people between that region of India and the 'Indian mainland', concerns, even tempers, ran high. Talk of diplomacy, trade and development, even a boosting of the economy with ambitious projects (like a localized version of the Delhi-Mumbai Industrial Corridor, billed as the 'Seven Sisters Corridor') was distilled down to one major concern. Would it lead to the greater movement (read migration) of people from Bangladesh into Northeastern India? If so, forget it.

But the migration is not going to stop. Livelihood needs will push this. Importation of religious belief, by virtue of Bangladesh's largely Islamic construct, may be a corollary, but religion has for long stopped being the motive for migration. The fact is that, unless rapid socio-economic transformation overhauls Bangladesh, both Bangladesh and India will be powerless to stem it. The ongoing, patchy exercise to fence India's 4,000 kilometre-plus border with Bangladesh will hardly prove to be a barrier.

In 2009, I had the opportunity to speculate about the future of this region in a position paper for the Kesroli Group, a collective of Indians and citizens of other countries but of Indian origin. They were—are—leaders or acknowledged experts, and promising youngsters, in business, economics, politics and public affairs from a wide spectrum of ideologies, the social sciences, technology, media, and so on. The brief I received was to 'max out' scenarios, projections based on current and logically extended futures—kite-flying, if you will. The purpose was to use best- and worst-case 'scenarios' and throw it open to discussion and circulation in rarified policymaking levels, offer a 'war-gaming' approach with the express purpose to offer solutions, mitigate 'worst-case' to 'manageable-case'. (Besides being presented to a select group of top executives and policymakers in a meeting hosted by the technology firm Infosys Limited, the paper was later published by the Mumbai-based foreign policy think-tank Gateway House and in part by the newsmagazine *OPEN*.)

In retrospect (this was the ancient era of 2009–2010 when head-in-the-sand was practically an official religion!) my take probably cut a bit too close to the bone. But I would stand by its alarm bells—and so has a referee of that paper who subsequently became a minister of substantial reach with the government of India—as long there is no evidence to the contrary, a need to bring the kite home, if you will. The combination of China and India, Bangladesh and India, and the violent ethno-political dynamics of the far-eastern arc of India make for an incendiary historical and geopolitical mix even without adding 'natural' causes—caused by nature and man alike.

What would happen if Bangladesh were to suffer a series of cataclysmic storms and severe inundation of its coastline? Unlike the relatively gentler inward migration forced by a similar inundation of the Indian coastline along the Bay of Bengal, the population pressure of Bangladesh, expected to be more acute than India's for several decades into the twenty-first century, would lead to its citizens literally forcing their way to every other point of the compass to escape the country's vastly vulnerable south. Bangladesh's borders would not be able to contain this migration.

India would be powerless to stem this migration. The steady trickle of migration to West Bengal and the bordering plains regions of Northeast India would turn into a flood. In this migration, livelihood needs—the brutal matter of survival—will surely precede the push of religion (such as riots engineered for political gain, and less cynical but equally dangerous religious extremism). There might even be the somewhat ironical instance of Bengali Mussulman migrants to Bengali-majority and Mussulman-majority districts of India bordering Bangladesh—Goalpara, Dhubri, Karimganj and Hailakandi in Assam, for instance, and nearly the entire strip along West Bengal's border—having to compete with ever newer arrivals.

In any case, such a future would turn migration into territorial usurpation. Driven by the influx from present-day Bangladesh,

Kolkata could implode. If this were to happen, the Government of India of the time would be compelled to deploy military along this area. This would be further west from the existing border fencing along India's border with Bangladesh in the territory of West Bengal. Such an eastern Line of Control—a cousin of the Line of Control along India's western border with Pakistan—could form the de facto eastern boundary of India, running north to south roughly from Barauni-Katihar in present-day Bihar and run continuously south along the eastern borders of present-day Bihar, Jharkhand and Odisha, and the mining rich areas west of present-day Bardhaman in West Bengal. This would be additional impetus to secure India's key mining and industrial belts against the influx. Economics as much as security would surely drive this cauterizing.

A scenario like this would hardly be restricted to the east. An influx from present-day Bangladesh into mainland India would certainly be accompanied by further religious radicalization among Hindus—the Bangladeshi 'explosion' would help to coalesce this trend. The Mussulman population elsewhere in India would be victimized.

India's urban spaces would be particularly vulnerable to strife, as it would need to absorb extra millions driven by the force of the migratory explosion. This migratory traffic would also place severe stress on present-day agrarian and rural spaces. Further, driven by the needs of the burgeoning population, there could be a continuing push to extend habitation, farming and industry deeper into what in the present-day context can be termed 'breathing rooms': forested areas.

Equally, to follow through with such an eventuality, India would be unable to prevent the breakdown of the entity collectively known as Northeast India. The states of Meghalaya, the territory of Assam south of the Brahmaputra, and the present-day state of Tripura could entirely be overrun by migrants from Bangladesh. The tribal and local populations of these areas, after a period of resistance, could be dominated by migrants. It is entirely conceivable that, cut off, the territories of Nagaland, Manipur and Mizoram could revert to their micro tribal states, with Myanmar and China dominating this political geography.

And what of the Chittagong Hill Tracts, swamped by Bengalis? What of China, with its eye on the Indian state of Arunachal Pradesh, and northern Myanmar? How much would the migration tip China's hand, and move it to secure its southern borders, even if that means effectively moving that border further south? ...

What of...?

What if...?

◆

And what if it all turns out all right, much of it at any rate? The future, while patchy across Banglasphere, does have some economic and geopolitical bright spots that might help cement some of the fault lines wrought by population pressure, migration and ethnic tension for some years—even some decades if things go well.

In the eastern aspect Hailakandi, of a largely agrarian economy, is among the most underdeveloped and poorest districts of India. Karimganj is largely agrarian too but has made a small push for industrialization. Cachar, also agrarian, is boosted by its tea and timber, and an entrepôt for states like Manipur and Mizoram. Modernizing railways offers better connectivity than before; and a lessening of ethnic conflict to the north and south of Cachar had brought relative stability and greater promise—for Silchar, for instance, as an aviation, railways, roadways and market hub for the region, a commercial waystation for the lower end of far-eastern India and northeastern Bangladesh alike.

That's a long-term bet of radial prosperity. Like many other areas of Assam—which, like West Bengal, ranks lower than India's national average in human development indices—these areas too are still largely driven by administrative development more than growth of industry, as Assam's Human Development Report for 2014 perceptively puts it. All three districts have life expectancies at birth lower than Assam's average of fifty-four years, according to the report—Cachar records the lowest. Except for Cachar, all Bengali-majority districts in Assam record lower than average years in school. Income levels in all these districts are lower than Assam's average. The three eastern districts rank among the lowest in Assam in terms of health. And, in the overall human development index they remain lower than Assam's average. All five Bengali-majority districts remain at the far end of poverty and 'asset-poverty' parameters among the province's twenty-eight districts. To call these places works-in-progress would be true, but would also be an exaggeration. To say that they have remained at the lower end of development priorities in Assam for several decades would not.

◆

Tripura is thus far the brightest spark in this easternmost arc of Banglasphere. Its unique geography, history as well as a go-getting attitude have pushed it to being among the best performing provinces of this region of India—indeed, India—in terms of human development parameters: giving it a large literate pool of human resource, and making it a bridgehead for sub-regional diplomacy and prosperity.

And, in what is surely a great irony, the long-festering sore of a swamping migration of Bengalis has placed this province at the forefront. At a talk in Guwahati in May 2014, I had proposed that, as part of India's Look East Policy (which the incoming Bharatiya Janata Party-led government escalated to 'Act East') and even for benefits that would accrue on account of location, these Indian states ought to boost economic contacts with Bangladesh and Southeast Asia, even establish representative offices in such countries—independently or in association with Indian diplomatic missions.

The suggestion was buoyed in part by what Tripura had already achieved with Bangladesh. I stress Tripura-with-Bangladesh as much as India-with-Bangladesh, because Tripura for all practical purposes has piggybacked on India's foreign policy gains, even contributed to it. Tripura's particular dynamic and restlessness to end its isolation ensured it. It wouldn't any longer remain isolated on account of the quirk of Partition which robbed it off direct access to Kolkata and the rest of India across East Pakistan—and later, Bangladesh.

Natural gas and the natural order of things led to Tripura's attitudinal and policy resurgence. After it was discovered in the 1970s, natural gas is today Tripura's one of two biggest tickets to prosperity. With the commissioning of a major power station in Palatana fuelled by that gas, the state is now able to handle its own power needs and contribute to its neighbouring provinces, and also lessen the need for expensive hydroelectricity projects that bring the attendant misery of displacement. Tripura now exports surplus electricity to Bangladesh—similar to an arrangement Bangladesh has with West Bengal.

India's evolving ties with Bangladesh is, in many ways, Tripura's lifeline. Indo-Bangladeshi relations really took off from 2009 when Sheikh Hasina again assumed the premiership. Bilateral trade more than doubled to $6 billion-plus between the 2009–2010 and 2014–2015 financial years. In 2011, India allowed duty-free access to Bangladeshi goods except for a handful of products. The issue of swapping enclaves (the bizarre reality of a total of 160 enclaves of Indian territory within Bangladesh, and Bangladeshi territory within India) gathered momentum during this time. It culminated in an agreement in May 2015 between the governments of Sheikh Hasina and her Indian counterpart Narendra Modi. India even moved several paces on another tricky issue, that of sharing river waters—as you know the Indian rivers Ganga, Brahmaputra, Teesta and Barak decant into Bangladesh.

Bangladesh, on its part, has massively curtailed sanctuary for rebels from nearby Indian states, most spectacularly with the arrest of several senior leaders of the United Liberation Front of Asom (ULFA)—and their subsequent, mysterious appearance in custody of Indian authorities. Bangladesh permitted the transshipment of equipment for India's premier exploration and production company, Oil and Natural Gas Corporation Limited's gas-based power plant in

Palatana, Tripura, in March 2011. This was followed in September 2011 by the first bilateral visit to Bangladesh by an Indian premier, at the time Manmohan Singh, in twelve years. Transshipment of rice by state-run Food Corporation of India to Tripura through Bangladesh is today an established precedent. Indian companies hope to score big in Bangladesh's infrastructure sector.

'These are all big gestures by both countries,' Abdul Matlub Ahmad, chairman of Dhaka-based Nitol Niloy Group that associates with Indian behemoth Tata Motors, told me in Agartala. We met there in July 2014—at the time he was also chairman of the India-Bangladesh Chamber of Commerce and Industry. But the two countries needed more innovative moves, he complained. 'For example, we are asking our government's permission to invest 5-10 per cent of our export earnings in India, specifically north-east India. Indian companies in Bangladesh must also export from Bangladesh.'

For its part India hopes to increasingly use Bangladeshi territory for the movement of people as well as goods. An Agartala-Dhaka-Kolkata bus service that would shave over 1,000 kilometres off a roundabout route, is one example. India is also eyeing greater connectivity to power grids in Bangladesh to trade and transport electricity; and hydrocarbon transshipment through pipelines, railways and roads. It has funded improvements to the road and rail link from Agartala to Akhaura, on the banks of the Titāsh—immortalized by the writer Adwaita Mallabarman and film-maker Ritwik Ghatak. Similarly, it is looking to improve the road and rail access south from Akhaura to Chittagong Port, the main attraction for Tripura and far-eastern India; and improving access to the river port of Ashuganj, only 40 kilometres from Agartala. A road and rail link south from Agartala to the border town of Sabroom is being boosted, and a bridge is being built by India to reach Chittagong, a little over 70 kilometres south of Sabroom. And eastern India, and several other regions in far-eastern India besides Tripura, would benefit from greater access of people and goods across Bangladesh, a near-seamless web that ceased with Partition.

I heard a former foreign minister of Bangladesh, Dipu Moni, talk up that mutual future in Agartala, leading a group of businesspersons like Ahmad, and diplomats and officials to a seminar called the Tripura Conclave, fronted by a Bengali emigrant to the United States from Tripura and organized by a well-known local journalist, also a Bengali from Tripura. The purpose was the overseas outreach of Tripura—really the geo-economic policy of Tripura.

Dipu Moni began her speech in polished, impeccable English, sharing greetings of her dear leader, whom she ingratiatingly addressed as 'Bongōbōndhukōnyā Sheikh Hasina', the daughter of Bongōbōndhu, and spoke loftily yet realistically of the 'enormous and incalculable potential' of Bangladesh, Tripura, far-eastern India and India working together.

After some minutes, she switched to Bānglā and stayed with it for the remainder of her speech, invoking the commonality of Bānglā between Bangladesh and Tripura, acknowledging Tripura's role in welcoming Bengalis in their times of trouble—this said without a hint of irony. She wasn't only playing with history; she was playing the crowd, playing the future. The crowd loved it. Those who didn't, like some Tiprasa tribal activists who pointedly asked questions in English about the future of their people in the greater scheme of things—for them, the Bengali scheme of things—first received an embarrassed silence, then a slightly belligerent rumbling from the largely Bengali audience, and were then ironically lectured to by the hosts about well-being for all. 'This is about us,' said one of the organizers, a Bengali. 'We should not be left behind.'

And so it will be in Tripura, the land near water—or, if you choose, of three realms—now inescapably part of Banglasphere.

◆

But the brightest spot of them all, so to say, the one thing that could go a long way to addressing a plethora of ills ranging from migration to extremism is economic growth. Bangladesh is today among the world's fastest growing economies, keeping pace with its larger neighbour India. In key human development indicators this country portrayed as that of the archetypically poor is a leader in South Asia, ahead of India, and ahead of West Bengal, which has spent much of this millennium trying to position itself as a manufacturing and services hub after more than four decades of economic disaster its governments visited upon it. Bangladesh runs among the largest and the most successful rural credit networks in the world. BRAC is today a global legend in poverty reduction, empowerment, microfinance and social enterprise, and so is its founder Fazle Hasan Abed. The country's trajectory is in a way emblematic of the manner in which BRAC has changed its avatars: from Bangladesh Rehabilitation Assistance Committee when it was established in 1972, after the war, to Bangladesh Rural Advancement Committee, to its current avatar, Building Resources Across Communities. The winner of the country's only Nobel thus far, Muhammad Yunus, won the Peace Prize in 2006 along with the pathbreaking microfinance organization he founded, Grameen Bank—today a commercial behemoth. Bangladesh is today a leading, respected exporter of expertise in microfinance and socio-economic empowerment in the developing world.

The largely agricultural country now has a fast-growing domestic manufacturing and services sector seen as among the most robust in the region. Bangladesh has evolved into a global textile export powerhouse.

◆

The chāshār désh, the country of peasants so dismissed by the snobs of West Bengal, has come of age, moved with aid in an attempt to move beyond aid. Some of the wealthiest Bengali businesspersons in South Asia today are of Bangladeshi provenance, riding the boom while the going is good. And it must remain good: socio-economic growth continues to be Bangladesh's greatest bulwark against a radical implosion, a calling card for its raison d'être, its very being.

In its economy lies Bangladesh's absolution.

Epilogue

Shéshér porbō

'Bengal is a small place that lived under a vast sky,' wrote my former colleague Sumit Mitra, a perceptive political observer of modern-day Bengal. 'Now its breadth is threatened.'

I would like to borrow Sumit-dā's evocative statement to make my own point. He used an article he wrote at the end 2015 as a plea for a land of liberal thought, cultural greatness and political vision that had been reduced to pettiness to rediscover its former greatness. He meant West Bengal. The scope of the article didn't permit a reaching into other places where Bengalis live, like Bangladesh, Assam and Tripura. It didn't include the Bengalis who didn't have the time or circumstance to display liberal thought and intellectual and cultural greatness to be included in the chronicles of history and media. I am talking here of the idolized and yet ignored folks of delicate watercolour paintings and documentaries and song, the masses of Bengali farmers and doers, the millions who live and die in anonymity. Those who even today hold up the economies of Banglasphere with their toil at home and in the world. They haven't had the time to be petty. They have been too busy by being the backbone and sinews and soul of the Bengalis as others have prospered being the professed brain of ideas and intellect. Chhōtōlōk, so bhodrōlōk can be.

This greater Bengal, which has for a thousand years been a vast place under a vast sky, is certainly threatened. Small-mindedness and the wash of history threaten us, as does petty squabbling—our squandering of so many chances to redeem ourselves. All we seem to do is cling to the dreams and intellect of giants—from over fifty, a hundred, a hundred and fifty years ago.

That could well be the leitmotif of the Bengalis, of Bengal—a desperate legacy married to a frenetic present and future of the greatest uncertainty, although if we have the courage and the vision it could be a future of the greatest possibility too.

Perhaps that is as it should be. The making of the Bengali happened here. The remaking of the Bengali is happening here, as it has for a thousand years and more. The unmaking of the Bengali could happen here too. Or we could evolve into a cosmopolitan, open-minded people—who will reject gratuitous chauvinism—and continue to evolve our language and culture as we once did—a continuing renaissance.

We don't have a starmap for our future, only a cautionary, evocative and querying navigation guide from Kazi Nazrul and a message of hope from his senior colleague, Rabindranath.

Kāndāri Hūshiār! Nazrul cautions. Beware, My Captain!

> You have to cross in the darkness of the night
> A desert vast and a hill of great height
> And a ocean, fathomless and dark
> Travellers, beware and look sharp
> The boat is trembling,
> The water is swelling,
> And the boatman is losing his way,
> Who will sit at the helm at this hour?
> Who has the courage and the power?
> The future calls you.
> Come forward, all who are bold and true.

And what alongside courage and power? What of faith in that courage and power, faith in deliverance with fortitude?

'Faith is the bird that feels the light and sings when the dawn is still dark.'

Bengalis claim the original was by Tagore, in Bānglā. The Chinese claim he was inspired by an ancient saying of theirs.

But why should anyone fight over beauty?

Acknowledgements

Even though I had for some years considered writing about what I call Banglasphere, a journey through the historical and socio-political landscape of West Bengal and Bangladesh, and had discussed it at one time with another publisher, a fuller book, a personalized biography of the Bengalis came together during a conversation with David Davidar of Aleph Book Company.

'Why don't you write this instead?' He suggested *The Bengalis* some years ago after we began our conversation about another book set elsewhere. 'Write that for us after.'

It became a homecoming of sorts: revisiting my roots, confronting these roots, revelling in a Bengaliness, a saturated Bāngāliyānā that I had not done in quite this manner, and doing so with heart and soul bared. It was also homecoming in another way. David read the early portions of my first book, the novel *Tin Fish*. He encouraged me to complete it, and introduced the manuscript and me to his successor at Penguin India. Here we are again.

Alongside David, Aleph's managing editor Aienla Ozukum has remained a pillar of encouragement, patience, dignity and professionalism. Their incisive and empathetic suggestions and editorial expertise have ensured *The Bengalis* emerged a much better book.

The work of numerous authors, writers and academicians has indubitably enriched mine. Although they are all acknowledged wherever their work appears in the narrative, and in the bibliography, I would like to particularly acknowledge several of them here.

Amitav Ghosh kindly permitted use of an excerpt from his

landmark novel, *The Hungry Tide*. Arunava Sinha shared with me an excellent translation of *Bōnōlotā Sen* by Jibanananda Das. Dr Carmen Brandt of Bonn University shared two work-in-progress essays on indigenous cultures and marginalization in Bangladesh, and made several suggestions for simplifying Bengali in Roman script for this book. Madhusree Mukerjee permitted me use of her path-breaking *Churchill's Secret War: The British Empire and the Ravaging of India During World War II*. Dr Nabanipa Bhattacharjee guided me to her searching and moving essays on Bengali speakers of Assam; these underpin my work on the Bengali language movement in Cachar. I thank my fellow authors at Aleph, Sisir Kumar Bose (*Subhas and Sarat: An Intimate Memoir of the Bose Brothers*) and Mihir Bose (*The Indian Spy: The True Story of the Most Remarkable Secret Agent of World War II*) for permitting use of some sections.

In addition, I would like to thank several writers and their publishers for adding priceless insight and nuance to *The Bengalis*. In particular, Professor Amartya Sen for his essay 'Tagore and his India' (*The New York Review of Books*); Vikram Seth for his poem 'A Morning Walk' from *Mappings* (Penguin Books India); Atul Kohli for his *Democracy and Discontent: India's Growing Crisis of Governability* (Cambridge University Press); Bharati Mukherjee for her essay 'Two Ways to belong in America' (*The New York Times*); Kumkum Chatterjee for her essay 'Goddess Encounters: Mughals, Monsters and the Goddess in Bengal' (*Modern Asian Studies*).

Nitish Sengupta's remarkable work, *Land of Two Rivers: A History of Bengal from the Mahabharata to Mujib* (Penguin Books India) was a constant companion alongside books by some of Bengal's greatest historians; as was Subrata Dasgupta's arresting work *Awakening: The Story of the Bengal Renaissance* (Random House India). Rabindra Ray's enduring *The Naxalites and their Ideology* (Oxford University Press) added layers to this book in a delightfully irreverent manner; as did Ranjon Ghoshal's essay 'Dada, Chap Neben Na!' (*Ma 2011*, India Today Group: a volume I thoroughly enjoyed editing). Rehman Sobhan's collection *From*

Two Economies to Two Nations: My Journey to Bangladesh (Daily Star Books) offered unparalleled insight. Sripāntho's trenchant, brilliant collection *Kéyabāt Méyé* (Ananda Publishers), a work I have treasured for several decades, is the true foundation of one of the chapters of this book. Sukanta Chaudhuri's *The Select Nonsense of Sukumar Ray* (Oxford University Press), which, like numerous works listed here and in the bibliography forms part of my personal collection, helped me to bring to you in English translation the genius of Sukumar-babu; in this case the icing is an introduction to the life and times of his father by Satyajit Ray.

I would be remiss to not acknowledge my twelve years at the India Today Group. As a writer and editor at *India Today* magazine I travelled to Bangladesh to expand the horizon for our readers at a time, the early- to mid-1990s, when the idea of South Asia was still in its infancy, and Bangladesh considered little more than a place of natural calamities and a source of refugees. The publisher and editor-in-chief of *India Today* at the time, Aroon Purie and two consecutive executive editors during my tenure, Inderjit Badhwar and Prabhu Chawla helped me to push these boundaries. *The Bengalis* contains excerpts and versions of some articles and essays on Bangladesh and Bengal's history I wrote for *India Today* in the 1990s; and references and quotes several articles and essays I commissioned, then and later, with the encouragement of AP (as we called Purie) on some of the greatest characters and moments of Bengal. I have also drawn from my several columns of reportage and analyses on West Bengal and the Maoist question, and political developments in Bangladesh, in *Mint*. Its sister publication, the *Hindustan Times*, commissioned me in mid-2009 to write a special feature on Lalgarh. The experience remains sharply etched in my mind, and finds expression in this book.

In a few instances, *The Bengalis* also draws on three of my previous books, *Red Sun: Travels in Naxalite Country*, published by Penguin Books India, and two books published by HarperCollins India, *Highway 39: Journeys through a Fractured Land* and *Clear.Hold.*

Build: Hard Lessons of Business and Human Rights in India. These works have some sections related to Banglasphere, from matters of identity, language and rebellion to the grinding politics of West Bengal. My sincere thanks again to Penguin Random House India and HarperCollins India for enabling these experiences, these books.

So many across Banglasphere, family, friends and colleagues, have shared their thoughts, insights, experiences and friendship over the years. So many who were not friends, but not foes either, elevated an interaction among strangers to a conversation between familiars on account of a shared history, or language, an idea, even a cup of chā or glass of lāl-chā.

In particular, I acknowledge my gratitude to Subir Chakravarti, Bellie Chakravarti, Deepankar Roy, Bansari Roy, Jyotirindra Roy, and Sunil Roy Paladhy in Kolkata and Santiniketan; and Nasreen Khan and Chhanda Farooq in Dhaka, for sharing their personal histories and observations. They are—and were—more than family: raconteurs are a gift for any writer.

Lubna Mariam guided me to several interesting sidelights of Bangladesh. Nellie Kar and her friend, Jharna Dhara Chaudhury, were the reasons for my being made welcome in the deepest recesses of Noakhali. Were it not for Abhijit Mazumdar I would not have been able to journey into the heart of Naxalbari and the mind of his father, Charu. Gopal Pratihar put aside his personal tragedies and remained by me as I travelled in 'Jongōlmohōl', and its rebellion and aftermath. Chandan Sinha and Zulfiqar Hasan guided me through some intricacies of West Bengal.

Subir, my father, shared with me the joys and horrors of Bengal. Together with Bellie, my mother who always insisted I write to her in Bānglā, keeping alive for me this core of Bengal in the places I lived in and journeyed to, he implanted a Bengaliness that more than three decades of travel and being away from Bengal has not diminished. My sister, Sumangali, and our cousins, Soma and Nasreen, remain my firmest links to Banglasphere, as are the writers, artists, musicians, directors and actors, spanning several generations—and blessedly too numerous to mention—whose work travels with me to new homes, on new journeys.

My daughter Maya remains the reason, besides David, why I attempted *The Bengalis*.

Oshésh dhōnnōbād.

Select Bibliography

Books

Addy, Premen, 'Global Indian,' *India Today Millennium Series*, Vol. 1, India Today Group (Ed. Chakravarti, Sudeep), 2000.

————, *Tibet on the Imperial Chessboard: The Making of British Policy Towards Lhasa (1899-1925)*. Kolkata: Academic Publishers, 1984.

Ahmad, Waheed, Ed., 'Address by Muhammad Ali Jinnah, Governor General of Pakistan, in Dacca, East Pakistan; March 21st, 1948', *The Nation's Voice*, Vol. VII: *Launching the State and the End of the Journey (Aug. 1947 - Sept. 1948)*. Karachi: Quaid-i-Azam Academy, 2003.

Anisuzzaman; Zamir, Muhammad; Islam, Syed Manzoorul (Eds.), *Bangladesh: Six Decades 1947-2007*. Dhaka: Nymphea Publication, 2010, 2014.

Anstey, F., *Baboo Jabberjee, B.A.* London: J. M. Dent & Sons Ltd., 1897.

————, *The Bayard from Bengal*. London: Methuen & Co., 1902 [Reprinted from *Punch*].

Bandyopadhyay, Kausik, '1911 in Retrospect: A Revisionist Perspective on a Famous Indian Sporting Victory', *Sport in South Asian Society: Past and Present*, Majumdar, Boria; Mangan, J. A., (Eds.). New Delhi: Routledge, 2005.

Bandopadhyay, Upendrakrishna (Ed.), *Leftenant Shuresh Bishshāsh: Chitrō Olōukik Ghotōnapurnō Ōtyashchorjyō Jbonkāhini*. Calcutta: Brajahari Dutta, 1899 [West Bengal Public Library Network]. <http://hdl.handle.net/10689/4288>.

Banerjee, Sumanta, *In the Wake of Naxalbari: A History of the Naxalite Movement in India*. Kolkata: Subarnarekha, 1980; Sahitya Samsad, 2009.

Barbosa, Duarte, *The Book of Duarte Barbosa: An account of the countries bordering on the Indian Ocean and their inhabitants, written by Duarte Barbosa, and completed about the year 1518 A.D.*, Vol. II (Dames, Mansel Longworth, trans. of *O Livro de Duarte Barbosa*). London: Hakluyt Society, 1921.

Basu, Sajal, *Politics of Violence: A Case Study of West Bengal*. Calcutta: Minerva, 1982.

————, *West Bengal: The Violent Years*. Calcutta: Prachi Publications, 1979.

Bose, Mihir, *The Indian Spy: The True Story of the Most Remarkable Secret Agent of World War II*. New Delhi: Aleph Book Company, 2017.

Bose, Nirmal Kumar, *My Days with Gandhi*. New Delhi: Orient Blackswan, 1974.

Bose, Sisir Kumar, *Subhas and Sarat: An Intimate Memoir of the Bose Brothers*. New Delhi: Aleph Book Company, 2016.

Brandt, Carmen, 'Projecting and rejecting indigeneity: From Bangladesh with love', final draft for *South Asian Indigenous Culture on Screen: Music Videos, Movies and Documentaries*, Maaker, Eric de; Schleiter, Markus (Eds). New Delhi: Orient Blackswan, 2017.

————, 'Writing Off Domination: The Chakma and Meitei Script Movements', Draft for *Script and Identity: The Politics of Writing in South Asia*, Brandt, Carmen; Sohoni, Pushkar (Eds), (South Asian History and Culture Special Issue), 2017.

The Administration of Bengal under Sir Andrew Fraser K.C.S. 1903-1908. The Bengal Secretariat Book Depot, Calcutta: Writers' Building, 1908.

The Bengal Club in History. Essays by Datta-Ray, Sunanda; Mitter, Bhaskar; Mukherjee, Rudrangshu; Ray, Bharati, (Sarkar, Malabika, Ed.). Kolkata: The Bengal Club Ltd, 2006.

Chakravarti, Subir, *Ak Gūchhō Jāpāni Kōbitā*, Kolkata: Grōnthāloy, 2001.

Chakravarti, Sudeep, *Clear.Hold.Build: Hard Lessons of Business and Human Rights in India*. New Delhi: HarperCollins India, 2014.

————, *Highway 39: Journeys through a Fractured Land*. New Delhi: HarperCollins India, 2012.

————, *Red Sun: Travels in Naxalite Country*. New Delhi: Penguin Books India, 2008.

Chatterjee, Manini, *Do & Die: The Chittagong Uprising 1930-34*, New Delhi: Picador, 2010.

Chatterji, Joya, *Bengal Divided: Hindu Communalism and Partition, 1932-1947*. Cambridge South Asian Studies (Book 57), Cambridge: Cambridge University Press, 2002.

Chatterji, Suniti Kumar, *The Origin and Development of the Bengali Language, Part I, Part II*. Kolkata: Calcutta University Press, 1926.

Chattopadhyay, Sayan, '"Things of Stylized Beauty": The Novels of Sudhin N. Ghose and the Fragments of an Indian Tradition,' *Ariel*, Vol. 43, No. 3, July 2012.

Chottōpādhyay, Shorōt Chondrō, *Shrikāntō*. Kolkata: Ananda Publishers, 1997.

Chaudhuri, Sukanta (trans.), *The Select Nonsense of Sukumar Ray*. New Delhi: Oxford University Press, 1987, 1993.

Chokrōborti, Mukundōrām (Kōbibor), *Kōbikonkōn Chōndi* (Edited and abridged by Obināshchondrō Mukhōpādhyāy). Kolkata: Purnochondrō Sheel, 1938; Bongabdō 1344 (Personal collection of the author, courtesy of Shorōtkāmini Debi, the author's great grandmother).

Chowdhury, Kabir, *Translations of the poems of Kazi Narul Islam, Bidrohi* (The Rebel) and *Kandari Hushiar* (Beware, My Captain). Dhaka: Nazrul Institute, 1997.

Colville, John *The Fringes of Power: Downing Street Diaries*, Vol. II. London: Weidenfeld & Nicolson (in Mukerjee, Madhusree, *Churchill's Secret War: The British Empire and the Ravaging of India During World War II*. New York: Basic Books, 2010).

Das, Sarat Chandra, *Indian Pandits in the Land of Snow*. Calcutta: Asiatic Society of India, 1893.

———, *Journey to Lhasa and Central Tibet*. Ed. Rockhill, London: W. W, John Murray, 1904.

Dasgupta, Subrata, *Awakening: The Story of the Bengal Renaissance*, New Delhi: Random House India, 2011.

Dasgupta, Sugata; Bhattacharjee, Ronen K.; Singh, Surendra V., *The Great Gherao of 1969: A Case Study of Campus Violence and Protest Methods*. New Delhi: Orient Longman, 1974.

Ferguson, Niall, *Empire: How Britain Made the Modern World*. London: Penguin Books, 2004.

Ghosh, Amitav, *The Hungry Tide*. London: HarperCollins, 2004.

———, *The Shadow Lines*. New Delhi: Ravi Dayal Publishers, 1988.

Ghosh, S. K., *Terrorism: World under Siege*. New Delhi: Nataraj Books, 2005.

Goldsack, The Rev. William, *A Mussalmani Bengali-English Dictionary*. 1923, New Delhi: Gyan Publishing House, 2007.

Goopy Gyne Bagha Byne, by Ray, Satyajit, Purnima Pictures, 1969 (based on a story by Roychowdhury, Upendrakishore, serialized in *Shondesh*, 1915-1916).

Hazra, Indrajit, *Grand Delusions: A Short Biography of Kolkata*. New Delhi: Aleph Book Company, 2013.

Hill, S. C., *Three Frenchmen in Bengal Or The Commercial Ruin of the French Settlements in 1757*. London: Longmans, Green, and Company, 1903.

Huda, Mohammed Nurul, *Poetry of Kazi Nazrul Islam in English Translation*. Dhaka: Nazrul Institute, 2000.

Hunter, W. W., *A Statistical Account of Bengal*, Vol. I; *Districts of the 24 Parganas and Sundarbans*. London: Trubner & Co., London, 1881.

———, *The Imperial Gazetteer of India*, Vol. II, *Bengal to Cutwa*. London: Trubner & Co., London, 1881.

———, *The Indian Musalmans*. London: Trubner & Co., 1876.

Huq, Muhammad Lutful, *Bāngāli Poltōn*. Dhaka: Prōthōma Prōkāshon, 2012.

Imam, Neamat, *The Black Coat*. New Delhi: Penguin Books India, 2013.

Irani, C. R., *Bengal: The Communist* Challenge. Mumbai: Lalvani Publishing House, 1968.

Jacobsen, Knut A., 'Scandinavia', *The Encyclopedia of the Indian Diaspora*, Ed., Brij V. Lal. Editions Didier Millet in association with National University of Singapore, 2006.

Jana, Arun K., 'Backwardness and Political Articulation of Backwardness in the North Bengal Region of West Bengal,' in *Rethinking State Politics in India: Regions within Regions* (Ed. Kumar, Ashutosh). New Delhi: Routledge, 2011.

Khalil, Tasneem, *Jallad: Death Squads and State Terror in South Asia*. London: Pluto Press, 2016.

Khan, Akbar Ali, *Discovery of Bangladesh: Exploration into Dynamics of a Hidden Nation*. Dhaka: The University Press Limited, 2001, 2012.

Khan, Mohammad Akram, *Moslem Bonger Shāmājik Itihāsh*. Dhaka: Oitijjhya, 2002.

Kling, Blair B., *The Blue Mutiny: The Indigo Disturbances in Bengal 1859-62*. Kolkata: Firma KLM Private Limited, 1966, 1977.

Kohli, Atul, *Democracy and Discontent: India's Growing Crisis of Governability*. Cambridge: Cambridge University Press, 1991.

Lapierre, Dominique, *The City of Joy*. New Delhi: Arrow Books, 1986.

Lakha, Salim, 'Australia', *The Encyclopedia of the Indian Diaspora*, Ed., Brij V. Lal. Editions Didier Millet in association with National University of Singapore, 2006.

Leckie, Jacqueline, 'New Zealand', *The Encyclopedia of the Indian Diaspora*, Ed., Brij V. Lal. Editions Didier Millet in association with National University of Singapore, 2006.

Maitra, Rajkumar, 'Boglā-māmā versus Dracula', *Topōbon*. Kolkata: Dev Sahitya Kutir, 1972.

Majumdar, R. C. (Ed.), *The History of Bengal, Volume I: Hindu Period*. Dhaka: The University of Dacca, 1943.

Mitra, Asok, *Calcutta on the Eve of her Tercentenary*, Kolkata: Abhinav Publications, 1990.

Mitra, Ashok, (Ed.), *The Truth Unites—Essays in Tribute to Samar Sen*. Kolkata: Subarnarekha, 1985.

Mōhini Mōhōn, A hagiography of Mohini Mohan Chakravarti, author's family collection, 1942.

Moorhouse, Geoffrey, *Calcutta*. London: Faber & Faber, 2008.

Mukerjee, Madhusree, *Churchill's Secret War: The British Empire and the Ravaging of India During World War II*. New York: Basic Books, 2010.

Mukherjee, Bimal, *Dūchākāy Dūniyā*. Kolkata: Swarnakshar Prakashani, 1986.

Mukul, M. R. Akhtar, *Āmi Bijoy Dekhechi*. Dhaka: Ananya, 2007, 2014.

Narayanan, T. G., *Famine Over Bengal*. Calcutta: Book Company Ltd, 1944.

Raleigh, Thomas, *Lord Curzon in India: Being a selection of his speeches as viceroy & governor general of India 1898-1905*. London: Macmillan and Co. Limited, 1906.

Raychaudhuri, Sarojkumar (Ed.)., *Terōshō-bāhānnōr Sherā Golpō*. Calcutta: Bengal Publishers, 1946.

Ray, Gautam (Ed.), *Nandigram and Beyond*. Kolkata: Gangchil, 2008.

Ray, Rabindra, *The Naxalites and their Ideology*. New Delhi: Oxford University Press, 2002.

Sarkar, Jadunath (Ed.), *The History of Bengal, Volume II: Muslim Period*. Dhaka:The University of Dacca, 1943.

Sarkar, Malabika (Ed.), *The Bengal Club in History*. Kolkata:The Bengal Club Ltd, 2006.

Sircar, Badal, *3 Plays*. Kolkata: Seagull Books, 1983; 2009.

Sen, Nabaneeta Dev, *Bhraman Samagra* (Vol., II): *A Collection of Travelogues in Bengali*. Kolkata: Dey's Publishing, 2010.

Sengupta, Nitish, *Bengal Divided: The Unmaking of a Nation 1905-1971*. New Delhi: Penguin Books India, 2007.

———, *Land of Two Rivers: A History of Bengal from the Mahabharata to Mujib*. New Delhi: Penguin Books India, 2011.

Seth Vikram, 'A Morning Walk', *Mappings*. Calcutta: Writers Workshop, Calcutta, 1981; New Delhi: Penguin Books India, 1994.

Sobhan, Rehman, *From Two Economies to Two Nations: My Journey to Bangladesh*. Dhaka: Daily Star Books, 2015.

Sripānthō, *Keyabāt Meye*. Calcutta: Ananda Publishers, 1988.

Tagore, Rabindranath, *Gitanjali* (with an introduction by W. B. Yeats). London: The Macmillan Company, 1913.

Timberg, Thomas A, *The Marwaris: From Jagat Seth to the Birlas*. New Delhi: Penguin Books, 2014.

Trojanow, Ilija, *Along the Ganga: To the Inner Shores of India*. New Delhi: Penguin Books, 2005.

Tunga, Sudhansu Sekhar, *Bengali and Other Related Dialects of South Assam*. New Delhi: Mittal Publications, 1996.

Van Schendel, Willem, *A History of Bangladesh*. New York: Cambridge University Press, 2009.

Zaidi, A. M., *From Syed to the Emergence of Jinnah, Evolution of Muslim Political Thought in India*, Vol. 1. New Delhi, 1975. <http://dspace.wbpublibnet.gov.in>.

Zakariah, Abul Kalam Muhammad, *Nobāb Shiraj-ud-Daulā*. Dhaka: Prōthōma Prōkāshon, 2015.

Articles & Essays

Ahmed, Khaled, 'Suhrawardy and Jinnah', *Express Tribune*, 1 January 2011.

'Aircraft accident Fokker F-27 Friendship aircraft 200 VT-DOJ Khulna Airport (KHL)', Aviation Safety Network. <https://aviation-safety.net/database/record. php?id=19690421-0>.

Akbar, M. J., 'Why Jyoti Basu could not be PM', *Times of India*, 10 January 2010.

Akhter, Shirin, 'Remittance Inflows and Its Contribution to the Economic Growth of Bangladesh', Niigata: Niigata University, 2016. <http://dspace. lib.niigata-u.ac.jp>.

Arif, Mohammad Kamrul Hassan, 'Legal Status of Bihari Community', *Daily Star*, 10 November 2015.

Assam Human Development Report 2014, United Nations Development Programme; Planning and Development Department, Government of Assam; NITI Aayog, Government of India.

Athreya, Venkatesh, 'Power to the People', *Frontline*, Vol. 27, Issue 3, 30 January–12 February 2010.

'Atisha Dīpamkara–The Treasury of Lives: A Biographical Encyclopedia of Tibet, Inner Asia and the Himalayan Region,' Shelley and Donald Rubin Foundation. <www.treasuryoflives.org>.

Bagchi, Nondon, 'Robi Remixed', *Ma 2011: Mood Music* (India Today Commemorative Issue), September 2011.

'IFA Shield Fina—100 Years Ago When Immortal Eleven Created History', 30 March 2011. <www.kolkatafootball.com>.

Bandopadhyay, Sabyasachi, 'Nirupam Sen owns up Nano project failure', 3 June 2010. <www.expressindia.com>.

Banerjee, Victor, 'Ananda Unlimited', *Ma 2011: Mood Music* (India Today Commemorative Issue), September 2011.

Banerjie, Monideepa, '200 houses burnt in Bengal village by mob protesting cleric's death', 22 February 2013. <www.ndtv.com>.

'Bangladesh Supreme Court confirms death for 2 Opposition leaders in war crimes case', *The Telegraph*, 18 November 2015.

'Bengal Summit: Mamata offers tax-friendly regime', *Business Standard*, 10 January 2016.

Bhabani, Soudhriti, '48 hours after communal riots, Kaliachak in Malda turns ghost town', 6 January 2016. < http://indiatoday.intoday.in/story/kaliachak-in-malda-turns-ghost-town-48-hrs-after-violence/1/563443.html>

Bhattacharjee, Manash Firaq, 'To Be, or Not to Be, Bengali,' 29 April 2017. <https://thewire.in/129658/bengali-tagore-nirad-chaudhuri/ >.

Bhattacharjee, Nabanipa, 'Language of Love and Death: Fifty Years of Assam's Language Movement', *Mainstream*, Vol L, No 9, 18 February 2012.

———, 'Negotiating Marginality: The Bangla-speakers of Assam', *Mainstream*, Vol LI, No 34, 10 August 2013.

———, 'Speaking the Devil's Tongue: The Bengalis of Assam', Abstract of lecture at Department of History and Culture, Faculty of Humanities and Languages, New Delhi: Jamia Millia Islamia, 24 January 2013.

Bhattacharyya, Sourish, '*Daab Chingri avec Vin, s'il vous plait,' Ma 2011: Mood Music* (India Today Commemorative Issue), September 2011.

Bhaumik, Subir, 'Book arson "a Taleban-style" act', 14 April 2005. <http://news.bbc.co.uk/2/hi/south_asia/4443565.stm>.

———, 'Disaster in Tripura', *Seminar*, No. 510, 2002.

'Bilateral Remittance Matrix 2014', 'Bilateral Remittance Matrix 2015', Migration and Remittances Data, The World Bank, October 2016. <www.worldbank.org>.

Brijanth, Rohit, 'Birth of a Hero'. <www.indiatoday.intoday.in, 20 October 1997>.

Buruma, Ian, 'The Last Bengali Renaissance Man', *New York Review of Books*, 19 November 1987.

Chakrabarti, Sumit, 'Space of Deprivation: The Nineteenth Century Bengali Kerani in the Bhadrolok Milieu of Calcutta', *Asian Journal of Social Science,* (From an abstract of the paper at Third Bremen Conference on Language and Literature in Colonial and Postcolonial Contexts, 15-18 March 2016. <www.bcll.uni-bremen.de>.

Chakrabarty, Bidyut, 'The "hut" and the "axe": The 1947 Sylhet referendum', *The Indian Economic and Social History Review*, 39, 4, London: Thousand Oaks, 2002.

Chakraborty, Debasis, 'Migration and Urban Informal Sector', (thesis submitted for PhD in Economics), Department of Economics, The University of Burdwan, 2014.

Chakraborty, Debjyoti and Bhattacharya, Ravik, 'Hired guns for polls: Meet the bomb-makers of West Bengal', *Hindustan Times*, 8 May 2016.

Chakravarti, K. C., 'Bongal Kheda Again', *Economic Weekly*, 30 July 1960.

Chakravarti, Sudeep, 'East By North-east: The Way Ahead for India's Security and Prosperity,'

Parts I, II, III, *The Sentinel* (14, 15, 16 May 2014), <*sentinelassam.com*> (Reprint of a talk delivered at The 1st Sarat Mahanta Memorial Lecture,

Guwahati, 1 May 2014).

————, 'From Calamity to Commerce,' *India Today*, 30 November 1994.

————, 'Hardline Danger in Bangladesh,' *Mint*, 9 August 2013.

————, *India's Demographic Tsunami*, position paper for the Kesroli Group, 2009; republished by Gateway House: Indian Council on Global Relations, July 2010. <www.gatewayhouse.in>; partially republished in *OPEN*, 10 July 2010.

————, 'Fundamental Problems;' 'Allah will help us', *India Today*, 31 August 1994.

————, 'The Migration Discourse', *Mint*, 27 July 2012.

————, 'Secure Dhaka to secure India', *Mint*, 5 June 2015.

————, 'The Past is Present', *Fifty-Fifty: Years of Hope and Despair*, India Today Commemorative Issue 1947-1997 (Ed. Chakravarti, Sudeep), 18 August 1997.

————, 'Lalgarh: A turf war among three Ms', *Mint*, 19 August 2010.

————, 'The next political battleground', *Mint*, 16 August 2012.

————, 'The Siege of Red Fort', *Hindustan Times*, 21 June 2009.

Chatterjee, Arup, '38 years on, "King of Football" Pele still humble in Kolkata', 13 October 2015. <www.mid-day.com>.

Chatterjee, Debjani, 'Kazi Nazrul Islam (1899-1976)', Disability Arts Online, 6 January 2015. <www.disabilityartsonline.org.uk>.

Chatterjee, Kumkum, 'Goddess encounters: Mughals, Monsters and the Goddess in Bengal', *Modern Asian Studies*, Vol. 47, Issue 05, September 2013, <http://journals.cambridge.org>.

Chattopadhyay, Sayan, '"Things of Stylized Beauty": The Novels of Sudhin

Chaudhuri, Subhasish, 'Bengali diaspora centre at varsity', *The Telegraph*, 26 June 2015.

Choudhary, Amit Anand, 'Grant citizenship to Chakma refugees within 3 months: Supreme Court', *Times of India*, 19 September 2015.

Choudhury, S., 'A "God-Sent" Opportunity', *Porous Borders, Divided Self*, *Seminar*, February 2002.

'Country-wise Inward Remittances', Bangladesh Bank, January 2017.

Damodaran, Harish, 'The Marwari Business Model', *Hindu Business Line*, 7-8 April 2013.

Das, Jibanananda Das, *Banalata Sen* (trans. Sinha, Arunava, 2012).

Das, Nabamita, 'Processes of negotiating intimate heterosexual identities and relations: Narratives of three generations of urban middle-class Bengalis living in Kolkata, India', (Thesis submitted to the University of Birmingham for the degree of Doctor of Philosophy, Department of Political Science and International Studies, School of Government and Society, University of Birmingham), March 2013.

Das, Sib Kumar, 'Odisha wages a literary struggle to claim rosogolla as its own', *The Hindu*, 6 June 2016.

Dasgupta, Biplab, 'The 1972 Election in West Bengal', *Economic & Political Weekly*, Vol. 7 No. 16, 15 April 1972.

Dasgupta, Swapan, 'The Modernist and the Guru', *India Today Millennium Series* Vol. 1, 2000.

Deb, Joyshree, Islam, Mohammad Shafiqul, 'Romantic par-excellence: Kazi Nazrul Islam's Selected Poems', *International Journal of Advancement in Research & Technology*, Vol. 2, Issue 5, May 2013.

Deb, Sandipan, 'The curious case of Byomkesh Bakshi', *Mint*, 4 Dec 2014.

'Denial of the present', Editorial in *The Telegraph*, 24 January 2016.

Dugar, Prodip Chand, 'Marwaris,' Banglapedia. <http://en.banglapedia.org/index.php?title=Marwaris>.

Emspak, Jesse, 'State of Matter: Bose-Einstein Condensate', 4 September 2016. <www.livescience.com>.

Etzold, Benjamin; Mallck, Bishawjit, 'International Migration from Bangladesh', Bundeszentrale fur politische Bildung, 30 November 2015. < www.bpb.de>.

Ferguson, Charles A., Preston, W.D., *107 Bengali Proverbs*, The Journal of American Folklore Vol. 59, No. 234 (Oct-Dec 1946), American Folklore Society, University of Illinois Press. <JSTOR.org>.

Ganguly, Arnab and Bhattacharyaa, Meghdeep, 'Hide, Didi, Hide', *The Telegraph*, 4 October 2015.

Ghosal, Aniruddha, 'Days before Jangalmahal votes, Mamata Banerjee takes on role of "saviour"', *Indian Express*, 27 March 2017.

Ghosal, Sutanuka, 'Lopchu tea: A brand that puts no stock in Harrods', *Economic Times*, 11 October 2014.

Ghoshal, Ranjon, 'Dada, Chap Neben Na!', *Simply Celebrate*, India Today Group, September 2011.

Goswami, P. C., 'Tragedy of Political Tactlessness', *Economic Weekly*, 30 July 1960, www.epw.in.

Governor-General of India (Attempted Assassination), House of Commons debate, 30 December 1912, Commons and Lords Hansard. <www.hansard.millbanksystems.com/commons>, courtesy of UK Parliament.

Graff, Violette and Galonnier, Juliette, 'Hindu-Muslim Communal Riots in India I (1947-1986), SciencesPo, 15 July 2013.

Goswami, B. B., 'India-Bangladesh border in Karimganj will be single-fenced, says BSF director general', *Times of India*, 4 June 2016.

Gupta, Abhijit, 'No one remembers the colonel', *The Telegraph*, 18 December 2011.

Gupta, Kanchan, 'The destroyer of West Bengal', *The Pioneer*, 10 January 2010.

Guha, Ramachandra, 'Why Bengal is to India what France is to the World', *The Telegraph*, 5 September 2015.

Hamilton, W. G., 'Lieut. Colonel N.S. Simpson', Letter to the editor of *The Spectator*, 3 January 1931. <www.archive.spectator.co.uk>.

Hazra, Indrajit, 'The Vikram Seth Show', *Hindustan Times*, 29 January 2012.

Hussain, Nazmul; Abbas, Md Zahir; Owais, Saba, 'Muslims in West Bengal: Trend of Population Growth and Educational Status', *Islam and Muslim Societies: A Social Science Journal*, Vol. 5, No. 1, 2012.

'Islamic State claims responsibility for Bangladesh bombings on Shias,' *Reuters*, 24 October 2015.

Jack, Ian, 'Rabindranath Tagore was a global phenomenon, so why is he neglected?', *The Guardian*, 7 May 2011.

Jain, Bharti, 'Two crore Bangladeshi immigrants illegally staying in India, Centre informs Rajya Sabha', *Times of India*, 17 November 2016.

Jalais, Annu, 'Dwelling on Morichjhanpi: When Tigers Became "Citizens", Refugees "Tiger-Food",' *Economic and Political Weekly*, Vol. 40, Issue No. 17-23, April 2005.

'Job Charnock not Kolkata's founder: Expert committee', *Press Trust of India*, 31 January 2003.

Joshi, Ruchir, 'Tracing Puppa', *Fathers, Granta* 104, 2008.

Kapadia, Novy, 'The death anniversary of Indian Football's first legend', 14 April 2013. <www.sportskeeda.com>.

Labour in West Bengal, Director of Information, Government of West Bengal, 1972.

'Letter from the Viceroy Lord Hardinge to Lord Crewe, Secretary of State for India, 24th August, 1911', *Hardinge Papers*. New Delhi: National Archives of India. <http://dspace.wbpublibnet.gov.in>.

Lorea, Carola Erika, 'Bengali settlers in the Andaman Islands', *The Newsletter*, No. 77, International Institute for Asian Studies, Leiden, Summer 2017. <www.iias.asia>.

Macaulay, Thomas Babington, 'Government of India', A Speech Delivered in the House of Commons on 10 July 1833.

———, 'Lord Clive,' *Critical and Historical Essays contributed to the Edinburgh Review*, 5th ed. in 3 Vols. London: Longman, Brown, Green, and Longmans, 1948.

——— 'Minute by the Hon'ble T. B. Macaulay, 2 February 1835', *Bureau of Education. Selections from Educational Records, Part I (1781-1839)*. Sharp, H. Ed. Calcutta: Superintendent, Government Printing, 1920. Reprint. Delhi: National Archives of India, 1965.

Magnussen, Kendall (Ed.), 'Atisha's Life Story', FPMT Education Services, 15 February 2009. <www.lamrim.com>.

'Malaysia hints at reviewing restriction,' *The Daily Star*, 30 April 2016.

'Maradona gets a tumultuous welcome in Kolkata,' *IANS*, 6 December 2008. <www.indiatoday.intoday.in>.

Mazumdar, Charu, 'China's Chairman is our Chairman: China's Path is our Path', *Deshabroti*, 6 November 1969; *Liberation*, Vol. III, No. 1, November 1969. <www.cpiml.org>.

Mitra, Sumit, 'Cinema's India', *100 People Who Shaped India*, India Today Millennium Series, Vol. 1, 2000.

———, 'Tripura: The Promised Land?', *India Today*, 1-15 August 1979.

———, 'West Bengal', *India Today*, 40th Anniversary Special, 9 December 2015.

———, 'Comrade papa's capitalist son', *India Today*, 31 December 1982.

Mookerjee, Sambhu Chandra (Ed.), *Mookerjee's Magazine*, March 1873; May 1873.

Mukherjee, Bharati, 'Two Ways to belong in America', *New York Times*, 22 September 1996.

Nachowitz, Todd, 'Identity and invisibility: Early Indian presence in Aotearoa, New Zealand (1769-1850)', Draft chapter for forthcoming volume *Indian Migration to the Pacific & Indian Ocean States* (Bandyopadhyay, Sekhar, ed.). Victoria University of Wellington, December 2016. <www.academia.edu>.

Nagchowdhury, Subrata, 'Why corpses of a 1982 killing are stirring again', *Indian Express*, 5 June 2015.

O'Connor, J. J., Robertson, E. F., 'Satyendranath Bose', School of Mathematics and Statistics, University of St Andrews, Scotland, October 2003. <http://www-history.mcs.st-and.ac.uk/Biographies/Bose.html>.

'Population of Overseas Indians', Ministry of External Affairs, Government of India, December 2016. <www.mea.gov.in>.

Poser, Adriana, 'The Scholar-Spy Who Saw Tibet's Densatil Monastery in All Its Glory', Asia Society, 11 April 2014. < www.asiasociety.org/blog/asia>.

Radice, William C., 'Lyrical Alchemist', *100 People Who Shaped India*, India Today Millennium Series, Vol. 1 (Ed. Chakravarti, Sudeep), 2000.

Ray, Balai, 'Evolution of the High Court at Calcutta and some Reminiscences', *The High Court at Calcutta Sesquicentennial Souvenir*, 2013. < www.calcuttahighcourt.nic.in>.

'Reinforcing Ties: Enhancing contributions from Bangladeshi diaspora members', Paper for Government of the People's Republic of Bangladesh by International Labour Organization, Swiss Agency for Development and Cooperation SDC, HDRC, Decent Work, 2015.

Roy, Subhajoy, 'Street short in name game', *The Telegraph*, 28 March 2014.

Roy, Subir, 'The legacy of Jyoti Basu', *Business Standard*, 20 January 2010.

Sarkar, Tithi, 'I'm indebted to my actors', *Ma 2011: Mood Music* (India Today Commemorative Issue), September 2011.

Schlund-Vials, Kathy, 'Revolutionary Arts and Political Poetics: Kazi Nazrul Islam', University of Connecticut; Asian American Studies Institute, 2010. <www.asianamerican.uconn.edu>.

Singharoy, Debal K., *Peasant Movements in Contemporary India: Emerging Forms of Domination and Resistance, Economic and Political Weekly*, 24 December 2005.

Sinha, Arunava (trans.), *Bonōlotā Sen* by Das, Jibanananda, 2012.

Sinha, Nirmal C., 'About Dipankara Atisa', 1984. <www.repository.cam.ac.uk>.

Sen, Amartya, 'Tagore and his India', *New York Review,* 28 August 2001.

Somvanshi, Kiran Kabtta and Barretto, Crystal, 'Companies that are the best wealth creators in East India,' *Economic Times*, 2 April 2012.

Talukdar, Sushanta, 'Less than 50 per cent Assamese speakers in Assam', *The Hindu*, 10 January 2008.

'Taslima Nasrin: "They wanted to kill me"', interview in *Middle East Quarterly*, Vol. 7, No. 3, September 2000. <www.meforum.org>.

'Tata pulls out of Singur, blames Trinamool stir', *Financial Express*, 3-4 October 2008.

The Annual Quality Assurance Report (AQAR) of the IQAC 2015-16 Part–A. University of Kalyani. <www.klyuniv.ac.in>.

'The Dying Race', *Karmayogin*, Vol. 1, No. 18, 6 November 1909.

'The Historical Triumph of 1911 IFA Shield', 24 July 2012, Mohun Bagan Atheletic Club. <www.mohunbaganclub.com/the-historical-triumph-of-1911-ifa-shield>.

'The West Bengal Land Reforms Act, 1955; West Bengal Act X of 1956 (As modified up to 1st January 1999) <www.banglarbhumi.gov.in> and <wbja.nic.in>.

'The World in 2017: How will the global economic order changer?', PricewaterhouseCoopers LLP, February 2017. <www.pwc.com>.

Thockchom, Khelen, 'Bengali script loses its only outpost', *The Telegraph*, 16 May 2005.

Tripathi, Sanjeev, 'Illegal Immigration from Bangladesh to India: Toward a Comprehensive Solution', Carnegie India, 29 June 2016. <www.carnegieindia.org>.

Tumbe, Chinmay, 'Remittances in India: Facts & Issues', Working Paper No.: 331, Indian Institute of Management, Bangalore, 2011.

Tata Motors Annual Reports, 2005-06, 2006-07, 2007-08, 2008-09, 2009-10, 2010-11, 2011-12.

Tata Motors Form 20-F, United States Securities and Exchange Commission, 2007, 2008, 2009, 2010, 2011, 2012.

Tata Steel Annual Reports, 2005-06, 2006-07, 2007-08, 2008-09, 2009-10, 2010-11, 2011-12.

Vaidyanathan, Siddhartha, 'Ganguly takes his shirt off', 30 August 2009. <www.espncricinfo.com>.

Venkatesh, Mahua, 'UP, Bihar, Bengal new hot destinations for foreign remittances', *Hindustan Times*, 28 March 2011.

Wali, Kameshwar C., 'The man behind Bose statistics', *Physics Today*, October 2006. <www. researchgate.net>.

'West Bengal tops chart in domestic violence', *Times of India*, 26 November 2015.

'Why tax rebate for painting houses blue-white, asks HC', *Times of India*, 28 March 2015.

'Was this spilling of blood not avoidable?' Statement of West Bengal governor Gopalkrishna Gandhi. <http://www.hindu.com/2007/03/15/stories/2007031521071600.htm>.

Zakaria, Saymon (Ed), *Bhabnagar: International Journal of Bengal Studies*, Vol.1, No. 1. Dhaka: Bhabnagar Foundation, August 2014.

Resources

banglastories.org

www.aurobindo.ru

sriaurobindoinstitute.org

en.banglapedia.org (Banglapedia)

www.bb.org.bd (Bangladesh Bank)

dictionary.cambridge.org/dictionary/english/gherao

dli.ernet.in (Digital Library of India)

www.epw.in (*Economic & Political Weekly*)

www.elite.se (Elite Hotels, Sweden)

Encyclopaedia Britannica (& britannica.com)

books.google.co.in (Google Books)

google.com/earth (Google Earth)

https://en.oxforddictionaries.com (Oxford Dictionaries)

gutenberg.org (Project Gutenberg)

www.questia.com

Ratan Tata Library, Delhi University

wbpublibnet.gov.in (West Bengal Public Library Network)

http://dspace.wbpublibnet.gov.in:8080/jspui/ (DSpace at West Bengal Public Library Network)

Index